Easter Island, Earth Island

The Enigmas of Rapa Nui

Fourth Edition

Paul Bahn and John Flenley

ROWMAN & LITTLEFIELD
Lanham • Boulder • New York • London

D1230814

Design
Rapanui Press Editorial
Eduardo Ruiz-Tagle

Investigation: Paul Bahn, Archaeologist, and John Flenley, Botanist
Design and Production: Eduardo Ruiz-Tagle, Rapanui Press
Coeditor: José Miguel Ramírez-Aliaga, Archaeologist, Centro de Estudios Avanzados,
Universidad de Playa Ancha
Editor: Rapanui Press, www.rapanuipress.cl

Credits and acknowledgments for material borrowed from other sources, and
reproduced with permission, appear on the appropriate page within the text.

Published by Rowman & Littlefield
An imprint of The Rowman & Littlefield Publishing Group, Inc.
4501 Forbes Boulevard, Suite 200, Lanham, Maryland 20706
www.rowman.com

6 Tinworth Street, London SE11 5AL, United Kingdom

Text © 2011 Paul Bahn and John Flenley
First Rowman & Littlefield edition published in 2017

Rapanui Press first edition
Rapa Nui, 2011

Rapanui Press second edition
Rapa Nui, 2014

Rapanui Press third edition, revised and expanded
Rapa Nui, 2017

ISBN 9781442266551 (cloth : alk. paper)
ISBN 9781538129784 (paper : alk. paper)
ISBN 9781442266568 (electronic)

♾™ The paper used in this publication meets the minimum requirements of
American National Standard for Information Sciences—Permanence of Paper
for Printed Library Materials, ANSI/NISO Z39.48-1992.

Printed in the United States of America

For Jos and Peter; and Eleanor, Frances and Yvonne

Contents

Photos: MAPSE colection

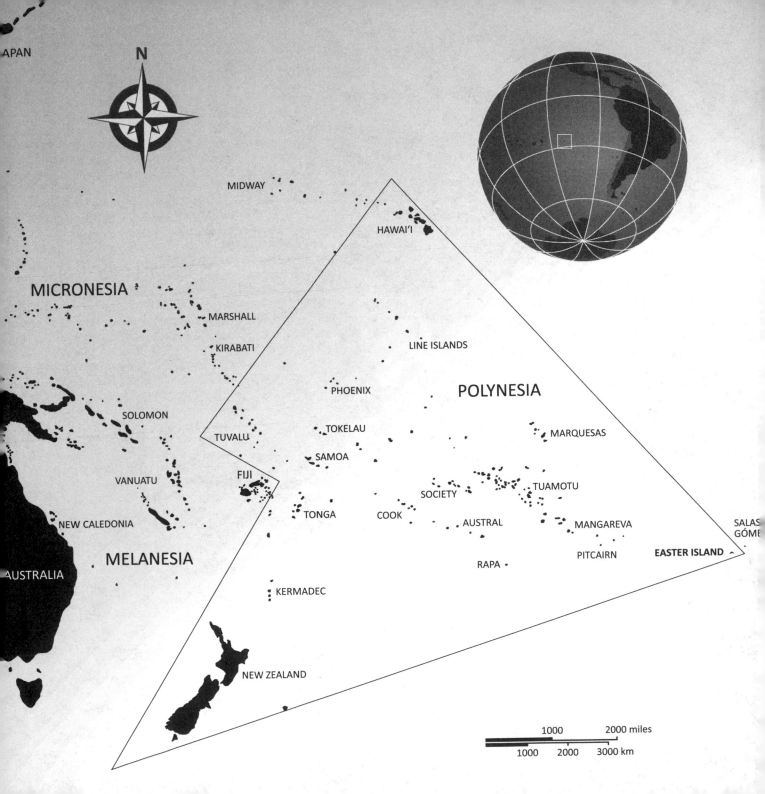

N

JAPAN

MIDWAY

HAWAI'I

MICRONESIA

MARSHALL

KIRABATI

LINE ISLANDS

PHOENIX

POLYNESIA

SOLOMON

TUVALU

TOKELAU

MARQUESAS

SAMOA

FIJI

SOCIETY

TUAMOTU

VANUATU

TONGA

COOK

AUSTRAL

MANGAREVA

NEW CALEDONIA

SALAS
GÓME

MELANESIA

RAPA

PITCAIRN

EASTER ISLAND

AUSTRALIA

KERMADEC

NEW ZEALAND

1000   2000 miles

1000   2000   3000 km

To the first edition
Easter Island, Earth island, 1992

*This tiny mote of land lost
in the endless empty seas
of the southeast Pacific.*

William Mulloy

The sheer remoteness of Easter Island is overpowering -it is five or six hours by jet from the nearest land; to reach it by boat takes days. The small island is pounded so hard by the ocean on all sides that, now that it has an airstrip, very few boats go there any more. Since the 19th century, the island has been known to its inhabitants as *Rapa Nui* (Big Rapa), a name owed to Tahitian sailors who thought it resembled the Polynesian island of Rapa, 3850 km (2400 miles) to the west. The early islanders themselves may never have had a real name for their island, which constituted their whole world. Yet somehow this remote, battered speck produced one of the world's most fascinating and least understood prehistoric cultures, a culture which has long gripped the public's imagination because of its unique, huge, stone statues or *moai*. These have become one of our 'icons' of the ancient world, instantly recognizable in their frequent appearances in cartoons or advertisements, where they are usually -and erroneously- depicted simply as blind, brooding heads gazing gloomily out to sea.

In view of the worldwide public fascination with the island, it is odd that no serious general account of its history and archaeology has appeared in English for over thirty years. Yet we now know far more about the development and downfall of its unique culture, and it is a story with an urgent and sobering message for our own times. There have been many popular books, but if one leaves aside those filled with fantasies about lost continents and visiting alien astronauts, they are dominated by the works of Thor Heyerdahl, which set out to buttress a single and now largely discredited theory. A more balanced and up-to-date account is badly needed, and it is hoped that the present volume will fill this gap.

Today, Easter Island is generally considered a strange, fantastic, mysterious place, and this is reflected in the titles of popular books and television programmes; indeed, one recent book about the island is even subtitled *The Mystery Solved*, though which particular mystery this referred to is not explained. For the archaeologists who have devoted their lives to the study of this fascinating place, there are no mysteries exactly, but there are plenty of intriguing questions to be answered. No one could fail to feel awe and wonder on contemplating the bare landscape of rolling hills; the huge craters with their reedy lakes; the hundreds of enormous stone statues toppled and scattered about the place; the abandoned quarries; the ruins of platforms, houses and other structures; and the rich rock art. Easter Island has been called the world's greatest open-air museum, and indeed the entire island can be seen as one huge archaeological site.

1. The Polynesian Triangle, and *Rapa Nui* which lies isolated in the Pacific Ocean.

At a conservative estimate, there are between 800 and 1000 giant statues or *moai* on Easter Island; the total is uncertain because survey work is still incomplete, and there are probably many lying hidden by rubble and soil at the island's quarry. More than 230 of the statues were erected on *ahu* (platforms), each of which might carry from one to fifteen statues in a row. Contrary to popular belief, the figures are not absolutely identical: in fact, no two are exactly alike in height, width or weight.

Despite variations in form and size, however, the classic *moai* consists of a human head gracefully stylized into an elongated rectangle, together with its torso down to the abdomen. Beneath the overhanging brow, the nose is long and straight or concave, the chin prominent and pointed, and the ear-lobes often greatly distended and carved to appear perforated, with discs inserted. The arms are held tightly at the sides, and the hands, their long tapering fingers (which have no nails) almost touching, rest on the protruding abdomen.

What motivated the islanders to create these extraordinary towering figures? Perhaps, as we shall see, on their platforms around the coast they served as a sacred border between two worlds, between 'home' and 'out there'. On a tiny island such as *Rapa Nui* the feeling of being alone and cut off from the outside world must have been overpowering.

How did the islanders transport the statues over long distances and erect them on the platforms? Were they *really* devoid of timber and rope, as the first European visitors thought? The answers are almost as diverse and contradictory as the variety of scholars working on the problem.

Further clues to the island's rich cultural development are provided by its cult of the 'birdman', which survived until the end of the 19th century. The birdman was seen as the representative on Earth of the creator god *Make Make* and was of enormous symbolic significance to these isolated people who could not come and go as the birds did. Indeed, the striking motif of the birdman appears repeatedly in Easter Island's abundant rock art, especially near the village of *Orongo*, which was the centre of the cult. One can even see birdlike features in some of the giant statues. But what prompted the rise of this enigmatic cult?

Scholars have searched for answers to this series of riddles in the *rongo rongo* phenomenon, the islanders' 'script' comprising parallel lines of engraved characters preserved on a series of wooden boards. According to legend, *Hotu Matu'a*, the first settler, brought sixty-seven inscribed tablets to the island with him. We shall explore just how much progress has been made in interpreting the twenty-five surviving tablets now scattered around the world's museums.

In this book, we take a look at these different topics, particularly in the light of the intense archaeological activity of the past four decades. We also address the issue of the islanders' origins. Where did they come from, and when? How many of them were there? How and why did they travel to the island in the first place? What did they bring with them, and how did they survive? More puzzling still is the question of why, not long after the first European visits to the island, the statues were toppled over and left in disarray, often deliberately beheaded. All the evidence points to a dramatic change in the islanders' way of life, which included the onset of violence and warfare. What cataclysm could have had such a devastating impact on the island's culture?

As we shall see, the answer to this last question carries a message that is of fundamental importance to every person alive today and even more so to our descendants. Given the decline of the island's culture, we should consider the parallels between the behaviour of the Easter Islanders in relation to their limited resources and our cavalier disregard for our own fragile natural environment: the Earth itself.

This is more, therefore, than an account of the rise and fall of an extraordinary prehistoric culture; if Easter Island is seen as a microcosm of our own world, then this is, indeed, a cautionary tale relevant for the future of all humankind.

To the second edition
The Enigmas of Easter island, 2002

In the ten years since the first edition of this book appeared, much new work has been done on many aspects of Easter Island's past, and many new publications have appeared. Some problems have become better understood, while others have deepened. And, as we write these lines, the death has been announced of Thor Heyerdahl. Whatever one's opinion of his theories, and of his attitude not only towards the ancient Polynesians but also towards those who disagreed with his views, his huge importance in this field should be readily acknowledged. Most researchers involved with Easter Island, ourselves included, first became interested in the island and its problems thanks to Heyerdahl's expedition in the 1950s, and the films and publications to which it gave rise. As our book already made clear in 1992, many fundamental contributions came from that Norwegian expedition; careful excavations, pollen analysis, the rescue of the *toromiro*, experiments in statue carving, transportation and erection, and, above all, the introduction of William Mulloy to the island.

Amid the wealth of literature that has been devoted to Easter Island's past over the last decade, there have been a number of papers which question the picture we outlined of massive deforestation caused by human factors. These criticisms are answered in this new edition of our book. But here we would just like to point out that ours was by no means a new view of what happened on the island. Even La Pérouse, in 1786, had suggested that the islanders themselves had imprudently cut down their trees: '...suppléent en partie à l'ombre salutaire des arbres que ces habitants ont eu l'imprudence de couper dans des temps sans doute très reculés... Un long séjour à l'île de France, qui ressemble si fort à l'île de Pâques, m'a appris que les arbres n'y repoussent jamais, à moins d'être abrité des vents de mer par d'autres arbres ou par des enceintes de murailles; et c'est cette connaissance qui m'a découvert la cause de la dévastation de l'île de Pâques. Les habitants de cette île ont bien moins à se plaindre des éruptions de leurs volcans, éteints depuis longtemps, que de leur propre imprudence' [1].

And William Mulloy, just before his death in 1978, had already come to suspect what had happened on the island. His excavations at *Akivi* had encountered root moulds, which led him to deduce that the '...area was once covered with significantly more vegetation than has been reported in historic times. Some of this vegetation must have been quite large, though its nature was not determined' [2].

Mulloy set out his preliminary assessment of the problem in two little-known papers which were republished by the Easter Island Foundation in 1997. In one, originally published in 1974, he mentioned the phenomenon of overpopulation and the finite environment, when the limits of food-producing potential are approached, and the hitherto efficient economic equilibrium disintegrates [3]. Here we see the seeds of Easter Island being considered a microcosm of, and a warning about, the current planetary situation, although Mulloy did not have any idea of the scale of the island's deforestation or any precise data about what constituted its forests.

In the other article, written in 1976, he wrote of: '...the notion that the environment has been progressively depleted by man since human occupation. Some evidence for this has already been accumulated, but more detailed research by palaeo-botanists is required. The extremely important studies of the pollen samples collected by the Heyerdahl expedition and made by Selling have not been published and perhaps should be repeated and extended' [4].

In short, Mulloy was remarkably prescient, noting the importance of Selling's initial but unpublished findings and calling for further work in this sphere. It is sad that this great archaeologist died just a few years before one of us (JRF) was able to carry out the very research he called for, and discovered the scale and timing of the island's massive deforestation, thus confirming his suspicions of what had occurred.

In accordance with current usage, our text has *Rapa Nui* for the island, but rapanui for the islanders and their language.

[1] La Pérouse 1997, p. 65.
[2] Mulloy & Figueroa 1978, p. 22.
[3] Mulloy 1974.
[4] Mulloy 1997a: 110.

To the third edition
Easter Island, Earth Island, 2011

Exciting new evidence has emerged since the previous (second) edition of this book. Further excavations have been reported, giving new insights into the prehistory of the island. New hypotheses have been put forward, and fierce arguments have erupted. Furthermore, there has at last been a public awakening throughout the world to the need to care for our environment, and to the dangers of not doing so.

When we published our previous edition, the publishers found the original title -*Easter Island, Earth Island*- far too green for them, and insisted that we change it to *The Enigmas of Easter Island*. Obviously the original edition had been ahead of its time for most people, although it was Highly Commended in the Sir Peter Kent Conservation Book Prize. We are delighted now to be able to revert to the original title for this third edition. Its time has finally come, we believe. We are encouraged in this belief by the adoption of Easter Island as the prime example used by Jared Diamond in his widely acclaimed book *Collapse* [1]. The author, having reviewed our previous edition in the New York Times Review of Books [2], uses Easter Island to illustrate his thesis that profligate over-use of resources is inevitably followed by collapse of civilization. His analysis is broad, in that it covers economics as well as ecology, which makes it even more relevant in this time of world economic recession. In selecting Easter Island, Diamond was using knowledge gained in a previous analysis of the attributes of many Pacific islands, in which, with archaeologist Barry Rolett, he evaluated the attributes of islands (such as size, latitude, climate, geology, elevation and isolation) which make them likely to exhibit collapse of culture [3]. Easter Island had come out top of the list, being one of the Pacific's most fragile environments, predisposed to species extirpations after human settlement because of its low relief, low rainfall, and its geographical isolation.

Our own conclusion that over-use of resources was the prime cause of the collapse of the megalithic civilization has not remained unchallenged. This is good. Science progresses by the questioning of hypotheses, so that they end up abandoned, modified or strengthened in the face of new evidence. That is why, when one of us (JRF) was asked by the editors of *Science* to referee the paper by Hunt and Lipo [4], he recommended that it be published, provided that a refutation could be published (by several authors) in the same issue.

The editors ignored this advice, and published the Hunt and Lipo paper, which argued that: (1) the date of colonization of Easter Island was around AD 1200, much later than previously thought; (2) the island was deforested primarily by introduced rats, rather than by people; (3) the collapse of the civilization was later than thought and resulted from European contact, not internal warfare. The last of these ideas had been proposed already by Rainbird [5] and Peiser [6]. Hunt subsequently re-iterated his arguments in two further articles [7].

These three arguments are carefully considered in the relevant sections of this book, and are all comprehensively rejected, using many lines of evidence. Hunt challenged the dating of the pollen evidence which favoured early colonization, so we re-dated it using modern techniques and found that it indicated colonization even earlier than we had previously claimed. The rats-only theory of deforestation was quite incompatible with the abundant evidence of charcoal in archaeological sites and in the pollen cores. The evidence for internal warfare leading to the collapse of megalith construction around AD 1650 (before European contact) has been re-examined and strengthened.

In fact, recent mathematical modelling [8] hypothesizes that there may have been not one collapse but several. Indeed, this could suggest that both the megalithic culture and the bird-man cult which followed its collapse were ingenious devices to sublimate internal warfare into more peaceful forms of competition. The analogy which springs to mind is the race between the USA and Russia to put a person on the moon, as a sublimation of the Cold War. Actually, as Gwynne Dyer [9] has pointed out, there has been a war in the western world roughly every 50 years since AD 1700 (counting the two World Wars as essentially one). The next one appears to be overdue, but perhaps this is because of increased longevity in the West. The 50-year cycle is to allow people to forget the horrors of war, and its ineffectiveness in solving problems. More old people (with votes) delay this process. What is needed in the near future is some clever device to avoid war by sublimating those competitive human tendencies. Perhaps a race to put a person on Mars could be the answer, or could international sporting competitions suffice? At least, we should be thanking the highly intelligent ancient inhabitants of Easter Island for suggesting the idea to us.

[1] Diamond 2005.
[2] Diamond 2004.
[3] Rolett & Diamond 2004; see also Diamond 2007.
[4] Hunt & Lipo 2006.
[5] Rainbird 2002.
[6] Peiser 2005.
[7] Hunt 2006, 2007.
[8] Cole & Flenley 2005, 2007, 2008.
[9] Dyer 2005.

To the fourth edition
Easter Island, Earth Island, 2016

In the quarter century since this book first appeared, a great deal of varied information has been learned about Easter Island, which we have endeavoured to summarise in each edition. At the same time, however, crazy theories about the island, as well as the basic ignorance of some members of the general public, continue to amaze us. For example, on the internet one can find a short video claiming that the entire island is man-made, apparently because its triangular shape must be linked to the Pyramids! And when Jo Anne Van Tilburg used her blog to present her re-excavation of two half-buried *moai* inside the Rano Raraku crater (statues previously uncovered by Routledge), there were 10 million hits, with people expressing sheer astonishment that the 'Easter Island heads have bodies! Who knew? What an astounding discovery!' [1]

Where more conventional views of the island are concerned, the new obsession, already reviewed and challenged in our 3rd edition, has persisted on the part of many people who are intent on arguing that all was well on the island until the Europeans brought terrible effects. 'Collapse' has almost become a dirty word since the best-selling book by Jared Diamond, and to use it in relation to the island's prehistory seems to be considered a profound insult to the islanders, since many people interpret it to mean 'total disintegration'. Yet when one consults the Oxford English Dictionary, one basic definition of 'collapse' is: 'Failure, "break-down" (of an institution, enterprise, established condition of things)', and we feel that this term can justifiably be applied to the pre-European culture of Easter Island. After all, the massive social and religious changes that took place on the island before the European arrivals – it should be remembered that the birdman race almost certainly began before 1722 [2] – are surely stark evidence that some kind of major crisis had hit the place, after centuries of apparent peace, harmony and cooperation. The 'established condition of things' had broken down.

It is undeniable that there were drastic changes in the social system, the religious system and the agricultural system, and each of these might be argued to be a 'collapse' if we had better information on the timing and duration of these transformations. But since our chronological data are so poor, it seems more sensible and cautious to adopt the term 'decline' with regard to each of these changes. The testimony by the Forsters as well as by other members of Cook's party in 1774 shows that the islanders were not doing very well, to say the least [3] – conditions were clearly far inferior to what had gone before – and one can justifiably wonder how long their new, more impoverished way of life could have lasted: for example, if the island had been hit by drought or some other natural disaster. We shall never know, since the arrival of Europeans eventually did cause a true collapse of a different kind. But it is clear that deforestation and soil erosion had major effects on the life and culture of the islanders, and that conflict arose where before there had been none, as far as we know. It is illogical to propose that these two phenomena were unconnected, as some have claimed.

During the period since our last edition, there have also been repeated assertions, in both publications and TV documentaries, that there was no violence on the island before the European arrivals, and that the *mata'a* were not weapons. We have therefore felt it necessary to devote more space in this edition to presenting the abundant and varied evidence that refutes these astonishing claims.

Some researchers have recently stressed that there were no abrupt detrimental changes on the prehistoric island, and instead have emphasised a marked 'continuity in cultural practices' [4]; but while we agree that the island's prehistory is indeed one continuous development, with no apparent influences from outside, the fact remains that the islanders not only made colossal changes in their social and religious life, but also adapted as best they could to the treeless landscape they had created – what other option was there for people who could not leave the island?

2. Sebastián Paoa in *Ana Te Pahu* cave.
Photo: Rocío Lafuente.

We are second to none in our admiration for what the islanders accomplished both before the crisis and after it – as we have always emphasised in earlier editions – but we do not see this in 'either/ or' terms. For example, why should the adaptability and survival of the islanders negate the so-called 'collapse theory'? They are part and parcel of the same phenomenon – indeed the very terms 'adaptation and survival' clearly imply that a major crisis had occurred and been weathered!

Another researcher has said: 'Is its history less a cautionary tale than a story of cultural resilience?' [5] – but why should it not be both? In fact the whole message of this book is that it is indeed both – a sobering lesson for our planet, but at the same time an encouraging example of human resilience and resourcefulness. Whether or not their culture 'collapsed' or simply 'declined' or underwent 'disruption', the islanders managed to adapt reasonably successfully to their new circumstances – and that is perhaps the most important lesson they offer the world.

[1] *Rapa Nui Journal* 26 (2), October 2012, p. 95.
[2] Edwards & Edwards (2013: 373) argue that the contest probably first took place in the early 1700s and perhaps even earlier.
[3] For the 1774 testimony, see Bahn 2015, pp. 149-50; Forster 2000; Foerster 2012.
[4] e.g. Mulrooney 2012, 2013.
[5] Boersema 2015, p. 7.

Perspectiva, vista desde el punto a, donde estuvo fondeado el Nav.º S. Lorenzo.

PLANO

de la Isla de S. Carlos (alias de David) Descuvierta por orn. del Exmo. Sr. Don Manuel de Amat y Juniet, Cavallero del Orn. de S. Juan del Consejo de S. M. Gentil Hombre de su R.l Camara con Entrada, Theniente General de sus R.s Exercitos, Virrey, Governador, y Capitan Gen.l de estos Reinos, y Provincias del Peru, y Chile, Haviendo para este fin hecho la Expedicion del Navio de S. M. el S. Lorenzo, su Comand.te D. Phelipe Gonzalez de Haedo, Capitan de Navio de la R.l Armada; y Fragata S.ta Rosalia, su Capit.n D. Antonio Daumonte, y embarcadose de Orn. de S. Ex.a por primero Piloto, y Practico de estos Mares D. Juan de Hervé Alferez de Fragata y Primero Piloto de la R.l Armada.

El dia 10. de Oct.e de 1770, salieron dichos dos Vageles del Puerto del Callao, y el dia 15 de Noviembre à las 7, de la mañana, se avistó dha. Isla, y se halló, p.r la latitud de 27. grad.s 6 m.s y por 264 gr. 30 m.s de long.d meridd. de Tenerife: dia 16. se dió fondo en ella en la Ensenada, que nombre de Gonzalez, en donde se mantuvo hasta el 21, que se hizo à la vela. Los que esta Isla vieron, hacen juicio que sus avitadores serán entre grandes, y pequeños de 900, à 1000. Personas; siendo el numero de los Hombres mucho mayor, q.l de las Mugeres. Estos son de cuerpo regulares: sus colores, como de Quarterones el pelo lacio, ojos buenos; muy agiles y nadadores, assi Hombres, como Mugeres: faciles en pronunciar la Lengua Castellana; todos andan desnudos, con solo un tapa rabo: Se pintan con distintas pinturas que de el terreno, que à no ser esto, y andar vestidos, como nosotros, parecerian Europeos. Toda la tierra de la Isla es negra, con algunas tierras distintas colores, que les sirve p.a pintasse; tienen una ...

... raiz, que tiñe de amarillo fino. Despues de aver dichos dos Vageles recorrido en diferentes alturas, y meridianos, ido al Puerto de Chiloe, vuelto à ver dicha Isla, y de ella regresado al Puerto del Callao, à donde llegaron dia 28 de Marzo de 1771, Navegaron desde que salieron del Callao, hasta su regreso 4177½ leguas; sin embargo de no aver naveg.do muchas noches, p.r la orn. è instrucciones, que tenia el Comandante de ellos.

EXPLICACION.

A.	Punta de S. Lorenzo.
B.	Los tres Cerros de las 3. Cruzes.
C.	Silla de S. Carlos.
D.	Ensenada de Gonzalez.
E.	Pan de Azucar, y Punta de S.ta Rosalia.
F.	Arenal, y Caleta de S. Juan.
G.	Punta de S. Juan.
H.	Punta de S.ta Ana.
Y.	Punta de S. Joachin.
J.	Punta de S. Joseph.
K.	Morro Negro.
L.	Caleta de Langara.
N.	Punta de los Callos.
N.	Cavo de S. Antonio.
O.	Farallones de Langara.
P.	Cavo de Christoval.
Q.	Cavo de S. Francisco.
R.	Caleta de la Cueva.
S.	Punta Negra.
T.	Punta Verde.
V.	Punta de Piedra.
X.	Caleta de la Campana.
Z.	La Campana.
Q.	Cavo de S. Phelipe.
a.	Fondeadero del Navio S. Lorenzo.
b.	Fondeadero de la Fragata S.ta Rosalia.
a.	Fondeadero de la Lancha.
AG.	Arena Gorda.
AP.	Arena y Piedra.
A.	Arena.
CP.	Coral y Piedra.

YSLA DE S. CARLOS

Escala de 2. Leguas Maritimas.

Escala de una Milla Maritima.

PLANO DE LA ENSENADA DE GONZALEZ EN LA ISLA DE San Carlos.

European discovery

Easter Island has been a source of both bafflement and fascination to the outside world ever since the first recorded visits by Europeans. Equally, nothing was ever quite the same after this European contact, and certainly not after the arrival of missionaries, the first Europeans to take up residence, in 1864 [1].

There are some Spanish claims of a visit to the island by Alvaro de Mendaña in his voyages to the South Pacific during the late 16th century; he certainly discovered some islands, including the southern Marquesas group, but there is no proof of a visit to Easter Island, and surviving records are not sufficiently precise to follow his route. Others think this was the island reported in latitude 27°S by the English buccaneer Edward Davis in 1687, though it scarcely matches his description of a low and sandy island only 500 miles from Chile, and with 'a long tract of pretty high land' some 12 leagues to the west. It is likely that he was wrong about the latitude; besides, none of his crew went ashore, and his account makes no mention of the numerous great monoliths which would certainly have been strikingly visible at this time.

We may never know for sure which, if any, vessels called at the island in the 17th century or earlier, but one scholar, Robert Langdon, believed that a lost Spanish caravel, the *San Lesmes*, which disappeared in 1526, was shipwrecked on a reef east of Tahiti, some of its crew intermarrying with Polynesian women; their descendants eventually reached Easter Island and donated Basque genes, which are still found there [2]. There is some genetic support for Langdon's theory: analyses of HLA (Human Leucocyte Antigen) groups, a tissue-typing system useful in the preparation of medical transplants, have revealed that eighteen people of 'pure' Easter Island stock possess a combination of genes that is frequent among Basques (the 'Basque haplotype'), although also found in many other areas [3]. They can be traced back to one 19th-century islander, and prove that one of his parents carried the (improperly named) 'Basque haplotype'. However, there is no chronological dimension to these analyses, and the date of the haplotype's arrival on the island will always be unknown: that is, one cannot assume that the 'Basque' genes arrived via the *San Lesmes* or any other early ship. There were hundreds of whalers in this part of the Pacific during the 19th century, and Basques were usually pre-eminent in this industry. We know virtually nothing about the routes or landfalls of all these doubtless lusty crews. Thus the officially accepted discovery by the outside world was made by the Dutch commander Jacob Roggeveen on 5 April 1722; towards 5 p.m., the island was spotted by the *Afrikaansche Galei*, one of a company of three ships under Roggeveen's command. The first sighting was noted in the ship's log [4]: 'About the 10th glass in the afternoon watch, De *Afrikaansche Galei*, which was sailing ahead, headed into the wind … giving signal of seeing land… a low flat island… we gave… to the land the name of the Paasch Eyland [Easter Island], because it was discovered and found by us on Easter Day.'

Roggeveen, then 63 years old and a lawyer by training, had the curious habit of baptizing islands with trivial names related to incidents during his visits. Needless to say, he rarely bothered to inquire what

2.1. Map by the Spanish expedition, 1770.

the natives themselves called their land. The next day columns of smoke were seen rising from various places, '...from which it may with reason be concluded that the island, although it appears sandy and barren, nevertheless is inhabited by people'. (The Dutchmen later found that what looked like sand from a distance was, in fact, '...withered grass, hay or other scorched and burnt vegetation'.)

Owing to '...very unstable weather, with thunder, lightning, heavy rain and variable winds from the northwest', a landing was not possible that day. Next morning, a canoe travelled the distance of nearly 5 km (3 miles) out to the ships, bearing a 'Paaschlander', a well-built man in his fifties, with a goatee beard. He was '...quite naked, without having the least covering in front of what modesty forbids being named more clearly. This poor person appeared to be very glad to see us, and marvelled greatly at the construction of our ship.'

On the following day, the Europeans did make a brief visit to the island itself, and provided the first recorded comments on its material culture: 'Concerning the religion of these people, of this we could get no full knowledge because of the shortness of our stay; we merely observed that they set fires before some particularly high erected stone images... these stone images at first caused us to be struck with astonishment, because we could not comprehend how it was possible that these people, who are devoid of heavy thick timber for making any machines, as well as strong ropes, nevertheless had been able to erect such images, which were fully 30 feet high and thick in proportion.'

It is ironic that Roggeveen had been searching for the island recorded by Davis thirty-five years before; Roggeveen's *Journal* did not appear until 1838, but his officer Carl Behrens did publish a romanticized, unreliable account in 1739 which exaggerated his own role.

One clue that the Dutch may not have been the first European visitors is the sheer lack of surprise shown by the islander who visited the ship. If the islanders had, indeed, had no contact with the outside world, and believed *Rapa Nui* to be the whole world, one would imagine that the arrival of three sailing ships full of white-skinned people would be akin to UFOs landing today and would arouse panic and terror; but Roggeveen's visitor displayed merely a friendly nonchalance and curiosity. As was noted by Cornelis Bouman, the captain of the second Dutch ship, the *Thienhoven*, whose account only came to light in 1910, 'The natives were not afraid of us at all' [5].

The early European explorers from Roggeveen onward made useful observations about the island's ethnography and antiquities, but their reports were prone to exaggeration (especially of the statues' dimensions) and contained frequent inaccuracies: the Dutch, for example, thought the statues were made of clay, and represented figures '...hung round with a long garment from the neck to the soles of the feet', and the Spaniards said the statues had lips stretching from ear to ear, and no hands [6], while the famous drawing produced during French explorer Comte de La Pérouse's visit in 1786 [7] (ill. 4) gives both the people and the statues a somewhat European appearance. Some made extremely brief visits (the Dutch only came ashore on one day, while the French, under La Pérouse, spent only ten hours on the island), or wrote down their recollections long afterwards. Others said little: the Spanish expedition from Peru in 1770 did not publish a word, leaving us with only the ship's log (ill. 2) which was not printed until 1908 [8].

Scientific study really began with Captain James Cook's visit of 1774 [9]. Cook had left Plymouth on 13 June 1772 with two ships, the *Resolution* and the *Adventure*, with the intention of sailing round the

3. Engraving of the confrontation between rapanui and members of the Roggeveen expedition. Journal published in 1728.

world along the most southerly latitude possible in the hope of finding the fabled southern continent. This expedition was the first in history to cross the Antarctic Circle, and sailed closer to the South Pole than anyone had before. However, the weeks sailing in those icy waters weakened the crew, and scurvy developed. Cook suffered a severe gall-bladder infection, and was saved by a broth of fresh meat made of the beloved dog of his naturalist Forster [10].

It was under these conditions that Cook ordered the expedition to sail north, hoping to reach some Polynesian island where the crew might recuperate. On 1 March 1774 they sighted Easter Island, and searched its rocky coast for a suitable landing place. The next day, two islanders in a small boat gave them bananas, while another came aboard and measured the ship's length. Cook and some men then went ashore to buy supplies, trading tinsel, nails, glass and clothing for sweet potatoes, bananas, sugar cane and chickens. Being still weak, Cook himself stayed on the beach, but a small detachment was sent inland to reconnoitre. Mahine, a Tahitian accompanying Cook's expedition, could converse with the natives to some degree.

Cook had been informed of the 1770 Spanish visit to the island just before he left England, but clearly his landfall here was not planned. The British rested at the island for four days, and then sailed on. As Cook himself recorded, 'We could hardly conceive how these islanders, wholly unacquainted with any mechanical power, could raise such stupendous figures, and afterwards place the large cylindric stones upon their heads.' Four years earlier, the Spanish captain Felipe González y Haedo -whose visit was the first since Roggeveen's- had written something similar in his own log, adding, 'Much remains to be worked out on this subject'.

The earliest known archaeological probings were carried out by men from the German gunboat *Hyäne*, commanded by Captain Wilhelm Geiseler, which visited the island for four days in September 1882 [11]. Although their main aim was to collect ethnographic material for Berlin's Kaiserliches Museum, they produced the first detailed ethnographic description we have from the island, and also excavated the floor of a house at *Orongo*, and some *hare moa* (stone 'chicken houses').

The first true archaeological work was done by an American team from the USS *Mohican* in 1886, and from then until recent decades concentration focused, inevitably, on the conspicuous and impressive remains: the statues, quarries, platforms and stone houses. The Americans (primarily paymaster William Thomson and ship's surgeon George Cooke) accomplished an extraordinary amount of work in only eleven days [12], including a reconnaissance survey that noted 555 statues; detailed recording of 113 platforms and of the ceremonial village of *Orongo*, as well as descriptions of many villages, caves, tombs, petroglyphs and paintings; brief excavations in the crater of *Rano Raraku*; the gathering of much information on legends and language; and the collection of many objects including two *rongo rongo* tablets.

A pioneering and courageous Englishwoman, Mrs Katherine Scoresby Routledge, spent an eventful seventeen months on the island during the First World War, a stay which led to an excellent book [13]; she also conducted extensive surveys and many excavations, as well as taking a series of superb photographs which form an invaluable archive of the island and its monuments at that time. She was so bent on retrieving as much information as possible before it was too late that she even ventured into the island's leper settlement to interview elderly Easter Islanders about their memories and customs.

4. Duché de Vancy, the artist on the French expedition to Easter Island in 1786, portrayed the islanders as having strangely European physiognomy and as being quick to steal any of the visitors' possessions that took their fancy. The expedition's leader, Comte de La Pérouse, is shown measuring a giant statue with its *pukao*, or stone head-dress, still in place.

In 1934/5 a Franco-Belgian expedition brought the archaeologist Henri Lavachery [14] and the ethnographer Alfred Métraux [15] to Easter Island for five months. The former concentrated his attention on the rock art, while the latter produced a monumental study of the island's technology and customs. *Rapa Nui*'s pastor, Sebastian Englert (1888–1969), made the first complete survey of the *ahu* and carried out invaluable work on language and traditions [16].

Then, in 1955, came a milestone in Easter Island studies, when the first expedition of Thor Heyerdahl (1914-2002) brought in a team of archaeologists, including William Mulloy (1917-1978) who was to become the foremost expert on the island's archaeology. This expedition carried out excavations in a variety of sites, developed a provisional three-period sequence, and obtained the first radiocarbon and obsidian dates. It also took pollen samples, and carried out interesting experiments in the carving, transportation and erection of statues. Two large monographs were rapidly published [17], as well as more popular works. Until his death in 1978 Mulloy continued his work on the island, involving not only excavation and survey but also (and most spectacularly) the restoration of several monuments and of part of *Orongo* [18]. His ashes are buried on *Rapa Nui*.

During the last few decades, a good deal of new research has been done on the island, often by people who studied under, or were otherwise inspired by, Mulloy; indeed, their work forms the nucleus of this book. By developing the work of their predecessors and investigating aspects of Easter Island history that had been neglected, they have made great progress in filling some of the gaps in our knowledge of the rise and decline of this unique culture [19].

[1] For the most complete list of early European visits to the island, see McCall 1990. Menzies (2003: 449) has claimed that the Chinese treasure fleets of the 15th century established supply bases on Easter Island and Pitcairn but, as far as we are aware, there is not a shred of evidence to support this statement.
[2] Langdon 1975.
[3] For the HLA studies, see J. Dausset in *Nouveau Regard* 1982, p. 228.
[4] For Roggeveen's account, see Sharp 1970; von Saher 1990, 1993.
[5] For Bouman's account, see von Saher 1990/1; 1993; 1994.
[6] For the Spanish texts, see Mellén Blanco 1986.

[7] La Pérouse 1997.
[8] According to Stephen-Chauvet 1935, p. 10, the Spanish not only visited the island in 1770, but also returned in January 1771 and October 1772 to complete their mapping.
[9] For Cook, see Beaglehole 1961.
[10] Forster 2000; Hoare 1982; see also von Saher 1992, 1999.
[11] Geiseler 1995.
[12] Thomson 1891.
[13] Routledge 1919; see also Love 1984.
[14] Lavachery, H. 1935, 1939.
[15] Métraux 1940, 1957.
[16] Englert, S. 1948, 1970.
[17] Heyerdahl & Ferdon 1961, 1965.
[18] Mulloy 1997.
[19] General books on the island's past include Stephen-Chauvet 1935; Orliac 1995; Lee & Catany 1995; Van Tilburg 1994; Ramírez & Huber 2000; Cauwe 2008; Pelletier 2012; Treister et al. 2013; and especially Fischer 1993. For the history of the island, see Conte Oliveros 1994; Fischer 2005.

Important collections of papers can be found in *Clava*, vol. 4, 1988, Museo Sociedad Fonck, Viña del Mar; *Circumpacifica. Band II, Ozeanien, Miszellen. Festschrift für Thomas S. Barthel.* (B. Illius & M. Laubscher, eds), 1990, Peter Lang: Frankfurt; *Journal of New World Archaeology* VII (1), August 1986, UCLA; Valenta 1982; and above all the indispensable *Rapa Nui Journal* (formerly *Rapa Nui Notes*) since 1986.

A number of major exhibitions have produced important catalogues: Esen-Baur 1989 (with Belgian edition in 1990: *L'Ile de Pâques: une Enigme?* Musées Royaux d'Art et d'Histoire, Brussels); Orefici 1995 (with a Catalan edition, 1995: *Els Moai de l'illa de Pasqua. Art i Cultures als Mars del Sud.* Fundació "la Caixa", Centre Cultural: Barcelona; and a French edition, 1996: *Voyage vers l'île Mystérieuse, de la Polynésie à l'île de Pâques.* Amilcare Pizzi Editore: Milan); Kjellgren 2001 *Easter Island: an Epic Voyage* (Montreal Museum of Archaeology and History, 2010); Wenger & Duflon 2011.

And a whole series of international conferences have produced volumes of proceedings: Cristino et al. 1988; Esen-Baur 1990; Stevenson et al. 1998; Vargas 1998; Stevenson et al. 2001; Stevenson et al. 2005; Wallin & Martinsson-Wallin 2010.

4.1. Petroglyphs located in *Orongo*.

Chapter 1

The island and its geography

No Nation will ever contend for the honour of the discovery of Easter Island as there is hardly an island in this sea which affords less refreshments and conveniences for shipping than it does.

Captain James Cook

Easter Island, a tiny speck in the South Pacific, is one of the most isolated pieces of permanently inhabited land on the globe, and the easternmost inhabited island of Polynesia [1]. It is located at latitude 27°S, longitude 109°W, some 2250 km (1400 miles) southeast of Pitcairn, its nearest inhabited neighbour and home to the descendants of the Bounty mutineers (1790). The nearest point in South America is Concepción in Chile, 3747 km (2340 miles) to the southeast. The Galápagos Islands, which played a key role in Charles Darwin's development of the theory of evolution by natural selection, are 3872 km (2420 miles) to the northeast.

To the south lies only the vast emptiness of the Southern Ocean, where countless mariners including Captain Cook once searched in vain for the supposed great southern continent. Eventually they found Antarctica, but much further south than predicted, and covered in the world's greatest ice sheet. Today, perhaps those scientists who live at the South Polar Station could claim greater isolation than the Easter Islanders. But the polar researchers have a transitory existence, and depend on a constant supply of resources from the outside world.

By contrast, Easter Island has been permanently inhabited for many centuries, for most of which time it was self-sufficient and probably in complete isolation.

Nowadays you approach the island at the end of a five-hour flight in a large jet belonging to LanChile, the Chilean airline. Leaving Santiago in the morning, you travel westwards only slightly more slowly than the sun, and thus arrive not much later than you set off. Alternatively, you start from Tahiti at the other end of the run, and face a similar length of flight. In this direction, however, the time change works against you, so that the six-hour flight takes more like ten hours on the clock. But be thankful for small mercies, at least you do not have to face the complication of crossing the international date line and thus arriving, like the lady in the limerick, before you set off. The date line is in the Pacific, but far to the west, between Tahiti and Fiji. The first sight of the island is a relief. Although you know the plane is guided by a radio beacon, there is always that slight tension in the guts. What if the plane overshot? Would it have enough fuel to go anywhere else? Suppose there was a storm or fog and the airport was closed?

5. *Rano Kau* engraving by A. de Bar, Alphonse Pinart expedition, 1877.

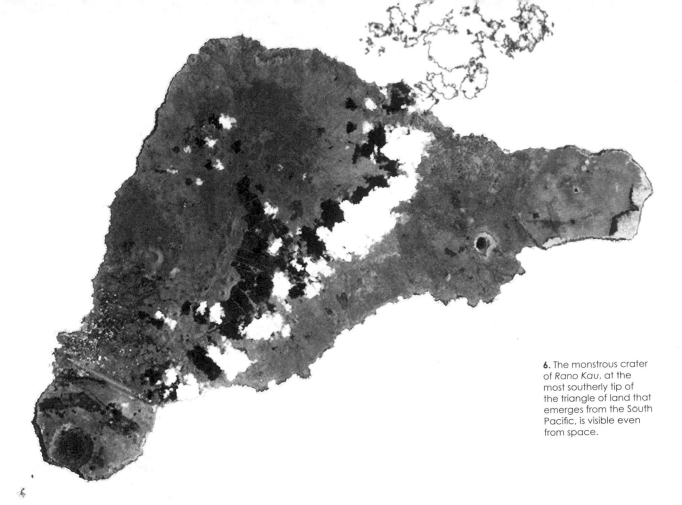

6. The monstrous crater of *Rano Kau*, at the most southerly tip of the triangle of land that emerges from the South Pacific, is visible even from space.

The landscape

When first seen from a plane window, the island gives little hint of the amazing sights in store. In general shape it is triangular and roughly symmetrical, with sides of 22, 18 and 16 km (13, 11 and 10 miles): it therefore covers only 163.6 sq.km or 63.2 sq. miles [2]. Its three main peaks -one near each corner of the triangle- are not like the craggy pinnacles of Hawai'i or Tahiti. Rather, they are firm and rounded, like the aptly named Paps of Jura in the Scottish Hebrides. The highest breast, *Terevaka* in the north, rises to 510 m (1674 ft) above sea level. The lesser pap of *Poike* in the east reaches only 460 m (1510 ft) and *Rano Kau* in the southwest only 300 m (985 ft).

As the plane draws closer, however, the strange details of the landscape appear. Cliffs along many parts of the coastline have been formed by the constant crashing of the waves, revealing black rocky columns reminiscent of Fingal's Cave on Staffa, another of the Scottish Hebridean islands. Caves are present here too, but mostly high up in the cliffs. *Rano Kau* is a pap with a serious problem, for in its centre is a monstrous circular crater, 1.5 km (c. 1 mile) across. Other smaller craters are now seen to be dotted about, which would give a slightly lunar appearance were it not for the obvious grassy vegetation. On *Poike* (which means 'Hill' [3]), as well as a small central crater, there are three strange rounded knolls in a line running to the coast. A few offshore stacks are pounded by the sea, especially the three at the southwestern tip of the island, *Motu Nui*, *Motu Iti* and *Motu Kao Kao*.

All too soon, the plane lands on the airstrip which crosses the island from west to east, and which has been extended in case it should be needed to receive the NASA space shuttle on an emergency landing. Any visiting geologist will soon be able to confirm the first impressions gained from the craters and columns seen from the air. The island is, indeed, volcanic in origin [4]. Despite desperate searches for granite or for sedimentary rocks such as limestone or sandstone, no trace of minerals derived from a continental formation has ever been found on the island. This is a blow to those searching for a 'lost continent', for granite and sedimentary rock are characteristic continental rocks. Volcanoes, however, may occur in continents or oceans, and most oceanic islands are considered by geologists to be volcanoes which have grown from the bed of the ocean until finally they have poked their noses above the water.

Modern geological theory accounts for such features rather well. All the major oceans have mid-ocean rifts at which liquid rock is constantly emerging from beneath the crust and solidifying. These rifts mark the boundaries between plates in the Earth's crust, beneath which upwelling convection currents bring the molten rock to the surface. A corresponding amount of rock is taken away from the crust at the edge of the oceans by a process of subduction, in which one tectonic plate slides under another. This leads to mountain building, in this case the Andes at the eastern edge and the Southern Alps of New Zealand at the western edge of the Pacific. Sometimes the ocean rifts branch, and at these points, known as 'hot spots', the upwelling is particularly active. Easter Island is over a 'hot spot', so it is not surprising that enough outpouring

of molten volcanic rock has occurred to build a mountain nearly 3000 m (nearly 10,000 ft) high -for that is the true height of the Easter Island volcano, as measured from the ocean bed. Were it not for the fact that over 2000 m (6500 ft) are covered by the sea, we should recognize Easter for the majestic mountain it really is.

Does this mean that Easter Island is still an active volcano which might burst into violent eruption at any time? Probably. The whole volcano -at least the part we can get at above the sea- is not very old by geologists' standards. According to the latest analyses [5], even the oldest part (*Poike*) is only about 0.5 million years old. Next oldest is *Rano Kau*, whose many outpourings of lava can be clearly seen as layers in the cliffs: the lowest -and therefore oldest- layers date to perhaps only 0.3 million years. *Terevaka*, the main eminence on the island, is less than 400,000 years old. It released a large lava flow on the southwest side very recently -only 2000 or 3000 years ago, according to one estimate. But the last major activity for which we have a date is c. 11 or 12,000 years ago, which geologically speaking is merely yesterday. This could have come from one of the numerous subsidiary cinder cones which dot the slopes of *Terevaka*; there are about seventy ancient eruptive centres on the island, each with its cone of ash. However, there has been little volcanic activity during the centuries of human occupation, and this is confirmed by the limited mentions of the phenomenon in the island's folklore [6].

Volcanoes produce a great variety of rock types, and a surprising range of these is present on Easter Island [7]. All three peaks are constructed mainly of basalt, which is simply solidified lava. Typically, it is a hard, almost black rock which might be mistaken for coal at a distance. It often occurs in layers representing distinct lava flows, a feature that is especially clear in the cliffs of *Rano Kau*. Vertical joints, producing the columnar appearance, are formed by the shrinkage of the lava as it cools and

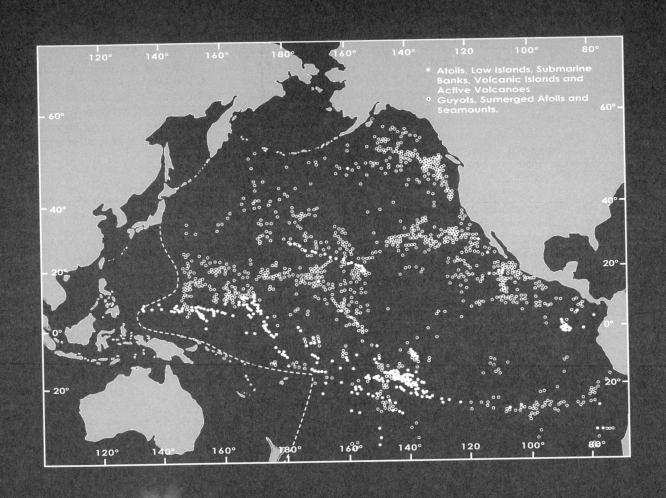

Atolls, Low Islands, Submarine Banks, Volcanic Islands and Active Volcanoes

Guyots, Sumerged Atolls and Seamounts.

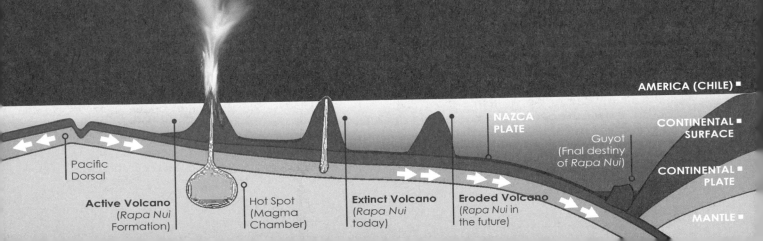

AMERICA (CHILE)

NAZCA PLATE

CONTINENTAL SURFACE

Guyot (Fnal destiny of *Rapa Nui*)

CONTINENTAL PLATE

Pacific Dorsal

MANTLE

Active Volcano (*Rapa Nui* Formation)

Hot Spot (Magma Chamber)

Extinct Volcano (*Rapa Nui* today)

Eroded Volcano (*Rapa Nui* in the future)

solidifies. The numerous caves, made famous in Thor Heyerdahl's book *Aku-Aku* [8], are mostly lava tubes. They are formed when an outpouring of lava solidifies on the outside, but the inside continues to flow downhill, leaving a tubular cavity. On *Terevaka*, some of the roofs of these caves have collapsed, revealing in each case a long cavern 10 m (33 ft) or more in height, with remaining areas of roof sometimes as thin as 30 cm (1 ft) (ill. 8). It is the abundance of these caves that causes most of the rainfall to drain away underground, contributing to the rather arid nature of large parts of the island. In fact, there are no permanent surface streams anywhere on the island; one stream does flow intermittently from *Terevaka* to the sea during heavy rainfall, but overall the absence of a high central plateau prevents gully erosion and the development of either streams or valleys.

In the past, the dense forest generated abundant precipitation that caused some perennial streams, which later became intermittent. In 1795 Captain Charles Bishop reported that '...we observed two very clear runs of water pouring over the rocks'. Even today in the rainy season some streams come down from Terevaka [9].

8. Interior of *Ana Te Pahu* cave, *Rohio* sector with its roof collapsed, and lush vegetation. Photo: Eduardo Ruiz-Tagle.

7. An apparently isolated island may be surrounded by numerous submerged peaks; the Pacific is known to contain hundreds of such 'hidden islands'.

Bottom: Volcanic islands such as Easter Island are formed by outpourings of molten rock from beneath the Earth's crust. Many of these islands, however, subsequently become submerged as the tectonic plate on which they rest is carried beneath an adjoining plate by the geological process of subduction.

In places the superficial basalt has a rough surface, giving it an appearance like a fresh lava flow. This is especially so near Maunga Hiva-Hiva (a small cone 3 km north-east of Hanga Roa) which has been dated to less than 2000 years old [10]. Surprisingly, the area shows signs of former intensive agriculture [11], perhaps because the fresh volcanic soils were rich in nutrients. Some of the basalt is extremely hard, and a deposit of it at Rano Aroi on Terevaka was exploited to make some of the hard tools used to carve the giant statues, as well as to make house-foundation slabs. Most of the tools that required a sharp edge, such as spearheads and woodworking implements, were made from obsidian, a black volcanic glass formed when lava cools so rapidly that it has no time to crystallize into basalt. There are numerous obsidian outcrops on the island [12]; the most important are around Rano Kau and on *Motu Iti* . The mineralogical characteristics of each source are distinctive, so we can tell that people thought the *Motu Iti* obsidian of sufficiently high value for them to make the risky boat trip out to the islet for the express purpose of obtaining this material.

The giant statues are, with some exceptions, made of porous volcanic tuff from *Rano Raraku*, a subsidiary cone on the side of *Terevaka*. Tuff is a rock formed from volcanic ash thrown out during an eruption, and subsequently compacted and hardened. It remains, however, much softer than basalt, which is doubtless why it was used for carving.

Most of the satellite cones of *Terevaka* are located on lines of weakness radiating from the peaks. They are mostly made of volcanic cinders or 'lapilli'. Sometimes these too have become compacted and hardened. It is one of these deposits of 'scoria' at *Puna Pau* (which means 'exhausted stream' in old rapanui [13]), coloured red with oxidized iron as volcanic rocks often are, which provided the *pukao* or 'top-knots' which surmounted many of the statues (see pp. 175-181).

The coastline of Easter Island is unusual in a Polynesian island in that it lacks a coral reef that reaches the surface. But this does not mean that there is no reef at all. A recent study [14] has shown that there are abundant corals, mainly of two species, *Pocillopora verrucosa* and *Porites lobata*, the latter dominating below 15 m depth. In some areas, especially off the north side of the *Poike* Peninsula and near Punta Cook on the west coast, the corals are built up into true reefs. Elsewhere they form just a veneer over the volcanic rocks. Most of the tropical reef-forming species are absent, because the ocean temperature falls to 21° C (70° F) in winter. There is nothing surprising in this, considering the latitude, which is outside the southern limit of the tropics. It does mean, however, that the coast is unprotected in storms. The result of the waves' ferocity has been erosion, leading to steep cliffs up to 300 m (985 ft) high around *Poike*, *Rano Kau* and the north side of *Terevaka*. Only the south coast seems to have escaped erosion on this scale, and has a gently shelving shoreline in many areas. Even this, however, cannot avoid the effect of exceptional wave action. Such an event occurred in 1960, following a powerful earthquake in Chile. This triggered an 8-metre tsunami (tidal wave), which carried fifteen statues weighing up to 30 tons each more than 150 m (500 ft) inland from the platform of *Tongariki*, and left them broken and covered by thousands of tons of *ahu* wall and fill [15].

The coastline has remarkably few sandy beaches. Only at *Anakena* ('Gannet cave' [16]) and *Ovahe* on the north coast, and less notably at La Pérouse Bay nearby, are these features found. This makes it difficult to land anything larger than a canoe in most areas, and tradition has it that *Hotu Matu'a*, the first discoverer of the island, circumnavigated it in his two canoes before landing at *Anakena*.

Under the influence of the subtropical temperatures and the moderate rainfall, Easter Island rocks have slowly weathered to give a variety of reddish or brownish soils that seem potentially quite fertile. On the oldest rocks (*Poike*) the soil is up to several metres

9. Aerial view of the island, showing its volcanic topography.

deep, whereas on the younger rocks of *Terevaka* it tends to be shallower. Recent research [17] has shown that in some areas the soils are at present rather poor in nutrients. But almost everywhere on the island, apart from the steepest parts of the cliffs and the youngest lava surfaces, there is soil sufficient in quantity and quality to support the growth of trees. This puts paid immediately to any suggestion that the present almost treeless nature of the island is the result of inadequacy in the soil.

Erosion of soil can be observed in numerous places today. This is most conspicuous at the cliff top on the south-west side of *Poike*, where a large area has been denuded almost down to bedrock. However, vertical faces about 1 m high in this area reveal a more subtle type of erosion which may have been in progress much earlier. This is slopewash, a relatively gentle process in which layers of topsoil progressively march downhill, burying those beneath. Radiocarbon dating of charcoal fragments in this material suggest that this process was active in many parts of the island between AD 1200 and AD 1650 [18]. It is a process commonly associated with deforestation by people.

The climate

Similarly, the lack of trees cannot be blamed on inadequacy of climate. In terms of temperature, conditions are almost idyllic for the growth of many species of tree. The mean annual temperature is 20.5° C (69° F), with only slight variation between seasons. The warmest months are January and February with 23.4° C (74° F), and the coolest are July and August with 17.8° C (64° F). Variation between day and night is only moderate, and frost is unknown. Rainfall is rather irregularly distributed throughout the year, with a mean of 1198 mm (c. 47 in). The wettest months tend to be March to June, and droughts may occur in several months, but especially in September which is commonly a very dry month. Rainfall also varies greatly from year to year (from 1550 mm [61 in] in 1948 to 766 mm [30 in] in 1953) as well as monthly. There are also marked differences over the island despite its small size, with the centre receiving far more rain than the north coast, as a result of the interplay of temperatures, topography, and the direction and intensity of winds.

The rainfall records are not very complete, but it is clear that severe droughts sometimes happen. Could these have prevented trees from surviving? Certainly this was not so in the 20th century, for there are introduced trees of considerable age, and of several species, round the main village of *Hanga Roa* and at other spots on the island. Whether the droughts might have been more severe in the past, as some scholars such as Australian ethnographer Grant McCall have suggested [19], is an open question at this stage, but one to which we shall return later.

The island is certainly a very windy place. Winds are a major climatic factor here, and few days are free of them. They blow mainly from the east and southeast between September and May, and from the north and northwest for the rest of the year. Severe storms are known, and the lack of a good harbour has caused real problems for shipping. Although these storms could have created difficulties for vegetation, there is nowhere in the world where wind alone can prevent the growth of woody vegetation. It may be limited to a wind-pruned scrub (as on many coastal cliffs in Britain, for instance), but it is not eliminated, even when the wind bears a damaging salt spray from the sea. In any case, there are locations on Easter Island, notably inside the crater of *Rano Kau*, which are totally protected from the wind. In fact, *Rano Kau* is a sort of natural hothouse, and its interior slopes support vines, figs and Bougainvillea which have flourished unrestrainedly since their introduction, possibly by Father Sebastian Englert. A more recent introduction, also thriving, is avocado. In general, then, Easter Island is potentially quite a fertile place. Large parts of it would be capable of supporting permanent agriculture or forest.

One drawback, however, is the lack of surface water. The high temperature and humidity cause rapid chemical weathering of the soil which, in turn, frequently leads to leaching; the high soil temperatures mean the evaporation rate is also high. The inevitable result of excessive evaporation and porous soils is weak moisture retention. The only reliable sources of freshwater naturally available to the first settlers were the three crater lakes (*Rano Aroi, Rano Kau, Rano Raraku*), apart from a few springs on the north coast, and pools formed in lava tubes. Not surprisingly, the settlers eventually pecked out some stone basins to catch and retain rainwater, as well as constructing some hydraulic monuments, cascades, embankments, canals, etc, on the slopes of Terevaka [20].

A description of Easter Island would be incomplete without mention of Salas y Gómez. This is a small reef, 415 km (260 miles) away to the northeast. It is only 300 m (985 ft) long at low tide, and shrinks to a mere 70 m (230 ft) at high tide. It is constantly swept by salt spray, and only four species of land plants grow there. There is a small depression which sometimes contains fresh water. Sea birds abound in the breeding season. Although it is possible to land only at times of exceptional calm, the Easter Islanders insist that they used to visit Salas y Gómez on a regular basis, to collect sea-bird eggs and young as a food supply. To achieve the return journey by canoe must have been a hazardous and exhausting affair, and there is actually no proof that the islanders went there in ancient times.

Fauna and flora

Islands are important natural laboratories, where evolution has carried out its work on a scale much easier to understand than on a large continent. Easter Island, thanks to its extreme isolation, has always been naturally poor in both fauna and flora. It has no indigenous land mammals [21], and only two small lizard species which are thought to have arrived as stowaways with the human settlers, who also almost certainly brought, deliberately, the edible Polynesian rat, later to be ousted by the European rat. On present evidence the settlers did not introduce the pig, which is surprising if they came from Polynesia, where this animal was commonly domesticated (Chapter 3). There is also no evidence that they ever had dogs [22], although they seem to have retained a memory of them, because when the cat was introduced they gave it the name *kuri*, which applies elsewhere in Polynesia to dogs. Rabbits enjoyed a brief abundance after their introduction in 1866, but had become extinct by 1911, wiped out by the islanders -indeed, this may be the only place in the world where rabbits were eaten before they could multiply! Sheep, pigs, horses and cattle were introduced in 1866 and survive to this day, in fluctuating numbers. Goats were also introduced.

10. The settlers also introduced two species of lizard, or *moko*. At right is the night lizard, *Moko Uru-Uru Kau* (Gekkonidae *Lepidodactylus lugubris*).

The only conspicuous land bird is a small hawk, which apparently survives mainly by eating insects. It too is introduced, as are the Chilean partridge and the South American tinamou. The human immigrants did bring with them the fowl *Gallus domesticus*, which was a major item of diet and was known by its Polynesian name *moa*. At times chickens have become feral in large numbers. Some Easter Island chickens still lay pale blue eggs, and it has been claimed that this is an original character. Similar eggs are laid by fowls in South America, which perhaps argues for a contact between the two places in the past; but whether it implies an immigration of people, and if so in which direction, is not so clear (Chapter 2).

Migratory sea birds used to come by, but their numbers and variety have now dwindled. Before human occupation, sea birds must have nested not just on offshore islets, as they do today, but also on the main island and probably in vast numbers, like those on the uninhabited Henderson Island far to the northwest. On the islet of *Motu Nui*, in the 1930s, Alfred Métraux collected not just the sooty tern for which the island is famous, but also petrels, grey terns, noddy terns, boobies, tropicbirds and frigate birds [23].

Sea mammals and turtles do not seem to have been abundant after the arrival of human settlers, judging from the scarcity of their bones in archaeological sites, though turtle shells were sometimes used to make decorative objects; fish were clearly less limited, since 126 species have been recorded, but compare this figure with the 450 species available in Hawai'i or the more than 1000 in Fiji! The lack of a coral reef also meant that shellfish were highly restricted in their numbers and variety, though they were heavily exploited [24].

The island's invertebrate fauna is also small and has some introduced forms. There are a few species of isopods, spiders, insects, worms, a snail; a cricket and scorpion are said to be introduced, like an irritatingly ubiquitous large type of cockroach. At least two species of ant are thought to have been accidentally introduced by humans.

Although the present-day visitor to Easter Island might, with a little searching, find well over a hundred species of flowering plants and ferns growing, there is no doubt at all that the majority of these are recent introductions to the island [25]. Many are ornamental plants, like the nasturtium and lavender; others are clearly crop plants, such as the avocado and the french bean. There are some large timber trees, including the blue gum and the Monterey cypress. Many are simply widespread weeds, like the fleabane and the dandelion. Sometimes the introduction is a matter of history, but more often it is unrecorded and -especially in the case of weeds- accidental. A few species are mentioned in the island's legends as having been introduced by the first settlers.

In 1917 the Swedish botanist Carl Skottsberg found only forty-six indigenous plant species, and two more have been added to the list since then [26]. There is no other oceanic island of comparable dimensions, geology and climate with such a poor native flora. Even allowing for some important species that are now extinct (Chapter 4), it is clear that Easter Island's environment was somewhat special. The study of the native flora rests on its taxonomy, means of dispersal and known distribution outside the island [27]. Certain species, for example, are endemic and, since they have no extra-island distribution, they must presumably be native. Others are known to occur on most tropical and subtropical coastlines. Their seeds float on sea water and remain viable in it, so there is no difficulty in believing them to be native too. In other cases, the likely means of arrival is by wind -this almost certainly applies to the ferns, whose spores are very light. A third possible method of arrival is by bird transport. This could include adherence to the feathers, feet or beak of a bird, or transport in its gut. A number of Easter Island grasses and sedges might well have been transported in the plumage of birds.

10.1. Petroglyph of a rooster.
The Rock Art of Easter Island, Georgia Lee and Paul Horley, Rapanui Press.

11. These Chilean palms in the National Park of 'La Campara' help us to visualise the original landscape of *Rapa Nui* where a very similar species covered the *Poike* peninsula. That area may have looked like this, but today all that remains is eroded soil, as can be seen in the inset photo.
Photos: Eduardo Ruiz-Tagle.

It is worth remembering that long-distance transport to Easter Island may have been less of an obstacle in the past than it is now [28]. We know that a number of species (the endemic ones) have been there long enough to diverge by evolution from their relatives elsewhere. We also know that the island is at least half a million years old, and for much of that period the Earth has been in the grip of successive ice ages. By removing water from the ocean to form massive polar ice caps, these ice ages lowered sea level by at least 100 m (328 ft), and possibly considerably more at times. Submerged islands (seamounts or guyots) abound in the Pacific (ill. 7, bottom). Although many of these are now too deep to have been exposed by the ice age lowering of sea level, the general history of Pacific islands is one of progressive lowering by a combination of marine and subaerial erosion and tectonic sinking (ill. 7, bottom), so that seamounts may have been higher in the past. All these factors combine to suggest that during much of Easter Island's existence, the possibility of 'stepping stone' dispersal would have been much greater than now.

It is also true that some of the mechanisms of dispersal may have been more powerful in the past. During the ice ages, the polar regions were subject to greater reductions in temperature than tropical regions. The difference in temperature between the tropics and the poles would therefore have been greater, and since this difference is what drives the 'Hadley circulation' (the basis of the trade winds), it is often argued that trade winds may have been more powerful in glacial times, although more latitudinally restricted. The westerly winds now prevalent in the forties latitudes may also have been stronger and there is evidence that this wind-belt moved towards the equator. Conversely, at times of higher temperature than now, such as the early to middle post-glacial (c. 9000 to 5000 years ago) and last interglacial (c. 120,000 years ago), cyclones extended to higher latitudes and may have been more frequent than now; we may be seeing the start of a similar phase, caused by the Greenhouse Effect. There is thus a strong possibility that the wind speeds available to carry plant matter to Easter Island were greater in the past.

Another, perhaps more important reason why dispersal could have been more effective in earlier times is that, on many islands, not only were bird populations greater in the past, but also the number of species was much higher. We shall see in Chapter 4 that discoveries of fossil bones on Easter Island and several Pacific island groups such as Galápagos and Hawai'i have demonstrated the former existence of species that no longer occur there. Many of these were endemic species, now extinct. On Hawai'i, about twenty-five species are known to have been eliminated since human immigration [29]. Some of these were apparently flightless, but others were perfectly capable of the long-distance migration that is common in birds. A number were ducks, a group for which the crater lakes of Easter could have been a suitable habitat.

It has been reckoned, therefore, that about half of Easter Island's native plant species could have arrived by bird, a third (all ferns) by wind and a sixth by water [30]. The question of *where* they came from will be considered more fully in the next chapter. It will suffice here to state that, according to Skottsberg [31], most of the island's flora came from southeast Asia via western Polynesia, and only to a small extent from South America.

We have already mentioned that Easter Island's environment is somewhat special. The remarkable fact is that Skottsberg found only one species of indigenous tree (2 per cent) and two of shrubs (4 per cent). This is quite out of line with other 'high' islands of the Pacific, which have a large woody flora (70 per cent), and has led to its flora being described as 'disharmonic' [32].

The indigenous tree that Skottsberg identified, *Sophora Toromiro*, is itself scarcely more than a shrub. It is endemic to Easter, although Skottsberg regards it as close to the species from the Juan Fernández Islands. The genus is common on islands of the southern oceans. The seeds of some sophoras can float in sea water for at least three years, and retain their viability for up to eight years [33]. Thanks to the depredations of the inhabitants, and the introduction of browsing and grazing animals by Europeans, the *toromiro* declined, so that by the time Thor Heyerdahl visited the island in the 1950s he could find only a single, almost dead specimen in the crater of *Rano Kau* [34]. Since then, no botanist has recorded it, and the species appeared to be extinct.

Miraculously, phoenix-like, it rose from the grave in Sweden. Seeds collected by Heyerdahl from the last surviving specimen on the island germinated in the botanic gardens at Göteborg [35]. The species is now flourishing there, as well as in the botanic gardens at the University of Bonn. Attempts have been made to reintroduce it to the island; the first attempts were unsuccessful, and there was concern that perhaps some vital ingredient was no longer present in the island soil. Later attempts by the Chilean Forestry Service are succeeding, but slowly. Recently the genetic diversity of the surviving specimens has been assessed [36], and it is clear that several cultivated specimens survived in Chile and elsewhere. A concerted effort to re-introduce the species is underway [37]. The outcome of the latest attempt is awaited with great interest.

[1] On climate and geography in general, see Zizka 1989. For general studies, Porteous 1981; McCall 1994.

[2] Cristino & Izaurieta 2006.

[3] Fischer 2005, p. 40.

[4] Baker 1967; Fischer & Love 1993; Vezzoli & Acocella 2009.

[5] Hasse et al. 1997.

[6] Baker 1967, p. 121.

[7] Baker 1993.

[8] Heyerdahl 1958.

[9] Fischer 2005. p. 25; Vargas et al. 2006, pp. 63, 289. For Bishop, see Roe 2005, p. 62.

[10] González-Ferrán, O. et al. 2004.

[11] Sonia Haoa, pers. comm.

[12] Stevenson et al. 1983/4.

[13] Fischer 2005, p. 42.

[14] Hubbard & Garcia 2003.

[15] Cristino & Vargas 1998, 1999.

[16] Fischer 2005, p. 20.

[17] Ladefoged et al. 2005.

[18] Mann et al. 2003.

[19] McCall 1993.

[20] Vogt & Moser 2010; Vogt et al. 2015. Loti (Rapa Nui 2009, p. 104) reported that fresh water was ultra-precious on the island, and that people kept it in gourds in which it fermented, and they often had to go without, resorting to stuffing themselves with lichens and sweet potatoes instead.

[21] Klemmer & Zizka 1993.

[22] In the 1992 edition of our book we mentioned (pp. 31, 91) a discovery of dog bones, as reported in the *Rapa Nui Journal* 5 (3), 1991, p. 45; however, this later proved to be a misidentification, as reported in the *Rapa Nui Journal* 7 (3), 1993, pp. 61-62. see also Vargas et al. 2006, p. 330.

[23] Steadman et al. 1994; Steadman 2006, pp. 248-52.

[24] DiSalvo & Randall 1993. According to Edwards & Edwards (2012, p. 64) whales were not hunted, but do beach roughly 2 or 3 times every 20 years today.

[25] Etienne et al. 1982; Zizka 1990; Flenley 1993.

[26] Skottsberg 1956; Alden 1990.

[27] Zizka 1990, 1991.

[28] Flenley 1993.

[29] Steadman 1989.

[30] Carlquist 1967.

[31] Skottsberg 1956.

[32] Van Balgooy 1971.

[33] Sykes & Godley 1968.

[34] Heyerdahl & Ferdon 1961.

[35] Alden 1982.

[36] Maunder et al. 1999.

[37] Maunder 1997. For the *Toromiro*, see also various papers in Esen-Baur 1990; C. Orliac 1993; and Liller 1995.

Children at school, Hanga Roa. MAPSE colection.

Part I

The original 'boat people'

...quite unexpectedly and to our great astonishment, four or five shots were heard in our rear... On this, as in a moment, more than thirty shots were fired, and the Indians, being thereby amazed and scared, took to flight, leaving 10 or 12 dead, besides the wounded.

Jacob Roggeveen, 1722

Chapter 2

Where did they come from? East or west?

*When the subject is enigmatic
Easter Island no man's knowledge
is either complete or secure.*

Father Sebastián Englert

The most fundamental question concerning the rapanui, the one on which many other issues depend, is where did they come from? Deeps surround this volcanic island for a radius of 15 km (c. 9 miles), and it is definitely not the remnant of a lost continent, so its inhabitants -like those of all other Pacific islands- must have arrived from elsewhere and colonized it. But where was this elsewhere? In view of the island's geographical position, there are two basic choices: east (South America) or west (Polynesia).

The idea that the Pacific islands were settled from the New World was initially put forward in 1803 by Father Joacquin de Zuñiga, a Spanish missionary in the Philippines; he based his view on the prevailing winds and currents. A specific link between Easter Island and the mainland was first suggested in 1870 when, at a lecture given by J. L. Palmer at London's Royal Geographic Society, Sir Clements Markham mentioned apparent analogies between the island's platforms and statues and those at *Tiahuanaco* (*Tiwanaku*), Bolivia. A number of German scholars in the 1930s also published papers seeing the origin of Easter Island culture in prehistoric Peru.

In the second half of the 20th century, the question of where the rapanui came from was dominated by the much publicized claims of the Norwegian explorer and adventurer Thor Heyerdahl. He accepted that Polynesians eventually reached the island from the west, and that it was their traits which dominated its anthropology and culture in recent periods; but he firmly believed that they were preceded by settlers from South America, to the east.

Since the question of where the islanders came from clearly has important consequences for the assessment of their cultural origins and development, we must begin by taking a look at the evidence for the two possible sources. The relevant evidence is varied, and little of it taken alone could be seen as decisive; as we shall see, however, the cumulative effect does point in one direction rather than the other.

Thor Heyerdahl and the *Kon-Tiki* Expedition

The prevailing winds and currents in this part of the Pacific are of crucial importance, for they were used by Thor Heyerdahl to support his claim that Polynesia could only have been settled from the New World. Indeed, the fact that southeast trade winds blow for most of the year encouraged Heyerdahl to attempt to prove his theory with the famous *Kon-Tiki* expedition of 1947 [1].

In a trip of great daring and imagination, Heyerdahl and his crew of five set out from Peru on a raft made of balsa wood, in order to demonstrate that a simple vessel could drift to eastern Polynesia on this 'one-way marine escalator'. Their supplies included canned foods and a solar still for making drinking water from the sea -essential equipment for a journey that was certain to last a number of months. On encountering powerful whirls at the eastern end of the South Equatorial Current, they were forced to west as much as possible to avoid being swept back. The six men -and a parrot- were crowded into a tiny bamboo cabin, sleeping on straw mattresses on reed matting. From a distance the vessel looked like '...an old Norwegian hay loft... full of bearded ruffians'. Initial anxieties about the logs becoming sodden or the ropes suffering from friction proved ill-founded, but the long heavy steering-oar often had to be wrestled with. There were dangers, such as a huge whale shark which had to be fought off with a harpoon, and occasional storms, during one of which a man fell overboard but was eventually rescued; the parrot, however, was washed overboard and never seen again.

The freshwater supplies became brackish after two months, but heavy showers replenished them. The ocean also provided food, since bonitos and flying fish would land on the deck, and once literally in the frying pan. Dolphins and pilot fish were constantly around the raft, and the crew amused themselves with the sport of luring sharks with tit bits and then hoisting them on board by the tail. Finally, having become one with the elements, and after months of perfect solitude, the crew knew that they were approaching land when they saw hundreds of sea birds. After 101 days at sea, the Kon-Tiki crashed on to a reef in the Tuamotus, east of Tahiti.

Following the apparent success of the Kon-Tiki voyage, Heyerdahl went on to expand and refine his theory. He had first seen Polynesia as having been colonized from the coasts of both South and Northwest America [2], but after Kon-Tiki he limited his theory to South America alone. Furthermore -and somewhat paradoxically- he decided that the Polynesians had indeed managed to arrive in canoes from the west, but quite late in Easter Island's prehistory, eventually massacring most of the Amerindian settlers. He even took this view still further, suggesting in his last book on the subject that Polynesians were, as he put it, '...brought to Easter Island, either with their consent or against their will, by navigators from a more culturally developed area of ancient Peru, using either force or cunning. Maybe the 19th-century Europeans were not the first to sail from Peru into the Pacific as slave raiders' [3].

The Kon-Tiki voyage, therefore, was of decisive importance in the archaeological study of Easter Island, for it led to what many considered to be Heyerdahl's obsession with his theory of colonization from the east. Clearly believing that the Kon-Tiki proved his theory concerning the '...permanent tradewinds and forceful companion currents', he bolstered his claim with selective evidence of the folk memory, botany, material culture, linguistics and physical anthropology of the island, building up a complex picture of the island's history [4], a picture that we must now examine more closely.

12. In 1947, Thor Heyerdahl set out to prove that Polynesia was first settled from South America. Carrying a six-man crew, the Kon-Tiki, a raft made of balsa wood, survived the onslaught of occasional storms and powerful currents to drift westwards for 101 days before being wrecked east of Tahiti. Despite the heroism of the expedition, it demonstrated no more than that a westward drift voyage was possible -and then only after a craft had been towed far out to sea to avoid the inshore Peruvian currents.

The map of prevailing ocean currents appears to support Heyerdahl's belief in the colonization of Easter Island from Peru -but the Peru coastal current tends to carry vessels north to Panama, while the ocean currents and winds often change direction.

NORTH EQUATORIAL CURRENT

EQUATORIAL COUNTER CURRENT

SOUTH EQUATORIAL CURRENT

Cook
Islands

Marquesas
Islands

Tahiti

Raroia

21 July

7 August

30 June

9 June

19 May

Departure
28 April

Pitcairn

Rapa Nui

HUMBOLDT CURRENT

PERU OCEANIC CURRENT

PERU COASTAL CURRENT

ANTARTIC CURRENT

13. Two illustrations by a member of the *Kon-Tiki* crew, the Norwegian artist Erik Hesselberg who published in 1949, *Kon-Tiki and I*, an interesting book about the expedition.

Heyerdahl presented, for example, the striking folk memory of an individual islander: Alexander Salmon, a half-Tahitian who lived on the island in the late 19th century, claimed that *Hotu Matu'a* came from a land in the direction of the rising sun in two big double-canoes with three hundred followers; they came from a group of islands to the east called *Marae-toe-hau* (Place of Burial), a very hot country.

These first South American settlers, as Heyerdahl saw it, introduced a series of plants to the island, including the sweet potato, *toromiro*, totora reed, chili pepper, cotton, and bottle gourd. He always believed that the totora bullrush (*Scirpus riparius*) -the dominant plant of all three crater swamps of Easter Island- was identical to that of Peru; he claimed that Olof Selling's (still unpublished) analysis found that its pollen suddenly began to deposit during the earliest human settlement period and was associated with soot particles. He also claimed that pollen from freshwater plants was absent before humans arrived, and that totora and *tavari* (*Polygonum acuminatum*, another aquatic plant) must have been brought in by humans because they generate only by new shoots from suckers, and not by seeds.

Over the years, Heyerdahl put forward a whole list of tool-types and features found on Easter Island which he believed to be characteristic of the New World (though not necessarily of any single archaeological complex), but rare or absent in Polynesia -for example, stone pillows, shallow grinding-stones, basalt bowls, stone picks, stone fish-hooks, and bone needles- and he placed equal stress on South American civilizations as sources of Easter Island's stonework and statues. In particular, it has often been suggested that the superb façade of closely fitted blocks at *Ahu Vinapu* I (ill. 14) is similar to Inca walls at Cuzco, Peru; and the kneeling statue 'Tukuturi' (ill. 20), discovered on the flank of *Rano Raraku* by Heyerdahl's 1955 expedition, has repeatedly been compared to kneeling statues from *Tiahuanaco*, and thus has been assumed to be an early prototype from which arose the more classic island statues, themselves compared somewhat paradoxically to standing statues from *Tiahuanaco*. Ironically, Heyerdahl himself once wrote that the classic *moai* have '...no similarity whatsoever to statues... on the continent to the east'! He saw the fitted stone blocks of Easter Island as Early Period structures different from any known Polynesian pattern of architecture ('...no Polynesian fisherman would have been capable of conceiving, much less building such a wall' [5]); and he considered three aberrant statue types on the island (boulder heads, rectangular pillars with human traits, and kneeling figures) to be characteristic of pre-Classic *Tiahuanaco*. Heyerdahl repeatedly pointed to superficial resemblances between the 16th-century Marquesas statues (see p. 127) and those of San Agustín in Colombia (of uncertain date, probably the early centuries AD), regardless of distance and chronology, although neither group has any specific resemblances with material from coastal Ecuador, which lies between them, together with 6400 km (4000 miles) of open sea! Furthermore, where domestic architecture is concerned, he saw two house-building traditions on Easter Island, with the Polynesians producing the boat-shaped pole-and-thatch dwellings (ills 44-45) and the Amerindians being responsible for the 'earlier' sophisticated corbelled structures.

In a somewhat tortuous argument, Heyerdahl also regarded *Rapa Nui*'s wooden carvings as non-Polynesian in inspiration and motif, especially the '...emaciated hooknosed long-eared goateed male figure' (ill. 87). Although he admitted that these carvings must be from the Late Period (by which time he accepted the Polynesians had arrived), he insisted that the objects display '...aberrant elements surviving from the Middle and even Early Periods'. Strangely enough, he saw the obsidian *mata'a* (spearpoints), which did not occur before the Late Period, as bearing a strong resemblance to tools in Peru and the Andes. He also made much of Edwin Ferdon's claim that four cupmarks on a rock at *Rano Kau* were a solar observatory, citing this as evidence of a heliolatry foreign to the rest of Polynesia and thus imported from sun-worshipping New World cultures.

The Easter Islanders' language provided Heyerdahl with further evidence; the islanders' term for the sweet potato, for example (*kumara*), is similar to the pan-Polynesian term *kuumala*, which has often been derived from the Quechua (South American) word *cumar*. He noted that both Routledge and Englert had heard fragments of an incomprehensible ancient language, but that even the islanders could not understand these words by the time missionaries settled there, so they were not recorded. Heyerdahl chose to assume that this ancient tongue came from South America; he believed that the original languages of *Tiahuanaco* and southern Peru were suppressed by the Inca long before they could be recorded, and hence it is impossible to find linguistic evidence for pre-Inca migrations from the mainland into Polynesia.

As for the *rongo rongo* 'script' preserved on a series of wooden boards, Heyerdahl tried to show some relationship with several South American scripts: for instance, he mentioned a picture writing of the Cuna Indians of Panama and northwest Colombia, who painted on wooden tablets used for recording songs. He also pointed to primitive writing systems found among the early historic (post-Columbian) Aymara and Quechua tribes of the Titicaca area who, like *rongo rongo*, use a 'boustrophedon' system, where the direction of lines is alternately reversed, so that one has to turn the tablet upside down at the end of each line. Similarly, he compared only selected motifs and signs from Easter Island's abundant rock art and script with the total array of alleged ideograms on the monolithic gateway at Tiahuanaco in Bolivia.

In his study of physical anthropology, Heyerdahl pointed out that the skeletal material we have is primarily or exclusively from the later periods, by which time Polynesians were well established on the island. So the race of the earlier populations was still, for him, an open question. Nevertheless, he also claimed that analyses of Easter Island skeletal material by American anthropologist George Gill had revealed '...traits that deviated from the Polynesian norm: many of the crania, for example, had curved 'rocking-chair' jawbones, an un-Polynesian feature known from the aboriginal population of America' [6].

Heyerdahl spent decades assembling evidence to support his theory of Amerindian cultural superiority, yet does it hold up under close examination? Careful scrutiny reveals the flaws in his apparently convincing argument; as we shall see, he relied on the selective use of evidence, which resulted in a misleading conclusion.

Kon-Tiki: The hidden evidence

The *Kon-Tiki* voyage, while in many ways spectacular, is in fact far from conclusive proof that Polynesia was first settled from South America. The *Kon-Tiki* herself was modelled on a type of craft developed by the Peruvians only after the Spanish introduced the use of the sail. Prehistoric Peruvians did voyage with small three-log rafts off their coast, but propelled them with paddles; they also used one- and two-man reed-bundle floats, and inflated sealskin floats, depicted in thousands of prehistoric (Lambayeque) representations -one never finds a depiction of a big raft or canoe or a sail [7]. Excavations by Heyerdahl at the Peruvian site of Túcume in the 1990s uncovered a clay bas-relief frieze of the Sipán culture (c. AD 1100-1200) which he interpreted, with a great deal of wishful thinking, as depicting a large reed vessel [8]. And he became fond of claiming that some Peruvian king had sent out 20,000 men in an entire armada of big reed ships, fanning out across the Ocean to find Easter Island [9]!

In fact, along the entire Peruvian coast there was no known prehistoric craft whose crew could conceivably survive a prolonged open-sea voyage. The desert coast of Peru lacked both the light woods needed for rafts and the large trees required for canoes. In southern Chile, sewn three-plank canoes existed (see below), but here too the sail was unknown, and propulsion was by paddle and drifting with currents [10].

It is possible that Easter Island may once have had rafts of palm-logs, because big log-platform vessels with triangular sails were known in Mangareva, and oral traditions there suggest that they had once been used for ocean voyaging [11]; so it is quite plausible that the very idea of ocean-going sailing rafts, and perhaps even an actual vessel, was taken to South America by Polynesians. To the west of Mangareva, bamboo rafts were the norm, while in South America balsa logs would have replaced the logs of Polynesian type.

According to Bittmann [12], a simple five-piece model of a wooden raft was found at the site of Cáñamo in northern Chile, dating to the 8th century AD, and constitutes the earliest solid archaeological evidence for a possible small predecessor of the large, complex balsa rafts known from the time of the first European contacts with northern Peru and Ecuador. But she does not believe that actual watercraft based on these small models would have been suited to long-distance open-sea voyages.

14. Detail of a wall at *Vinapu* I or *Ahu Tahiri*, showing the delicate and precise work on the masonry. Inset is a detail of an Inca wall in Cuzco, Peru. Photos: Eduardo Ruiz-Tagle.

Coastal watercraft may well have been present earlier in these regions of South America, and may have been an independent development here, but nevertheless one can make a strong case for influence from Polynesia in the development in Ecuador of ocean-going sailing rafts with triangular sails, like those of Mangareva. Similarly, a strong case has now been made for the technology of sewn-plank canoes having been brought to both southern Chile and the Chumash of the south Californian coast by Polynesians, in the latter case by Hawaiians around AD 700 [13].

Furthermore, the *Kon-Tiki*'s encounter with the South Equatorial Current -and the fact that she was towed out fifty nautical miles from the Peruvian coast- means that her journey cannot truly be termed a drift voyage;

15. Polynesian mariners used canoes and vessels with sails to cross vast stretches of the Pacific. An engraving of a A war canoe of New Zealand by John Hawkesworth, Cook expedition, London, 1773.

Eugene Savoy's 1969 attempt to repeat the trip without being towed away from the coast led to his raft being caught in the 250-mile wide Humboldt current and carried to Panama. Subsequent experiments have confirmed that, at best, the South Equatorial Current and the southeast trade winds would carry a vessel from Peru to the Marquesas or the Tuamotus, not to Easter Island. In any event, the comparison of *Kon-Tiki* with the drift voyage of a prehistoric vessel is hardly fair; *Kon-Tiki* was an intentional navigated voyage with a known, if general, destination, and the crew had the benefit of radios, maps and sophisticated navigation instruments. We must conclude that *Kon-Tiki* showed nothing more than that, by using a post-European-contact kind of sail-raft and modern survival equipment, it is possible to survive a 101-day voyage between Peru and Polynesia [14].

In a harsher assessment, Paul Theroux [15] has written that '...in a lifetime of nutty theorizing, Heyerdahl's single success was his proof, in *Kon-Tiki*, that six middle-class Scandinavians could successfully crash-land their raft on a coral atoll in the middle of nowhere.'

Winds, currents and navigation

Heyerdahl's argument relied on the prevailing easterly direction of the winds and currents in the region, yet this is by no means a constant: Heyerdahl, like de Zuñiga before him, overlooked the fact that the easterlies are not, as he claimed, 'permanent', but are subject to seasonal and annual variation, when the direction of winds and currents is from west to east. For example, Roggeveen, as we have seen, was prevented from landing on the island on 7 April 1722 by stormy winds from the northwest, and William Thomson noted that while in summer the wind blew from the southeast, in winter it blew from the southwest or west. There are also the 'El Niño' events to be considered -cyclical changes in the circulation of the ocean and atmosphere over a large part of the South Pacific, so named ('The Child') because they commonly occur around Christmas- westerly wind reversals that can become the prevailing wind over much of the region for a considerable period (see Chapter 3). During these episodes, the South Equatorial Current slackens or even reverses.

If the winds and currents can tell us little in themselves, we must turn to the navigational skills of the ancient Polynesians and South Americans, to see which group was best qualified to make the long and hazardous journey to Easter Island.

We have abundant, excellent, documented evidence of the amazing navigational skills of the ancient Polynesians who travelled across vast stretches of the Pacific carrying people and resources, colonizing such far-flung islands as Hawai'i and New Zealand, and usually progressing in a generally easterly direction, albeit with some counter movements. In fact, we know from the journals of explorers and missionaries that Polynesian mariners of the 18th and 19th centuries knew how to sail against the wind; prevailing southeasters posed no obstacle to sailing canoes or other sailed vessels, which simply tacked or lay close to the wind, and were helped by their long steering-oar or by paddles; and the Polynesians were well acquainted with the westerlies and frequently used them to sail eastward. Indeed, the exploits of the Polynesians throughout their history in colonizing every habitable island over 30 million sq. km (c. 11.5 million sq. miles) of Pacific Ocean have been described as 'the great seafaring saga of all time', one that we shall examine more closely in Chapter 3.

On the other hand, we have no solid evidence for any ancient South American ocean voyaging of this type; there is no indication that in the early centuries AD (or indeed later) South American Indians had the capacity to move themselves and their domesticates over such great distances. Instead, their vessels seem to have hugged the shore, although finds of pottery indicate that some South Americans did reach the Galápagos Islands, 960 km (600 miles) west of Ecuador. It is known that this part of northwest South America, unlike Peru, did have prehistoric sailing rafts, with centre-boards and sails, that were capable of long voyages and

could have reached the limits of the Peruvian coastal current [16]. However, there are thousands of miles of open ocean between South America and Polynesia, broken only by the Galápagos and a few other islands offshore; so these empty seas with their few islands near the South American coast offered very little inducement or encouragement for the development of long-distance off-shore voyaging [17]. Most South American sailing took place in the zone of very settled weather -the winds and currents only become strong well out to sea. After the *Kon-Tiki* expedition, Heyerdahl learned from South Americans how to steer a raft by manipulating the centre-boards and sail, so that the vessel could be handled as easily as any boat and could sail in any direction. But if the South Americans could do this, why not also the Polynesians? In addition, it is worth remembering that sailing off this continental coast is very different from voyaging between islands, in that you always know where you are, and you merely have to sail east to reach some point of the shore.

There is also the extreme isolation of Easter Island, so remote that it is pretty unlikely that it could be found more than once with any degree of reliability. And even if a very occasional stray vessel did reach that tiny speck from east or west, there is little chance that it could have gone to its homeland and back, let alone directed other vessels to the island. Most specialists consider two-way voyaging from the island to have been impossible during its prehistory, and many believe that it was settled only once.

Yet despite these facts, Heyerdahl was asking us to believe that not only did some enterprising voyagers from ancient Peru make it to Easter Island, but that they also went further west, kidnapped some Polynesians and brought them back. Assuming that the Peruvians maintained contact with their mother country, this all implies that the South Americans were fully capable of sailing eastward despite the prevailing currents and winds!

It is, clearly, far more sensible to base oneself on the proven skills and long-distance voyages of the ancient Polynesians, and to assume not only that they were fully capable of reaching *Rapa Nui*, but also of sailing further eastward to South America and returning safely to Polynesia: certainly Irwin sees this as a more likely scenario than what he calls 'Heyerdahl's American diversion' [18]. There are some prehistoric finds in Chile, for example, which could well be of Polynesian origin, though finds of Easter Island *mata'a* (spearheads) there are difficult to date, carry insufficient archaeological guarantees and may simply reflect the export of the island's artifacts since the 19th century [19]. In addition to the technology of sewn-plank canoes, mentioned above, it is likely that Polynesians also introduced the compound bone fish hook to the New World [20]; some human skulls and jaws from Isla Mocha off Chile are of Polynesian type [21]; and most recently bones of Polynesian chickens have been unearthed at the Chilean site of Arenal (see p. 72) [22]. So any possible New World influences in Polynesia may not necessarily have had anything to do with Amerindian voyaging.

The navigational skills of the ancient Polynesians are clear, therefore, and feature in a number of the Easter Islanders' compelling traditions and legends; indeed, virtually all the islanders' rich folk memories and legends support the case for colonization from the west.

Oral traditions

One of the best-known legends of *Rapa Nui* is that *Hotu Matu'a*, the island's first king, came from the west, heading for the sunrise, and that his home was an island called *Hiva*. It is noteworthy that this name occurs several times (Nuku Hiva, Fatu Hiva, Hiva Oa) in the Marquesas Islands, 3360 km (2100 miles) northwest of Easter Island, because Father Sebastian Englert, one of the 20th century's foremost experts on the island's culture, believed that this is where *Hotu Matu'a* came from [23]. It would be ironic if Easter Island had been colonized from Fatu Hiva, the very place where Heyerdahl first began his quest to prove the opposite.

Furthermore, it is said that when *Hotu Matu'a* felt death approaching, he went to the sacred site of *Orongo* (the island's westernmost point) and called out to his homeland. In fact, Polynesian tradition sees the westernmost part of a land as the departure point of souls. Routledge heard that tale, and specifically noted that *Hotu Matu'a* '... looked over the islet of *Motu Nui* towards *Marae Renga*... his old home'. Similarly, according to Alfred Métraux, the islanders only knew the name of the land of their first ancestor, '...a big island located to the west called *Marae-Renga*. It was warm there and had lots of trees' -this was certainly a Polynesian island. Surgeon Palmer of HMS *Topaze*, which called at *Rapa Nui* in 1868, said that the islanders of his day believed that the island of Rapa, 3850 km (2400 miles) to the west, was their original home. Geiseler, in 1882, reported one story that the ancestors had come from Rapa and landed at *Vinapu*, and another that they had come from the Galápagos and landed at *Anakena*, but generally they were believed to have come from the west [24].

A leading specialist in Polynesian archaeology, Yosihiko Sinoto, having worked in the Marquesas for many years, remarked that '...when I first visited Easter Island it was like going home.' The two places have so many similarities in their material culture and language, as will be seen below, that Kenneth Emory, the eminent specialist in Polynesian archaeology, became convinced that the prehistoric culture of Easter Island could have evolved from a single landing of Polynesians from a Marquesan island, fully equipped to colonize an uninhabited volcanic island [25].

15.1. An engraving of Otaheite fleet by William Hodges, Cook expedition, 1777.

Heyerdahl's approach to oral traditions was extremely selective: his model started from a myth, and then he tried to support this picture with concrete evidence. He thus chose to dismiss legends that the islanders came from the west (i.e. East Polynesia). The fact that all the island's folk-tales only began to be collected in the late 19th century, by which time the population had come very close to extinction, and that the few survivors may have had a less than perfect knowledge of the old traditions and legends, and besides had acquired terrible knowledge of Peru's existence through slave raids, should encourage the greatest caution, but Heyerdahl firmly believed his chosen scenario.

However, 'memory material' in modern anthropology is interpreted mainly as a clue to contemporary social relations, and its value as a historical record is very limited. Many scholars are reluctant to use this material to cover deficiencies in archaeology, but while scientists prefer to work from the archaeological and ethnographic evidence, using oral traditions -which tend to be allegorical and metaphorical- only to provide confirmation or colour here and there, Heyerdahl did the precise opposite. Even within the selected story that Heyerdahl chose to believe, he regarded some parts as reliable (the direction from which the colonists came, the description of their land), but rejected others as allegorical (for example, that the first two separate arrivals were brothers, and the fact that even the legend pointing to an eastern origin says the homeland was a group of islands).

In fact, there is very little reason to pay the slightest attention to Heyerdahl's tale; for a start, it claims that *Hotu Matu'a* found the island empty, but also contradicts this by saying that his brother *Machaa* was already there, having set out two months previously. The chances of two such voyages managing to reach the same isolated speck just by heading west beggars belief. We shall see below

that botanical evidence also destroys some aspects of these tales. But even more crucially, Thomson recorded the story in 1886 after a mere eleven days on the island; yet only twenty-eight years later Mrs Routledge, who spent sixteen months there intensively gathering information, *never encountered that story* [26]. Instead, her informants either did not know (like most of Thomson's) or claimed that their ancestors came from two neighbouring islands known as *Marae Renga* and *Marae Tohio*. Métraux insisted that the Salmon/Thomson data concerning an origin in the east were extremely questionable and undoubtedly of very recent date [27].

In short, it is extremely dangerous to rely on oral traditions: as Mrs Routledge wisely pointed out, '...It was even more difficult to collect facts from brains than out of stones... it is particularly difficult to arrive at the truth from the untutored mind...when memory was vague, there was a constant tendency to glide from what was remembered to what was imagined... The information given in reply to questions is generally wildly mythical' [28]. Elsewhere she added that '...the Polynesians are notoriously inexact in their statements. They frequently do not themselves know when they are speaking the truth and when they are relying on imagination' [29].

So all the recorded folk tales from the island need to be taken with a large pinch of marine salt. But if oral tradition is to be included, as Heyerdahl insisted it must, then his preferred version of the islanders' origins seems to be wildly inaccurate, inconsistent and aberrant; all the other versions gathered both before and after point to the west.

Folk memories can be equally misleading in the study of the island's plants: pollen analysis has shown, for example, that *toromiro* (*Sophora Toromiro*) and *hau hau* (*Triumfetta semitriloba*) trees were on the island thousands of years before humans arrived, yet oral tradition says that these species, along with all other

16. Detail of a Nukutavake canoe (Tuamotu islands), collected by Wallis, 1771. The hull is composed of forty-five sections of wood bound together with continuous lengths of plaited cordage covering battens of coconut leaves split midrib. A similar technique was used by the rapanui.

17. Engraving of rapanui *Vaka Ama* canoe, Comte de La Pérouse expedition, 1786.

useful plants, were introduced by *Hotu Matu'a*, the first king: so much for the reliability of oral traditions! Since the island's legends frequently contradict each other and cannot be seen as decisive evidence, perhaps we can make some progress by taking a look at the more tangible botanical information that is available.

Botanical evidence

Taxonomy provides a clear challenge to Heyerdahl's theory of colonizers from the New World, in that the island had no maize, beans or squash -staple resources in South America- at the time of the European arrival or even in the first pollen analysis done for Heyerdahl's own investigation. It also disputes Heyerdahl's claim for the Peruvian origin of the totora (*Scirpus riparius*), for the island's variety of totora is distinct from Peruvian ones (though similar to a Chilean kind), and it can reproduce by seeds, which could therefore have been transported to the island by the wind, the ocean or on birds' feet [30]. There is nothing bizarre in such a method of transport. Charles Darwin washed the seeds of fifty-two species of plants from the feet of water birds. The *tavari* (*Polygonum acuminatum*) also probably reproduced by seed, and could have been introduced by birds from any number of places. Indeed, the fact that it occurs in South America does not prove Heyerdahl's case, for it could have been transported on birds' feet from South America to, say, the Marquesas in some distant time period, only to be taken by people from there to Easter Island. This would not be surprising, for the plant is credited with medicinal value. Pollen evidence is unclear about this plant's antiquity on the island.

The name for *totora* is the same in Hawai'i as on Easter Island, revealing that the word must have been carried from a common homeland where a similar reed was present before these islands were settled. In any case, all this argument became academic after pollen analysis by John Flenley showed that the reed has been present on Easter Island for at least 30,000 years! It provides no evidence whatsoever for a link with the New World. Besides, we know that during Roggeveen's visit in 1722 natives '...came swimming on bundles of tied reeds' -they had no reed boats of the type associated with this plant in South America.

Heyerdahl's theory of the South American origin of the chili pepper is equally dubious. According to the Spanish account of 1770, chilis were brought out by the islanders together with sweet potatoes and bananas; Heyerdahl asserted that no other plant on the island could possibly be confused with chili peppers, while others suggested that it was probably confused with the indigenous plant *Solanum forsteri* whose native name of *poporo* or *poroporo* is also applied to the chili peppers now growing on the island. It is especially noteworthy that Captain Cook's botanist, George Forster, who devoted rather more time to such observations only four years later, never reported chili peppers.

In fact, the Australian researcher Robert Langdon believed that the whole chili pepper story rested on a mistranslation of the word *guineos* as a noun, rather than as an adjective describing the bananas ('guinea plantains') [31]. However, he also believed that a different mistake had masked the presence of the American plant manioc (tapioca/cassava) on Easter Island: in the original Spanish account of 1770 the word yuca was used, which was translated as *taro* or left untranslated. Little credence can be placed in Langdon's theory: for a start, it relied on the testimony of a couple of 18th-century Spanish pilots, neither of whom presumably was very skilled at botanical identification. Secondly, Forster, the first botanist to visit the island, clearly recorded *taro* rather than cassava only four years later; and Langdon himself pointed out that Thomson made no mention of the plant in his careful list. It is hardly a crop that can be missed, for it is not seasonal, and has a large and distinctive top growth; yet it does not appear in any account until the thorough botanical survey of 1911! Langdon was driven to imagine a scenario whereby the final Polynesian settlers who came to the island neglected the plant, which was unfamiliar to them; so the manioc supposedly reported in 1770 became extinct, but the plant was reintroduced before 1911... Clearly, an awful lot of assumptions were being made here [32].

As for cotton, none of the first three European expeditions (Roggeveen, González, Cook) reported seeing any, and we know that La Pérouse, the next European visitor in 1786, sowed some cotton seeds. The first botanical survey of the island, in 1911, found a few isolated semi-wild specimens of cotton, and claimed these had been introduced in the 1860s. Moreover, no word for the plant was recorded in the early dictionaries or vocabularies of the island. The only textiles seen by the first European visitors in 1722 were made of *tapa*, the beaten bark of the paper mulberry: at that time, even Polynesians who knew the cotton plant (such as Tahitians) did not know that it could be spun and woven, whereas the prehistoric Peruvians were the greatest experts the world has ever seen in spinning and weaving cotton. The total absence and ignorance of woven textiles on Easter Island is damning evidence against any link with Peru.

The one remaining possible botanical link between the island and the South American mainland is the sweet potato (*Ipomoea batatas*), which was certainly present on the island by the 15th-17th century (see Chapter 4, p. 108), and indeed a few other undated remains of the plant have been encountered in prehistoric sites on *Rapa Nui*; Heyerdahl implied that it came direct from South America, though he also admitted it

might have come from the Marquesas. Even if it reached there from the New World, this would in no way imply any direct contact between Easter Island and the mainland. As yet we simply do not know how or when the plant reached the island; or how and where it was introduced to Oceania from South America [33], if that is indeed what happened (there are wild species in Southeast Asia). Many scholars believe it could have been distributed by birds or other natural means. On linguistic evidence, according to specialist Douglas Yen, it is probable that it was carried to central East Polynesia sometime between the 3rd and 8th centuries AD and was widely dispersed from there [34]. Unfortunately, although its pollen grains are large and distinctive, they do not seem to preserve well in sediments, and few have been recovered from Easter Island's crater-cores that could shed light on its history in *Rapa Nui* (see Chapter 4, p. 108). The question will doubtless be resolved one day when we have a thorough DNA analysis of every species cultivated there.

Recently, new evidence of cultivated plants has been derived by Mark Horrocks from all three swamps on the island (*Rano Kau, Rano Raraku* and *Rano Aroi*), using not only palynology but also phytoliths and starch grains of characteristic shapes. The occurrences of these were radiocarbon dated, and were usually fairly late (for further information, see chapter 9).

The latest thinking is that little solid evidence exists for the transfer of any known plant between the New World and Polynesia apart from the sweet potato. And even if that plant was somehow obtained from the New World, this is very different from the transfer of a whole range of Amerindian material culture and religion, as well as of adequate numbers of Amerindians themselves. These are the areas to which we must now turn our attention.

18. *Mangai*, bone hooks; composite (*vere vere*) and stone (*maea*).

Bottom: *Patia*, harpoon found in 1987 at *Anakena*, very similar to those found in the Marquesas Islands.

Art and artifacts

What can archaeology itself, in the form of artifacts, art and structures, tell us about the origin of the Easter Islanders? The studies and excavations of the 20th century, and especially of the past few decades, have led almost all specialists in the archaeology of the South Pacific to see *Rapa Nui*'s artifacts as clearly of Polynesian origin, and thoroughly familiar within the context of east Polynesian material culture, and displaying no cultural break [35].

For example, many of the earliest European visitors, including the Spanish in 1770, Forster in 1774 (who even made a drawing ill. 88), and La Pérouse in 1786, mentioned that the islanders' canoes had an outrigger fixed to them -and since the outrigger is an invention of the Austronesian-speaking peoples who spread from Southeast Asia, this is yet another indication of where the islanders came from [36].

Rapa Nui's one-piece fish-hooks (despite Heyerdahl's claims) are typically and distinctively Polynesian, displaying continuity at least back to a group dated at *Ahu Vinapu* to AD 1220, and therefore on balance argue against any significant non-Polynesian element in Easter Island culture [37]; for example, the use of sharply incurved points, in contrast to the barbed forms of Hawai'i and New Zealand, is also characteristic of early periods in the Marquesas. The two-piece hook, on the other hand, was a local development, comparable to innovations in Hawai'i and New Zealand. It is particularly noteworthy that the *Kon-Tiki* Museum's excavations in the 1980s at *Anakena* -traditionally believed to be the site of Easter Island's first settlement and where Heyerdahl was confident that some link with South America would be found- in fact encountered a 6 cm bone harpoon head of a type identical to specimens found in the Marquesas [38] at the bottom of the stratigraphy (c. AD 1200), along with Polynesian coral files and bones of the Polynesian rat and the red Asian jungle fowl (chicken). Since even Heyerdahl accepted that the island was full of Polynesians when Europeans arrived, and since Polynesians were also clearly there from the start, where are the South Americans? He never addressed this dilemma.

The island's stone adzes correspond to the simple forms of a very early stage (pre-AD 1100) in east Polynesian adze development (as found especially in the Marquesas, as well as the Society Islands, Samoa and Tonga). *Rapa Nui* seems to have been isolated before the development of fully tanged forms in the rest of east Polynesia, but had some later innovations of its own, such as a quadrangular pecked adze with a deeply grooved butt. Much of the island's other material culture likewise reflects affinities with east Polynesia (particularly the Marquesas), innovations due to long isolation, and adaptation to local conditions (such as a comparative scarcity of large shells for tools, and an abundance of obsidian). The absence of Polynesia's typical food-pounders on Easter Island, like that of certain adze types which developed by AD 1000 in central Polynesia, points to a colonization in the first centuries AD.

Heyerdahl did find evidence of repeated South American visits to the (far closer) Galápagos Islands in the form of over 2000 fragments from at least 131 pots, 44 of them clearly pre-Inca types from South America. But, just as there is no trace of

textiles, not a single prehistoric potsherd has ever been found on Easter Island -yet these are the two most characteristic and abundant products of Peruvian culture. Even if South Americans had brought no pottery with them, they could still have manufactured some on the island: Carlyle Smith, one of the archaeologists taken to *Rapa Nui* by Heyerdahl in 1955, found a source of excellent potter's clay on the island, in a damp area on the west slope of *Rano Raraku*. He made a small pottery vessel with it, and fired it successfully [39]. Clearly any Amerindian potter could have done so too.

The same argument does not apply to Polynesians, however; although the early prehistory of western Polynesia is characterized by decorated *Lapita* pottery, which developed into a plain ware by the first millennium BC, pottery seems to have disappeared entirely by AD 200 in Samoa and Tonga, and by AD 300 everywhere else. In fact, after that date, it is probable that no society anywhere in Polynesia made pottery at all, perhaps because of the comparative poverty of clay resources on these basalt and coral islands. In other words, any Polynesian colonizers of Easter Island would be unfamiliar with pottery-making, unlike the Amerindians.

Ironically, at one point it appeared that pottery had been found: Heyerdahl showed the islanders potsherds from Peru, hoping that similar material might turn up on *Rapa Nui*. Sure enough, before long, a man produced some polished red sherds from a single vessel, which he claimed to be from a looted grave at *Ahu Tepeu*. The archaeologists found no pottery there, and indeed the episode turned out to be a hoax, the sherds being from an old pot from Chile. The islanders had been anxious to find what 'el señor *Kon-Tiki*' needed, and an excited Heyerdahl understandably could not believe his ears when he learned the truth, so badly did he want pottery to be found [40].

It is worth noting that some prehistoric pottery has been found in the Marquesas Islands, which were settled by the 1st century BC, but it was all imported from the west. Some stone bowls on Easter Island are identical in rim-shape to coarse-ware pottery bowls from Samoa; it has been suggested that such stone bowls, which appear to be replicas of late Polynesian plain ware ceramics, may be a tantalizing clue to early settlement of *Rapa Nui*.

A further argument against strong South American influence is the complete absence of the pressure-flaking technique on stone tools throughout Polynesia [41]. This technique, involving 'pushing' flakes off a core, as opposed to striking them, was widespread in the New World; it appeared early and lasted a very long time, so any Amerindians reaching Easter Island would undoubtedly have used it, especially as the island's obsidian is eminently suited to the method. This was one piece of negative evidence which left William Mulloy -previously known for his work on Amerindian culture- '...unconvinced an American Indian had ever set foot on the island'. And of course Heyerdahl had nothing to say about the total absence of South American metalwork on Easter Island!

So much for artifacts. But what of the monumental platforms and carvings? There are indeed some superficial similarities visible here and there between Easter Island and South American forms -after all, there are only so many shapes which simple monolithic human statues can take- but there was also much contradiction, wishful thinking and subjectivity underlying Heyerdahl's assertions. Even the few American anthropologists who strongly believed in contact between the New World and other parts of the Pacific found it very peculiar that Heyerdahl should be pointing to resemblances between *Rapa Nui* and the Tiahuanaco culture centred on Lake Titicaca in the highlands of Peru and Bolivia, rather than with a coastal complex. Moreover, the 'Imperial'

Tiahuanaco phase begins in the 8th century AD, and its influence on the coast starts somewhat later, so if the first settlers reached Easter Island before AD 400, as Heyerdahl believed, how could they bring Tiahuanaco culture across with them? This was the period of Mochica culture on the Peruvian coast. To overcome the contradictions, he would have had to dismiss the two dubious early *Rapa Nui* radiocarbon dates (AD 318 from reeds in a grave at *Ahu Tepeu* I, and AD 386 from charcoal in the *Poike* ditch) as being invalid (e.g. the charcoal could be natural) and place the first settlement at the next earliest date of AD 690 (from *Tahai*), but that is still too early for classic Tiahuanaco influence [42].

Secondly, the accurate mortarless fitting of large polygonal blocks began in Peru after AD 1440, but Easter Island has similar dressed stonework before AD 1200 (at *Tahai*). Heyerdahl assigned *Vinapu* I (with fitted blocks) to the Early Period, but it has been shown that it probably dates to AD 1516, whereas *Vinapu* II is actually earlier (AD 857) and displays a rougher, typically east Polynesian facing of vertical slabs -in fact, a block from *Vinapu* II is actually incorporated in the foundation of *Vinapu* I. So while a later date for *Vinapu* I corresponds better to the age of fitted blocks in the Andes, it postdates a clearly Polynesian structure on the same site.

In any case, Easter Island's platforms conform to the tradition and plan of the *marae* (shrines to ancestral gods, and socio-religious centres) of east Polynesia, not to those of Andean temples: in fact, *Ahu Tepeu* I (which produced the 4th-century date) bears a very marked resemblance to a *marae* on Timoe Island, near Mangareva [43]. Indeed, Mangarevan *marae* are more similar to Easter Island's platforms than to any other stone structures in Polynesia, suggesting a connection or, at least, a common origin. As for the stone walls, Andean specialists have pointed out that they cannot match the type exactly among classic Inca masonry. Moreover, unlike the solid blocks

19. The great trilithon on Tonga Island, one of the most impressive monuments in Polynesia.

20. Above: *Moai Tukuturi* during excavations of Heyerdahl. He repeatedly compared *Tukuturi* (left) to a kneeling stone figure from Tiahuanaco (right), the pre-Inca sun-worshipping centre in the Andes, but the similarities are not proof of Amerindian influence on *Rapa Nui*.

used in Peru, the Easter Island 'walls' are actually a facing of slabs that masks a rubble core, so any resemblance with Cyclopean blocks is equally superficial. Métraux emphasized the falseness of this analogy [44].

It has been suggested that the islanders' skill with stone was derived from their expertise in carpentry and woodworking, such as in producing the planks needed for canoes [45]. But it was not a skill unique to *Rapa Nui*, since house platforms in the Marquesas, described as the finest in Polynesia, were built with beautifully fitted but unshaped Cyclopean basalt blocks: the dance-platform of Uahake-kua was built of stones weighing 3 to 5 tons each. One can also mention the immensely tall -5 m or 16 ft- stone trilithon 'Haamonga a Maui' of about AD 1200 on the island of Tonga (ill. 19), reminiscent of the Stonehenge trilithons, and made of quarried coral blocks weighing 30 or 40 tons. The Polynesians were no strangers to stoneworking or Cyclopean blocks. They were also quite capable of producing sophisticated corbelled structures, whatever Heyerdahl's claims; there is no strong evidence that these were earlier than the boat-shaped dwellings (indeed, some of those at *Orongo* incorporate kerbstones from the boat-shaped houses in their stonework!) and, in fact, it is far more likely that the stone houses with corbelled roofs are a local invention stimulated by the availability of abundant flat, thin basalt slabs and, perhaps, a growing scarcity of materials for pole-and-thatch dwellings -perhaps even by the necessity of producing structures which could better withstand the elements. In any case, corbelling also exists in Hawai'i, and was clearly within the repertoire of 'Polynesian fishermen'. The boat-shaped houses certainly resemble elliptical structures of Mangareva, Rapa and the Tuamotus; the stone kerbs that outline some on Easter Island also occur in Mangareva and the Society Islands.

Furthermore, Heyerdahl's 'boulder-heads' are, in fact, recarved fragments of *Rano Raraku* tuff that used to be intact statues of classic type. The rectangular humanoid pillars appear to have been in use in the 19th century at *Vinapu*, and are thus more likely to be a very late form than very early.

Where the kneeling statue *Tukuturi* is concerned, it has often been pointed out that there is no evidence for its early date -we have no idea about its original position- and several scholars, including Sebastian Englert, have seen it as stylistically a very late sculpture that resembles a Polynesian *tiki* (its posture is well known on Easter Island, and is used by singers in festivals). An attempt to pinpoint it led to four radiocarbon dates, two recent, one early, and one in-between, so the question remains unresolved [46]. The kneeling statue of Tiahuanaco cannot be said to share more than its posture with the Easter Island example, and the latter's face is in any case too weathered for sound comparisons to be made. The treatment of *Tukuturi*'s body is far less angular and more naturalistic, and its face is at quite a different angle: the more one looks at the two, the less alike they seem.

Very few specialists in either Polynesian or South American sculpture have been even remotely convinced by Heyerdahl's analogies. Heyerdahl also compared much of Easter Island's other art with that of South America, and here, some of his examples were more plausible than others. Unfortunately, a few features such as supposed 'felines' and a 'turkey' seem to be figments of the imagination: William Thomson found that a single petroglyph of a birdman at *Orongo* with the face of *Make Make*, the main deity, was similar to a decorated stone he knew from Peru (though he stressed that he knew of no other similarity between the island's relics and those of Peru). However, his cursory sketch of that figure lacks its bird-beak (in fact, he failed to mention birdman figures at all), while his unfortunate and inaccurate

21. A net float from the Solomon Islands likewise portrays a seated human with a bird's head.

22. An Easter Island rock carving portraying the 'birdman'. A Hawaiian rock art figure which, although lacking a beak, is astonishingly similar to its counter-part on Easter Island.

23. A typical Easter Island 'eye-mask' motif. Centre: A rock carving of a face from Hawai'i. Bottom: The recurring 'eye-mask' face also appears in the Marquesas Islands.

description of claw-like hands and feet was seized on by Heyerdahl as indicating 'feline' features and hence a link with the New World (although it has been argued that even if feline images were found on the island, they could easily post-date European contact, and in any case prove nothing about cats in Polynesia, let alone an American origin) [47].

A further error of this type was Lavachery's illustration of a painted face in a cave on *Motu Nui* with 'tear-streaks' -another South American trait for Heyerdahl, although, in fact, the lines on the face simply define the shape of the nose.

As for Heyerdahl's attempt to link Easter Island's famous 'birdman' motif with the New World, there are equally good, if not better, analogies in other directions, such as some remarkable resemblances between the Easter Island motifs and others in the Solomon Islands, where seated humans with frigate-bird heads are carved as net floats and canoe prows. Moreover the birdman motif is relatively abundant in, and intrinsic to, the arts of Marginal Polynesia (i.e. Easter Island, Hawai'i and New Zealand) [48], and American rock-art specialist Georgia Lee has studied petroglyphs in the Hawaiian Islands, depicting squatting anthropomorphs in profile, some in bas-relief, which 'bear an uncanny resemblance' to the birdmen of Easter Island. Rather than jump to simplistic conclusions about direct contact between the two places, however, she sensibly prefers to see the similarity as reflecting a shared Polynesian heritage [49].

Another factor which has come to light is that Hawaiian rock art includes an 'eye-mask' motif, which bears a remarkable resemblance to those of Easter Island as well as to numerous big-eyed faces in the art of the Marquesas.

The wooden statuettes of male figures on *Rapa Nui* recall certain wooden images of Hawai'i with similarly emphasized ribs and backbones, while elongated earlobes with earplugs are also prominent in the Marquesas and Mangareva -two factors that render Heyerdahl's ascription of American origins highly questionable. Furthermore, closer examination of the cupmarks at *Rano Kau*, cited by Edwin Ferdon as evidence of heliolatry on the island -a claim seized upon by Heyerdahl- reveals that they would be a hopelessly inaccurate solsticial observatory, especially since the horizon is obscured at this location [50]. Hence, another New World trait proves to be a mirage.

Ramírez has pointed out how Heyerdahl had to mix together examples from very distant locations and times -Tihuanaco, Sican, Inca- to build his theory, and has also dismissed the evidence of the clay frieze at Túcume (it 'should be disregarded. His "birdman" holding an egg is a Moche bird holding something like an egg') as well as the depiction at Túcume of a double paddle, which 'is just a Moche paddle' [51].

All in all, the available archaeological evidence shows strong continuities leading up to the recent, better-known and undoubtedly Polynesian materials: these continuities, in artifacts and in the siting, planning, building and use of typically Polynesian ceremonial platforms, are in sharp contrast to the 'clear break' necessary to Heyerdahl's theory of the arrival of two totally different populations. Even if one were to allow some of Heyerdahl's resemblances to South American specimens, it is clear that the vast majority of Easter Island's material culture points to an origin in the west. Can the fields of language and physical anthropology cast further light on this matter?

Linguistics

Almost all recent work on this topic derives the language of Easter Island entirely from Polynesia: some of the words, such as *poki* for child, are unique to the island, and are symptomatic of the islanders' long isolation from their roots (it is generally reckoned that Easter Island became isolated from the rest of eastern Polynesia before the colonization of Hawai'i and New Zealand); however, Thor Heyerdahl inevitably regarded these local words as being non-Polynesian, from an alien (i.e. New World) substratum. For example, he pointed to the words for 'one' to 'ten' recorded by the Spanish visitors in 1770; yet, as Métraux showed, the Spaniards were on the island for only six days and were totally unfamiliar with Polynesian languages, so any information obtained by them is almost certainly garbled. Only four years later, Cook -who had a Tahitian with him, who could converse with the islanders- recorded correct proto-Polynesian words for one to ten on *Rapa Nui*, and Forster noted that the words for parts of the body were similar to those on Tahiti [52]. It has recently been found that Heyerdahl was correct to trace the word *kumara* to a South American origin -there was a term like this in coastal Ecuador- but this may simply indicate the landing place of the Polynesians who perhaps took the sweet potato back with them [53].

A few other researchers, notably Robert Langdon and Darrell Tryon [54], also tried to turn the old *Rapa Nui* tongue into a link between Polynesia and South America: they claimed that, at the time of contact, *Rapa Nui*'s language was made up of three elements, one of west Polynesian origin, one from east Polynesia, and the third of unidentified origin. The first two elements were allegedly fused on the island of Ra'ivavae, 500 km (311 miles) south of Tahiti, and this language was then carried to Easter Island no earlier than the 16th century. The third element, comprising words unknown in other Polynesian languages, was the remnant of a non-Polynesian tongue which could only have come from the east in ancient times.

However, other specialists such as Roger Green and Steven Fischer [55] have shown that there is only weak and selective evidence for this view, and, in fact, no satisfying evidence at all for the existence of a pre-Polynesian language or a so-called 'Second Wave of Polynesian Immigrants' on Easter Island. No other specialists have adopted this hypothesis. Langdon and Tryon conjured up a very complex picture, with influences going back and forth across the ocean, and with repeated borrowings which are unmarked and undetected in Easter Island linguistics. The standard, orthodox view is far more straightforward and accounts for the evidence more economically and quite satisfactorily: this is, therefore, a case for applying Occam's razor and choosing the simpler, common-sense explanation: i.e. the language of Easter Island is a member of an eastern Polynesian subgroup.

Certain words in the island's language show clear links with the 'Central Eastern' group of Polynesian languages, while others seem linked to western Polynesia, and not the central eastern area. All place-names are Polynesian. Attempts at glottochronology, using changes in language to estimate the length of time since the islanders became cut off from their homeland, point to their having parted company with eastern Polynesia between AD 300 and 530, probably around AD 400. On linguistic grounds, an argument has even been made for differentiation as early as the 1st century AD, although this does not give any clue as to when it reached the island. However, it has been said that this '...may be the greatest example of isolation, in terms of both geography and time-depth, known to linguistics' [56].

The language does stand apart from the others of the region in a number of ways, because it retains many features that have been lost or replaced on other islands. It seems to have a transitional or 'developmental' position between the tongues of western and eastern Polynesia. This suggests strongly that, together with Mangarevan, it was the first language to split off from eastern Polynesia; and in the course of its long isolation it experienced internal alterations of the autonomous language, losing some features and adopting others, while the other islands innovated a shared set of new features or lost inherited ones.

Heyerdahl's comparison of Easter Island's rock art and script with those of Bolivia was as dubious as his theory concerning the island's language: in fact, there are far more remarkable similarities between some *rongo rongo* motifs and designs employed in the Solomon Islands, which have led some scholars to believe that the Easter Island 'script' originated in Melanesia. Although the implied theory of a direct migration from there to Easter Island is no longer tenable (the Marquesas Islands and/or Mangareva are now seen as the obvious source), it is still clear that there were related influences at work here.

All specialists, such as the Russians Butinov and Knorozov [57], say that the island's 'script' is clearly Polynesian, with its signs reflecting local environment and culture; they noted the use of boustrophedon (named after the way an ox ploughs a field) in Peru, but saw no affinity between signs in the two places, concluding that Easter Island did not borrow its 'script' from Peru, although there remained the possibility of some influence in either direction.

The foremost *rongo rongo* scholar, Thomas Barthel of Germany [58], said that the names, phrases and allusions so far deciphered on the Easter Island boards are unequivocally of Polynesian origin: he found references to Tahiti, Bora Bora, Pitcairn, and to common Polynesian plants that have never grown on Easter Island. Consequently, he believed that the 'script' originated elsewhere in eastern Polynesia -perhaps on Huahine or Raiatea- and came to *Rapa Nui* with *Hotu Matu'a*.

But is there any evidence of the arrival of two different peoples on the island? Or should one assume, as has been argued, that arriving voyagers or castaways would probably have been killed or enslaved rather than allowed an opportunity to introduce new behaviour patterns?

Physical anthropology

From the very start of anthropological analysis of the island's human remains, the results have always pointed west: measurements of skulls led a number of scholars, including leading British anatomist Sir Arthur Keith, independently to indicate a Melanesian origin rather than a Polynesian, though Polynesian types were present; while the 19th-century French scholar Hamy found affinities between the island's skulls and those of Papua New Guinea. More recent analyses have shown that Easter Island head shape and dentition have close affinities with those of Hawaiians. Current thinking is that the Easter Islanders are undoubtedly Polynesians, with no original admixture with other groups; any morphological extremes found can be attributed -like those in language or material culture- to long development in isolation.

Analysis by Rupert Murrill of the bones collected by Heyerdahl's Norwegian expedition concluded that the islanders are and were Polynesian. Studies of blood groups led some scholars to suggest, with reservations, that South American Indians could have been a source of the island's population, but Murrill deduced from the same data that both the islanders and the Amerindians came from the same gene pool in east Asia: so much for blood groups! Roy Simmons studied the blood-group genetics of living islanders and other Polynesians, and suggested that they were the products of drift voyages from every direction, including South America, but stressed that such conclusions cannot really be deduced from blood-group, gene-frequency comparisons.

In short, blood typing alone is meaningless for a comparison of two groups of people whose other physical features are as dissimilar as the 'short, coppery, barrel-chested Peruvian with round head, straight hair and slightly hooked nose' is from the 'tall, brown, stocky Polynesian with a wide range of head shape, wavy black hair, and a rather flat, wide nose' [59].

Heyerdahl's attempt to link the islanders' crania with those of the American continent using George Gill's analyses was a complete misrepresentation of Gill's results: Amerindian skulls display a flat jaw-base, a broad flat nasal root and a straight suture of the palate and it is Polynesian skulls that have the 'rocker jaw', a deeply depressed nasal root, and a jagged, arched suture of the palate. Indeed, the rocker jaw is the most characteristically Polynesian skeletal trait known to physical anthropology, one that is considered virtually diagnostic of Polynesian ancestry. Its frequency of occurrence on almost all islands from New Zealand to Hawai'i ranges from 72 to 90 per cent, but it is extremely rare among Amerindians.

The Easter Island skeletal material Gill has examined so far is of Polynesian type in all these and other features, though its percentage of rocker jaws is comparatively low (48.5 per cent), indeed the lowest known in Polynesia [60].

Gill's preliminary analysis of fifty skulls, together with his reinterpretation of Murrill's data, suggested close ties between Easter Island and the Marquesas. The skeletons were clearly those of Polynesians, and although he had scarcely begun evaluation of possible Amerindian traits, he felt that 'any Amerindian genetic contribution detected is going to be a small one'. At the 'Rapa Nui Rendezvous' conference of 1993 at Laramie, he and his team presented their latest findings and put forward a new theory in an attempt to account for the overall

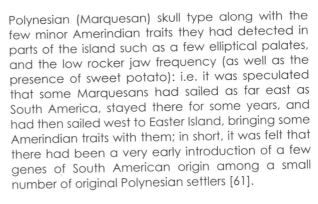

Polynesian (Marquesan) skull type along with the few minor Amerindian traits they had detected in parts of the island such as a few elliptical palates, and the low rocker jaw frequency (as well as the presence of sweet potato): i.e. it was speculated that some Marquesans had sailed as far east as South America, stayed there for some years, and had then sailed west to Easter Island, bringing some Amerindian traits with them; in short, it was felt that there had been a very early introduction of a few genes of South American origin among a small number of original Polynesian settlers [61].

Others, however, on the basis of new genetic studies which found a total lack of South American DNA on Easter Island [62], found this theory difficult to accept, particularly since it would also mean that the voyagers from the New World must have totally forgotten, or been ignorant of, all the characteristic implements, materials and techniques of that world. Instead, it was suggested that the low frequency of rocker jaws was probably due to the Founder Effect (i.e. to random chance in the genetic composition of the original founders), and that perhaps this might also apply to the other cranial traits in question [63].

By the Albuquerque congress of 1997, Chapman was leaning heavily towards the Tuamotus as the Easter Islanders' point of origin, having found a closer anatomical relationship with that island group than with the Marquesas ('All metric analyses show a relatively homogeneous population of East Polynesians occupying all of Easter Island by Late Prehistoric and Protohistoric times'), while Gill was stressing that the supposedly Amerindian discrete cranial traits might prove to exist elsewhere, as analyses were expanded to other parts of the Pacific. The 'thread of Amerindian trait' which he had found, especially in the northeast part of the island, seemed pervasive but not extensive, whereas if, as Heyerdahl believed, lots of Peruvians had sailed to Easter Island, one would find them in the metric analyses (with their shorter heads, smaller skulls, etc) -but one doesn't [64].

By the Hawai'i Congress of 2000, things had evolved even further. Gill pointed out that the islanders' high, long, large crania and facial characteristics are distinctive, and tie them directly to other East Polynesians, and especially to the Gambier Islands, although there was still a possibility of a very small genetic element or simply minor cultural influence from South America [65]; new studies by Chapman and Stefan showed that all islanders represented by skeletal remains are homogeneous throughout late prehistory and protohistory. Chapman even stressed that, in contradiction to Heyerdahl's speculations, and to his own previously reported results from non-metric studies, the latest analyses do not support any settlement from or gene flow with South America; he attributed the similarities reported in 1993 to observer error in data collection, and suggested that the most likely ancestral homeland was either Mangareva or the Tuamotus [66]. Stefan's analysis of the craniometric data likewise indicated that the prehistoric islanders had their strongest affinities with the Gambier Islands (i.e. Mangareva), followed closely by the Tuamotus; there was very little similarity to coastal Peruvian samples, so there had been no extensive contact with, or colonization from, that part of the world [67].

Heyerdahl had made much of selected early descriptions of the islanders' physical appearance, in particular their fair skin -light skin colour was much admired by them. Although the earliest voyagers give conflicting accounts of the islanders' racial characteristics, as on so many other points, the perceptive Captain Cook wrote that '...in colour, features and language, they bear such affinity to the people of the more western islands, that no one will doubt that they have had the same origin', while the Spanish in 1770 wrote that 'They in no way resemble the Indians of the South American continent' [68].

24. Left, engraving of tattoos in New Zealand from Cook's expedition of 1769/70; right, a rapanui called Tepano, by Stolpe 1899. In both we can see the use of facial tattooing which was very common in Polynesia.

The most recent genetic work in Polynesia, particularly using HLA (Human Leucocyte Antigen) blood grouping, has shown clearly that Polynesians are mainly derived from a southeast Asian population, and that east Polynesians display considerable homogeneity and are probably derived from a small number of founders. No evidence has been found at all for gene flow between South America and Polynesia -many genes found at high frequency in the one place are not found in the other- and the few similarities between them can be attributed to their source populations in Asia [69]. Heyerdahl's view, in other words, receives no support whatsoever from genetic analyses.

The DNA from the bones of ancient Easter Islanders is entirely of Polynesian type. Since the present population on *Rapa Nui* is descended from the 155 survivors of the 19th-century disasters (see p. 217), with considerable uncertainty as to whether there was genetic admixture in the past, studies of the DNA of living islanders cannot be regarded as totally reliable indicators of origin. The most recent analyses of the DNA of present-day islanders have found that their genetic ancestry is c. 75% Polynesian, 15% European and 10% Native American, but the timing of the admixtures is highly uncertain. The genes of European origin suggest admixture after the European contact began in 1722, and it cannot be excluded, for example, that the Amerindians were among the crew of some visiting European ship in the early 1800s or earlier [70].

Since the above is inconclusive, a better approach may be to study ancient DNA from dated bones of the commensal animals brought by people. This has been done for the bones of the Pacific rat (*Rattus exulans*), which was carried by people everywhere in the south-west Pacific, and was an item of food (see p. 200). The modern DNA of this species has been studied throughout Polynesia, in sufficient detail to produce a relationship diagram which groups together gene combinations of likely common origin: a sort of family tree, in fact [71]. The ancient rat bones from Easter Island are most closely related to those from Mangareva and the Marquesas [72], suggesting they may well have been brought from either of those places. Unfortunately, *Rattus exulans* has never occurred in South America, so we have no comparison with that location.

However, a comparison is possible if we take another commensal, the chicken. In 2007, a group from the University of Auckland [73] found that a chicken bone from El Arenal, an archaeological site in Chile, had a radiocarbon date around 600 years old, which is about 100 years before Columbus. This was surprising, as it had always been thought that the Spanish introduced chickens from Europe to South America. Furthermore, the DNA from the bone contained a rare gene similar to one found in ancient chicken bones from Tonga and American Samoa, suggesting early Polynesian contact with South America -a kind of *Kon Tiki Fried Chicken*! [74]. The find has been criticized on various grounds [75], and new relevant data are awaited with interest.

Conclusion

The earliest scholars to visit *Rapa Nui*, such as Katherine Routledge, had no obvious preconceptions about the origins of the islanders; after a full and fair assessment of the available evidence, she, like others before and after her, concluded that they had come from Polynesia, not from South America. Likewise, the scholars brought to the island by Thor Heyerdahl in 1955, although fully aware of his beliefs, were open-minded about the issue, while he, to his credit, wanted people who would not necessarily agree with him but who would evaluate the evidence in a fair and unbiased manner: as Ferdon put it, '...when we jokingly asked Thor if he wanted us to dig up a South American pot to prove his theory of American Indians' having populated parts of Polynesia, he saw nothing funny in it' [76]. Their investigations eventually led them to the conclusion that '...most of what is known of the prehistoric culture, as well as the surviving language, suggests Polynesian immigrants from islands to the west', though a few elements might possibly be American in origin. Nevertheless, thanks to the power of public relations, popular books and television programmes, Heyerdahl's view is still the best known among the general public, and was given another airing in his ten-week television biography.

Bengt Danielsson, a member of the *Kon-Tiki*'s crew, described Heyerdahl's theoretical procedure as follows [77]: 'Thor builds his pyramids upside down.' This simple metaphor is perfectly accurate and was extended by Christopher Ralling, who wrote: 'The whole structure of Thor's thought sometimes rests on a single, slender premise... he has grown impatient with those who build their pyramids the right way up, and never get beyond the bottom layer'.

In this chapter, we have examined all the different kinds of evidence relevant to the problem of origins, and found that Heyerdahl's theory of a South American source for Easter Island culture was indeed a tottering edifice precariously based on preconceptions, extreme subjectivity, distortions and very little hard evidence. In putting it together so singlemindedly over the years, he came to resemble someone who had painted himself into a corner with no means of escape, but was loath to admit it. As Kirch has said, 'Heyerdahl's theory was never taken seriously by scholars, since it ignores the mass of linguistic, ethnographic, ethnobiological and archaeological evidence' [78]. According to his biographers, even though he had no formal academic degree, he 'had no qualms in disregarding professional advice when it went against his expectations', and he showed no respect for the research of others. 'He was more of

a true believer than an open-minded scientist in search of the truth. He knew the answers before the job was done' [79]. His hypotheses that the South Americans were the first to populate Polynesia had 'become an absolute truth. Even in the light of counter veiling evidence he was unwilling to discuss the hypotheses. By this he also violated elementary scientific method....He openly admitted that his deliberate method had always been to irritate and provoke his opponents' [80].

On the other hand, Heyerdahl's work certainly caused scholars to check their assumptions, and above all his first expedition was the direct cause of much of today's research. The fact that his theories aroused deep scepticism or vehement rejection reflected not so much any prejudice about the source of Polynesian culture, but rather the selectivity of his data and his cavalier disregard of the problems of dating and distribution, as well as for the work of those whose findings contradicted him. In the eyes of virtually all specialists, any contact that the island may have had with the New World did not precede its settlement by Polynesians, and influences from South America, if any, had a minimal impact on the island's cultural and anthropological development.

Forty years ago it was still possible to claim that the evidence linking certain elements of Easter Island with South America was the same as that used to derive others from Polynesia, so that scholars who supported either hypothesis while rejecting the other were applying double standards. Today, however, the variety and solidity of the Polynesian case contrasts strikingly with the tenuousness and subjectivity of the evidence for links between *Rapa Nui* and South America.

The inescapable conclusion is that, while there may perhaps have been sporadic contact between the two places -and, as mentioned above, there is a rapidly growing body of evidence for Polynesian visits to the New World coast- Peruvian culture is notable by its absence. If Amerindians had the place to themselves for centuries, there should be far more physical evidence of them and their culture. However, as Roger Green has emphasized in recent syntheses of the evidence [81], virtually everything -whether oral traditions, biological anthropology, simulated and real voyaging (see Chapter 3), flora and fauna, or archaeological material- now points firmly to East Polynesia, and particularly to what he calls a 'Mangareva interaction sphere source'. It is still possible, indeed probable, that the more remote ancestral home was the Marquesas, in view of the numerous similarities and links with those islands; but the most likely immediate source for the island's prehistoric population is Mangareva. As Green has stressed, in many of their architectural features Easter Island's religious sites are closely related to those of the Tuamotus, Mangareva and Pitcairn, and the initial stages in the development of *ahu* and *marae* (see above, p. 62) are very similar; and a tremendously strong body of archaeological evidence points to a basic cultural continuity throughout the whole of Easter Island's prehistory.

No reliable sign of any American component in material culture has been encountered, let alone any trace of an original or subsequent irruption of settlers from the New World. In the light of recently revived theories about Polynesians sailing east to South America and bringing back ideas and genes, it is worth remembering that Katherine Routledge in 1919 had already concluded not only that the island was not populated from there, as mentioned above, but also that if there had been any influence, it had been in the other direction, i.e. from eastern Polynesia to the New World [82]. One must keep an open mind, but it would require clear and diagnostic anthropological, biological, linguistic and archaeological data to confirm that any group of American Indians was ever in residence on the island, and after a century of research no such evidence has turned up. It therefore has to be accepted that Easter Island was colonized only from eastern Polynesia.

[1] Heyerdahl 1950.

[2] Heyerdahl 1952.

[3] Heyerdahl 1989, p. 173.

[4] Heyerdahl 1958, 1989.

[5] Heyerdahl 1989, p. 233.

[6] Heyerdahl 1989, p. 229.

[7] Lanning 1970.

[8] Heyerdahl et al. 1995.

[9] Bahn 1993a, p. 47.

[10] Lanning 1970.

[11] Green 2001.

[12] Bittmann 1984.

[13] Jones & Klar 2005; Ramírez-Aliaga & Matisoo-Smith 2008; Jones et al. 2011.

[14] Suggs 1951, chapter 16; see also Howells 1973, pp. 216-18; Emory 1972.

[15] Theroux 1992, p. 455.

[16] Lanning 1970.

[17] Irwin 1992, p. 62; Finney 1993.

[18] Irwin 1992.

[19] Smith 1961a, pp. 270-71; Mellén Blanco 1986, p. 150.

[20] Jones & Klar 2005.

[21] Ramírez-Aliaga & Matisoo-Smith 2008, pp. 89-90.

[22] Storey et al. 2007, 2011; Fitzpatrick & Callaghan 2009. According to Edwards & Edwards (2013: 30), early contact is supported by the fact that, of all continental Chile, only the people of the Arauco peninsula in the south marked ownership of fowls by cutting the phalanxes of chickens into different patterns, as the Rapanui did for centuries.

[23] Englert 1970, pp. 47, 49, 86.

[24] Geiseler 1995, p. 80.

[25] Emory 1972.

[26] Routledge 1919, p. 282.

[27] Barthel 1978, p. 22.

[28] Routledge 1919, pp. 211-12.

[29] Routledge 1917, p. 332.

[30] Heiser 1974.

[31] Langdon 1988.

[32] Bahn & Flenley 1994.

[33] Ballard et al. 2005; Roullier et al. 2013.

[34] Yen 1974.

[35] Golson 1965/6 (especially p. 80); Green 1998, 2000, 2001.

[36] von Saher 1999.

[37] Golson 1965/6, p. 63.

[38] Wallin 1996; Martinsson-Wallin & Wallin 1994, p. 162.

[39] Smith 1988; see also Routledge 1919, p. 272.

[40] Ferdon 1966, p. 60; Smith 1988.

[41] McCoy 1976a, p. 333.

[42] See Tihuanacu, une civilisation des Andes. Dossiers d'Archéologie 262, avril 2001.

[43] Golson 1965/6, pp. 77, 79.

[44] Métraux 1957, p. 227.

[45] Skinner 1955.

[46] Englert 1970, p. 123; Skjølsvold & Figueroa 1989; see also Bahn 1990. According to Østreng (2014: 92), Englert told Heyerdahl that Tukuturi's posture was used by islanders when singing in choirs on special occasions, a tradition of historical times, so that this statue had to be much younger than the others. Despite the importance Heyerdahl normally attached to folklore and legend, he ignored Englert's explanation, and decided the statue had nothing to do with local traditions.

[47] For an account of all these errors in rock art interpretation, see Lee 1992.

[48] Balfour 1917; Routledge 1919, pp. 296-98; Barrow 1967; Barrow 1998.

[49] Lee & Stasack 1999, pp. 153-54.

[50] Lee & Liller 1987.

[51] Ramírez & Huber 2000, pp. 22-23.

[52] Hoare 1982, p. 466.

[53] Scaglion 2005.

[54] Langdon & Tryon 1983; for a review, see Clark 1983.

[55] Green 1988; Fischer 1992.

[56] Du Feu & Fischer 1993.

[57] Butinov & Knorozov 1957.

[58] Barthel 1978.

[59] Heyerdahl & Ferdon 1965, pp. 255, 333.

[60] Gill 1990, 2015.

[61] Gill & Owsley 1993; Gill 1994; Baker & Gill 1997; Chapman & Gill 1997; Gill et al. 1997.

[62] Hagelberg 1993/4, 1995; Hagelberg et al. 1994.

[63] Bahn 1994.

[64] Gill 1998; Chapman & Gill 1998; see also Bahn 1997.

[65] Rapa Nui Journal 14 (2), 2000, p. 58; Clow et al. 2001; Gill 2001.

[66] Chapman 1998, p. 170; Stefan & Gill 2015.

[67] Stefan 2001; Stefan & Gill 2015.

[68] Ruiz-Tagle 2006, p. 93.

[69] Hill & Serjeantson 1989.

[70] Thorsby 2010, 2012, 2014; Moreno-Mayar et al. 2014; Hagelberg 2014, 2015.

[71] Matisoo-Smith et al. 1998.

[72] Barnes et al. 2006.

[73] Storey et al. 2007.

[74] Eric Powell, pers. comm.

[75] Gongora et al. 2008; Storey et al. 2011.

[76] Ferdon 1966, p. 38; see also Smith 1993, p. 79; Heyerdahl 1989: 175.

[77] See Ralling 1990, p. 282; and an article in The Listener, 19 April 1990, p. 6. According to Østreng (2014: 80), 'As one of his field companions claimed, Heyerdahl seemed to draw his conclusions first and then looked for highly selective evidence of confirmation.' When Skjølsvold found a rat's leg bone in the lowest stratum of excavation, Heyerdahl disregarded and suppressed it – the find was important in that it showed remains of Polynesian culture in the lowest strata.

[78] Kirch 2000, p. 238.

[79] Kvam 2013; Østreng 2014: 93.

[80] Kvam 2013: 214, 324; Østreng 2014.

[81] Green 1998, 2000, 2001.

[82] Routledge 1919, p. 291.

Chapter 3

How did they get there, and why?

*Sailing into the unknown with women
and pigs aboard to find an island
has always seemed to me a
foolhardy business no matter
how intrepid and adventurous
the Polynesian might be.*

Edward Dodd

Days, weeks at sea, at the mercy of the waves, without a glimpse of land. Braving the elements. Kept going through faith in their leader, *Hotu Matu'a*, a group of people -scores of them, men, women and children- were crowded into a catamaran with their animals and plants, their material possessions, and food for a journey of unknown duration. Their navigator stood by the upturned bow of the long vessel and scanned the eastern horizon for tell-tale signs of the 'promised land' which could be their new home...

Having decided that Easter Island was colonized from eastern Polynesia, we must now turn to the fascinating question of how such an amazing and hazardous journey was accomplished, and speculate as to the possible reasons that lay behind it. In the absence of written records, alas, the precise nature and cause of the journey can only be a matter of informed guesswork, based on a knowledge of Polynesian ethnography as well as on the islanders' own legends which, though not wholly reliable for details as we have already seen, nevertheless give a flavour of the likely events.

'Star-Compass' navigators

Ethnographic study of prehistoric Polynesia does, indeed, provide us with intriguing glimpses of the way of life of the first Easter Islanders. In the colonization of the world, modern people had settled in New Guinea and Australia by at least 50,000 years ago, and had reached the northern Solomon Islands c. 28,000 years ago, but there is no evidence of any settlement in Polynesia until many millennia later, presumably because further exploration had to await the required navigational expertise enabling people to sail far offshore and survive [1].

In western Polynesia, where the islands are rich, comparatively large and close together, the early settlers (installed by c. 3200 years ago) were able greatly to develop these new navigational skills in conditions of comfort and relative safety. They could then spread further east (for example, to the Marquesas by 150 BC), where the islands were poorer in natural resources, smaller and further apart, requiring greater risks in exploration. It is thought likely that voyages of exploration occurred before actual colonization took place,

25. Tahitian boats in
Matavai Bay (Tahiti),1773.

using a strategy of 'search and find' or 'search and return home safely if unsuccessful'. In short, the spread involved a developing strategy of directed exploration that laid emphasis not on the fastest rate of advance but, understandably, on the best chance of survival [2].

The Polynesians were, in fact, among the most highly skilled seafarers and navigators the world has ever seen. They had an astounding knowledge of the night sky, and could steer by star paths using 'star-compass' techniques that are still practised over much of the Pacific; some had individual names for about two hundred stars, but recognized and used many other associated stars. They had an amazing ability to detect surface currents and compensate for them. And they had the almost uncanny skill of steering by wave motion, guided by the barely perceptible swells reflected from islands beyond the horizon: as David Lewis remarks, 'The skilled navigator comes to recognize the profile and characteristics of particular ocean swells as he would the faces of his friends, but he judges their direction more by feel than by sight' [3]. The most advanced practitioners of this art would enter the water to judge the swells against the most sensitive part of the body, the scrotum [4], thus giving a whole new meaning to the term 'ball-bearings'.

The most sophisticated navigational concepts were restricted to selected initiates -this was closely guarded knowledge, handed down only within the navigator families. The ocean was not the daunting barrier it appears to landlubbers, but, as Thor Heyerdahl often rightly stressed, a highway on which violent storms or the danger of death were no greater a risk than a car accident is today. The inhabitants of Pacific islands spent a great deal of time paddling or sailing in their lagoons or visiting neighbouring islands, and trading over quite large distances. Water was their element.

It is not surprising that the Polynesians' economy was based on the intensive exploitation of marine resources, together with shifting cultivation of a wide range of tubers and fruits. The commonest crops were the *taro*, yam, sweet potato, coconut, breadfruit and banana, while pigs, dogs, chickens and rats provided meat. The Polynesian islands comprised territorial divisions (sometimes individual islets) which usually incorporated a portion of coastline and stretched to the mountainous interior. Settlements, concentrated along the coast or in the more fertile valleys, consisted of homesteads scattered among plantations, and often clustered around chiefly dwellings. The concept of aristocracy was highly developed in Polynesian society, with the chiefs having the power of life or death, and usually tracing their lineage back through a series of first-born sons to the tribal founder-ancestor [5].

What could have been the Polynesians' motive for long-distance voyaging to new lands? Romantic explanations abound in the literature -the spirit of adventure, the roving seafarer, the conqueror, the supposed stimulus of astronomical events such as stellar novae and supernovae- but Polynesian ethnography provides us with plenty of more mundane and more realistic choices. All of them may hold some truth, since no single explanation can account for the numerous Polynesian voyages of colonization over the centuries.

There may have been drastic reasons for departure: volcanic activity, tidal waves, hurricanes, earthquakes, freak droughts, famine, overpopulation or epidemics must have created refugees from time to time, and small and isolated atolls are especially subject to depopulation through these factors. Equally drastic, and no doubt more frequent, was violence: warfare, raiding, and violent family disputes leading to enforced or voluntary exile. The native histories of the Pacific are full of references to the flight of defeated parties before their enemies -the first 'boat people' seen on this ocean.

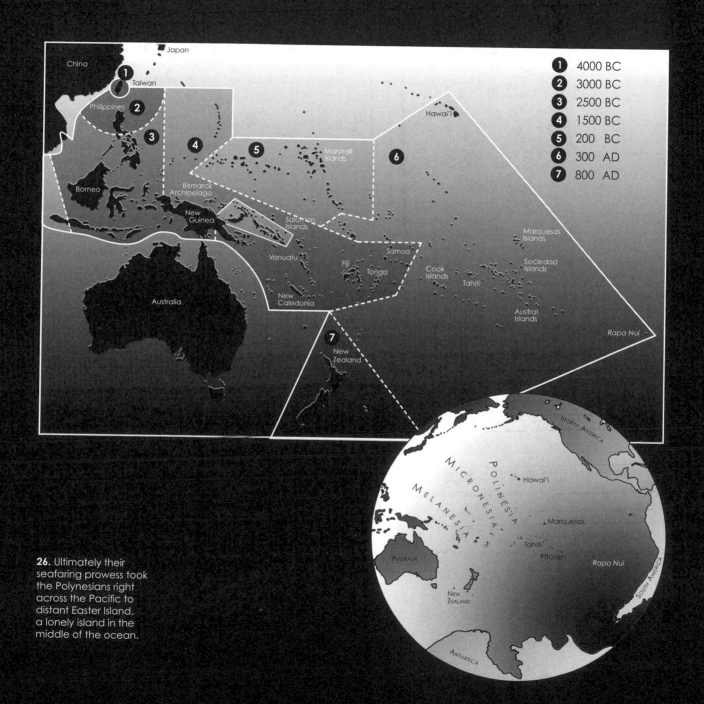

1	4000 BC
2	3000 BC
3	2500 BC
4	1500 BC
5	200 BC
6	300 AD
7	800 AD

China
Japan
Taiwan
Philippines
Borneo
New Guinea
Bismarck Archipelago
Marshall Islands
Salomon Islands
Hawai'i
Vanuatu
Fiji
Tonga
Samoa
Cook Islands
Tahiti
Marquesas Islands
Sociedad Islands
Austral Islands
Rapa Nui
New Caledonia
Australia
New Zealand

NORTH AMERICA
POLYNESIA
MICRONESIA
MELANESIA
Hawai'i
Marquesas
Tahiti
Pitcairn
Rapa Nui
SOUTH AMERICA
AUSTRALIA
NEW ZEALAND
ANTARTICA

26. Ultimately their seafaring prowess took the Polynesians right across the Pacific to distant Easter Island, a lonely island in the middle of the ocean.

27. Engraving of a Nuka-Hiva warrior.

Many people were set adrift in rafts or small canoes for crimes and misdemeanours such as murder, adultery, insults, breaches of etiquette, or even juvenile mischief. It is known that a considerable number of such 'criminals' might be deported together: could the first Easter Islanders be a Polynesian equivalent of the British convicts sent to Australia? Men of abnormal physical strength or influence, of whom people were jealous or afraid, might also be sent into exile.

There were other social reasons for the 'budding off' of new communities: in many islands, the chief's first-born son inherited the land, so restless and ambitious younger sons, seeing no chance of advancement at home, often set out in canoes '...well provisioned with fruits, animals, women and male helpers', as Dodd put it [6], to seek fame and fortune in a new homeland. Some may well have gone out of sheer curiosity, or to seek new materials or partners for trading purposes. Occupants of some Polynesian islands are known to have gone very considerable distances, looking for raw materials or suitable types of stone for toolmaking or tomb-building.

Oral traditions from Easter Island itself paint a vivid picture of its first settlers, who, as we have seen (p. 53), are said to have come from a large, warm, green island to the west called *Hiva*, probably Mangareva or an island in the Marquesas. One tale relates that they left because of a cataclysm, when most of their land was submerged beneath the ocean. However, the most common tradition is that *Hotu Matu'a*, a chief, was forced to flee that island after being defeated in war -either at the hands of his own brother, or because of his brother's misconduct with a rival chief's woman. One of *Hotu Matu'a*'s entourage, a tattooer called *Haumaka*, had a prophetic dream of an island to the east with volcanic craters and pleasant beaches, on which six men could be seen. *Hotu Matu'a* therefore sent a canoe with six picked men to search for the island and await his arrival there, in order that the dream might be fulfilled. He himself followed in a double canoe, and landed on the beach of *Anakena* after a voyage of six weeks. The details of this tale may be mythological, but there is a good chance that it contains a sound framework of truth; in particular, the political circumstances leading to *Hotu Matu'a*'s flight are quite believable, being typical of Polynesian history.

Apart from his human entourage, perhaps dozens of people, his vessel must have been well supplied with tools, food, and plants and animals. Its two canoes would have been joined by a bridge bearing a mast and a shelter. There would have been a supply of drinking water, to be replenished from downpours during the voyage. Provisions would have included fruits, coconuts, vegetables, and also preserved fish since, apart from flying fish, it would have been difficult to obtain seafood over the farthest deeps. A lot of cooking could have been done at sea, with a sandbox carried on board and a small bed of embers constantly nursed. It has been reckoned that even a modest double canoe, c. 15 m (c. 50 ft) long, could carry about 18,000 pounds, so there would have been no problem carrying plentiful supplies in addition to the passengers. On the shelter-floor and in the canoes would be the plants to be used for food, together with medicine, clothing, jewellery and vessels. In small cages or simply tied to the bridge were probably pigs and dogs, and certainly some chickens and rats -the latter were considered a delicacy by the elders. All Polynesian colonizers had learned over thousands of years to bring such items along, in case their new home did not have them -and Easter Island was certainly to prove bereft of many of the resources needed to support a Polynesian colony.

Found by chance?

As with the question of the source of the colonizers, there are two principal views about their journey to Easter Island: some scholars believe that it was a skilfully navigated voyage, like other island colonizations in the Pacific, whereas others claim that Polynesian voyages were haphazard affairs, which sometimes struck lucky and found habitable islands.

In one sense, this debate is of little consequence to us, since the crucial point is that people did reach Easter Island, whether purposely or accidentally. But it is worth examining the two sides of the argument for the insights they provide into the culture and capabilities of these Polynesian colonizers.

The main proponent of the 'accidental' theory, Andrew Sharp, argued in a series of books and articles that deliberate navigation to and from remote ocean islands was impossible in the days before courses could be plotted with precision instruments [7]. In other words, he shared Captain Cook's own suspicion that the more isolated islands of the Pacific were settled by accident.

Sharp rightly pointed out that to talk of a 'deliberate navigation' actually implies three voyages: a preliminary journey of reconnaissance, a navigated voyage back home to report the discovery of the new island, and finally the navigated voyage to bring the settlers to their new home. As we shall see, a triple trip of this kind is extremely unlikely in the case of Easter Island.

The doubts about the possibility of deliberate navigation rest not only on the variability and unpredictability of winds and currents, but also on the frequent invisibility of stars or other heavenly bodies. Another important factor is the minute target presented by the small Pacific islands scattered through an area of 30 million sq. km (11.5 million sq. miles) of ocean, bigger than Africa, bigger even than the former Soviet Union and China combined: the distance from New Zealand to Easter Island represents one quarter of the entire circumference of the globe. The Marquesas group spans 400 km (250 miles), the Hawaiian archipelago some 600 km (370 miles), and New Zealand, 1500 km (930 miles). But Easter Island's mere 23 km (14.25 mile) span, lost in the Pacific, is a real needle in a haystack. The slightest miscalculation in course would miss it by a huge margin.

Hence, while 'local' two-way voyages of a few hundred kilometres- such as the islanders insisted they regularly undertook to Salas y Gómez, 415 km (258 miles) away- might be feasible since winds and currents would be familiar and relatively predictable, supposed two-way voyages over thousands of kilometres are far less likely: in golfing terms, it is like the difference between putting (where the hole provides a comparatively large target) and scoring a hole in one. The chances of Easter Island being reached even once were extremely limited; to imagine it being reached several times over vast distances is beyond belief.

Lewis, and later Finney [8], repeatedly stressed that while it is possible (though unlikely) that many canoes managed to reach Easter Island, it is far more unlikely that there was regular, intentional 2-way communication between the island and eastern Polynesia. It would have been easy -had timber for good canoes been available, which was probably not the case- for Easter Islanders to sail westwards towards the East Polynesian archipelagos using the prevailing winds: indeed, in the 1940s and 1950s the islanders sometimes stole rowboats from the Chilean Navy or used makeshift sailboats, and headed west, successfully reaching central East Polynesia. But any return journey would have been phenomenally difficult, requiring not only westerly winds, but also the ability to find a tiny lone island lost in a vast ocean without any surrounding archipelago. Nevertheless, in recent years some researchers, unwilling to accept the notion of a single settlement followed by such isolation, have insisted that the Easter Islanders

probably did maintain regular 2-way contacts with east Polynesia, albeit less repetitive and continuous than elsewhere in the region, and possibly even with South America; some believe that this only happened during the early occupation phase, while others have even claimed that isolation only began around AD 1600 [9]. Obviously, one cannot disprove this, and one must keep an open mind, but for the moment there is absolutely no evidence for it (and, as we have seen, common sense argues strongly against it): If the island did indeed maintain such contacts, then why did its language remain so archaic? Why has no foreign or exotic stone ever been found there (and conversely, why is there no solid evidence for the plentiful *Rapa Nui* obsidian turning up on other islands)? Why are there no later forms of Polynesian fish-hooks, or later forms of adzes with tangs, or typical Polynesian food pounders? And above all, why did the islanders never use these contacts to make good the island's total lack of pigs and dogs, so crucial and common in the Polynesian way of life? In short, we feel that Mulloy was absolutely correct when he saw isolation as a central fact of *Rapa Nui* prehistory, and it is worth recalling the words of Cornelis Bouman, one of the first Dutch visitors of 1722: 'I must conclude from the characteristics of these people that they have never seen any other nation, except the one that lives on their island' [10].

Andrew Sharp was undoubtedly right that all far-flung islands must have been encountered accidentally before their first settlement, for the simple reason that nobody knew beforehand that they were there. However, the real debate centres on the degree of navigation or luck involved in these voyages of exploration [11]. They have often been called 'drift voyages', which is an unfortunate term implying no guidance at all.

In any case, drift alone is most unlikely to have led settlers to Easter Island. Using a series of computer programmes simulating Pacific voyaging and incorporating many variations and a wealth of data on winds, currents and island locations, three scholars (Michael Levison, R. Gerard Ward and John W. Webb) found that the likelihood of a drift or accidental voyage to Easter Island from South America was virtually nil [12]; likewise, no simulated drifts from the nearest inhabited islands such as Mangareva or the Tuamotus reached Easter. Only two voyages from Pitcairn got anywhere near. In fact, of 2208 simulated drifts, not one reached Easter Island, and only three came within 320 km (c. 200 miles) of it. It was concluded that the island's settlers were probably following an intentionally easterly course at the time, and were lucky enough to find land; simulations modified to allow for sailing on a preferred course did reach Easter Island.

It is worth noting that this work also established that Pitcairn itself could have been reached by an accidental drift voyage from Easter -perhaps by a fishing vessel carried off in a storm. Such occurrences are by no means unknown even today: one Easter Island fishing boat was caught by a storm in 1947, and ended up in the Tuamotu archipelago thirty-seven days later.

Subsequently, a massive programme of computer simulations, involving tens of thousands of canoe voyages, was carried out by Irwin which looked at what was feasible in Polynesian navigation, emphasizing the practicalities of deep-sea sailing and incorporating details of weather and currents, the relative accessibility and remoteness of the island targets, very specific data on the distances between islands, and the behaviour and capabilities of boats [13]. Where Easter Island is concerned, the simulations of voyages from Pitcairn found that the odds against finding *Rapa Nui* were still high; indeed, Pitcairn itself was hard to reach, and the few successes occurred in the winter, with the help of westerlies of sub-tropical origin (see below). One-way simulated voyages from Pitcairn to Easter

Island took 21 days, but the success rate even when sailing in the very best direction was only about 30% for *Rapa Nui*.

The proponents of deliberate Polynesian long-distance voyaging argue that it is our modern technology which blinds us to the more traditional ways of doing things: our experts, astronomers, mathematics, clocks, instruments, compasses, maps and calendars have ended our reliance on the heavens for time and directions, and make it impossible for us to believe that people could go confidently across oceans without our artificial aids. We assume instead that vessels normally hugged coasts, and ventured elsewhere through accident and misfortune.

Ethnography provides plenty of evidence to the contrary, and the extent of the Polynesians' geographic knowledge suggests that deliberate two-way voyages were accomplished almost routinely over an impressive range: local histories show that Polynesian outliers were frequently visited by huge ocean-going canoes from Samoa and Tonga, and until quite recently there were two-way voyages of up to 1300 km (c. 800 miles) without intervening islands, and 2240 km (c. 1400 miles) with a single intermediate island (Raiatea to Niuataputapu). There were also multiple voyages between eastern Polynesia and New Zealand (as shown by finds there of New Zealand obsidian). Polynesians thought nothing of being at sea for two weeks or more.

One important factor is that pinpoint accuracy was not required: a radius of 80 to 120 km (50 to 75 miles) around an island brings one within the area where birds, winds, land-clouds and the altered swell patterns of the ocean can be used as guides [14]. By 'expanding' the difficult targets in this way, it was possible simply to steer for entire archipelagos, and then use the 'radius phenomena' as one approached (ill. 29). Even the tiny Easter Island is extended tenfold by these indicators, still a small target, but easier to find than if one relied simply

28. The island of Tahiti, from the 2nd voyage of Cook, 1772-75. Note the sail and the row of double canoes.

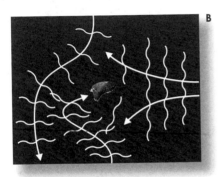

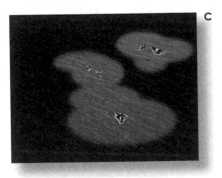

29. Techniques employed by Polynesian mariners included the **A**; observation of changing cloud formations, **B**; variations in swells and wave patterns around an island, which meant that **C**; within a radius of about 50 miles around an island group, the seafarers could detect the presence of land even without sighting it.

on visual contact with the land: Pacific islands are visible only from a distance of 100 km (c. 60 miles) at best, and most from far less, some a mere 24 km (15 miles). Whereas Easter Island's highest peaks (510 m) were only spotted from a distance of 35 sea miles (1 nautical mile=1.85 km) by the Germans in 1882, the Spanish in 1770 saw sea birds several days before reaching the island [15] -and the island's originally great quantities of seabirds, fanning out in all directions every day, would certainly have expanded the island's 'visibility' far more for the first settlers [16].

Andrew Sharp and others have pointed out that these 'radius phenomena' are unreliable and may be deceptive: cloud effects are not always present over islands, and are frequently found over tracts of ocean without land. Sea birds do not always congregate near land, and even then are only detectable in close proximity.

Nevertheless, reliable or not, it remains true that Polynesian navigators could and did use indicators such as these to direct their vessels safely and accurately to chosen destinations. Another useful phenomenon was subsurface luminescence (thought to be a form of bioluminescence triggered by a backwash wave): these streaks of light that dart out from the directions in which land lies are best seen from 100 to 160 km (60 to 100 miles) out, and it was customary to steer by them on overcast nights when the heavens were invisible.

The active alternative to Heyerdahl's passive 'migration by drift', following prevailing winds and currents, and Sharp's passive 'migration by chance', where colonizations were accomplished through accidental blow-away voyages, is to see the settlement of the Pacific islands as a long, slow, skilful, systematic and largely premeditated affair, which steadily built on accumulating knowledge of geography, the elements, seamanship and provisioning [17]. Over the centuries, it is probable that a faith was born from the distribution of islands, a virtually continuous series of island chains strung out from west to east, that there were always new lands to be found: eastward, ever eastward.

Had the colonization been entirely by accidental voyages, one must suppose a staggering percentage of losses at sea, with perhaps only one boat in a hundred or even a thousand getting through. No maritime people could tolerate such losses, and their explorations would soon have ceased. The persistence of the Polynesians' expansion, together with their efficient and well-equipped vessels, argue that -despite some inevitable losses- they were eminently successful in their explorations, going boldly in their starsteered enterprises.

Since they could not rely too heavily on winds and currents, they built their vessels -the double canoe or 'catamaran' (a Malay word that originally meant 'tied logs')- for speed rather than stability. Captain Cook reported with wonder how the Tongan chiefs literally sailed rings around his ship even when she was doing her best in a fair breeze. With a sail and a favourable wind these canoes could cover 160-240 km (100-150 miles) per day, and thanks to the Polynesians' ability to preserve foods for long periods, a range of 8000 km (c. 5000 miles) was feasible.

The aerodynamically efficient sails and slim hulls would permit the canoes to sail windward, though probably not for long distances if heavily laden: no sailor, even today, wants to spend days or weeks pushing hard into wind and current. This is why some scholars have argued that much of the Polynesians' spread from west to east was accomplished not by tacking against the prevailing southeast trade winds but by awaiting and using the periodic westerly wind reversals (see p. 52). During the past two centuries, such 'El Niño' events with prolonged westerlies have occurred at intervals of one to eight years, with major ones every seven to sixteen years. New evidence suggests that extreme El Niño–Southern Oscillation events were very frequent in the period AD 800 to AD 1200 [18]. This could have provided favourable winds at times, as well as stimulating migration from East Polynesia because of drought conditions there.

Thanks to the journals of European explorers and missionaries in the Pacific, we know that the 18th and 19th-century Polynesians were well acquainted with these westerlies, which were especially frequent in the summer, and did use them to sail eastward. Cook, for example, was told that when Tahitians wished to sail eastward they waited for the westerlies of November to January. They could even foretell other periodic spells of westerly wind by a day or so. There is no reason to assume that their ancestors were any less competent. In 1986, a Polynesian voyaging double-canoe, the *Hokule'a*, was sailed successfully from Samoa to Tahiti in an experiment to show that it was possible for such a vessel to sail from west to east by using westerly wind shifts.

The use of occasional westerlies, in the summer or during El Niño, might also accord some feasibility to the theory that Polynesians may have sailed to South America and back (see Chapter 2); on the other hand, the Humboldt Current could not have been used for the return westward, as has been suggested, for the simple reason that it would take one north along the South American coast; as seen in the *Kon-Tiki* case, one has to cross that current in order to reach the winds and currents out to sea [19].

However, while anomalous westerlies would have been a great help in colonizing many Polynesian islands, they were not needed where Easter Island is concerned. At 27° S, the island lies in a transitional zone between the southeast trades and the westerlies of higher latitudes; as we have already seen, in winter *Rapa Nui* is often subjected to unsettled, rainy weather with spells of strong westerly winds. A vessel that strayed south out of the trade wind belt could have been caught by these westerlies and carried to the island. This would require an extraordinary combination of luck and seamanship, not to mention the ability to endure a cold and stormy voyage, and helps explain why *Rapa Nui*, far from the mainstream of Polynesian voyaging, was to remain the most isolated of colonies, largely or totally cut off from the rest of Polynesia.

The fact that animals and plants were always transported to the new settlements argues strongly against the colonization being accidental: would offshore fishermen, unexpectedly caught by a storm, happen to have not only their womenfolk but also dogs, chickens, pigs and rats on board as well as banana sprouts and a wide range of other useful plants? The transporting of complete 'landscapes' to new islands suggests organized colonizing expeditions. Only in those few cases (e.g. Pitcairn, Henderson) where small island settlements were abandoned or their inhabitants died out could one argue for colonization after accidental, unprepared voyages, though it is equally likely that these too were normal colonizations which simply failed owing to an impoverished environment or some other cause -indeed, it has been speculated that they were abandoned because they had been deforested, so that the inhabitants could no longer build and maintain the large voyaging canoes which were needed for inter-island exchange with Mangareva [20].

So were the voyages all deliberate or all accidental? As usual in prehistory -and despite the legend of *Hotu Matu'a* voyaging to a known destination- the truth probably lies in a combination of both theories: it is doubtful that many successful colonies could have been started by fishermen or coastal voyagers blown off course, but it is equally extreme to envisage nothing but systematic voyages of exploration. The Polynesian spread, whatever its degree of planning and purposefulness, must have been a hazardous and uneven affair, relying heavily on luck in unpredictable conditions and unknown seas. To realize this point only increases one's admiration for the skill and daring of these pioneers who were willing and able to face such terrible risks.

As we saw in Chapter 2, the ultimate origin of the rapanui may have been the Marquesas, but it seems unlikely that they came directly from there: 19th-century sailing ships never went directly from the Marquesas to Easter Island, but went from Mangareva or Pitcairn [21]. The reason is obvious, to go directly from the Marquesas would require the crossing of almost 2000 miles of open ocean, whereas a voyage from Mangareva would involve only 1450 miles, during which one could encounter a scattering of atolls and the high island of Pitcairn, east of Mangareva, which further cuts the gap by 300 miles. Even from Pitcairn, however, Easter Island is 1150 miles away, and to travel this distance against the easterly trade winds and currents would have meant actually sailing more than 4000 miles, constantly pushing against wind and sea [22]. This is another strong reason to suppose that the settlers made the journey in a period of anomalous westerlies.

In June 1999, the *Hokule'a* sailing canoe left Hawai'i for Easter Island. By mid-July it had reached the Marquesas; it then sailed to Mangareva in the Gambiers, taking 33 days for that leg of the voyage. It reached *Rapa Nui* in October after a voyage of only 17 days from Mangareva [23] (whereas Irwin's simulations, as mentioned above, had predicted 20-21 days from Pitcairn to *Rapa Nui*, during winter westerlies). However, a note of caution has been sounded by Anderson [24], who feels that modern experimental double-canoes like the *Hokule'a* are far more powerful than the early historical vessels and employ forms which probably never sailed in prehistory, so that it is hard to accept their data on speed, their ability to sail windward, etc. He points out that Maori and Hawaiian canoes could not go to windward at all, and that while some historical Polynesian vessels were considered flexible and

30. Down: Priests traveling across Kealakekua bay for first contact rituals. Cook expedition.

Right: Navigation map made with wooden sticks and shells, Marshall Islands.

robust, others were fragile and liable to come apart. In short, it is likely that the prehistoric vessels would have been far slower than the *Hokule'a*, used a combination of downwind sailing, drifting and paddling, and needed very long periods at sea -thus facing difficulties of provisioning, materials stress and voyaging hazards. His conclusion, that long-distance sailing must have been far more difficult for Polynesians than modern experiments suggest, and that marginal East Polynesia must have been far less accessible, underlines how miraculous it was that *Rapa Nui* was found even once, and how incredibly unlikely it is that it maintained contacts with the outside world.

The first Easter Islanders, henceforth marooned at the 'end of the world' (*Te Pito Te Henua*, literally 'land's end' or 'fragment of the earth', but sometimes translated as 'The Navel of the World' [25]), probably began their new life with, in the words of Patrick Kirch, a full 'transported Polynesian landscape'. However, many of their plants, as well as the pigs and dogs, became extinct, the plants, no doubt, through environmental difficulties, and the animals through accidental or purposeful extermination, or perhaps through failing for some reason to survive the voyage to the island.

It is time, therefore, to look at the life of -and the traces left by- these first human beings ever to set foot on Easter Island: what they found there, how they adapted to the conditions and then altered them quite drastically.

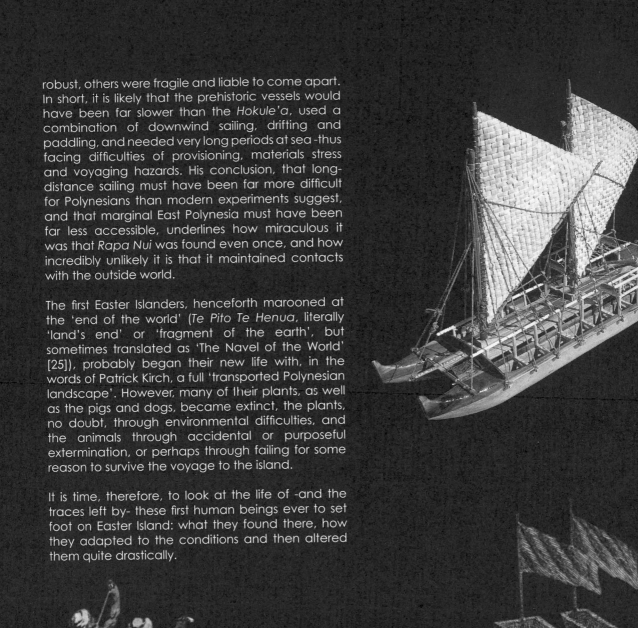

[1] For Polynesian prehistory, see Kirch 2000, 1984; Bellwood 1978, 1987; Jennings 1979.

[2] Irwin et al. 1990; Irwin 1992.

[3] Lewis 1972, 1974.

[4] Lewis 1974, p. 752.

[5] Kirch 1984.

[6] Dodd 1972.

[7] Sharp 1957, 1961.

[8] Lewis 1972, p. 307; Finney 2001, 1993, p. 4.

[9] Green 1998, p. 109; Green 2000; Martinsson-Wallin & Crockford 2002; for the AD 1600 claim, Vargas et al. 2006, p. 22.

[10] von Saher 1994, p. 100.

[11] Golson 1962.

[12] Levison et al. 1973; but see Finney 2001, pp. 172-73.

[13] Irwin 1992; but see Finney 2001, p. 173.

[14] Lewis 1972, pp. 102-3, 175.

[15] Geiseler 1995, p. 16; Mellén Blanco 1986, p. 123. Lisjanskij (2004, p. 122) reported that 'at fine weather, it seems to be visible some 60 miles away', and also (p. 119) that 'before reaching the island, we saw many small birds... which fly like pigeons, but are smaller in size; from this we concluded that we were not so far from the island'.

[16] Finney 2001, p. 175.

[17] Irwin 1992, Irwin et al. 1990.

[18] Finney 1985, 1991, 1993; Finney et al. 1989; Irwin 1989, 1990; Caviedes & Waylen 1993; Moy et al. 2002.

[19] Finney 1994.

[20] Finney 1994a.

[21] Irwin 1992, p. 93; Green 2000, p. 72.

[22] Finney 1993.

[23] Finney 2001; Finney & Kilonsky 2001.

[24] Anderson 2001.

[25] Barthel 1978, p. 5.

31. The *Hokule'a,* replica of a Polynesian double canoe, has carried out numerous important voyages in the Pacific over the past thirty years, using the stars and wave formations as navigational aids.

32. Engraving of Tahitian war canoe by Hodges. Voyage of Captain Wallis, 1766-1768.

1400 years of solitude?

In attempting to retrace the islanders' prehistory, our first task is to determine when that prehistory began. As we have seen, it is extremely improbable that the island could have been reached more than once before the arrival of the Europeans. Yet genealogical studies, involving the listed names of previous chiefs back to *Hotu Matu'a*, led Sebastian Englert to conclude that the latter and his followers had arrived no earlier than the 16th century AD, while on the same basis Métraux placed their arrival in the 12th century [1]. But archaeology has subsequently suggested, through radiocarbon dating, that people were already on the island by AD 690, and possibly even by the 4th century (though isolated single dates always need to be treated with caution): this would fit with another tradition that there had been 57 generations of kings since *Hotu Matu'a*, which, allowing an average of 25 years per generation, would take one back to AD 450. But where do the persistent tales of conflict between the *Hanau E'epe* and the *Hanau Momoko* populations fit in?

Thor Heyerdahl sought links with South America in the famous legend of the 'long-ears' (*Hanau E'epe*) and the 'short-ears' (*Hanau Momoko*), seeing the former as the descendants of the first (Amerindian) colonizers, and the latter as the more recent Polynesian arrivals. Hence he saw the 'long-ears' as having their ear-lobes elongated and perforated for disc-ornaments, a practice still current when the Europeans first arrived (though Mrs Routledge was informed that the term 'long-ears' conveyed to the natives not the custom of distending the ears but having them long by nature [2]). According to Heyerdahl's selected story, the 'short-ears' massacred all but one 'long-ear' (who subsequently had descendants) in the 17th century at the 'battle of the *Poike* ditch'.

Yet Sebastian Englert emphatically denied that these Polynesian terms referred to ears: having studied the older form of the islanders' language in more detail than anyone else, he stressed that the terms meant 'broad/strong/corpulent people' and 'slender people', respectively [3]. In view of the widespread notion in Polynesia associating physical size and corpulence with leadership and *mana* (spiritual power), this would suggest that the *Hanau E'epe* were the upper class, and the *Hanau Momoko* the lower. Once again, the evidence for supposed links with the New World evaporates -and in any case, as shown above, elongated ears and disc ornaments are well attested in the Marquesas Islands, and are therefore not exclusively a New World phenomenon.

Furthermore, Englert believed that the *Hanau E'epe* were latecomers who designed the platforms, and that the *Hanau Momoko* created the statues, while Thomas Barthel, after exhaustive study of the island's oral traditions, decided that *Hotu Matu'a* arrived from Polynesia long after an initial colonization from the same direction -he was chief of the *Hanau*

33. An engraving of a long-eared rapanui by William Hodges, Cook expedition, 1774.

Momoko, but brought some *Hanau E'epe* prisoners with him as a labour force to work on the land. They were settled on *Poike*, away from the *Momoko* lands. Although the terms mean 'slender' and 'stocky', respectively, the tales concerning the two groups contain no indication of racial or cultural differences. It is far more likely that the relationship between them was one of victors and vanquished, or of lofty versus lowly status, although this clashes with the normal Polynesian association of stockiness with *mana* and the upper class.

Any attempt to fit the traditions to the archaeology is admirable, but we have already shown that they are factually unreliable: at least six different genealogies have been recorded [4], for example, containing different names and numbers of kings, and these were gleaned from a few surviving natives from the late 19th century onwards, by then a decimated, demoralized and culturally impoverished population which had lost most of the collective cultural-historical memory. Besides, they would mean that the island was reached not once but twice -or even three times if the tale of *Hotu Matu'a*'s advance party of explorers were to be accepted. While that is theoretically possible, the most probable hypothesis is still that of a single early colonization from Polynesia, led by a chief, a culture hero who has been given the name *Hotu Matu'a* (i.e. Great Parent). The island's archaeological record is certainly one of continuous artifactual and architectural development, with no trace of a sudden influx of new cultural influences from outside.

Besides, any supposed new arrivals after the first colonization would have been few in number compared with the established population, and could have made little impact culturally other than with an idea or two -indeed, as E. P. Lanning reminds us, small groups arriving by sea would probably have been 'knocked on the head or put to work cleaning fish' [5]. One can hardly envisage them imposing a new religion or political organization without a fleet-load of warriors. In the absence of any hard evidence for further immigration, let alone invasion, it must be assumed that the island's cultural developments and elaborations were produced by internal forces.

The earliest archaeological radiocarbon date obtained so far, as we have seen, is AD 386 ± 100 from charcoal on a buried land surface at the *Poike* ditch; this may indicate very early forest clearance, but the result is considered very doubtful since an obsidian sample from the same provenance gave a date of AD 1560! An even earlier 4th-century result (AD 318) came from a sample of totora reed in a grave at *Ahu Tepeu* I, but a bone sample from the same grave gave AD 1629. So the earliest really reliable radiocarbon date is reckoned to be that of AD 690 ± 130 from the first construction phase of *Ahu Tahai*, a few kilometres to the south of *Tepeu* [6]; but since these platforms were already large and stylized the first settlers probably arrived long before, sometime during the first centuries AD. The earliest date for a house was obtained on charcoal of *Thespesia populnea* (*mako'i*) from a rectangular dwelling excavated on *Rano Kau*: AD 770 ± 239 [7]. Some specialists prefer to discard all the early dates as lacking clear cultural associations or being on unsuitable materials, and claim that the island, like the rest of East Polynesia, was first settled towards the end of the 1st millennium AD; however, others see palaeoenvironmental evidence for human colonization of remote Oceania before AD 300-600, while linguists still insist that their data point to human arrival on Mangareva and *Rapa Nui* by the first few centuries AD [8].

These 'Late' and 'Early' chronologies have become less and less compatible in recent years. The 'Late chronologists', led by Atholl Anderson from Canberra, Australia, apply a process of 'chronometric hygiene', which eliminates dates that are in any way doubtful. This is basically a good idea. They conclude that New Zealand, for example, was uninhabited by people until AD 1200, though there could have been earlier visitors. For *Rapa Nui* the Late chronology has been championed by Terry Hunt, whose excavation at *Anakena* [9] has dates starting abruptly at AD 1200. These identical dates from two vertices of the Polynesian triangle (New Zealand and Easter Island) fit neatly with the idea of drought-enforced migrations out of Central and East Polynesia [10]. There are, however, many problems with the Late chronology [11]. On *Rapa Nui*, the *Anakena* excavation has a geological unconformity at the base where it rests on a buried soil. This suggests a gap in deposition of perhaps 1000 years or more below the AD 1200 date [12]. If one is going to have chronometric hygiene one must have geological hygiene also. Therefore the gap in deposition means that the AD 1200 date can only be a minimum age for colonization. The late date for New Zealand has similar and other problems [13]. In both cases it is accepted that there may have been substantial immigration around AD 1200: the question is, were there any people there already? For further study of this question, we must turn to evidence of pollen and charcoal.

Fossil pollen grains and fine wind-blown charcoal may be preserved in lake sediments as we shall discuss in the next section. The sediments can be radiocarbon dated, and when we find changes attributable to early human agricultural activities (such as a first significant decline in trees and a first rise in charcoal above background level) those dates may well indicate a minimum age for human arrival. Such well-dated evidence has come from the core collected in *Rano Raraku* by Daniel Mann [14] (see p. 252 for more details). It shows a simultaneous decline of tree pollen and rise of charcoal dated to about AD 1200. There are, however, some problems in interpreting this as the actual date of human arrival, rather than a minimum age. Immediately below this date we have a gap in deposition suggesting a drought that lowered the lake water level, possibly to zero. In a drought period, *Rano Raraku* would not have been a good place to live, because of lack of water supply. It is therefore possible that the edge of the much larger crater lake, *Rano Kau*, would have been the place where early settlers found a living.

Recent re-dating by modern techniques of a core from Rano Kau taken by John Flenley and Jim Teller (aided by Earthwatch volunteers) suggested a more likely date for first settlement was AD 100 [15]. This evidence for first forest decline is based on several dates which are well placed in relation to each other. Although they are derived from sediment carbon rather than macrofossil carbon, they seem to be reliable and apparently indicate forest burning which took about 200 years to recover. However, we accept that it is uncertain whether this was caused by people, as there is no independent evidence of human presence at that time. And given that we have evidence of slight volcanic activity around 3000-2000 BP, the possibility of a volcanic fire cannot be totally ruled out as yet.

A further core taken from Rano Kau in 2005 has been beautifully dated, using only totora fruits, to yield 16 calibrated dates in perfect sequence. The magnetic susceptibility trace from this core shows that there had been severe soil erosion around AD 650-700 [16], which could prove to be a realistic date for early agriculture within the crater. These pre-AD 1200 dates are also more in line with a mathematical model for population growth on the island constructed by Anthony Cole [17]. In fact the pollen and charcoal record in Rano Kau suggests there could have been at least three periods of population growth and collapse on Rapa Nui, and perhaps as many as six. These collapses could have been related to periodic droughts, or to rapid declines in the soil of freshly deforested areas.

In addition to the above-mentioned radiocarbon dates and the evidence from pollen and linguistics, in recent years there has been a more accurate calibration of obsidian dates, some of which point clearly to settlement considerably before AD 1200 -indeed, they begin at c. AD 700 [18].

Overall, the evidence available points to an early centre of habitation on the island's southwest corner, more or less where the population is gathered today. *Anakena*, where *Hotu Matu'a* is supposed to have landed, has been revealed by excavations to have had its earliest habitation in the late 8th or 9th century AD with platforms present by 1100 [19], while the south coast seems to begin a rapid build-up of population and construction only around AD 1300.

In what kind of environment would the first settlers have found themselves?

Reconstructing the environment

Pollen analysis provides us with vital information concerning the vegetation of Easter Island at the time of the earliest human settlement.

Each year, in the *Rano Raraku* crater lake, microscopic algae grow and later die. Their dead bodies fall to the bottom of the lake, mixing as they do so with any clay or silt washed into the lake from the slopes surrounding it, and any particles such as pollen grains falling in from the air. Each year, a new layer of sediment is thereby added on top of what has already accumulated. This process has been going on ever since the lake first formed over 37,000 years ago. In recent millennia the process has accelerated because of the totora reed (*Scirpus riparius*) growing around the edge of the lake, and in dry periods extending its growth right over the sediment surface. The dead totora leaves and rhizomes contribute even more rapidly to the growth of sediment. Another sub-aquatic plant, *tavari* (*Polygonum acuminatum*), is also contributory in this way.

Sediments of these types -i.e., the fine detritus muds (gyttja) formed mainly from algae, or the coarser detritus muds and peats formed from larger plants-have become well known in many parts of the world for providing a record of environmental history: a book whose pages record, in faithful detail, what was happening in and around the lake or swamp in which they are formed. *Rano Raraku* is not the only such site on Easter Island. *Rano Kau* is potentially even better, and *Rano Aroi*, near the summit of *Terevaka*, provides a third one. It is probably no accident that *Rano Raraku* and *Rano Kau* are each near major archaeological sites (the statue quarries and *Orongo*, respectively). The likely explanation for this is that they are the major sources of fresh water on an otherwise rather dry island, and would thus have been obvious centres for human activity. These two sites, therefore, have the potential to reveal much about the palaeo-environment of the island, and of human impact on it. They are both in the lowlands: the addition of *Rano Aroi*, which can provide similar information from the uplands, makes Easter Island one of the finest places in the world for integrating archaeology with the history of environment; furthermore, we may come close to solving the mystery of the island's decline by charting the rise and fall of its forests.

The first attempt to discover the history of the environment on Easter Island was made by Thor Heyerdahl's expedition in 1955, which collected short sample cores from the swamps at *Rano Raraku* and *Rano Kau* and passed them to Olof Selling, a Swedish palynologist, for analysis. Selling had already made detailed studies on Hawai'i, so he was familiar with many Pacific pollen types. He concluded that the toromiro (*Sophora toromiro*) had formerly been much commoner on the island. He also found

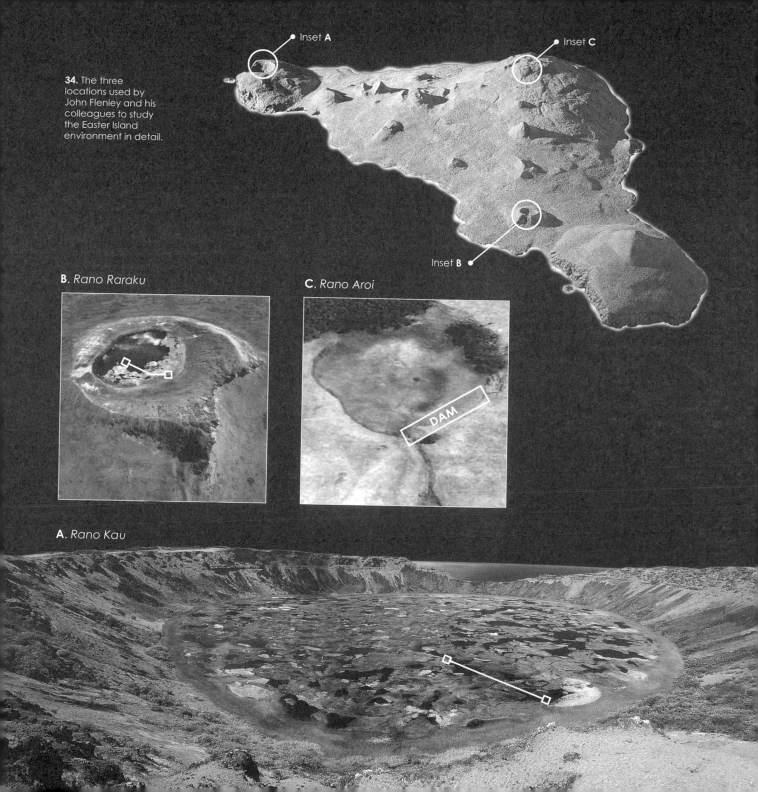

34. The three locations used by John Flenley and his colleagues to study the Easter Island environment in detail.

Inset **A**

Inset **C**

Inset **B**

B. *Rano Raraku*

C. *Rano Aroi*

DAM

A. *Rano Kau*

abundant pollen of a palm tree [20]. In this family (the Palmae) many pollen types are rather similar (at least as seen under ordinary microscopes), so it was impossible to identify the pollen with a particular species, but Selling made the suggestion that it could be a species of the genus *Pritchardia*. This was a reasonable guess, for *Pritchardia* is common on Hawai'i and other Pacific islands [21].

Selling also found pollen of *Compositae*, which was probably derived from shrubs, and he concluded that Easter Island had once borne a forest. Unfortunately no radiocarbon dates were obtained, so it was impossible to say when the island had been forested. Equally unfortunately, the work was never published, although it is mentioned in the expedition monographs. Shortly afterwards Selling retired from academic life, and no further analyses of these samples were made. The problem therefore remained: what was this mysterious palm which had once been so prevalent on the island that Selling reported its pollen 'filled every cubic millimetre of the bottom strata in the (*Rano Raraku*) crater lake'?

Pursuing the palm

John Flenley's first sight of *Rano Raraku* in 1977 convinced him that it was an ideal site for pollen analyses (palynology). In the first place, there were no inflow or outflow streams to the crater swamp; this meant that pollen would arrive mainly by aerial rather than water transport (which could have washed in older sediments), and that once in the crater it could not be washed out again. Secondly, with its diameter of c. 500 m (c. 1625 ft), it was just about the right size: previous research in New Guinea had taught that larger sites collected pollen from too great an area for easy interpretation and that smaller ones might well be too young, because swamp growth is so rapid in the tropics and subtropics.

Thirdly, it was a swamp, and no longer the lake c. 6 m (20 ft) deep pictured in Routledge's and Heyerdahl's publications, because the water level had recently been lowered (by perhaps 6 m) by the pumping out of water for domestic animals. A large trench had been dug through the lowest point of the crater rim, and a pipe inserted leading to a tank outside the crater. This was a tragedy, an act of unwitting palynological vandalism, for the diggers had destroyed possible geomorphological evidence of any former overflowing of the lake, which would have been a clue to past climate. Also, the exposed sediment at the edges was rapidly drying and oxidizing. On the plus side, however, this saved a lot of work, for it proved possible to walk out c. 75 m (c. 250 ft) on to the swamp to obtain the cores, without the need to make a raft. On a subsequent visit in 1984 with Professor Jim Teller, of the University of Manitoba at Winnipeg, Canada, Flenley was relieved to find that the pumping had stopped and the water level had partially recovered, back to a depth of c. 3 m (10 ft). The result, however, was that it was necessary to make a raft in order to obtain further cores from the centre of the basin.

Another reason why the site was outstanding was its proximity to the archaeology. The statue quarries extend not only over the outside of the crater, but also down the inside on the southern side. Numerous statues, finished apart from their eye sockets and the carving on their backs, stand looking out over the lake (ills. 35 and 58). It seemed likely that when the quarries were in use there must have been so many people active on the southern bank of the lake that the vegetation must have been modified, if not totally destroyed. The result would probably have been soil erosion, and the eroded soil should have ended up in the lake. The decision was therefore taken to carry out the sampling on the southern side of the lake, and proved a correct one (ill. 34 B).

35. The lake inside *Rano Raraku* volcano, with one of the *moai* from the interior quarry. Photo: Eduardo Ruiz-Tagle.

36. The Chileans' prized wine palm, *Jubaea chilensis*. Note the bulging shape of its trunk, totally different from the typical elongated Polynesian coconut (see note 33, p. 123). Below, a line of *rongo rongo* writing, with the possible symbol of the palm highlighted.

A peak of pollen believed to be *Solanum* (*poporo*) occurred at 70 cm (27.5 in) depth (i.e. possibly 70 years ago, and certainly within the last 200 years) [22]. If this pollen came from *Solanum forsteri*, it could represent actual cultivation of this plant within the crater. This cultivation in former times was mentioned by Métraux.

Immediately below the layer of inwashed sediment at 1.1 to 1.2 m (c. 3 ft 7 in to 3 ft 11 in) depth, there was a striking change in the pollen spectra. Grass pollen was less common, and the grass grains were larger. Pollen of the *toromiro* became quite common. But the big change was the *sudden appearance of palm pollen as the dominant type* -indicating, of course, that after this point living palm trees had suddenly disappeared. The grains were now well preserved and, although one could not be certain, they did not seem quite like the reference pollen of coconut. Palm grains are notoriously difficult to identify, so advantage was taken of a visit to Flenley's laboratory by G. Thanikaimoni, at that time the world expert on palm pollen. He could only confirm that the pollen was probably from a palm of some kind, but he refused to be more specific. It seemed pretty sure that this must be the pollen type which Selling had referred to as *Pritchardia*, so a scanning electron microscope study was now undertaken of the fossil and of various palms, including *Cocos* and two species of *Pritchardia*. The Pritchardias had a smooth surface with pits in it, whereas the fossil had a ropey (rugulate) surface: *Pritchardia* was therefore eliminated. The fossil grain had a surface like that of *Cocos* and also of *Jubaea chilensis*, the Chilean wine palm which is in the same subfamily (Cocosoideae) [23].

Further interpretation of this pollen type might have been impossible had it not been for a fortunate accident. During Flenley's stay on the island in 1983, the then governor, Sergio Rapu, had shown him a bag containing some objects found by a party of visiting French cavers. They had been exploring one of the lava caves in the northeast side of *Poike* at *Ana O Keke*, when they had come across what appeared to be a cache of nuts. They had collected thirty-five nuts, which Señor Rapu allowed to be photographed. Each was almost spherical and about 2 cm (3/4 in) across, with three lines running around it like lines of longitude on a globe. Somewhere near the middle of each 'segment' was a small pore: in some cases a depression, in others a hole right through the wall of the nut. This was reminiscent of the three pores near one end of a coconut, although the positioning of the pores was different. Señor Velasco, a respected agronomist who was also present, immediately suggested that these nuts were similar to those of the Chilean wine palm [24].

Flenley was permitted to take away several of the nuts, and sent some to Kew to be examined by Dr John Dransfield, the world expert on palm taxonomy. He telephoned in some excitement to report that the nuts must belong to a Cocosoid palm. There are eight genera of Cocosoid palms, but only two, *Jubaea* and *Jubaeopsis*, have fruits roughly resembling the fossil. After comparing the fossils with dried plant material and with fruits from the enormous specimen of *Jubaea chilensis* in the Temperate House at Kew (the largest glasshouse plant in cultivation anywhere in the world), Dransfield concluded that the French cavers had discovered what was probably an extinct species of the genus *Jubaea*, for the fossil fruits were slightly larger and more oblate than those of the living species. In any case, even if the fruits had been identical, it would have been rash to assume that all other parts of the plant would have matched those of the living species; they could have been quite different. Dransfield subsequently named the Easter Island palm *Paschalococos disperta* [25]. However, Jacques Vignes, leader of the French expedition, bought fresh wine palm fruits in the street in Santiago,

where they are sold as food, and these turned out to be much closer to the fossils than are the fruits grown at Kew. So the possibility increases that the Easter Island palm was at least closely related to *Jubaea chilensis* and possibly of the same species: the Chilean wine palm may, therefore, turn out to be the vital evidence for which archaeologists have been searching.

Known in Chile as *cau cau* (*glilla*), the Chilean wine palm is the largest palm in the world. It has a smooth trunk with a diameter often up to 1 m (3 ft) or more, and it is at least 20 m (65 ft) tall. The trunk is cylindrical, tapering towards the top, and sometimes with a slight bulge about one third of the way up. The leaves are large and feather-like, as in a coconut, and the fruits are borne in clusters among the leaves. Each fruit is, like a tiny coconut, provided with an outer fibrous layer, with a hard shell beneath [26].

37. Fossil palm nuts with clear evidence of having been bitten by the Polynesian rat, *Rattus exulans*.

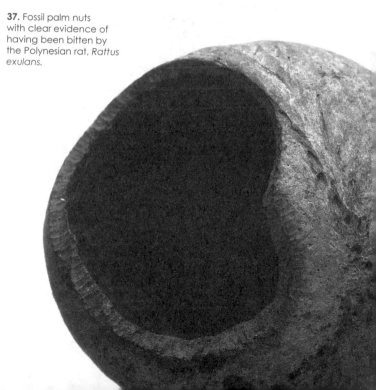

38. A scanning electron microscope picture of an Easter Island palm pollen grain.

39. American geologist Charles Love discovered these root channels lined with carbon in *Rapa Nui* soil; their small, unbranched nature and even width conform with roots of the Chilean wine palm, which can be seen in the following photo.

The Chileans regard this, their only species of palm, as of great importance, and not surprisingly so, for it is the source of four important comestibles. The nuts contain an oily kernel which is regarded as a delicacy. The tree's abundant sugary sap can be obtained by cutting off a flower or fruit inflorescence, and attaching a receptacle to receive it. Alternatively, if a tree is felled uphll onto a slope, sap will continue to flow from the cut for a week. It can then be concentrated by boiling to give palm honey (*miel de palma*), which is highly prized in Santiago. Further boiling reduces the product to a brown sugary mass (*sucre de palma*), which may be eaten straight or used in cooking. Alternatively, the sap may be allowed to ferment: this occurs naturally, through the agency of wild yeasts, and yields a highly alcoholic palm wine (*vino de palma*). A tree would provide enough liquid (and some nutrition) for a single person for a week. Given that many areas of Rapa Nui are without streams or springs, this could have been an important means

of survival (see below, p. 107). Such a rate of felling would, however, have speeded up the eventual extinction of the species on the island.

Jubaea chilensis is no longer a common tree in the wild, and it is good to know that it has conservation status. It does occur, however, near the road from Santiago down to Valparaiso at c. 33° S and down to 36°S, and is cultivated down to 40° [27] and it grows well where planted in Tenerife in the Canary Islands (27° N). It therefore seems likely that it (or a near relative) would have experienced no difficulty in growing in the lowlands of Easter Island (27° S), since it is likely that *Jubaea* would have migrated north in South America during Quaternary glacial periods.

The late Dr Juan Grau demonstrated that *Jubaea* fruits float in sea water and retain their viability for a number of weeks [28]. It is also relevant to point out that there is a line of sea-mounts providing a connection between South America and *Rapa*

40. Carbonised sweet potato found in excavations of an *umu pae* by Michel & Catherine Orliac.

41. The holes found in solidified lava by Gerardo Velasco. Their inside bears ringed marks very similar to those on the trunks of the Chilean wine palm, and it seems certain that the tubes are the casts of the trunks of palm trees. Photo: Eduardo Ruiz-Tagle.

Nui. Some of these would have been above the water surface during periods of lowered sea level in Quaternary glacial periods and could have provided "stepping stones" to the island.

Inspired by seeing the fruits from the caves, one of Flenley's 1983 party, Mike Symonds, discovered a further fruit in a crevice within the structure of *Ahu Maitaki Te Moa* on the island's north coast. Although in a poor condition, this was clearly recognizable as the same plant group, and the find was important as suggesting the survival of the species up to the time of the construction of the platforms (a Middle Period one, c. AD 1100-1680) or even later.

Sergio Rapu reported that many broken fragments of the same nuts had been recovered from his archaeological dig at *Anakena*, but of course this did not necessarily indicate where the tree had been growing. The fruits have since turned up in various other places, however. Jacques Vignes found sixteen in caves within the *Rano Kau* crater

on a return visit to the island in 1986, while Edmundo Edwards, a resident of the island, found a large number in a cave on the island's north side. French archaeologist Michel Orliac found two in 1988 on the south side near *Ahu Vinapu*, where colluvium was exposed at the coast in the mouth of a gully [29]. A small cache of nuts was found by Yoshinori Yasuda in a crevice in the cliffs at *Te Pora* on the west side of the island, during his visit in 1995. In recent years, burnt specimens recovered from various sites have been used for radiocarbon dating (see below).

The nuts and pollen are not the only evidence of the palm. Linton Palmer reported [30] that during his visit in 1868 he had seen the boles of large trees which he assumed to be coconuts -given the latitude, coconuts are unlikely, but *Jubaea* is not. This evidence was confused by Métraux [31], who reported that Palmer had seen large wooden 'bowls', but the original clearly has 'boles'. In the London Times of 1869 it was reported that 'In one spot on the island there are a few stumps of a large palm, but the trees no longer exist' [32]. The island's rock art features a couple of probable representations of the palm: one seems to be the trunk of a large tree, while another looks like a palm frond [33].

Palm tree roots are distinctive. The trees do not produce the large, much-branched roots characteristic of broad-leaved forms. Instead, they produce very large numbers of thin, unbranched roots emanating straight from the base of the tree; and those of *Jubaea* are particularly small, narrow and numerous, compared with the roots of most palms, especially coconut palms. At *Ahu Akivi*, William Mulloy reported finding root moulds, of undetermined nature, but which showed that the area had once been covered by quite large vegetation (see p. 11) [34]. Subsequently, American geologist Charles Love found numbers of root channels lined with carbon in soils on Easter Island (ill. 39). These channels do not taper or vary in width

42. *Jubaea chilensis* in its natural habitat in the Chilean National Park; and in the 'La Campara' National Park. Photo: Eduardo Ruiz-Tagle.

as would broad-leaved tree roots: in size, density and branching they appear to conform perfectly with the morphology of present-day *Jubaea* roots and not at all with those of *Cocos*.

Love found these root casts in various lowland (under 200 m [656 ft]) sites, but especially in the deep soils of *Poike*. They may easily be seen by any visitor searching the area of bad soil erosion on *Poike*'s southern side. Some are visible in the erosion platform, from which the topsoil has been removed.

Others are visible in the vertical face where erosion is still proceeding: in this case, the root casts are visible only in the lower part of the section, where the original blocky soil structure is still intact. Another good place to see them is on the north side of the road from *Vaitea* to *Anakena*. In July 2001, Love also found several root moulds of large trees, with roots 15 to 20 cm in diameter, twisting and radiating out from a central point; their sizes suggest trunks 30 to 50 cm in diameter [35].

This evidence was further strengthened by a discovery made by Gerardo Velasco in the western cliffs at *Te Pora*. Cylindrical holes run horizontally into the basalt for up to 6 metres (ill. 41). These are not the 'lava tubes' which form when lava flows solidify on the outside but continue to move inside. There are numerous lava tubes on the island, but they are up to 5 m in diameter, and of irregular shape. The holes which Velasco found are straight and mostly around 40-50 cm in diameter. Their inside bears ringed marks very similar to those on the trunks of the Chilean wine palm. Furthermore, they mostly lie just above a layer of orange clay which is clearly a buried soil. It seems certain that the tubes are the casts of the trunks of palm trees which were growing in the buried soil and were pushed over and entombed by the advancing lava [36]. Later the palm wood burnt or decayed away to leave the hollow casts. Given that these casts are mostly about halfway down the cliff which sections the *Terevaka* lavas, dated to less than 400,000 years ago, the palms must have lived during that period. So it seems clear that palm trees may have lived on Easter Island for a very long time.

It now appears possible that there was more than one species of palm. Examination of phytoliths (biogenic opal particles produced by plants) preserved in soil has revealed two kinds of phytolith. The common one is similar to *Jubaea chilensis*, but there is another type which could be a separate species [37].

Charles Love also found a fragment of carbonized palm wood which provided a radiocarbon date of c. AD 930. The palm fruits from *Ana O Keke* were radiocarbon-dated by Dr Harkness at East Kilbride, giving an age of c. AD 1130, i.e. within the Middle Period of the island's prehistory. Those found by Michel Orliac were dated to AD 1212-1430 and AD 1300-1640. The specimens discovered by Professor Yasuda were dated to AD 1290-1410 and AD 1295-1415. A date of 705 BP (AD 1260-1400) has been obtained on a burnt specimen from an *umu* (see below, p. 116) at *Ahu Heki'i*; a fragment from *Akahanga* was in a layer dating to 340 BP (AD 1450-1650); while fragments from *Maunga Tari* also suggest that some palm trees survived into the 16th century [38].

These results were sufficiently close to the present day to make one speculate that the tree might have survived into protohistoric or even historic times. A talk with Sergio Rapu confirmed these hopes: a tree called *nau-nau-opata* (literally, 'the nut tree that hangs by the cliffs') had formerly grown on the island, especially near the sea. This tree had now disappeared. Skottsberg's account of the island's botany also made reference to it. In fact, he had been sent nuts that the island children used as tops, and which were also worn around the neck as decorations, threaded through two small holes made in the shell. Skottsberg concluded the nuts were of *Thespesia populnea* (*mako'i*), a tree still found on the island; but examination of this species revealed its nutshells to be thin and fragile, quite unsuitable as tops. It seems possible that the holes which Skottsberg observed were two of the three natural holes in every *Jubaea* shell, and that children were still wearing them in the 19th century when the necklace he examined was collected.

Attempts are now being made by several laboratories to extract ancient DNA from the palm fruits found in the caves, and to compare this with the DNA of the Chilean wine palm. Results are eagerly awaited.

The recent research by Dr Candace Gossen [39] on cores from *Rano Kau* has proved extremely interesting, but has raised several problems. She claimed to find four distinct types of palm pollen in her cores. But all other researchers on *Rano Kau* (Flenley, Horrocks, etc) and other sites on the island have allocated all their palm pollen grains to a single taxon. Gossen's thesis includes pictures of all her pollen taxa; they are somewhat different, but are they sufficiently different to represent separate palm tree taxa? We cannot be certain.

It is clear, therefore, that at the time of the first human settlers, Easter Island was covered by some kind of forest. There have even been suggestions that there was once dense forestation, perhaps even rainforest: in 1983, Patrick Kirch discovered that there once existed a small snail -named *Hotumatua anakenana* after the legendary first king- of a group now confined to moist forest conditions [40]. More recently, Catherine Orliac, examining over 30,000 charcoal fragments associated with archaeological sites, has found 13 more species of tree and shrub which are now extinct on the island [41]. Most of these have living relatives in the rainforest, patches of which still survive on a few other Pacific islands such as Tahiti and Rarotonga. It may thus be concluded that rainforest existed on Easter Island when people first arrived.

The dominant tree in this forest was almost certainly the palm in most areas. The carbonized stumps found by Bork and Mieth [42] made it possible to measure the distance between palm trees on the *Poike* Peninsula, the average distance being only 2.6 m. This gives an estimate of approximately 1400 palm trees per hectare. Since more than 80% of the island was covered like this, and up to an altitude of 500 m, they use the density and distribution of

palm root casts to calculate a total population of c. 16 million palm trees. Love, on the other hand, estimates a forest at the time of Polynesian arrival of between 600,000 and 1.5 million trees [43].

Another possible attribute of the palm trees may be of importance. As mentioned above, if they are indeed close to (or identical with) *Jubaea*, they would have provided a valuable possible food resource: the sugary sap. Bork and Mieth [44] estimate that if the trees were felled first, to obtain the sap, and only burnt later, then about 2 litres of calorie-rich, nutritional sap could have been consumed by every inhabitant (estimating 8000 people at the maximum) over a period of seven or eight centuries. They could even have fermented the sap into palm wine, with even more interesting repercussions.

Mieth and Bork [45] point out that the palm sap could even have been sufficient to provide drinking water requirements for those people not living near one of the few good sources of fresh water, and thus constitute an alternative to the crater lakes and the brackish coastal water sources. In Chile the palm trees are felled to extract the sap, but one wonders if this was the only possible method with the *Rapa Nui* palm. In South East Asia (where the Polynesians originated) palm sap is obtained from many species by cutting off the inflorescence and attaching a gourd or other receptacle. The tree survives this treatment for a long time.

What evidence is revealed by archaeology and ethnography concerning the day-to-day life of the first Easter Islanders? Until the last few decades, interest in Easter Island's archaeology understandably focused almost exclusively on its spectacular sculptures, platforms and rock art, as well as on the origin of its people. Even in recent years, these features have still been the centre of attention, though a few notable studies have been devoted to the prehistoric islanders' domestic and economic life; consequently, more is now known about these neglected areas of research [46].

An 'Earthly Paradise'

What was this new world in which *Hotu Matu'a* and his followers were marooned? One legend has it that the party was in some distress by the time it arrived; their vessel broke up on the shore, and they then cooked their first meal for a long time. But there is no reason to suppose that they starved, despite this rude transfer from a lush, warm island to a cooler, windy one.

Traditions claim that for the first three months the Easter Island settlers had nothing to eat but fish, turtles, ferns and fruit including 'sandalwood nuts' (which are now extinct -it seems likely that palm nuts were being referred to). During the initial phase, while their plants and seedlings were being nurtured, the settlers undoubtedly relied heavily on the island's natural resources of fish, birds and shellfish. The same occurred on every other colonized Polynesian island, leading in many cases to swift extinction or impoverishment of a whole range of species, most notably in New Zealand, where at least 37 native bird species and subspecies went extinct, including 12 kinds of flightless moas, as well as a bat, lizards and frogs, during the period of Polynesian settlement [47].

Indeed, Steadman has estimated that the faunal collapse in Oceania involved a loss of 8000 species or populations, in what has been called a 'dreadful syncopation' of human arrival and faunal extinction in Oceanic islands [48]; he has analysed bird bones from sites throughout the Pacific islands, and constantly found that, before the arrival of humans, they had a much richer bird fauna than that which was historically documented, and that humans caused extinctions of up to half of the known land birds throughout the tropical Pacific through predation, habitat alteration, competition and predation from introduced rats, and introduced avian diseases [49].

It seems Easter Island was no exception: the excavations at *Anakena* unearthed over 6000 identifiable bones, of which 2583 were porpoise (most common in the early levels, with a marked decline later). According to Steadman, it appears this was once the richest seabird island in the world when Polynesians arrived, with probably more than 30 resident species from the tropic, temperate and sub-arctic zones, 14 of which are now extinct on *Rapa Nui* while the rest mostly breed on the islets and only one (the red-tailed tropical bird, *Tavake*) struggles to survive on the island today; half a dozen species of landbirds were also originally present, but today there are no endemic or indigenous landbirds at all. The early human settlers on Easter Island ate sooty terns, storm petrels, albatross, fulmar, booby, shearwaters, rails, pigeons, doves, herons, parrots and barn owl. There was a massive reduction in bird numbers, with species lost through this human predation, as well as diseases introduced by chickens, habitat destruction, and the arrival of rats -as happened throughout the Pacific [50].

The breadfruit, basis of the Polynesian diet, was presumably brought but could not survive in this climate; the coconut did not fare well either. However, recent excavations by the Orliacs have recovered 32,961 plant samples from species including more than 200 food plants, many of which had not been detected in pollen samples; they also found three whole sweet potatoes (ill. 40), dating to the 15th-17th century, as well as other fragments of them [51].

Analysis of agricultural soils for microfossils of crop plants has revealed some interesting finds, including sweet potato (a single pollen grain), Pacific island

42.1. *Manavai*, (place with water) were the most efficient solution to protect crops from weather. They were built on the surface or underground, depending on the nature of the terrain. Even today they are used by rapanui.

cabbage tree (*Cordyline*) and possible paper mulberry (*mahute*); starch grains of *taro*; and a probable banana phytolith [52]. Collating this with more recent work at *Te Niu* on the northwest side [53], we now have starch grains and/or pollen of four introduced crop plants: the common yam (*Dioscorea alata*), sweet potato, *taro* and bottlegourd (*Lagenaria siceraria*).

In many areas it now appears that cultivation was aided by stone mulching [54]. This technique involves the placing of stones of various sizes on top of the soil, between the crop plants, to minimize water loss by evaporation. On an island as windy as *Rapa Nui*, this would have been of great benefit for the conservation of soil moisture. Nowadays, these agricultural areas are mostly overgrown by grasses and sedges, but are easily recognised by their abundance of ankle-twisting stones. About 70% of the island surface was covered with stones in this way (see also Chapter 8) [55]. Detailed study of soil temperatures beneath lithic mulch has shown that temperatures are consistently lower than for bare soils, and are much less variable, thus providing a more stable growing environment [56].

A thorough analysis of the garden types shows that they differ in the size of stones used for mulching, and there is a relationship of this with altitude, and probably also with the crop being grown. It appears the lowland gardens were intensively cultivated and upland ones progressively more extensively cultivated [57].

A great deal about the development of island agriculture has been revealed by study of the soils. Indeed it has proved possible to develop a complete landscape history [58]. This was done for the eastern peninsula, *Poike*, which has the deepest soils because of its greater geological age. The palm root channels and carbonised rootstocks exposed by recent soil erosion show that the palms had originally been very close together: a dense palm forest in fact. This was destroyed by fire around AD 1250-1300. It seems that intensive agriculture was then practised for about 100 years. This included the development of planting pits about 35 cm deep, lined with charcoal and ashes, and filled with loose sand and remnants of palm nuts. This intensive use led to soil erosion upslope, burying the site in slopewash. Stone mulching was not practised in this area, as there was no suitable supply of stones nearby. Later, gully erosion began, and has been exacerbated in recent times through heavy grazing by sheep and cows.

At later dates (AD 1400-1700), it appears that agriculture was focused increasingly on upland sites, perhaps because of higher rainfall there [59]. The purpose of this seems to have been to produce an agricultural surplus, so that the architectural construction activities in the lowlands (*ahu, moai,* etc) could be supported.

If, as might be expected, pigs and dogs were brought over, they either did not survive or were eaten before breeding. The chicken did manage to flourish, and eventually assumed huge importance in the island's economy. This also explains why human bones (from the thighs of deceased fishermen) were used for making fish-hooks -they were the only large mammal bones available- though the island's most common bone artifact, the small-eyed needle used to sew bark cloths together, was made of chicken, sea-bird or occasionally fish bone. Finally, the settlers' introduction of edible rats was to have dire consequences (Chapter 9).

A great deal of important information about the early islanders can be gleaned from the eye-witness accounts by the first European visitors: the Dutch reports of 1722 are obviously crucial, being our very earliest glimpses of *Rapa Nui* when it was, as far as we know, as yet unaffected by the outside world.

Roggeveen stated that the islanders were well proportioned, generally large in stature, very sturdy with strong muscles, and extremely good swimmers. Many had stretched and perforated ear-lobes, and both men and women were extensively tattooed (ills. 24 and 43). They were outstandingly strong in the teeth and even old men could crack large, hard, thick-shelled nuts with them (presumably the fruits

43. Rapanui woman and man with tattoos, engraved by Pierre Loti, 1872.

of the mysterious palm; see above). Yet physical anthropologists have consistently reported that the early islanders' teeth were in poor shape: Sir Arthur Keith, for example, found decay in every adult skull he examined from the island, and remarked, 'Tooth trouble is even more prevalent in Easter Island than in the slums of our great towns.' In fact, the islanders had the highest rate of caries seen in any prehistoric people. By the age of fourteen, carious lesions were already in evidence, and increased steadily; by their twenties, the islanders all had cavities, and by their thirties the frequencies of decay, especially in women, were far higher than in other Pacific agricultural groups [60].

This was probably caused not only by poor oral hygiene but also by an inadequate diet, particularly in later periods, and by food high in carbohydrates that was baked in earthen ovens and eaten unpounded. Caries were even high in the front teeth, an unusual phenomenon probably produced by the habit of sucking sugar cane to relieve thirst. Sugar-cane juice was used as a liquid substitute to overcome the island's limited supply of fresh water; Captain Cook's botanist Forster reported sugar cane stalks '...about 9 or 10 feet high'.

Recent analyses of the bone chemistry of skeletons from islanders of the 17th-19th centuries have revealed that they ate more land protein (chicken, rat, eggs) than other Pacific islanders, with an average of one third of protein coming from the sea. Men consumed more protein than women, and teeth from *Ahu Nau Nau* show more consumption of meat and/or fish. Dental microwear shows traces mostly of tubers and sweet potatoes. The study by Commendador et al. concluded that there was a decline in/depletion of available terrestrial proteins through time -possibly due to slash-and-burn reducing soil nutrients and leading to a breakdown of soil porosity and structure, and hence reduced soil stability. The increased soil erosion led to decreasing soil quality of an already nutrient-deficient landscape, with repercussions throughout the island's ecosystem. Such landscape modifications could have constricted available terrestrial animal protein sources. The new gardens, etc, increased nutrient levels compared to surrounding soils. These innovations helped to stabilize a marginal landscape, and plant intake increased as terrestrial animal consumption decreased [61].

Although his visit came only fifty-two years after Roggeveen's, Cook noted that the islanders were not well built; according to Forster, there was '...not a single person amongst them who might be reckoned tall'. All the early visitors saw a wide range of skin tones, from white or yellow to reddish. Light skin was much prized, as in other parts of Polynesia, and it is claimed that youngsters, particularly girls, were sequestered in caves like *Ana O Keke* to enhance the whiteness of their skins, as an indication of high status.

The earliest 'portraits' were produced during Captain Cook's visit (ill. 33), but some prehistoric islanders have been 'brought back to life' by the technique of reconstructing the face on a cast of the skull. In this way, American sculptor Sharon Long was able to recreate the faces of three islanders [62]. Although inevitably approximate in some details, her reconstructions are so lifelike and accurate that excited modern islanders were able to identify the lineage of one male head from the head-shape and facial features. The family identified was descended from the royal *Miru* tribe of the *Anakena* region, and investigations later proved that this skull had indeed come from the *Ahu Nau Nau* area, associated with that tribe!

Physical anthropologists have found further evidence of distinct social groups on the island in their analyses of skeletal material. George Gill, of the University of Wyoming, has detected some anomalies: skeletons from the area around *Anakena*, but from nowhere else, had the very rare genetic condition of a defective patella (the kneecap has a corner missing), while sacro-iliac (pelvic) fusion is very common on the south coast but quite rare elsewhere [63]. There were clearly strong social boundaries between these families which maintained their peculiarities, at least in late periods. The *Anakena* population in particular, thought to be of the *Miru* tribe or royal lineage (descendants of *Hotu Matu'a*), remained genetically isolated through inbreeding; it did not tolerate the entry of outsiders into the group by marriage.

Different parts of *Rapa Nui* also had different roles. The Dutch reported that the other side of the island (i.e. from La Pérouse Bay, where they landed) was the main place for cultivation and fruit trees, and all the produce brought to the Europeans seems to have come from there. The islanders divided their arable land into square fields with furrows [64]: the lack of dividing walls thus makes them very hard to detect archaeologically, and little attempt has yet been made to study them from aerial photography.

Cornelis Bouman, Roggeveen's captain, stated that '...of yams, bananas and small coconut palms we saw little and no other trees or crops' [65]. Roggeveen's personal judgment, however, was more favourable: 'We have found it... outstandingly fruitful, producing bananas, sweet potatoes, sugar cane of special thickness, and many other sorts of produce, although devoid of large trees and livestock, apart from fowls, so this land, because of its rich earth and good climate, could be made into an earthly Paradise if it was properly cultivated and worked, which at present is done only to the extent that the inhabitants are required to for maintenance of life.'

The Dutch accepted about sixty fowls and thirty bunches of bananas from the natives, although

Bouman recorded that '...they were not very well provided with these'. In 1770, the Spanish visited a banana plantation near *Vinapu* which they claimed '...stretched about a quarter of a league in extent and was about half that distance in breadth', but Aguera wrote that 'Los campos están incultos, menos algunos pequeños rincones de tierras en que se hayan plantíos de yucca, nema, y camotes...pero todo muy insipido, como que carece de cultivo'. In 1774 Cook reported only a few scattered plantations of sugar cane and sweet potatoes (although the latter were the best he had ever tasted), while Forster observed bananas growing in holes a foot deep or in natural cavities to collect and preserve rainwater; their party could see that other parts of the island had once been under cultivation, but all emphasised that the land was now extremely poor and often sterile, the plantations sparse and with small crops [66]. By 1786, La Pérouse found that only one tenth of the island was cultivated, but the fields were tended with great care, being weeded, watered and fertilized with the ash of burned stalks. Bananas grew in regular lines. At the time of the Russian Lisjanskij's visit in 1804, he noted that every house was planted around with sugar cane and bananas [67].

Bouman informs us that '...they cut their bananas with a sharp little black stone. They first cut around the branch and then twist it off' [68]. This stone was clearly obsidian, the islanders' chief raw material for tools and, later, weapons [69]. Unlike other Polynesians they were unable to make much use of bone, as we have seen, or of shell, since they had few molluscs big enough to provide raw material. The main obsidian outcrops occur at the southwestern part of the island, in particular the 90 ha (222 acre) scatter at *Orito*, but also the islet of *Motu Iti* which, though not easily accessible, was worth the trip since it consists almost entirely of an obsidian that is particularly good for flaking. Preliminary analysis of retouch and dulling on some of *Rapu Nui*'s flake tools indicated that they were employed in shaving wood, while more detailed microwear analysis of obsidian flakes from the upland agricultural complex of *Maunga Tari* on the southern slope of *Terevaka* has recently revealed that about 25% were used for scraping sweet potatoes, and 25% for cutting plants, while activities of lesser importance included the scraping of soft woods (11%), plants (9%) and fish (9%) [70].

Work is currently being done on identifying the different mineral inclusions and banding of Easter Island's obsidian types, so that in the near future it will be possible to quantify and date how each source was used, and assess the distribution of its material across the island. Thanks to the constantly improving method of measuring 'hydration layers' (minute layers formed in fractured obsidian surfaces by the absorption of water from their surroundings; they increase in thickness through time), obsidian dating is proving an extremely valuable complement to radiocarbon dating for the island's later prehistory, though earlier periods are still somewhat problematical for the technique.

A series of archaeological excavations has begun to build a clearer picture of the more mundane aspects of the island's prehistory, although many results of the work carried out by Heyerdahl's team in the 1950s still await publication (notably the faunal and pollen data), and the information we have mostly concerns the last few centuries before European contact rather than the island's early occupation phase. A further problem is that most artifacts recovered are surface finds, with no date or context, or come from the fill of structures or from cremation pits that cover long periods; and of course, the vast majority of perishable items have completely disintegrated and hence elude the archaeologist. Nevertheless, the stratigraphic excavations carried out in the past few decades should eventually help us to obtain a clearer view of developments in the island's material culture through time.

The basic domestic unit of the island appears to have comprised a dwelling (a house, rock overhang or cave), plus a selection of associated features: earth ovens, stone chicken houses, and stone garden enclosures [71]. Most settlements consisted of two or three such dwellings dispersed in and around the agricultural plantations. Their frequency, status, house-size and quality of construction decrease away from the coast -inland they tend to be on rocky eminences or hill slopes- and they seem to have slightly higher densities around springs and the more fertile soils of the inland and upland, as one might expect. Settlement as a whole had a strong coastal bias, but with exploitation of inland resources because the coast had poor soils as well as winds and salt spray: this framework of a coast-to-inland strip closely resembles the patterns of land use and ownership throughout eastern Polynesia.

There were also 'village complexes', clustered around a religious/ceremonial site with its altar-platform, and, c. 50 to 100 m (c. 165 to 330 ft) away, five or more elliptical houses, with dressed kerbstones, for priests, chiefs or other people of high rank. Commoners' dwellings stood a further 100 or 200 m (330 or 660 ft) inland from these élite coastal structures, and usually comprised elliptical houses (though without dressed stones) associated with *umu*, *manavai* (see below, p. 116) and *hare moa* (see below, p. 117), indicating a dependence on agriculture and horticulture.

The finest elliptical houses (*hare paenga*) had a foundation outlined with a kerb of cut basalt stones, an expression of social rank and wealth because of the considerable time and effort required to carve them -in fact, *paenga* means both 'cut stone' and 'large family'. The stones were from 0.5 to 2.5 m (1.5 to 8 ft) long, 20 or 30 cm (8 or 12 in) wide, and at least 50 cm (20 in) high; small holes in them held the thin uprights of curved branches, which formed a series of arches attached to a ridge-pole and supporting the superstructure of plant materials (ills 44 and 45). Many had a crescent-shaped lateral pavement of beach stones outside, where the people worked, ate and chatted.

44. Reconstruction for the movie *Rapa Nui* of a finished *hare paenga*.

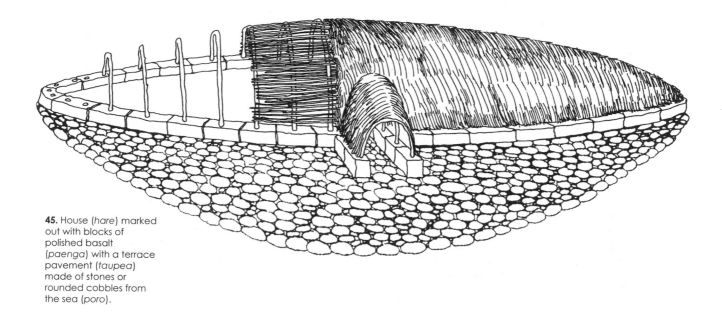

45. House (*hare*) marked out with blocks of polished basalt (*paenga*) with a terrace pavement (*taupea*) made of stones or rounded cobbles from the sea (*poro*).

Hare paenga are almost always found near platforms, and often clustered in a semicircle just inland from those on the coast, with very few in the island's interior [72]. Being so close to the sacred area reflected the high social status of their occupants, and in fact Aguera, one of the Spanish visitors of 1770, noted that '...others (whom I believed to be their ministers) occupy dwellings close to their statues'. These houses were first described by the Dutch visitors of 1722, who saw them as 'built of a sort of straw looking like beehives or as if a Greenland sloop has been turned upside down'. The concept of boat-shaped houses is widespread in Polynesia, and extends back across the Pacific into southeast Asia. It clearly underlines the primacy of boats in the islanders' heritage, and it is noteworthy that almost all house entrances faced the sea, and have their ovens and other structures on the seaward side.

Most had a single tunnel-entrance, up to 1 m (3 ft) high, into which one had to crawl. These offered protection from the cold and the blowing rain; small statues of wood or stone sometimes stood at either side of this entry. Some of these structures seem to have been, or become, communal, and inside there was space for dozens of people to eat and sleep. Islanders told Mrs Routledge that the evening meal was consumed inside, and that they slept parallel to the length of the house, their heads towards the door, with the old folk in the centre (which was up to 2 m [6 ft] high) and the younger people at the ends (which were less than 1 m [3 ft] in height).

Most of the elliptical houses, being for commoners, had no stone foundation-kerb; their poles were stuck directly into the ground, though they still had a stone pavement set flush against the front of the house.

They averaged 12 to 14 m (40 to 46 ft) in length and 2 m (6 ft) in width, though in 1786 La Pérouse mentioned one that was 100 m (330 ft) long and could contain at least two hundred people. These structures seem to have become smaller, narrower and lower in later periods, probably due to timber becoming scarcer [73].

Since these were essentially night-time sleeping shelters, with most daytime activities taking place outside, there was little need or room for furnishings, as Roggeveen's remarks confirm: 'We found absolutely nothing... no furniture at all and of utensils only calabashes in which they keep their water. I tasted it and found it to be very brackish' (Cook's party, on the other hand, drank spring water from the west part of the island and pronounced it sweet and delicious). Cook confirmed that the natives had very few gourds, so that a coconut shell was a very welcome gift. The houses also had reed mats on the floor, and some stone pillows, often decorated with engravings.

All of our eye-witness accounts come, of course, from the very end of the island's prehistory, but most of our domestic archaeological data also come from the later phases; this is simply because the islanders had a tendency to build their houses on top of or very near previous habitations, so that older evidence is usually masked quite effectively.

The island's most ubiquitous archaeological feature is the *umu pae* (stone-lined earth oven): hundreds have been found, the vast majority of which are in coastal areas; the earlier ones seem to have had no stones, the stone-lining being a late adaptation to the gradual scarcity of wood as fuel [74]. The Dutch reported that the islanders prepared chicken '...in holes in the ground in which they had stones that were heated glowing hot by burning bushes', while La Pérouse observed small windbreaks enclosing the ovens.

The *umu pae* have a wide range of shapes (round, rectangular, pentagonal) and sizes since some were single-event structures, others were permanent fixtures for family or community use, while the biggest were for communal feasts. Even the largest, however, were only up to 1 m (3 ft) across: the islanders did not need huge ovens since they lacked large mammals to cook in them. Most are in front of the houses (on the seaward side) but some specialized cooking centres are known, such as one on *Rano Kau* comprising thirty-three large ovens. Domestic examples, however, were simple pits which, like the houses, were maintained in the same spot over the centuries -a series of three superimposed ovens spanning 250 years was found in one artificial mound, which was probably created by the successive clearing out of food residues and heat-fractured stones. Such trash mounds can be up to 10 m (33 ft) across and 50 cm (20 in) high.

Manavai or garden enclosures were either walled or subterranean -about 1450 of them have been recorded. It is thought that they provided favourable micro-environments for the paper mulberry and bananas by protecting from the wind, helping to retain moisture and affording shade (*manavai* means 'place of water'). Their proximity to houses suggests that they could also have functioned as toilets.

Certainly, they are located primarily in the coastal zone, where there was a greater need to protect plants from the desiccating effects of the winds from offshore. Inland settlements may simply have used natural depressions or found them less crucial in sheltered areas: hence they are archaeologically less visible inland, apart from the crater of *Rano Kau*, which can be seen as a giant natural enclosure, providing protection from wind and a lush micro-environment -little wonder that it contained a complex of houses and terraced gardens on its steep inner slopes.

These garden enclosures, always found 10-30 m from elliptical houses, appear in many different forms and are either isolated or in clusters of two to fifty [75]. On average they are 3 to 5 m in diameter, though some were far bigger. They comprise rubble walls, about 1.5-2 m high, and are similar to structures in Hawai'i. Basalt hoes have been recovered in excavations of one residential site. Circular garden plots are also known, but since excavations inside them have occasionally revealed refuse, cooking places and tools suggesting a long occupation, it is thought that many were originally stone houses with a reed roof: González noted in 1770 that elders and leaders lived in the long houses, while 'priests' lived in little stone houses near the statues.

The *hare moa* ('chicken houses'), almost impregnable to robbery, were long thought to reflect the crucial importance of this fowl to the islanders' food supply and gift exchange system. They were solid, thick-walled, flat-topped, rectangular drystone cairns, up to 2 m (6 ft) high, 2 or 3 m (6 or 10 ft) wide, and between 5 and 20 m (16 and 66 ft) in length, with a low, narrow chamber running down the centre; their small entrances at ground-level could be blocked with stones at night, supposedly so that any attempt to get at the fowls would be heard in the nearby houses.

More than 1230 of these structures have been recorded on the island, almost all in the coastal zone. It was Palmer in 1868 who first reported that he had been told they served as 'hen houses', and that chickens were inside them; but he also expressed his doubts about this, as he had seen very similar structures which he had been told were tombs. Geiseler in 1882 dissected one of them, and found bones of birds and humans inside -he was told it was a tomb, and the birds had just flown in; at this time, he also reported that chickens were running wild over the island, with innumerable nests everywhere- however, it should be recalled

that in the late 18th century, Cook and La Pérouse said chickens were scarce, and visitors in the 1820s mentioned none, so it is quite possible that poultry had disappeared from the island by the 1820s, and had to be reintroduced in the 1860s [76].

It was Routledge who was told by her informer, Juan Tepano, that they were intended for safeguarding chickens, so that a thief could not steal them without making a noise in removing the stones. Routledge speculated that such chicken houses could have been turned into ossuaries, but today most specialists suspect that the reverse was the case [77] i.e. that the vast majority of the structures were ossuaries, whose long, narrow chambers could have contained several secondary burials, and that some of them were later used by chickens, with or without human agency. So the question arises: which came first, the chicken or the dead? There are two main types which are very different inside: some late ones could be tombs, and human bones have been found inside; but those with a low narrow chamber consistently contain guano, feathers, bones and eggshells [78].

A further source of confusion is that human skulls have sometimes been found in the 'chicken houses': these *puoko-moa* (fowl heads) from the royal *Miru* clan were thought to have the power to increase egg yields, and about twenty engraved 'egg heads' are known of both sexes [79]. A belief in the fertilizing power of chiefs' skulls has also been documented in the Marquesas. Oddly, however, *Rapa Nui*'s wealth of rock art includes only thirteen representations of chickens and eight of plants, which shows that this art was not a simple record of food resources but was a religious and social phenomenon tied to ritual and to things of the spirit rather than of the stomach.

In the interior zone, high inland, are found the poorest commoners' houses, smaller and humbler

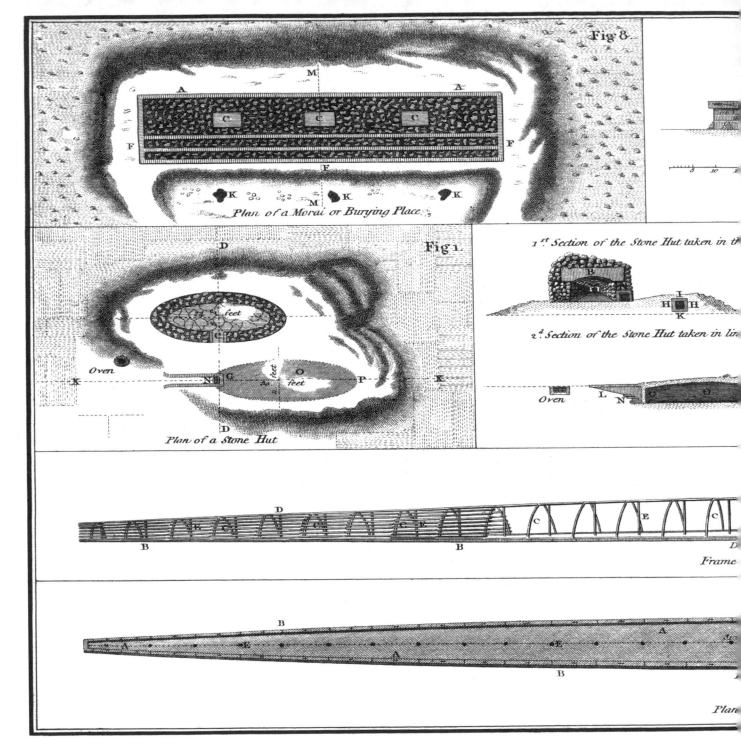

Fig 8.

C C C

A A

M

F F

F

K K K

M

Plan of a Morai or Burying Place.

5 10

Fig 1.

D

feet

Oven

X N G O P K

feet

D

Plan of a Stone Hut.

1ˢᵗ *Section of the Stone Hut taken in th*

H H
K

2ᵈ *Section of the Stone Hut taken in li*

Oven L N O

D

B C C C E C E C

B D

Frame

B

A E A E A

B

Plan

46. Geometrical details of the monuments of
Easter Island, La Pérouse expedition, 1786.

Published as the Act directs Nov.

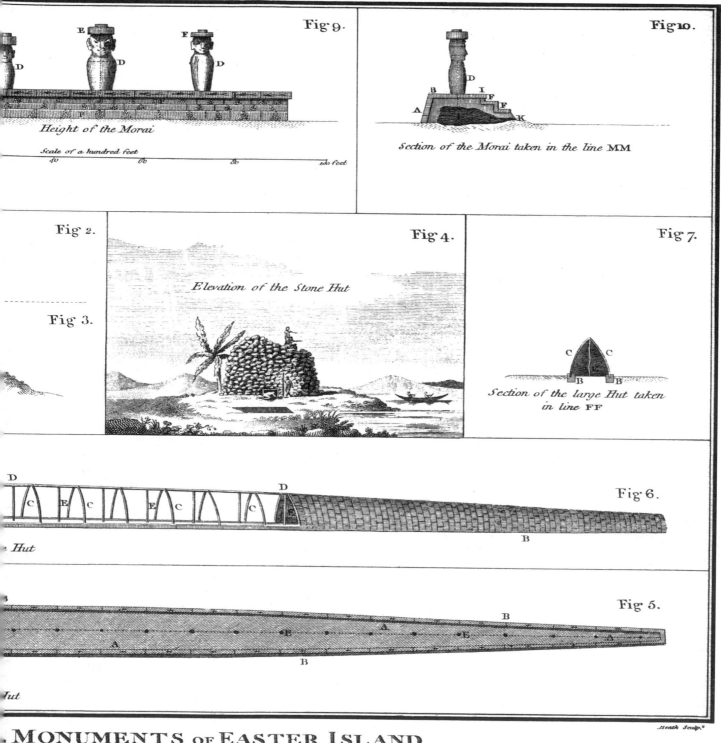

Fig. 9.

Height of the Morai

Scale of a hundred feet
40   60   80   100 feet

Fig. 10.

Section of the Morai taken in the line MM

Fig. 2.

Fig. 3.

Fig. 4.

Elevation of the Stone Hut

Fig. 7.

Section of the large Hut taken
in line FF

Fig. 6.

Hut

Fig. 5.

Hut

Heath Sculp.

MONUMENTS OF EASTER ISLAND

Robinson Pater Noster Row London.

constructions which designate their lower status: these comprise both rectangular (4-5 m long, 2-2.5 m wide) and circular (1.8 to 3.75 m in diameter) forms [80].

Along ravines at the foot of Mount *Terevaka*, about four hundred square and rectangular house foundations have been identified which seem to be early in date (c. AD 800-1300 according to results from obsidian) and resemble structures in the Marquesas; they would have had a superstructure of vegetation, and are associated with crude platforms, red scoria statues and exterior pavements, all on a small scale. Excavations inside them have uncovered woodworking tools, and it is therefore probable that these were habitations -perhaps short-term or seasonal- for those who harvested the great trees that used to grow on the mountain: *Terevaka* literally means 'to pull out canoes'. An island that was once so heavily forested would certainly have required a large labour force to be involved in the felling and working of timber for canoes as well as for the statue industry (Chapter 6). In the Marquesas it is known that four hundred men might be engaged in the construction of a single large canoe, and throughout Polynesia canoe-building involved both specialized craftsmen and communal efforts.

Over eighty rectangular house foundations are also known at *Vai Atare*, on the opposite side of *Rano Kau*'s crater to the ceremonial village of *Orongo* [81]. This was the area where the slabs for house foundation-kerbs were quarried, so that this cluster of houses was probably for the quarrymen.

In 1886 Thomson reported seeing a village of elliptical stone houses extending for over a mile along the west coast, north of *Tahai*; their entrances all faced the sea, and each had a little cave or niche at the back. Like the ceremonial houses at *Orongo* (Chapter 10) they were corbelled, with a keystone on the top; but whereas the *Orongo* houses were quite late, these seemed to Thomson to be the oldest on the island, especially as his guides knew nothing of the place, not even its name. Sadly, no trace of this village remains, but it provides evidence that stone houses and corbelled superstructures were a long-lasting tradition on *Rapa Nui* rather than a late intrusion.

Caves were also lived in occasionally, especially in the later phases of prehistory -for example, by fishermen exploiting the coastal zone- the always late material found in the caves excavated so far suggests strongly that for much of the island's prehistory, when it still had a heavy vegetation cover, most caves were so full of plant life, water and dampness as to be unsuitable for occupation. Even under today's relatively dry conditions, they are typically damp. A similar phenomenon is known in Hawai'i, where cave occupation seems to have begun four hundred years after the earliest settlement.

Not surprisingly, coastal caves yield more fishing tools and fish remains than inland caves, where chicken bones are far more prominent. Fire-pits and charcoal concentrations tend to be just outside cave entrances, whereas bone and shell remains form middens both inside caves and extending outside.

One large cave on the south coast has been excavated, and its earliest occupation level yielded very high densities of food remains such as rat, chicken and fish bones, shells, and fish scales, together with obsidian tools. Thomson in 1886 reported finding little univalve shells in all the ruins and caves he explored, as well as on the beach: this resource was still highly prized as food by the islanders. Shellfish were gathered for food despite their small size (up to 4 cm [1.5 in]), being readily available to hand-gathering in the rocky surge zone; they were eaten raw, or cooked in water. Crustaceans such as crayfish and crabs were also probably taken, as well as bird eggs from the offshore islets -several early visitors, including Cook, remarked on the scarcity of land and sea birds on the island itself (see above, p. 108). As late as 1968, however, thousands of sea birds in very large flocks would still visit the island occasionally.

Turtles have never been a common occurrence, owing to the cold climate and the lack of sandy beaches, but there are thirty-two represented in the island's rock art, which implies that they were considered of some importance (only two sharks and thirteen octopuses are depicted). A few turtle-shell ornaments have been found, and it is worth noting that throughout Polynesia turtles were connected with royalty and with special ritual practices. Seals were equally rare on the island, though some seal bones were discovered during recent excavations of early levels at *Anakena*, and twenty-three petroglyphs (rock carvings) may represent this animal [82].

Archaeological evidence of fish-hooks suggests that long-line fishing was of minimal importance, especially in areas such as the south coast where the shallow water permitted the effective use of nets. Overall, our knowledge of fishing techniques is limited, since so much of the equipment is perishable and does not survive archaeologically [83]: for example, the only clue to the use of nets is the presence of basalt net-sinkers and of bone netting needles. But in any case, without a lagoon, many types of large-scale communal netting operations were impossible on Easter Island. Whereas co-operative lagoon fishing with nets and sweeps up to 150 m (c. 500 ft) long took place on Mangareva, and over 1 km (c. 0.5 mile) long at Tubuai in the Rapa group, communal shore fishing on Easter Island was comparatively infrequent and

small in scope. Only one net appears in the island's rock art, and only one ancient draw-net over 20 m (65 ft) long, its meshes made of paper-mulberry fibres, survives in Washington, collected by Thomson in 1886. Geiseler reported seeing a net 60 m (200 ft) long in 1882, but most scholars think that figure is an exaggeration [84].

The great diversity of hooks found -of stone or human bone, and manufactured with the help of obsidian drills and coral files- was employed primarily for shore fishing of small fish rather than for open-sea exploitation. This is confirmed by the remains of marine fauna, which are dominated by small inshore species of fish and eel. The oldest hooks dated so far are bone specimens from *Vinapu* and *Tahai*, and come from the early 13th century AD; we still lack relevant data for earlier periods, though, as mentioned earlier (pp. 60-61), excavations at *Anakena* (by the *Kon Tiki Museum* expedition of 1987) uncovered an early bone harpoon of a type used in the Marquesas. Of course, many basic methods such as trapping, snaring, and hand collecting will have left no traces. A *rongo rongo* tablet given to Bishop Jaussen of Tahiti in the 19th century was wrapped in 6 m (19 ft) of the human hair cording that was used for fishing at that time.

Fish-hooks have been found in greater numbers on the north coast than on the south; It is thought that fish were more abundant and offshore fishing better in the north, which has yielded most of the larger and two-piece fishhooks from the island: these were probably used for deep handline fishing by experts, and it is noticeable that the forms found change from deep-sea to inshore types through the archaeological record. Moreover, of the 381 fish-hook motifs so far found in *Rapa Nui*'s rock art, no less than 93 per cent are on the north coast (58% are at *Ahu Ra'ai*), and all are the kind used for deep-water fishing, especially of tuna [85].

The fish-hook motif is totally absent from whole sections of the island which are, and presumably were, excellent fishing locations. A considerably greater percentage and variety of fishbone have been found in middens at sites such as *Anakena* in the north than on the south coast, where the small shellfish seem to have been correspondingly more important. Broadly speaking, then, the north/ west part of Easter Island specialized in fishing while the south/east part had the intensive dry-field agriculture, together with the terraced cultivation inside the lush, protected crater of *Rano Kau*. This brought about institutionalized exchange mechanisms between these areas as well as between coastal and inland zones, especially as fishing vessels may eventually have required wood from the *toromiro* trees of the south coast, and caulking mosses from the crater lakes.

We know from the island's ethnography that there were restrictions (*tapu*) on marine resources, which were controlled by the high-status *Miru* clan of the north; this explains why most petroglyphs not only of fish-hooks but also of sea creatures are located on the north coast. The island's highest chief redistributed the prestige fish (a common phenomenon in Polynesia), while resources of great economic value, such as tuna, turtles, seals and dolphins, were reserved exclusively for the aristocracy at certain times. Only the *Miru* nobles could continue to enjoy larger fish like tuna during the *tapu* months from May to October, and lesser mortals would supposedly be poisoned or develop asthma if they too tried to eat them then. This reflects the political domination of the *Miru*, their monopoly of these resources and perhaps, at the same time, the growing difficulties experienced in exploiting the open sea (Chapter 9).

However, undoubtedly the most remarkable display of respect for the island's élite is embodied in the great statues, to which we must now turn our attention.

[1] Englert 1948; Métraux 1940.

[2] Routledge 1919, p. 282.

[3] Englert 1970, pp. 88, 93; see also Mulloy 1993; Meroz 1995.

[4] Englert 1970, p. 87.

[5] Lanning 1970, p. 175.

[6] For radiocarbon dating, Ayres 1971; for obsidian dating, Stevenson 1988. For both, Vargas et al. 2006.

[7] McCoy 1973; see also Vargas et al. 2006, p. 307.

[8] Spriggs & Anderson 1993, p. 210; for an earlier date, Kirch & Ellison 1994.

[9] Hunt & Lipo 2006, 2011.

[10] Allen 2006; Flenley 2010.

[11] For a variety of critiques of the AD 1200 claim, see Flenley & Bahn 2007; Flenley et al. 2007; Weisler & Green 2008; Shepardson et al. 2008. In particular, Shepardson et al. show that Hunt & Lipo's application of 'chronometric hygiene' was selective and their statistical analysis unjustified, since an alternative analysis of the same samples points to a date of AD 900.

[12] Flenley et al. 2007. Edwards & Edwards (2013, p. 40) have pointed out that Anakena has been severely affected by tsunamis during the past 100 years, and today several house foundations in the left part of the bay are under water, indicating that early settlements may have been located beyond the present shoreline.

[13] Sutton et al. 2008.

[14] Mann et al. 2008.

[15] Flenley et al. 2007.

[16] Gossen 2007.

[17] Cole & Flenley 2008.

[18] Vargas et al. 2006, pp. 228, 243, 276; oddly, these authors nevertheless suggest (p. 399/400) an initial settlement at AD 800, but they do not rule out an earlier arrival (p. 403).

[19] Skjølsvold 1993, 1994; Martinsson-Wallin & Wallin 1998a, 2000.

[20] For Selling's work, see Heyerdahl & Ferdon 1961, p. 519, footnote.

[21] Heyerdahl & Ferdon 1965, p. 149.

[22] The full study of the island's pollen diagrams is in Flenley et al. 1991, Butler & Flenley 2001, and Horrocks et al. 2013, 2015.

[23] Flenley & King 1984; Dransfield et al. 1984.

[24] Dransfield et al. 1984.

[25] In Zizka 1991.

[26] M. Orliac 1989, 1993; Zizka 1989a; Arnold et al. 1990.

[27] Grau 1996, 2000.

[28] Grau, pers. comm.

[29] M. Orliac 1993.

[30] Palmer 1868, 1870, 1870a.

[31] Métraux 1940.

[32] Powell 1869 (see *Rapa Nui Journal* 21 [1], May 2007, p. 58).

[33] Lee 1992, p. 121. In the first edition of this book (pp. 86, 89) we followed Orliac (1989) in proposing that some of the *rongo rongo* characters resemble palm trunks and that some even feature the characteristic bulge of *Jubaea*. However, it has now become clear that what looks like a palm tree glyph is merely the superimposition of an X sign over a toa or sugarcane sign (or sometimes the toa superimposed on an X), so that the resemblance to a palm tree is mere illusion (S. R. Fischer, pers. comm.).

[34] Mulloy & Figueroa 1978, p. 22.

[35] *Rapa Nui Journal* 15 (2), 2001, p. 125; Mieth & Bork 2003, p. 35, 2004.

[36] Bahn 1995; according to Edwards & Edwards 2013, p. 43, there are 203 palm moulds on the coast -- the oldest were created by a 50,000-year-old lava flow, whereas moulds further inland date to 6,000-10,000 years ago. The fact that there are no significant changes between the density or characteristics of the moulds produced during three successive lava flows in the area indicates that the palms regenerated successfully and did not undergo any major transformations during that time.

[37] Stevenson 1997, pp. 57-8; Orliac & Orliac 1998, p. 200; Martinsson-Wallin & Wallin 1998, p. 172; 2000, p. 32.

[38] Kirch et al. n.d. See also Vargas et al. 2006, p. 327.

[39] Gossen 2007, 2011.

[40] Bork & Mieth 2003.

[41] Love 2004.

[42] Bork & Mieth 2003; Mieth & Bork 2012; 2015: 95.

[43] Love 2004.

[44] Bork & Mieth 2003; Mieth & Bork 2012; 2015: 98.

[45] Mieth & Bork 2005; Mieth & Bork 2012; 2015: 98-99.

[46] Martin & Steadman 1999, p. 50.

[47] Steadman 1995, 1997, 1999, 2006; Martin & Steadman 1999; Kirch 2000, p. 61.

[48] Steadman 2006, pp. 248-52; Steadman et al. 1994; Martinsson-Wallin & Wallin 1994, p. 170; see also *Rapa Nui Journal* 7 (2), 1993, p. 62.

[49] Orliac & Orliac 1998.

[50] Cummings 1998.

[51] Horrocks & Wozniak. 2008; Wozniak et al. 2010.

[52] Stevenson & Haoa 1998; Wozniak 1999; Stevenson et al. 1999.

[53] Bork et al. 2004.

[54] Gossen & Stevenson 2005.

[55] Bork et al. 2004; Mieth & Bork 2015: 101.

[56] Gossen & Stevenson 2005.

[57] Baer et al. 2008; Ladefoged et al. 2010.

[58] Mieth & Bork 2003, 2004; Mieth, Bork & Feeser 2002; Mieth & Bork 2015: 100/1.

[59] Long & Gill 1997.

[60] Gill 1988; 2000, p. 118.

[61] Polet 2015; Commendador et al. 2013.

[62] Long & Gill 1997.

[63] Gill 1988; 2000, p. 118.

[64] von Saher 1990/1, p. 51.

[65] Ibid., p. 51.

[66] For Bouman, Ibid. For Aguera, Foerster 2012, p. 124. For the Forsters, see Bahn 2015, Forster 2000. For the analogous reports by Joseph Gilbert, William Wales, Richard Pickersgill and Charles Clerke, see Foerster 2012, pp. 194, 198-99, 206, 209.

[67] Stevenson 1997, p. 51.

[68] Vargas 1998a; Vargas et al. 2006.

[69] Stevenson et al. 1983/4, 1988; McCoy 1976a.

[70] Ibid. p. 200.

[71] Ibid., pp. 114, 118.

[72] Vargas 1998a, p. 124; Vargas et al. 2006, p. 119.

[73] Fischer 1993a.

[74] Ferdon 2000; see also Geiseler 1995, p. 73-4; Vargas et al. 2006, p. 126.

[75] Vargas et al. 2006, p. 128.

[76] Routledge 1919, pp. 241-41.

[77] Vargas 1998a; Vargas et al. 2006, pp. 102-4.

[78] McCoy 1973.

[79] Lee 1992, pp. 95-96; 2004.

[80] Ayres 1979.

[81] Métraux 1957, p. 69; Geiseler 1995, p. 73.

[82] Lee 1992, pp. 95-96; 2004.

[83] Ayres 1979.

[84] Métraux 1957, p. 69; Geiseler 1995, p. 73.

[85] Lee 1992, pp. 113-15; 1997.

Rapanui in front of the church, Hanga Roa.

Part II

**Ancestors of stone:
A petrified dream**

*In Easter Island ...
the shadows of the departed
builders still possess the land
... the whole air vibrates with
a vast purpose and energy
which has been and is no
more. What was it? Why was
it?*

Katherine Routledge, 1919

Chapter 5

Statues and ceremonies

*...empty repetition, like a caged animal going
round and round and making always the same
thing,
these frozen faces, these frozen frames
in a film that's running down...*

Jacob Bronowski

'Living Faces'

The most famous and most astonishing feat of the Easter Islanders' Stone Age culture was the production of hundreds of standardized gigantic stone statues -the *moai*- without the use of metal tools. How and why did they do it?

The Easter Islanders' origins partly explain their motivation: even some of the 19th-century visitors to *Rapa Nui* compared its statues to those of other Polynesian islands: for example, the Forsters in 1774 said that 'The statues which are erected in honour of their kings, have a great affinity to the wooden figures... on the chief's marais or burying places at Taheitee' (ill. 53) [1].

The carving of large, human figures in stone was not common in Polynesia, in part perhaps through lack of suitable material: all Pacific statuary is in igneous rock. In the Marquesas, where volcanic tuff was used, there are large ancient stone statues of rotund men associated with ceremonial platforms -a massive statue called 'Takaii' on the island of Hiva Oa, for example, is 2.83 m (9.25 ft) high- these figures are unlike those of *Rapa Nui*, but certainly hint at a shared heritage and

tradition of statue-carving. Herman Melville, in *Typee*, relates how, in the Typee valley of the Marquesas, he came upon a huge wooden statue with staring eyes, standing on a stone platform [2].

The Australs too have monolithic stone sculpture At Ra'ivavae, there was a *tiki* figure some 2.3 m (7.5 ft) tall (Moerenhout in 1837 reported that the *ti'i* of Ra'ivavae, stone images on *marae*, were almost as colossal as the *Rapa Nui moai* [3]); and it is known that Pitcairn Island also had hard red tufa statues standing on shrines: unfortunately, the Bounty mutineers threw them off a cliff! However, investigations by Mrs Routledge and others showed that the Pitcairn platforms were smaller versions of those on Easter Island, with a similarly sloped inner façade 12 m (39 ft) long; and one surviving fragment of a statue, found under the veranda of a modern house there, was a torso with large hands clasped on its abdomen [4]. Recently, a *moai* fragment found in the rubble of the *Ahu Tongariki* likewise had its arms across its mid-section in the same pose as in the Marquesas and Australs [5]. Parallels have also been drawn between Easter Island's statues and

47. Forster's sketch of a *moai*, the earliest drawing known of one of these statues. Cook second voyage, 1774.

a type of pumice figure from New Zealand, with a narrow rectangular head, jutting brow and long curving nose.

The vast majority -about 95%- of the Easter Island statues (890 have been inventoried so far, including 397, almost half of them, at *Rano Raraku*) are made of *Rano Raraku* tuff [6], including all those erected on platforms (164), but about fifty-five are made of other stone (and are smaller than the average size of 4.05 m high and 12.5 tons): red scoria (eighteen), basalt (fifteen), or trachyte (twenty-two), a dense white stone from *Poike* -- indeed, a recent survey has discovered dozens of previously unknown statues on *Poike*, but only a couple of them are made of *Rano Raraku* tuff.

The finished statues on platforms range from 2 to almost 10 m (6 to 33 ft) high, and it has been estimated that their average weight and height are 10 tons and 3.8 m [7]: the biggest, at *Ahu Hanga Te Tenga*, is 9.94 m (32.5 ft) long, but appears to have fallen and been broken in the course of being erected, since its eye sockets were never cut. The statue known as *Paro* (which was erected on *Ahu Te Pito Kura*) is almost as long, 3.2 m (10.5 ft) across the shoulders, and weighs 82 tons.

There might be up to fifteen *moai* in a row on a statue platform; it is a common misconception that they were absolutely identical, whereas, in fact, no two are exactly alike: 'Since the concept of realistic individualized art did not exist in ancient Polynesia, no *moai* bore an individualized appearance' [8]. A certain amount of variety can be seen within the rows; some platforms (ill. 50) seem to have had all their statues erected in one episode, while other rows were built up over time.

The largest statue ever made, nicknamed 'El Gigante', was a monstrous 20 m (65 ft) in length, weighing up to 270 tons, and it is generally reckoned to have been well beyond even the remarkable ingenuity of the Easter Islanders to move it, let alone erect it somewhere (the obelisk in Paris's Place de la Concorde is not much taller, at 22.8 m [75 ft]). Lying unfinished in the *Rano Raraku* quarry (ill. 51), it represents an enigma in itself: was it a commission from some power-mad individual or group? Did the workers abandon it once they recognized the futility of carving a figure they could not possibly move? Was work on it simply abandoned as part of the general cessation of statue building? On the other hand, Vince Lee has argued that fewer than 300 people could have moved it, upright, using levers, on a sled over a wooden ladder-trackway [9].

Islanders told Thomson in 1886 that the platform Tahiri was the last to be built and had been intended for that statue. Or was it, as some scholars believe, never intended to be a standing statue, but simply an enormous petroglyph, like the recumbent funerary statues in European cathedrals? [10]

Dozens of statues have detailed designs in bas-relief on their backs that may represent tattooed signs of rank: for example, curved lines at each shoulder plus a vertical line for a spine appear to make the kind of abstract human face that is widespread and significant in the island's art (for example, on wooden ceremonial paddles) and elsewhere in Polynesia. On statues at *Anakena* there are also bas-relief spirals on the buttocks.

Between the fingertips and below the navel of a typical statue is a feature in bas-relief believed to be a *hami*, the fold of a loincloth. Lines that curve across the small of the back (ill. 49) are likewise thought to represent the *maro*, the sacred loincloth of authority, which was important in denoting the rank of chiefs and priests throughout Polynesia. Specimens of *maro* were recorded in 19th-century Easter Island, made of *tapa* or of human hair.

48. *Ahu Nau Nau moai, Anakena,* representing one of the best works in stone from the island.

129

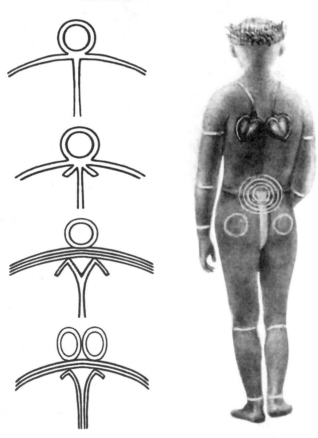

It is generally assumed that most of the figures are male, though in fact the vast majority are unsexed: a gender can only be assigned safely to the few (in the quarry and at *Tongariki*) with a goatee beard, or to a couple of specimens with a vulva marked [11]. Some scholars see the *hami* as indicating a male. Others have seen the occasionally very developed nipples as a sign of femininity, but this is unfounded. One or two statues have well-rounded breasts but no other sign of being female, whereas at least one of those with a vulva has nothing at the bust that gives the slightest hint of its gender. The vulva may have been a later addition, and in any case sexual ambiguity is by no means uncommon in Polynesian art.

A clear distinction can be drawn between those statues which were erected on platforms, and those -whatever their intended function- which were not. Apart from the fact that only the figures on platforms were given eye-sockets, head-gear, and perhaps colouring, the average height of the platform-statues is 4 m (13 ft), whereas that of those not on platforms is 6 m (20 ft); and many of the platform figures are stockier and less angular than those at the quarry, with less accentuated features and less concave or prominent noses and chins. Some believe that the earliest statues had more rounded and naturalistically-shaped heads, because such types were often used as building material in platform structures [12].

The eye sockets had generally been assumed to have remained empty, adding to the brooding appearance of the figures, although Lt Colin Dundas stated in 1871, 'Although we could not find any specimen, I believe that [the eye sockets] were intended to be filled with eyes of obsidian, in the same manner as the eyes of the small wooden figures' [13]. In 1978, excavations by Sonia Haoa, a native archaeologist, uncovered fragments of white coral and a circular red scoria pebble under

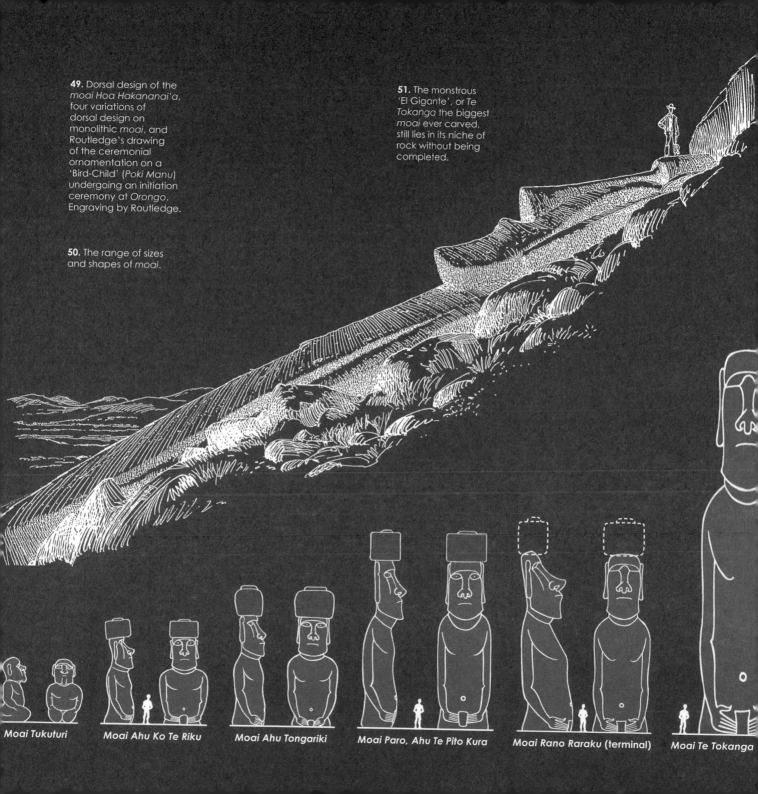

49. Dorsal design of the *moai Hoa Hakananai'a*, four variations of dorsal design on monolithic *moai*, and Routledge's drawing of the ceremonial ornamentation on a 'Bird-Child' (*Poki Manu*) undergoing an initiation ceremony at *Orongo*. Engraving by Routledge.

50. The range of sizes and shapes of *moai*.

51. The monstrous 'El Gigante', or *Te Tokanga* the biggest *moai* ever carved, still lies in its niche of rock without being completed.

Moai Tukuturi

Moai Ahu Ko Te Riku

Moai Ahu Tongariki

Moai Paro, Ahu Te Pito Kura

Moai Rano Raraku (terminal)

Moai Te Tokanga

52. Reproduction eyes fitted in erect *moai* at *Anakena* showing how they gaze slightly upward. It was once thought that the statues had always been 'blind' (Photo: MAPSE), but in 1978 fragments of white coral and red scoria were discovered under a fallen statue of *Anakena* -when pieced together, they formed an eye that fitted the statue's empty socket perfectly.

a fallen statue at *Anakena*; when fitted together they formed an oval eye of cut and polished coral, about 35 cm (14 in) long, which fitted the empty socket of the figure (ill. 52). When restored to their original appearance, the statues with fitted eyes provide a startlingly different image from that to which the world had grown accustomed [14].

When reproduction eyes were fitted, it was found that the statues had stared not directly at the villages before them -which would doubtless have been rather disconcerting- but slightly upward, perhaps explaining a Mangarevan name for the island, *Mata-ki-te-Rangi*, meaning literally 'eyes towards the heavens'. Less romantic observers have commented that the eyes make the statues 'look like a worried businessman at tax time'!

The reason that so few of the coral eyes had survived the toppling of the statues is that islanders had burned the coral fragments found around wrecked platforms to make whitewash for their houses: coral was scarce, since the island has no lagoon, and the only supply came from fragments washed up on the shore. William Mulloy found an almost intact eye under a fallen statue's face at *Vinapu* in the 1950s, but it was very eroded, and its round shape led him to think it was a fragment of a '...beautifully made coral dish' which had been elliptical with pointed ends [15]. Since Sonia Haoa's discovery in 1978, fragments of eyes of white coral or pumice have been found in a number of sites, some of them with pupils of obsidian rather than of scoria [16]. One curious fact, however, is that none of the European explorers who saw statues still standing on their platforms ever mentioned these eyes, and in fact González in 1770 stated that '... the only features of the face are simple cavities for the eyes'. Is it possible, therefore, that these eyes, embodying consciousness and intelligence, were only inserted at certain times or for particular ceremonies to 'bring the figures to life'?

At *Ahu Nau Nau, Anakena*, numerous coral eye fragments have been recovered in excavations, along with some other artifacts of coral or algal nodules. These have now been radiocarbon dated, with the 'marine correction' to allow for the ancient CO_2 dissolved in the ocean. Twenty-six of the dates are between AD 1000 and AD 1600, but one is earlier, possibly AD 700 [17]. Using 'chronometric hygiene', this date must be excluded. The other dates fall into groups which appear to correspond with the phases of construction of the *ahu*.

The outside world's first recorded comment on the famous statues appears in the *Journal* of Cornelis Bouman, one of Roggeveen's captains, who wrote,

on 8 April 1722: 'On land we saw several high statues in the heathen fashion' [18]. Whereas the Spanish in 1770 at first mistook them from out at sea for big shrubs symmetrically set up! Roggeveen's log states that the islanders '...set fires before some particularly high erected stone images, and then, sitting down on their heels with bowed heads, they bring the palms of their hands together, moving them up and down'. It has been suggested that the fires the Dutchmen saw may simply have been preparations for earth ovens, so that food could be offered to the unexpected guests, but Bouman's account shows that the Dutchmen saw chickens being cooked in the ground, so they could presumably differentiate the two phenomena.

53. Background engraving: a temple in Hawai'i, with three of its statues highlighted. Third voyage of Captain Cook.

54. Left: *moai Ahu Vai Uri, Tahai* complex, and right; *moai Hoa Hakananai'a*. Photo: Eduardo Ruiz-Tagle.

Many of the first European visitors expected the giant statues to be gods, although La Pérouse wrote in 1786 that '...we never came across traces of any cult and I do not think that anyone could suppose the statues to be idols, although the islanders do show them respect'. None of the statues is known to have had the name of a deity. Instead, they were all known by the collective name *aringa ora* (living faces): they are clearly generalized rather than individualized portraits. Captain Cook's party heard the term *ariki* (chief) applied to some, while others had nicknames such as 'Twisted Neck', 'Tattooed One' and even 'Stinker' (even today, the islanders frequently use nicknames for each other and for visitors). Geiseler reported in 1882 that '...even today every older rapanui man knows well the name of each of the many statues, regardless whether these are still standing or have already fallen down, and displays great respect toward them'; they still thought the idols had special attributes and possessed great powers' [19].

From the islanders' testimony and other Polynesian ethnography, it is virtually certain that the statues represented high-ranking ancestors, often served as their funerary monument, and kept their memory alive, like the simple upright slabs in front of platforms in the Society Islands, which represented clan ancestors, or the statues dominating the terraces of sanctuaries in the Marquesas, which were famous old

chiefs or priests. Indeed, the Spanish pilot Moraleda in 1770 reported that the *moai* represented people of particular merit, worthy of being commemorated [20].

This would explain the special features of the platform images: one can speculate that statues were commissioned during the lifetime of elders -rather like the pyramids or tombs of Egyptian pharaohs- but their eyes were left uncarved to indicate the person was still alive. Only after death was the statue moved to its platform and erected, the sockets hollowed out, and its eyes and sometimes a head-dress set in place, perhaps to 'activate' its *mana* (spiritual power); if this is correct, then the eyes had far more than an occasional ceremonial significance.

But in addition to their 'identity', the statues may also have incorporated distinct symbolism of other kinds: display is a constant in Polynesian culture. These towering vertical figures on their horizontal platforms around the coast served as a sacred border between two worlds, as intermediaries between the living and the gods, between life and death -transitional areas of this kind tend to be of ritual significance in all human societies. The ancestor figures, facing inland towards the villages and with their backs to the sea, probably provided considerable reassurance and protection. One can compare the Indonesian island of Sulawesi, where wooden effigies of the deceased, wearing clothes and head-gear, and with staring inlaid eyes, are placed on high balconies in cliffs so their spirits can forever watch over their village.

It has been suggested that the Easter Island statues' location, as close to the shore as possible, implies a role in preventing encroachment by the sea, particularly if the legend about *Hotu Matu'a* and his followers fleeing a partly submerged island has any basis in fact. In that case, however, one might expect the ancestors to be placed facing the potential threat rather than with their backs to it, and the location might equally well be explained as a convenient way of keeping these structures away from the limited agricultural land available; there was little point in having fields by the shore, where heavy salt spray would damage the crops.

Max Raphael, the German art historian, pointed out that the sheer monumentality of the figures, their grandeur in relation to the viewer's relative smallness, fulfilled the need to feel protected, and must have created a sense of security and repose: monumentality always commands respect and awe [21]. These were not works of art that carried on some dialogue with the individual, they were repositories for conserving the ancestors' spiritual power -concentrated in the head or eyes- which protected the community. The attraction exerted by each individual figure is limited, since they are so stereotyped, but in groups their effect is greatly magnified.

Raphael noted how the back of the head is flat, the cheeks and ears are 'static', but the nose and mouth jut forward aggressively; moreover, the straightness or concave curve of the nose contrasts markedly with the frequently arched noses on the island's wooden figures. He therefore believed that, consciously or unconsciously, the nose was shaped as a symbolic phallus, a vertical part above a horizontal part whose base bulges at both sides (phallic noses also occur in petroglyphs, as well as on some wood carvings), while the 'pouting' or protruding thin lips with a groove between them suggest the form of a vagina. In short, he saw these heads as sexual symbols -monuments to dead men that were somehow involved in the process of rebirth. Other scholars have seen the entire *moai* as symbolic of the phallus and procreative power -there is at least one legend on the island that the penis provided the model for the design [22]- and we have already pointed out the statues' inherent ambiguity of gender.

54.1. European measuring a *moai*. Engraved by Noel Eugene Sotain, 1816. Memoria Chilena.

The winglike hands resting on the stomach may also have specific meaning. In the traditional Maori carving of New Zealand the hands were placed there to protect ritual knowledge and oral traditions, because it was believed these were carried in the belly. Figures with hands on the abdomen are also common in the Marquesas and elsewhere in Polynesia.

In many societies around the world, the very presence of the ancestors, whether as images or in the form of their bones (or both), frequently serves as a group's best evidence that the land has always belonged to them. The figures can therefore, in a sense, be seen as literally staking a claim, connecting a lineage to its ancestral land through a founding father (or mother). Moreover, the roles assigned to the eminent dead in this way may bear little resemblance to the roles they performed while alive: it is very common for individuals or groups in pursuit of power and authority in a changing society to call upon the dead to help them and bolster their claims. The deifying of great men who were either direct descendants of the gods, mighty warriors or people with great prestige was a deeply rooted characteristic of Polynesian culture. In Polynesia, only the nobility had ancestors and a genealogy stretching back to the gods, and Polynesian art as a whole is dominated by almost stereotyped portraits of these ancestors.

However, on Easter Island it seems that the statue carving was done not by a population under the control of some central power, but rather by a number of fairly independent kin groups from different parts of the island. It is likely that they were in competition with each other, trying to outdo their neighbours in the scale and grandeur of their religious centres and ancestor-figures. There is some evidence of an overall tendency for the statues being carved to increase in size over time.

But exactly how was the carving accomplished with a simple Stone Age technology?

[1] von Saher 1992.
[2] Routledge 1917, p. 344.
[3] Cain & Bierbach 1997, p. 106.
[4] Routledge 1919, pp. 313-4.
[5] *Rapa Nui Journal* 9 (3), 1995, p. 90.
[6] Van Tilburg 1986, 1994; Bahn 1993; Liller 1993; Ramírez & Huber 2000, p. 64; Vargas et al. 2006, p. 165; Shepardson 2013. In an interview (Pelletier 2012, p. 137), Van Tilburg states that her inventory, begun in 1982, has now reached 1045 sculpted items. It is therefore most puzzling that Hunt & Lipo (2011, p. 171) claim that theirs was the first extensive survey of *moai* since that of Thomson in 1886!
[7] Edwards & Edwards 2013, p. 320.
[8] Fischer 2005, p. 34.
[9] Lee 2012, 2013.
[10] Métraux 1957, p. 165.
[11] Barthel 1958.
[12] Skjølsvold 1996.
[13] Dundas 2000, p. 38.
[14] Vignes 1982. Hunt & Lipo (2011, p. 83) erroneously attribute the eye's discovery to S. Rapu.
[15] Mulloy 1961, pp. 156, 177, fig. 46.

[16] Seelenfreund 1988, p. 79; Steadman et al. 1994, p. 88; Martinsson-Wallin 1996. According to Edwards & Edwards (2013, p. 325), a Chilean sculptor and artist, Germán Ruiz, found a complete eye of carved coral with a hole in the early 1970s in a cave, but nobody believed his claims, and its whereabouts are now unknown.

[17] Beck et al. 2003.

[18] von Saher 1990/1.

[19] Geiseler 1995, pp. 35, 24; see also Beaglehole 1961, p. 340.

[20] Mellén Blanco 1986, p. 159.

[21] Raphael 1988.

[22] Edwards & Edwards 2013 p. 322.

55. *Ahu Akivi restored by William Mulloy and Gonzalo Figueroa, 1960.* Photo: Eduardo Ruiz-Tagle.

The statues' maternity ward

The volcanic crater of *Rano Raraku* is one of the world's most extraordinary and evocative archaeological sites, filled with unfinished statues and the empty niches from which hundreds of others have already been hacked out. If you are lucky enough to have the whole place to yourself, rather than swarming with visitors, its stillness and silence become eerily overwhelming. But imagine this unique quarry bustling with activity on the inner and outer slopes, with many different groups of tattooed and painted workers, the rhythmic noise of countless hammers striking rock, and no doubt songs or chants ringing out...

In our modern age, with its advanced technology and its emphasis on speed and impatience, it is hard to understand how prehistoric people could spend vast amounts of time and hard manual labour on carving, transporting and erecting huge stones, whether they be the megaliths of Western Europe or the *Rapa Nui* statues. On the other hand, it can be argued that in prehistoric times -and particularly on a small isolated island- there was little else to do, and stone-carving became a ruling passion; in 1786 La Pérouse reckoned, perhaps somewhat optimistically, that three days' work in the fields annually was all that each islander needed to do in order to obtain food for the year, while in the 1860s the missionary Eugène Eyraud reported that the islanders did no real work at all. A day's exertion assured them of a year's supply of sweet potatoes. The other 364 days of the year were spent 'walking about, sleeping and visiting'. They made their own entertainment in those days!

It is the lack of comprehension by modern people of what can be achieved with simple technology, lots of time and muscle-power, and some ingenuity, which has permitted the lunatic fringe of archaeology to flourish. The most obvious example is the theory, proposed by the Swiss writer Erich von Däniken and others, that the prehistoric world was visited sporadically by extraterrestrial astronauts who are responsible for anything in the archaeological record that strikes us as impressive or enigmatic [1]. In addition to being a lazy and simplistic *deus ex machina* solution to supposed ancient 'mysteries', this view provides the comforting reassurance that 'we are not alone', and that human progress is being monitored and occasionally nudged in the right direction by some benevolent power in the universe.

It is therefore somewhat ironic that the Easter Islanders' own efforts to reassure themselves -through their colossal carvings- that they were not alone have been seized on and distorted by the proponents of ancient astronauts or lost/ drowned supercivilizations. Such views ignore the real achievements of our ancestors and constitute the ultimate in racism: they belittle the abilities and ingenuity of the human species as a whole.

Von Däniken's view of the Easter Island statues is very simple: being made of 'steel-hard volcanic

56. An engraving of the inner quarry at *Rano Raraku*, 1869.

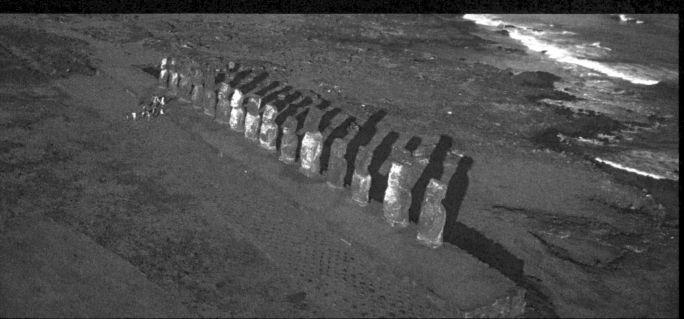

57. An aerial view of the *ahu Tongariki*

58. *Rano Raraku* lagoon and interior quarry

59. Aerial view of *Rano Raraku*

60. An aerial view of *ahu Vinapu*

63. Routledge's view of the quarry's southeastern inner slopes, seen from across the lake, which revealed the large number of *moai* already completed, and others in the process of being carved.

Right: Member of the Heyerdahl's expedition wielding a toki in front of the keel of a moai, and rapanui during the carving experiment.

stone' they could not have been made with '... rudimentary tools. ...Nobody could ever have freed such gigantic lumps of lava with small primitive stone tools... The men who could execute such perfect work must have possessed ultra-modern tools.' He proposed that a small group of 'intelligent beings' was stranded on the island, taught the natives various things, made the statues -he emphasizes their 'robot-like appearance'- and were then rescued before all the figures were finished. The natives tried to complete the carvings with stone tools, but failed miserably.

The yellow-brown volcanic tuff of *Rano Raraku* (Raraku was the name of a local ancestral spirit) is made of ash and lapilli. It is, indeed, steel-hard on surfaces exposed to the weather: the Spanish visitors of 1770 struck a statue with a hoe or pickaxe, and sparks flew. Underneath, however, it is not much harder than chalk, being formed of compressed ash, and can be cut and shaped quite easily even with stone tools: Métraux found that '...the modern sculptors consider this material easier to work than wood. With nothing but an axe they cut out a large block of tuff in a day and in a few hours transform it into replicas of the great statues' [2]. The quarry is littered with thousands of flaked and pointed stone picks (*toki*) of compact basalt: if von Däniken's theory were correct, it seems bizarre that so many of these should have been made by the islanders before they realized the tools were useless! In fact, no less than 504 were located at the base of two *moai* recently re-excavated by Van Tilburg [3].

During Thor Heyerdahl's expedition in the 1950s, he discussed with the islanders how the statues were carved, and they insisted that these picks had been used for the task; it is uncertain whether any of the tools were hafted on handles, though one or two hafted adzes are known in the island's rock art [4]. In a now famous experiment, Heyerdahl hired six men who used some of these tools to outline a 5 m (16 ft) statue [5]. It was first measured out on the rock-face in arm and hand lengths, and then the bashing began, each blow raising a bit of dust. The rock was frequently splashed with water to soften it (the spongy rock also absorbs rainwater, which makes the statues fragile and hard to preserve today), and the picks quickly became blunted and had to be sharpened or replaced. It took three days for these unpractised men to produce a statue-outline, and on the basis of this somewhat scanty evidence it was somehow calculated that six men, working every day, could have completed a figure of this size in twelve to fifteen months, allowing one sculptor every half-metre (Katherine Routledge, the first person to make a detailed study of the quarry, had estimated that a statue could be roughed out in fifteen days, while Métraux had thought this figure too small).

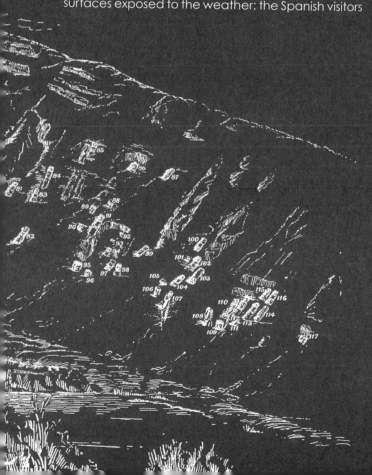

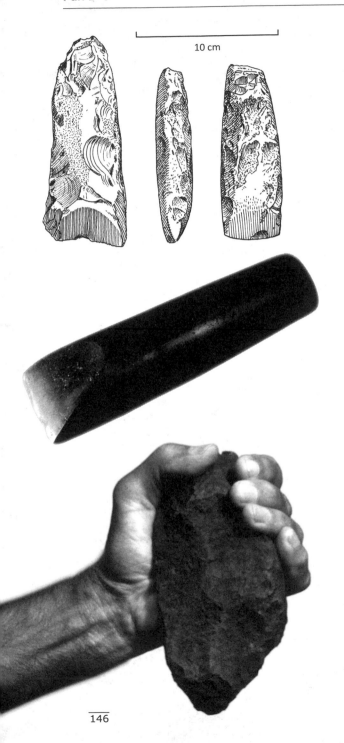

10 cm

Rano Raraku: **The quarry**

It follows that twenty practised workmen, perhaps in alternating teams of ten with plenty of elbow-room, could have produced any of the island's finished statues, even *Paro*, in a year. Allowing a thousand statues on the island, and an estimated period of at least five hundred years of carving activity (from c. AD 1000 to 1500, based on radiocarbon dates from Norwegian excavations at the quarry), it is clear that even a small population could have achieved this number of figures. But since the *Rano Raraku* quarry contains so many unfinished statues, of a variety of sizes and types, it seems likely that there were numerous different groups at work, and the timespan necessary to account for a thousand statues could be far shorter. The high number of unfinished figures at the quarry also implies that carving them was much easier than moving and erecting them, and production was far outstripping demand. Excavations have revealed the abundant foundations of houses both inside the crater and, in regular terraces, between *Rano Raraku* and the coast, which are thought to be those of the numerous quarrymen.

What is certain is that specialized master-craftsmen were at work here; the islanders reported that the sculptors had been a privileged class, their craft being hereditary in the male line, and that it was a matter of great pride to be a member of a sculptor's family. According to legend, the statue carvers were relieved of all other work, so that the fishermen and farmers had to provide them with food, especially valuable seafood; the carvers were also paid in fish, lobsters and eels.

64. Three of the thousands of basalt *toki* which were used to carve the *moai*. They often fit the hand very comfortably.

65. Engraving of the *Rano Raraku* quarry by Routledge.

66. *Moai* in the process of carving.

67. *Pu Makari*, some of the postholes which are thought to be part of a statue-lowering system high on the crater rim of *Rano Raraku*.

Large areas of the quarry lie hidden under slope deposits, so it was actually bigger than we can recognize today (it should be remembered that this quarry was the 'maternity ward' for over 90 per cent of the island's statues). At present, it is c. 800 m (c. 2600 ft) long, and contains numerous now empty niches from which statues were once removed, as well as 397 figures visible on the outer and inner slopes illustrating every phase of the carving process (ills. 59, 63, 65 and 68); as Geiseler wrote, the unfinished idols '...permitted the clear recognition of the steps used in idol making' [6]. The information they provide shows us just how systematic this process was.

The figures were carved on their backs, with their base usually pointing down-slope (though some point the other way, others lie parallel to the mountain, and some are almost vertical). The space between a started statue and the cliff wall was generally about 60 cm, wide enough for one man to work in [7]. As they were cut away, a keel was left along the back, keeping them attached to bedrock (ill. 63 and 69). All the basic details of the head (except the eyes), the hands and so on were carved at this stage, and the surface smoothed, probably with pumice, of which fragments have

been found: the tuff, while excellent for carving and smoothing, is not good for polishing.

With the statue held firm by a packing of stones and fill, holes were punched in the keel, until it was completely pecked away [8]. Some were probably broken at this point, and it is noteworthy that the quarry displays abundant evidence of breakage or of figures abandoned due to defects in the stone. The tuff was in plentiful supply, so it was simpler to abandon a faulty statue and begin a new one than to persist with a bad one. Carving might also be abandoned if there was a slip during the work, which in Polynesia was seen as a sign of evil affecting the carver's *mana*.

The next task was to move the statue down the slope (of about 55 degrees) without damaging it. Depressed runways or channels of earth seem to have been used, with the remains of the keel serving to maintain the statue's direction. The islanders claim that cables were used, perhaps attached to the statue's neck (ill. 69).

On the rim of the crater, 150 m (c. 500 ft) above the plain, though apparently only of use to operations at one part of the inner slope, are some pairs of

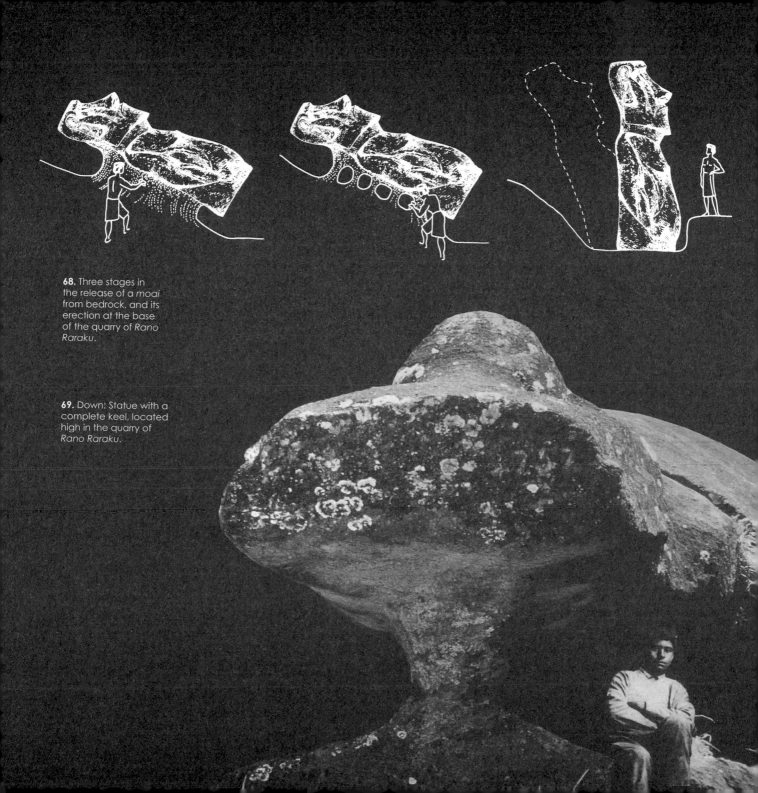

68. Three stages in the release of a *moai* from bedrock, and its erection at the base of the quarry of *Rano Raraku*.

69. Down: Statue with a complete keel, located high in the quarry of *Rano Raraku*.

pecked cylindrical holes over 1 m (3 ft) in depth and width, with horizontal channels connecting them at the bottom [9]. Scars suggest that ropes. 7.5 to 10 cm (3 to 4 in) thick were fastened here, and the islanders have confirmed this. Since the revelation that large trees were readily available (Chapter 4), it is also thought probable that large trunks stood in these holes, with the ropes around them: the islanders themselves had told their German visitors of 1882 that colossal tree trunks had been set in these holes, and held cables used to lower statues down to the places intended for them, by giving '...an anchorage point to the men who from here controlled with long ropes the downward movement of the completed idol' [10]. Ropes may also have been attached to horizontal wooden beams set transversely in the channels leading down the slope: traces of these runways and of beam-seats remain in the quarry.

Some accidents certainly happened: at least one head was left in place while its body continued down the slope. But, by and large, the system seems to have worked well.

Once down from the quarry, the statues had the carving of their backs completed. But as Ramírez & Huber have pointed out, one of the unfathomable mysteries of the island is why the sculptors did not simply cut out rough blocks, and then haul them to a more comfortable working place. And why did they do most of the carving before moving the statues, and even before bringing them down the quarry slope? [11]

Over c. 400 m (c. 1300 ft) of the bottom of the exterior slope stand about seventy essentially completed statues erected in pits in the ground: it is these figures, buried up to their shoulders or even chins by sediments, and with their backs to the mountain, which have produced the classic cartoonist's view of Easter Island heads gazing out to sea. Excavations by Katherine Routledge and, more recently, by Thor Heyerdahl's teams revealed that these are, in fact, full statues like those on the platforms, and the tallest is over 11 m (36 ft) in height [12]. It has been assumed that these were figures of people not yet dead, or that they had not yet been moved to *ahu* because of lack of room on the platforms or simply lack of resources for the transportation.

At the edge of the adjacent plain about thirty more statues lie on the surface, mostly on their fronts. Others are scattered along prehistoric 'roads' heading vaguely southward and westward along the south coast.

We now arrive, therefore, at the question that has perplexed every visitor to the island: how were these figures brought down from the quarry and transported, sometimes miles, to their final destinations?

[1] von Däniken 1969, and several other titles of the same kind.
[2] Métraux 1957, p. 164. Routledge was told by a descendant of a master carver that the stone was softer when it was first extracted. They waited for them to harden before transporting (Edwards & Edwards 2013, p. 332).
[3] Van Tilburg & Arévalo 2012, p. 78.
[4] Lee 1992, p. 117.
[5] Skjølsvold 1961, pp. 368-69.
[6] Geiseler 1995, p. 27.
[7] Ibid.
[8] Routledge 1919; Mulloy 1970; Lee 2012, 2013.
[9] Mazière 1969, p. 213.
[10] Geiseler 1995, pp. 28-32.
[11] Ramírez & Huber 2000.
[12] Routledge 1919, p. 185; Heyerdahl 1989.

69.1. *Moai, Rano Raraku.*
Moai, Brett Shepardson, Rapanui Press.

REYZE naar het ZUYDLAND.

Chapter 7

Rocking or rolling:
How were the statues moved?

*[They] seemed to be triumphing over us,
asking:
'Guess how this engineering work was done!
Guess how we moved these gigantic
figures down the steep walls of the volcano
and carried them over the hills
to any place on the island we liked!'*

Thor Heyerdahl

Over the years some ingenious or far-fetched explanations have been put forward as to how the finished statues were moved from the quarry. In 1722 Roggeveen, clearly not a geologist, was misled by the tuff's colour and its composite nature (the numerous lapilli embedded in it) and claimed that the statues were in fact moulded *in situ* from some plastic mixture of clay and stones; some of Cook's officers in 1774 came to the same conclusion. In 1949 a psychologist, Werner Wolff, even Imagined that the figures were roughed out, then blown from erupting volcanoes to the platforms, and finished where they fell! [1] Others have suggested electromagnetic or anti-gravitational forces and, as we have already seen, visiting extraterrestrials.

The islanders themselves cling to a legend that the statues walked to the platforms thanks to their spiritual power, or at the command of priests or chiefs. It was said that the statues walked a short distance each day towards their platforms, and also that they walked around in the dark and uttered oracles!

It may be true that faith can move mountains, but archaeologists have sought more mundane explanations. The first point to be made is that the problem in transportation was not necessarily the statues' weight (this could be considerable, though the average is no more than about 18 tons) but their fragility, since the *Rano Raraku* tuff is not very dense (its specific gravity -i.e. the ratio of its density to that of water- is light, only c. 1.82), and it was important not to damage the elaborate detail already carved on the figures [2].

Hundreds of statues were moved from the quarry, some of them as far as 10 km (6.25 miles) though it is noticeable that only the smaller ones were moved quite so far, a potent argument against spiritual forces alone being responsible! No doubt, the effort and distance involved in setting up particular statues added to the ostentation of their size, further enhancing their prestige and that of their village.

To early observers, who thought that the island had always been bereft of wood or material

70. The earliest known depiction of *Rapa Nui*, Roggeveen expedition, published in1728.

for cordage, the method of moving the statues remained obscure. The first real progress on this topic came during the Franco-Belgian expedition of 1934 when a 6-ton statue was moved by sledge, using 100 islanders. Later, in the course of Heyerdahl's expedition of the 1950s, an experiment was carried out with a 4 m (13 ft) statue weighing around 10 tons. Following the elders' instructions, the islanders made a wooden sledge out of a tree fork and lashed the statue on its back on to it; ropes of tree bark were attached to it. About 180 men, women and children came to feast and dance, before setting about the task of pulling the statue a short distance on its sledge, using two parallel ropes [3].

Since 180 people could pull a 10-ton statue, then 1500 could certainly have moved even *Paro*'s 82 tons (plus its heavy sledge); as we shall see (p. 218), such a number is well within the estimated prehistoric population. Sledge transportation could have been rendered much smoother and more efficient -reducing the required workforce by one third- by applying lubricants to the track: *taro*, sweet potato, totora reeds or palm fronds could all have been used, and there is an oral tradition on the island that mashed yams and sweet potatoes were indeed used as lubricants for moving the statues -naturally, the mash would not have gone to waste, as chickens could have eaten it later.

A Czech engineer, Pavel Pavel, has carried out important experiments with a 9-ton replica *moai*. It was placed on its back on a sledge on grass, but thirty men were unable to move it. Using 800 kg of potatoes made the pulling easier, and the men were able to move it 6 metres (which used up 30% of the mashed potatoes). However, when the sledge was placed on beams 2 m long and 20 cm in diameter, only ten men were needed to pull it [4].

Since we know that timber was once in plentiful supply (Chapter 4), it should thus be borne in mind

that the work -and the workforce- could have been almost halved again by dragging the sledge over a lubricated wooden track rather than over the ground.

William Mulloy suggested a simple and economical method of transportation involving a curved Y-shaped sledge, made from the fork of a big tree, on which the statue would rest face-downwards [5]. A large pair of shearlegs is attached to the figure's neck by a loop, and as they are tilted forward, the rope partially lifts the statue and takes some weight off the sledge (ill. 75). The statue therefore follows the shearlegs, in a kind of rocking movement caused by the bulging abdomen.

Mulloy estimated that, by this method, *Paro* could have been moved the 6 km (4 miles) to its platform by only ninety men. Specialists in ancient technology have pointed out that a flat-bottomed sledge would serve just as well, and that the estimate of ninety men for *Paro* is much too low. It has been calculated that, while possible (assuming the presence of trees big enough to serve as shearlegs, palms being flexible and unsuitable for the job), Mulloy's method is no more efficient than other techniques [6]. It also puts special stress on the statues' fragile necks. Besides, most of the statues apparently abandoned in transport do not have the protruding stomachs ideal for this method, which suggests that it was not the one being employed.

Von Saher has described how, on the island of Sumba (Indonesia), a sledge made of two tree trunks forming a wedge shape was used to transport a 46-ton stone, pulled by 1500 people -the men from seven villages- taking turns. Using 10 heavy vine-ropes, 1000 men pulled at one time. They received no pay, but were given plenty of food, music and entertainment, and had a tremendous sense of 'belonging'. Many pigs were slaughtered for the occasion, which conferred great prestige on the owner of the stone [7]. Perhaps this kind of event provides us with some insights into the cooperative projects on Easter Island.

The simple sledge method has become a little more plausible now that we know about the presence of the palms, since they could be used for both sledges and rails or trackways. Palm wood is not very durable, on the whole, and the trunks of most species split on drying, and rot in a damp environment. The timber used would therefore need replacing frequently, so if the palms were used for statue transportation, this activity probably contributed heavily to the depletion of this resource; it is worth noting, however, that the present-day *Jubaea chilensis* or Chilean wine palm -the modern species closest to that which was once prolific on the island- is quite resistant to decay: its outer bark, although only 5 mm thick, is very dense. A further obvious use for palm trunks is as rollers or rails, provided they were at least 20 cm (8 in) across: as mentioned earlier (Chapter 4), modern specimens of *Jubaea* can reach a height of over 25 m (82 ft) and a diameter of 1 to 1.8 m (3 to 6 ft), and although the trunk consists of a spongy, fibrous mass (less dense and more fibrous than that of coconut) within a thin hard rind (ill. 71), it dries out to considerable hardness -it has been calculated that the outer hardwood of the bottom part of a mature palm can support about 6 tons [8]. To be really efficient, rollers or rails must be fairly uniform and run on (or form) a well-constructed track. British and French experiments in moving prehistoric megaliths have found that this technique reduces the workforce required to about six or seven men per ton. Hence to drag *Paro* on palm rollers would need 500 to 600 people. On roughly made tracks, rollers can jam, but a well-constructed track plus lubrication –perhaps using seaweed– can make the task relatively easy.

A different technique for moving the largest statues horizontally was suggested by the French architect and archaeologist Jean-Pierre Adam [9]. Observing fishermen of the Ivory Coast, he saw two men move a very heavy canoe up the beach with the greatest of ease, whereas four people could not have dragged it. One man sat on one end, to raise the other enough for a single roller to be placed beneath; the other man could then swivel the whole canoe through 180 degrees (ill. 75). They then changed places and repeated the operation until the canoe had travelled the required distance. If a series of rollers were to await each statue at the base of the runway down from the quarry, then the figures would be slightly raised above the ground. The rollers would have to be beneath the centre of gravity or almost under the axis of rotation. The head would then be weighted with rocks in bags, and a post or rock solidly planted in the ground next to it. With ropes attached to the base, it would then be simple to swivel the whole figure through 180 degrees. The ropes, counter-weight and post would have to be moved for each subsequent operation. Adam calculated that, by this method, *Paro* could have been moved by 590 men, just over a third of the total needed for the sledge method. Both this technique and Mulloy's also require only short bursts of pulling, with welcome rests in between, unlike sledge-dragging.

It is worth noting that a little-known Dutch drawing (ill. 70) produced in 1728, just a few years after the island's rediscovery and probably based on information from Roggeveen's companions, shows a big sculpture (bearing no resemblance to a *moai*) being moved by only nine natives; it is difficult to assess the method used, but the block seems to rest on a stone slab, and may well have rollers beneath it, so this might add weight to Adam's suggestion.

Van Tilburg [10] believed firmly that the statues were transported on their backs, feet first, and she first carried out computer simulations to investigate their transportation; unfortunately, the average platform selected for her experiments was *Ahu Akivi*, a very untypical specimen since it stands inland, and can thus be approached from either the

71. A cross-section of a Chilean wine palm, showing the thin, hard rind and fibrous interior.

72. Scene from the film *Rapa Nui* by Kevin Reynolds, showing the massive use of ropes and logs.

front or back. The coastal platforms, however, could only be approached from the front, so the statues would have had to be turned around before being raised, if they arrived feet first on their backs. And of course, computer simulations are all very well, but moving huge rocks for real is a very different thing. In a 1998 experiment for television, she directed the movement of a 9-ton replica statue on the island; forty men pulled it on a sled on slides for 50 m. But inevitably she was forced to change its position from supine to prone, because a supine statue would have had to be erected from behind the platform, which, as just mentioned, was impossible in most cases. However, as engineer Vince Lee pointed out, even her newly adopted method posed numerous problems, because where do the columns of pullers go as the sled nears the platform [11]? In Lee's more sensible, practical and experienced view, only the use of levers can solve this dilemma, so one needs surfaces against which levers can push. In the Andes, Egypt and elsewhere, large rocks have likewise been found in places which are far too constricted for the large numbers of pullers needed to drag them -levers must have been used to push the stones from alongside and behind.

In an impressive experiment directed by Lee on the island, twelve men levered a 6-ton rock 15 feet in an hour and a half; each man was thus moving 1000 lb of rock, with no pullers required, and they could thus have moved the rock about 80-100 feet per day, the same rate as achieved by Van Tilburg with 4 to 6 times as many people, and of course they could have reached any platform without anyone working on the seaward side! [12]

The statues, if transported on their fronts or backs, must have required considerable wrapping and padding with vegetation because of their fragility and to protect their decoration. But what if they were moved upright, to reduce the friction surface, perhaps swivelling on their bases like a refrigerator?

Katherine Routledge had '...seriously considered whether they could have been moved in an upright position' [13]; Heyerdahl was told by the islanders in the 1950s that the statues had 'wriggled along' (this was displayed with the feet together and stiff knees), while a few years later French explorer Francis Mazière was told by a native '...that the statues moved standing upright, making half turns on their round bases' [14].

In the 1980s, two independent experiments were carried out into the feasibility of this technique. Pavel Pavel began with a 26 cm (10 in) statue of clay, which proved to be very stable owing to the large circumference at the base and the narrower upper section, placing the centre of gravity at about one third of the total height. He then made a 4.5 m (15 ft) concrete statue weighing 12 tons, and in 1982, at Strakonice (Czech Republic), carried out experiments in moving it upright; it was given a slightly convex base for easy swivelling (a flat base would result in longer 'steps'). Ropes were fastened around the head and the base, and seventeen people in two groups tilted the figure on to its edge and pulled it forward. With practice, good progress was made, the team working rhythmically and without strain [15].

In 1986, Pavel was able to repeat the experiment on the island using two real re-erected statues. First, a 2.8 m (9 ft) statue of 4 or 5 tons was tried (with padding to protect it from the ropes); only three men were needed to tilt it, and five to pull it forward. Next, at *Tongariki* (ill. 74), a 4 m (13 ft) statue of 9 tons was moved. It proved so stable that it could tilt at 70 degrees to either side without falling. Only sixteen people were required to move it a distance of 6 m (20 ft): seven tilting and nine twisting forwards. Pavel therefore concluded that, with practice, this figure could have been moved 200 m (c. 650 ft) per day, and that even the largest statues on the island could have been transported in this way -though moving

73. Aerial view of part of Charles Love's recent excavations of sections of road.

Charles Love's *moai* in Wyoming being moved on a sled and rollers.

Paro's 82 tons for 6 km (4 miles) over rough terrain is a very far cry from a small figure moving 6 m (20 ft). He believes that the *moai* were probably moved in the wet season, to reduce friction and wear on their bases. Thor Heyerdahl estimated that a 20-ton statue could move an average of 100 m (c. 330 ft) per day by this method [16].

American geologist Charles Love also had a replica of a giant statue made in Wyoming; the 4 m (13 ft) concrete figure weighed 10 tons, being denser than *Rano Raraku* tuff, and is equivalent to the smallest 20 per cent of the island's figures. With two hemp ropes, each 2.5 cm (1 in) thick, attached to its brow, he found that crews of fourteen to twenty-two men could move it a few feet by alternate pulling, which caused chips to come off the front of its base (ill. 73). This was a precarious method, and the figure toppled over twice, so it is likely that this simple technique was used only for moving very short distances or for the statues' final positioning. Placing logs under the lateral edges stabilized the statue and protected its base, but made it no easier to move forward. However, a breakthrough occurred when Love's statue was placed upright on two green logs carved into sled-runners to fit its base, and then raised on to a track of small wooden rollers. The statue could now be moved 45 m (148 ft) in two minutes using twenty-five men and two ropes -indeed, the problem was not moving the figure but stopping it [17]! This appears to be the best method for long-distance transportation: it is convenient, stable, and fast, causes no damage, and requires little wood, not much rope, and few people (ill. 73). Pavel's tilt-and-swivel technique is more likely to have been employed for final positioning. Certainly, Lee has emphasized that a *moai* upright, with guy ropes to the four corners of its sled, requires the least manipulation of the load, and avoids the problem of walking it along the ground [18]. Besides, as Love has pointed out, Van Tilburg's method -quite apart from the problems mentioned above, as well as serious omissions in the television version of her experiment- requires taking a standing statue at the quarry, tipping it over onto a sledge, and then raising it again at the platform; such operations would have been highly dangerous both for the *moai* and the islanders, whereas the Pavel and Love experiments have shown the efficiency of upright transportation [19].

There are three major questions concerning upright transportation: first, as shown above, swivelling damages the base [20], and it has been said that the friction would have worn the soft tuff so severely that the statues would have been down to their nostrils in no time. Clearly, however, if Love's method were used, this would not be the case. Secondly, what of hilly terrain? Would the statues not topple as they tried to ascend or descend a slope? In fact, the statues have a slightly forward-slanting base -stones had to be placed under some of those on reconstructed platforms to prevent them leaning forward- and this would help to counter-balance an ascending slope of 10 or 12 degrees; on the descending side, the statue could simply be turned around and moved backwards. Horizontal figures or sledges, on the other hand, would lose contact with some rollers on hilly terrain. Thirdly, no rope marks have been found on the statues' necks and no wear on their bases; this could be explained simply by the use of effective padding beneath the ropes, and, as we have seen, Love's roller method causes no damage to the bases.

A vital ingredient in all these methods of moving the statues is a plentiful supply of strong rope. If one assumes that *Paro* was pulled using only 10 ropes, each having to resist the combined force of at least 50 and perhaps even 150 people, as shown earlier, it has been calculated that the ropes would have to be several centimetres in diameter, and they would need to be about 80 m (260 ft) long: in other words, hundreds of metres of very thick rope were necessary, weighing a ton or more. The more efficient the transportation method, the less cordage is needed, but a section of the population must have been engaged in permanent rope-making to meet requirements, especially as rope deteriorates even faster than wood and would have to be constantly replenished. The only good rope-making material known to have existed on the island was the inner bark of the *Triumfetta semitriloba* shrub, which the islanders called *Hau hau*, and possibly also the crowns of the now-extinct palm. *Hau hau* is a remarkably strong fibre, and was much used in historic times for small twisted cordage, but it no longer exists in quantities sufficient to provide the kind of ropes mentioned above, and no accounts survive of the heavy cordage that must have been made. It is quite possible that a decline in availability of heavy-duty rope contributed as much as the scarcity of timber to the end of statue-building.

Much attention has been paid over the years to the statues at the foot of *Rano Raraku* and those between the quarry and the platforms, in the hope of obtaining clues to the particular transportation method used. Since many of those on the quarry slopes are standing in pits, while others on the plain

have clearly broken after falling from an upright position, it has sometimes been assumed that all were being transported upright. Many scholars, however, believe that most of them were not being transported at all, but were set upright in these positions either temporarily (for their backs to be finished, for rituals to be performed, or to await the death of the person they represented) or permanently, lining the avenues of approach to the quarry. A few may also have simply been abandoned in the course of transportation, perhaps because of strife, or a failed ritual, or the commissioning group's inability to muster the necessary manpower.

Many of the intact horizontal statues in this area lie face-down, which might support Mulloy's idea of transportation in this position (as opposed to being moved on their flat backs on rollers), while others lie face-up and broken, which suggests that they were set upright along the road and later

74. Pavel Pavel's experiment in 1986.

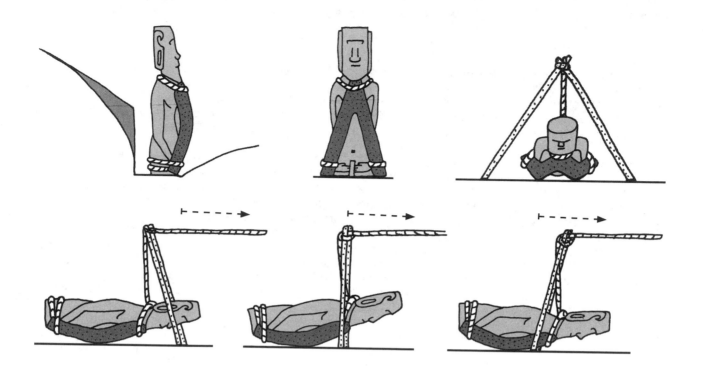

75. The enigma of how the prehistoric islanders could have moved the giant statues, often over long distances from the quarry, and erected them on platforms, has provoked a host of theories and experiments. Above: stages in William Mulloy's bipod method.

Down: Adam's 'canoe-swivel' method as applied to a *moai*.

thrown down -or perhaps that they fell and broke while being transported upright. Certainly, Love's examination of more than 40 *moai* abandoned along the roadways suggests strongly that they were transported upright [21].

In fact, statues are found along the ancient roads on their backs, fronts and sides. At points where they were apparently being moved uphill they are generally on their backs with their base towards the hill; where going downhill, they are usually on their fronts, again with their base towards the hill. Many have their heads pointing away from the quarry, but there is no fully consistent pattern. In some cases, groups of two to four statues are fairly close to each other, in varying positions, occasionally even at angles to one another.

Mrs Routledge believed that *Rano Raraku* was approached by at least three magnificent avenues, each lined at intervals by statues with their backs to the hill, and that none of the figures now lying around the island was in the process of being moved [22]. Support for her view came from excavations in 1986 by Thor Heyerdahl's expedition, which found that a 7.8 m (25.5 ft) statue of 40 tons, lying face down near *Rano Raraku* along Routledge's 'southern road', had an irregular circular pavement or pedestal of basalt stones behind it, bearing clear traces of the statue's base; it was therefore probable that this *moai* had been carefully and purposely set up at this spot [23]. The buried face of the figure was unweathered, suggesting that it had not stood upright for long. However, excavation of a statue of similar size, also face down, some 700 m (2300 ft) away, found no trace of such a pavement. At least some of the upright statues buried at the foot of *Rano Raraku* still stand on stone pavements.

Routledge was also the first to notice rainfall-erosion patterns on these roadside moai which showed that many of them had been vertical for a long time; and this has recently been supported by a study by Cauwe and De Dapper, who argue that the erosion indicates that they were upright for at least several decades and probably more. Most of these fallen *moai* were not being transported but had been set in place along the roads [24].

The island's 'roads' are still visible by the slanting light of the setting sun [25]. These tracks, slightly raised on lower ground and depressed through higher ground, are c. 3 m (c. 10 ft) wide, and radiate out from *Rano Raraku*, generally following the lie of the land and avoiding sharp alterations in terrain. They must certainly have been cleared of any unevenness and of stones, but today, thanks to decades of neglect and of sheep grazing, they are again covered in small stones, though clear of boulders.

The condition of the roadbed must have been critical: the clay surface becomes very hard and stable if pressed heavily, but soft or muddy going would make statue transportation impossible. This implies that transportation took place during the drier summer, and was perhaps completely interrupted by wet wintry conditions (the very opposite of Pavel's suggestion, mentioned above): if so, and if statues were being moved upright, it is possible that those which had reached soft or potentially wet ground (like the first of those excavated by Heyerdahl in 1986) would have been given a stable temporary pedestal to prevent their tipping over; those on drier or solid ground (like the second) would not need a platform.

Recently, however, Love has examined about 20 km of the 40 km of roads built from *Rano Raraku* to various areas (ill. 73), primarily focusing on 3 main roadways plus several branch roads, and has excavated a total of 210 m (in 5 sectors) of the southern roadways; his preliminary findings are startling. They traverse old basalt flows and the shallow valleys between them, and have a basic cut-and-fill construction; excavation of 10 m and 20

75.1. Abandoned *moai* next *Rano Raraku*. Moai, Brett Shepardson, Rapanui Press.

m stretches has revealed how they were cleared, cut. graded and, in many places, filled with soil. Various grades up and down slopes were cut and filled to help the statue movers, and it is clear that a great deal of cooperative labour was required for these roads -in the valleys, the fill construction can be built up to a metre or more with layers of clayey soil to make a flat surface about 5 m wide. In at least one area, a pavement was made, apparently to facilitate the movement of *Paro* through a section of rough bedrock. Some stretches of road were carved into the surface of the higher basalt flows, apparently to avoid a flat surface, with paths cut into a shallow V or a broad U shape, about 5.5 m wide and 30 cm deep (though in other places the roads seem half-worn into the ground surface, presumably by centuries of footwear, rather than cut into bedrock).

Some segments of road have long rock alignments along the shoulders, which seem to be kerbstones set into the backfill, while others have numerous post holes dug into bedrock outside the kerbstones -presumably to accommodate some kind of contraption for pulling and prising the statue and its framework forward in places (thus perhaps confirming Lee's insight, mentioned above). Such features seem most common where the roadway slopes upwards [26].

Another possibility that has received little or no attention -perhaps owing to the constant crashing of the waves (though it did occur to the Americans in 1886)- is that some figures might have been transported the short 500 m (c. 1600 ft) distance from the quarry to the shore and then floated on timbers or rafts around the coast to the platforms where they were required. At several points around the coast there are lava-flow causeways, and also some paved ramps, which run into the sea. These *apapa* (which literally means 'unload') are generally seen as canoe-ramps, places for large vessels to land or unload: there is one next to *Paro*'s platform (*Ahu Te Pito Kura*), and Mulloy restored a fine sloping ramp of beach boulders at *Tahai*. It is therefore quite possible that some large blocks, and perhaps some statues,

75.2. *Moai*, on the interior slopes of the *Rano Raraku* statue quarry.
Moai, Brett Shepardson, Rapanui Press.

were transported by water. It is also worth noting that fragments of *Rano Raraku* tuff at a platform-like structure dating to AD 1174 on the offshore islet of *Motu Nui* have led to claims that at least two small statues were taken there [27]. Most specialists doubt the idea, but there are at least three submerged *moai* at the bottom of the sea [28].

One can only conclude, as so often in archaeology, that no single explanation suffices for all the statues: the giant statues found between the quarry and the platforms vary from 1.77 to 9 m (c. 6 to 30 ft) in length, and there is no reason to suppose that the same method of transportation was used for the smallest as for the biggest. Different techniques were probably used according to the size and style of figure, the distance to be travelled, and the manpower, timber and ropes available. As Pavel has pointed out, it is the weight and proportions of the statues which were the most important criteria in selecting the mode of transportation, because a 4 m statue is twice as tall as a 2 m specimen, but 8 times as heavy [29]. Love agrees that the road-form must have depended on the maximum weight of the next statue to be transported, and that doubtless the methods of moving the *moai* changed as larger and larger specimens were carved.

But in any case, we need to go back to the drawing board, because researchers have always assumed that the island's road bed surface was flat and the road horizontal, but, as his work shows clearly, none of the *moai*-moving theories or experimental methods presented so far can cope with the structure of the roads he has excavated! The cut parts of the road are not conducive to rollers or skids or tilting a statue along, and any contraption used would have to accommodate both the flat fill surfaces and the V-shaped surfaces [30].

So the mystery of statue transportation remains intact...

[1] Wolff 1948.
[2] Métraux 1957.
[3] Skjølsvold 1961, pp. 370-71.
[4] Pavel 1995, p. 72; 2009; Bahn 1995.
[5] Mulloy 1970.
[6] Cotterell & Kamminga 1990, pp. 226-32.
[7] von Saher 1994a.
[8] Gurley & Liller 1997.
[9] Adam 1988.
[10] Van Tilburg 1996, 1994.
[11] Fisher & Fisher 2000, pp. 98-133; Lee 1998, 1999; Love 2000; see also MacIntyre 1999.
[12] Lee 1998.
[13] Routledge 1919, p. 195.
[14] Mazière 1969; for another early suggestion regarding the 'refrigerator method', see *Rapa Nui Journal* 4 (2), 1990, p. 29.
[15] Pavel 1990, 1995, 2009.
[16] Heyerdahl et al. 1989; Pavel 1995, 2009.
[17] Love 1990.
[18] Lee 1998.
[19] Love 2000, p. 117. A recent experiment by Hunt & Lipo (2011; Bloch 2012; Lipo et al. 2013) once again showed, rather unnecessarily, that Pavel's swivel method can move an upright *moai* some metres.
[20] See letter by A. Padgett in *Rapa Nui Journal* 9 (4), 1995, pp. 124-5.
[21] *Rapa Nui Journal* 15 (1), 2001, p. 50.
[22] Routledge 1919, p. 194.
[23] Heyerdahl et al. 1989.
[24] Routledge 1919, pp. 194-96; Cauwe & De Dapper 2015.
[25] Lipo & Hunt 2005.
[26] Love 2000; see also *Rapa Nui Journal* 14 (2), 2000, pp. 61-2; 14 (3), 2000, p. 99; 15 (1), 2001, p. 50; 15 (2), 2001, p. 125; and C. M. Love, The Easter Island Mystery, *Discovering Archaeology* Nov/Dec 2000, p. 12.
[27] *Rapa Nui Journal* 5 (1), 1991, pp. 6-7; Edwards & Edwards 2013, p. 400.
[28] von Saher 1993a, p. 31; Sonia Haoa, pers. comm., December 2008. In a recent interview (Pelletier 2012, p. 134), Van Tilburg has likewise argued, in relation to the numerous canoe motifs carved on *moai*, that some were transported by sea; whereas Hunt & Lipo (201, p. 57), for some reason, consider the sensible notion of floating some *moai* on rafts a 'wacky idea'!
[29] Pavel 1995, 2009.
[30] Love 2000; *Rapa Nui Journal* 14 (3), 2000, p. 99.

So far, then, we have a large statue that has somehow arrived from the quarry: where is it to go? At this point, it is worth pausing to consider the phenomenon of the *ahu*, the rectangular platforms which have tended to be overshadowed -literally and metaphorically- by the statues [1]. Even without any statues on them, *Rapa Nui*'s platforms would be an archaeological wonder, for they are remarkable pieces of massive communal engineering, sometimes requiring the moving of 300 to 500 tons of stone: for example, the *Tahai* complex comprised three structures requiring about 23,000 cubic metres (c. 30,000 cubic yards) of rock and earth fill, estimated to weigh 2000 tons.

This tiny island has at least 313 platforms, which form an almost unbroken line round its coast except for areas of high cliffs (though a few are on cliff-edges), with distinct clusters around coves or good landing places and areas that are specially favourable for habitation. They range in size from quite small to over 150 m (c. 500 ft) in length and up to more than 4 m (c. 13 ft) in height, and comprise a rubble core faced with masonry, for which no mortar was used. The seaward façades often seem to have been placed as close to the shore as possible, and parallel to it, forming impressive walls which seem to rise straight out of the sea. These façades vary from uncut local stones to precisely carved and fitted blocks. To the landward side was a ramp, paved with lines of beach boulders and sloping down to an artificially flattened plaza (ill. 77): one such 'court' at *Tahai* measured 55 by 40 m

(180 by 130 ft). Around the coast, there seem to be major platform complexes on average every 0.7 km (c. 0.5 mile), marking boundaries and serving as residential and socio-political and religious centres. *Rapa Nui*'s platforms are very clearly variations of the *marae* -platforms of central and eastern Polynesia- this word, which clearly postdates the departure of the Easter Islanders from Polynesia since it is not part of the old *Rapa Nui* tongue, originates from the proto-Polynesian *malae* meaning 'meeting place', and different island groups have used such open spaces and platforms for similar purposes throughout the area: for example, the *heiau* of Hawai'i. In the Tuamotu, Society and Austral Islands, the word *ahu* referred only to the raised platform at the end of a rectangular court, whereas in the northern Marquesas and on Easter Island it meant the whole ceremonial centre. Numerous Polynesian *marae* are found inland, but many are coastal platforms, usually parallel to the shore.

A few platforms on Easter Island seem to have been built specifically to contain burials. This does not seem to have been the original function of the image-platforms, though Thomson's investigation of the immense *Tongariki* structure revealed a narrow corridor at its centre, full of human remains; instead, the normal *ahu* had multiple functions such as serving as a social and ritual centre, and a lineage and boundary marker. Burial seems to have been the exception rather than the rule in early periods on *Rapa Nui*, since no early skeletons have yet been found: cremation was far more common,

76. Engraving of an *ahu*, Cook expedition, 1774.

and elaborate cremation pits have been found behind the central platform at many complexes such as *Akivi* or *Ahu O Rongo* (although the lack of reddened rock indicates that the actual cremation took place elsewhere) [2]. These contain fragments of human bone mixed with beach pebbles, bits of obsidian and charcoal and a variety of artifacts such as fish-hooks, and occasional bones of chickens and rats. This therefore seems to be a mixture of cremation and of votive offerings and hence presents an analogy with the slab-lined pits placed next to Polynesian *marae* for the disposal of offerings and sacred paraphernalia. Cremation, however, was not practised in the rest of eastern and central Polynesia.

The study of *Rapa Nui*'s platforms is made especially difficult because many have been plundered over the years for building blocks and foundation stones, leaving what at first sight seem to be featureless piles of rubble. However, detailed examination of the remains can shed much light on their construction. Hydration dating (obsidian) and radiocarbon dating (charcoal) have established that some platforms were built in a single episode while others have constructions spanning centuries: most 'image *ahu*' have more than one construction event, and some have seven or eight [3]. At *Anakena*, for example, several generations of platform seem to have been built on top of each other, with the structures being enlarged over the centuries. Modifications to platforms would often incorporate old statues or old house-foundation slabs in their construction -for example, at *Tongariki*, where there was a complex sequence of expansion and recycling involving several platforms and pavements (ill. 78), and with earlier types of statues as blocks or fill [4]. This poses problems, since so many construction events remain undated in each *ahu*, and there is such continuity and diversity of architectural elements, that the few dozen platforms excavated so far cannot yield a clear picture of the evolution of the image

ahu form, and moreover, recent reconstructions of platforms may combine architectural features from more than one construction episode, and hence influence both archaeologists and the public, thus muddying the waters [5].

Nevertheless, in the opinion of those archaeologists who have excavated and studied the island's *ahu*, they reflect an overall stylistic continuity derived from the early Polynesian settlement, starting with small platforms which gradually increased in size and complexity as the statues changed from naturalistic forms to the highly stylized *moai* of ever-growing proportions. The three-stage chronological classification of *ahu* structures developed by the Norwegian expedition of the 1950s was later questioned by Mulloy & Figueroa, who saw no sharp changes, but rather a single period of uninterrupted development '...characterized by gradual introduction of new ideas, expansion of themes and improvement of capacities' [6].

The islanders took the basic Polynesian architectural form and gradually developed their own local elaborations, such as adding the ramps, as well as lower lateral extensions at either side. Excavations have revealed changes in form over time, with overlapping, abutting or out-of-line architectural features; these were not, however, contemporaneous or island-wide changes, which casts grave doubt on provisional sequences developed from the excavation of a very few platforms such as those at *Vinapu*: subsequent excavations at *Akivi*, for example, showed that it belonged to a far later period than expected. Some platforms were partially and deliberately destroyed before careful modifications took place -certain architectural features are not found all over the island but are very localized, emphasizing the rivalry between different clans or kin groups, perhaps each producing their own variation of the monuments.

77. Principal structures of a classic *ahu moai*:

1 Central Platform: Here the statues (1-15) were placed on foundations sculpted in basalt. Generally the front wall presents elaborate well-fitted rectangular basalt slabs (*paenga*). These are occasionally built over a cornice of rectangular blocks made of red scoria.

2 Wings: These were built from the ends of the *ahu* extending towards the sides of the central platform. Sometimes there are lower platforms and sloped ramps paved with round stones (*poro*) delimited by a rear and terminal wall.

3 Sloped ramp (*tahua*): This is paved with round stones of marine origin (*poro*).

4 Plaza: A ceremonial place which sometimes includes a stone circle used for ritual purposes (*paina*).

5 Moai: Statues made of volcanic tuff mostly carved at the *Rano Raraku* quarry.

6 Pukao: Hats or headdresses made of red scoria carved at the *Puna Pau* quarry.

7 Crematoria: These are lined with fine debris, fragments of red scoria and remains of charred bones.

8 Avanga: This is a chamber for depositing the whitened bones of clan members, and corresponds to later burials in the *Rapa Nui* cultural sequence.

9 Canoe ramp: These are located at some small wharfs near the *ahu*.

10 Hare paenga: These boat-shaped houses, also called *hare vaka*, were used by high-ranking islanders.

The very earliest platforms on the island may have been simple open-air altars without statues on them -it is very hard to tell because of all the subsequent changes they have undergone- or they may even have carried wooden figures like some in the Marquesas. Some had courtyards marked out by walls or a piece of levelled ground. The earliest such structure dated so far (AD 690) is the first phase of *Ahu Tahai*, which was a narrow, flat-topped platform of rubble fill surrounded by masonry; it was later extended by lateral wings, and may possibly have had a red scoria statue on it rather than a *moai* of later, classic type. Such a scoria figure was indeed found here, and its rounded, naturalistic features, circular eyes and normal 'human' ears, together with its raw material are all reminiscent of some *tiki* figures of the Marquesas. A similar statue was exposed in the fill of *Ahu Tongariki* after that was destroyed to its foundations by the 8 m tsunami (tidal wave) of 1960 (caused by an earthquake off Chile); and two partial figures were incorporated in the late-phase wings of *Ahu Heki'i*. It is probable that such small red figures were the precursors of the *moai*, and stood on top of, or in front of, the earliest platforms just like the small statues or simple upright slabs that represent chiefs at the *marae* elsewhere in Polynesia.

The few scoria statues found on the island seem to span at least as long a time as the *moai*, and regardless of whether they ever stood on early platforms themselves, they are often closely associated with the structures and the cult activities that took place there. Red scoria [7] was also used as a landward facing for certain platforms (*Akahanga, Vinapu*), and Linton Palmer said in 1868 that there was at least one 'pillar statue' in this stone (like the one found at *Vinapu*) at every image platform. In other words, scoria statues were probably made throughout the prehistoric period, both before and alongside the giant statues as a separate but related phenomenon.

The first phase of *Ahu Akivi*, unusual because it is located inland and faces the sea, seems to have been a simple 35 m (115 ft) *ahu* with two 20 m (65 ft) lateral wings but no evidence of statues; instead, it is possible that a large polygonal slab (found in the fill of the later phase) had been set upright on it like on a Polynesian *marae*, and the same may be true of a small, 1 m (3 ft) high image of *Rano Raraku* tuff found in the same fill. Around AD 1460, this platform was rebuilt to support seven large statues on pedestals, and the wings and ramp were raised substantially, with rows of beach stones added [8].

The earliest known 'classical' statue of *Rano Raraku* tuff that originally stood on a platform is located just north of *Tahai*, and dates to the 12th century AD. It is over 5 m (16 ft) high, weighs 20 tons, and shows that the quarry was operating by this time, and that the classic statue form was already well developed; the latest date we have for a platform with a statue is c. AD 1650, a figure at *Hanga Kio'e*, over 4 m (13 ft) high and weighing 14 tons. In other words, we know that statue quarrying was carried out at *Rano Raraku* for at least five hundred years and probably rather more.

Despite the early date from *Tahai* (see above), the latest orthodoxy, based largely on the excavations at *Anakena*, is that ceremonial sites began c. AD 1000-1100, with a subsequent expansion phase. Certainly, the building of platforms seems to have become an obsession by c. AD 1200, and this 'golden age', the peak construction time for both platforms and statues, lasted until the end of the 16th century [9].

It is important to note that, according to astronomer William Liller, between 15 and 20 platforms show at least reasonable evidence of having been oriented or positioned astronomically, mostly towards important sunrise or sunset positions [10]. More than 90 per cent of coastal platforms were built with their long axis closely parallel to the shore, as elsewhere

78. Cross section of an *ahu*:

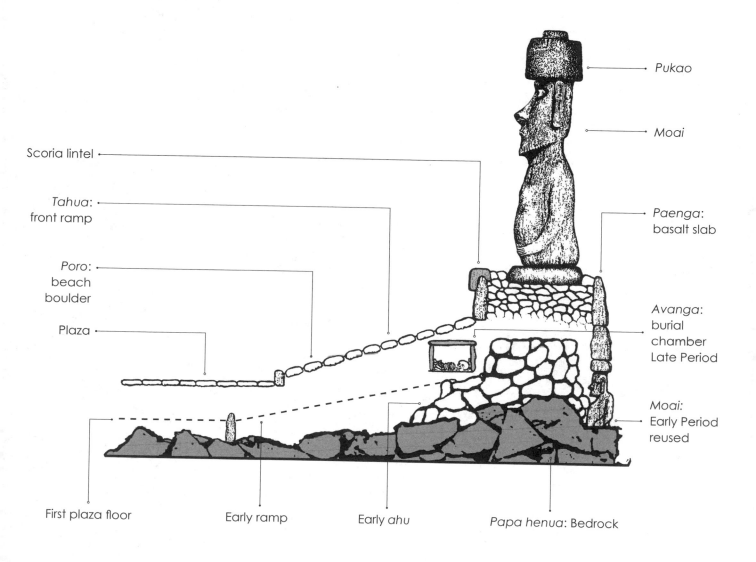

Pukao

Moai

Scoria lintel

Tahua: front ramp

Poro: beach boulder

Plaza

Paenga: basalt slab

Avanga: burial chamber Late Period

Moai: Early Period reused

First plaza floor

Early ramp

Early *ahu*

Papa henua: Bedrock

in Polynesia where they were useful navigational aids; but six coastal platforms that are not parallel to the shore have their long axis aligned North–South and face the rising equinox. Some inland platforms seem to be directed towards the rising winter solstice, marking the time when days are shortest and the sun is lowest in the sky. It is noteworthy that the three most outstanding monuments on the island -*Vinapu*, *Tongariki* and *Heki'i*- have all five of their central platforms oriented to the rising solstice or equinox. The summit of *Poike* was probably used as a calendar indicator since the winter solstice sun rises over it as seen from *Orongo*. Oral traditions record that priests also watched the rising and setting of particular star constellations which signalled the times for certain rituals, feasts, and agricultural or fishing activities (and it is worth mentioning that a cluster of fifty-six small cupmarks at *Matariki* on the northwest coast resemble a kind of star map). The islanders would have found it crucial to know the onset of the seasons for crop-planting, owing to their subtropical, somewhat temperate climate, while birds, fish and turtles all followed seasonal patterns of appearance.

The platforms were, as already mentioned, a mass of rubble encased in retaining walls of varying quality. There is now no doubt that the famous precisely fitted and smoothly pecked basalt slabs that form a façade on the seaward side of some platforms, such as *Vinapu* (ill. 14) and one or two others, were the final stage in their construction, and in some cases were added as a finishing touch after the statues were already standing: their mass, together with that of the ramp at the other side, enables the platforms to resist the immense lateral push exerted by the weight of the statues. This is not, therefore, an archaic feature, and in no way points to any connection with Andean civilizations.

On Easter Island, the best façade slabs commonly weigh 2 or 3 tons: at *Vinapu* one slab measures 2.5 by 1.7 m (8 by 5.5 ft), and probably weighs 6 or 7 tons, while one at *Ahu Vai Mata* is 3 by 2 m (10 by 6 ft), weighing 9 or 10 tons. Such feats of construction are by no means unique in the region, however. In the 19th century, European visitors wondered how Tahitians could move huge masses, such as 3-ton logs, over great distances with just levers and rollers; and some of the logs transported by New Zealand's Maori to make their canoes often weighed far more than *Rapa Nui*'s statues. Similar prodigious feats can be found all over Polynesia, and Tahiti's *marae* of Mahaiatea is over 100 m (over 325 ft) long, while platforms in the Marquesas can be 120 m (c. 390 ft) long and 30 m (c. 100 ft) wide, comprising blocks of more than 10 tons [11]. It has been estimated that even modest platforms could require months of work by at least twenty people.

The frequent finds of large quantities of obsidian flakes within the fill of excavated *Rapa Nui* platforms suggest that they played a role in the construction, perhaps in cutting or trimming fibres for rope (the islanders claim that stone blocks were moved around on sledges), smoothing levers, or simply in food preparation [12].

The last type of platform to be built on the Island seems to have been semipyramidal, a dramatically different form usually superimposed on the earlier, classic statue-bearing types and often constructed of stones torn from these predecessors. Fewer than 75 semipyramidal platforms are known, in contrast to the more than 125 image-platforms. They never carried statues, and are mostly made from stones that would rarely require the cooperation of more than 2 or 3 men (in contrast to the image *ahu*, where many stones -let alone the *moai*- must have required the cooperation of dozens of men) [13]. All of them seem to have been ossuaries, designed purely to receive burials, like some of the earlier non-image platforms.

79. *Ahu Nau Nau*, at *Anakena* beach.
Photo: Eduardo Ruiz-Tagle.

Assuming that we have a platform that has been strengthened in preparation, how did they get the statue up there? Captain Cook reckoned that the figures were raised little by little, supported by stones. Receveur, a priest accompanying La Pérouse in 1786, agreed, suggesting that the figures had been raised quite easily by using levers and progressively slipping stones underneath. Most speculation since then has concurred, envisaging the gradual construction of a ramp of earth and stones on which the statue would be raised and then tipped over into place.

This technique was first tried out on the island in 1955 when William Mulloy, during his excavations at *Vinapu*, needed to replace in the platform wall a fallen slab weighing over 2 tons, which lay 2 m (6 ft) in front of, and 1 m (3 ft) below, where it should be. Six islanders using two long levers set about raising each side of the slab, and sliding material beneath it to make a masonry platform, until it lay above its destination. Then it was gradually tilted, levered and pushed into place. The whole operation took one hour.

In another important experiment carried out during Heyerdahl's expedition of 1955, a fallen statue of 25 tons at *Anakena* (ill. 79) was raised 3 m (10 ft) in the same simple way; by using two levers (5 m [16 ft] long) and slipping stones underneath, twelve islanders built a ramp under it, and had it standing on its platform in only eighteen days [14]. It was first raised horizontally until it had reached the same height as the platform; then its head alone was raised, until the sloping figure could be simply slid forward and tilted to a vertical position. Since the levers were used against the statue itself, large scars were caused, suggesting that the original builders might have protected the figures with padding. However, they may not always have done so, because Love has found that tilting a statue to its place on an *ahu* produces marks that match what one sees elsewhere: i.e. toppled statues often have chipped bases, but only on their lateral edges, where sometimes gigantic pressure flakes have been driven off upward from the base; and many of those fallen along roadways likewise have huge chips driven upward from their lateral edges [15].

There are few archaeological traces of massive ramps on Easter Island: at *Akahanga* the remains of a masonry mound lie to the landward side of a platform and a statue seems to have fallen off it; other platforms, such as *Te Pito Kura*, do have tremendous numbers of stones nearby which may be the traces of raising operations. Ramps would also have involved colossal amounts of extra labour in their construction and removal. However, the ramp idea largely arose because of the island's alleged lack of wood. Since we now know that timber was once in plentiful supply, it has also been suggested that an alternative method might have been used, namely the construction of simple, solid wooden scaffolds of criss-crossed beams; such a scaffold would have been just as effective as a ramp, but would take less time and effort to set up and dismantle. During the restoration of *Ahu Akivi* in 1960, Mulloy's team did use a rectangular timber armature against which the levering was done -it is worth noting that excavations in *Akivi*'s plaza found many post holes up to 2 m (6 ft) deep. It took a month to erect the first of *Ahu Akivi*'s seven 16-ton statues, but the seventh took less than a week, showing the benefit of experience for unpractised hands. It is safe to assume that the prehistoric islanders knew exactly how to set up the figures with a minimum of effort.

But so far, all experiments and theorizing on this topic have involved horizontal statues; what if the figures arrived upright at their platforms, as discussed above? There seems no good reason to doubt that, with care, these very stable figures could have been raised in the same gradual way, being tilted first one way and then the other, as stones or logs were inserted beneath them.

Even more extraordinary than the raising of the statues, followed by the insertion of their eyes into the sockets, was their crowning glory, the *pukao*: a soft red scoria cylinder from the quarry of *Puna Pau*. These seem to have been a late addition, associated only with statues on the largest and most important platforms of late phases, since most platform statues (e.g. those of *Akivi*) do not have them, and fewer than 100 are known to exist (Englert counted 58 fallen from statues on platforms -although there were 164 *moai* erected on *ahu*- plus 31 *pukao* still in their quarry). They should be seen perhaps as a sign of the continuing rivalry between villages or kin-groups, determined to 'keep up with the Joneses' and outdo each other in the splendour of their monuments and in their homage to the ancestors with further symbolism: in the Marquesas, a great stone was placed on the image of a dead

man as a sign of death and mourning, and the *pukao* may have had a similar meaning.

Debate continues about the precise nature of these cylinders; in the past, some scholars have suggested they represented grass-hats or a kind of turban made of painted paper-mulberry or *tapa* (cylindrical head-dresses are found in much of Polynesia), others that they were dressed and stained top-knots of hair, or wigs; it goes without saying that von Däniken saw them as space helmets! Red was a significant colour associated with ritual and chiefly power throughout Polynesia, and hair was sometimes coated with red ochreous earth in Melanesia. At present, the most likely explanation is that they are a stylized version of the *hau kurakura*, a red feather head-dress worn by warriors -the early European visitors saw islanders wearing feathers on their heads, and some circular

80. The experiment undertaken by twelve islanders for the Norwegian expedition of 1955. A 25 ton statue at *Anakena* was raised In 18 days, by using two levers and slipping stones beneath it to build a ramp.

81. Restoration work at the *Ahu Tahai* in 1968. The same crane was used later to install the *pukao*.

or cylindrical feather head-dresses have actually survived. Throughout Polynesia, red feathers were identified with the spiritual power of the gods [16].

For a long time it was uncertain how the scoria head-dresses were set in place, and those to be seen today on restored statues were all put there by cranes, not without difficulty (ill. 81). It would be a major undertaking to raise any *pukao*, but what of *Paro*'s monstrous specimen -almost 2 m (6 ft) across, 1.7 m (5.5 ft) high, and weighing about 11.5 tons? Even bigger examples lie in the quarry. Cook suggested that ramps or scaffolding were used. Some scholars, such as Mulloy and Adam [17], even proposed that the cylinders might have been raised at the same time as the statues, and that they were solidly lashed together; most scholars, however, feel this is far too risky, and that the red cylinders were almost certainly a later addition -for example, one unfinished cylinder now lies abandoned 150 m (nearly 500 ft) from the single-statue platform (*Ahu Ature Huke*) for which it was intended.

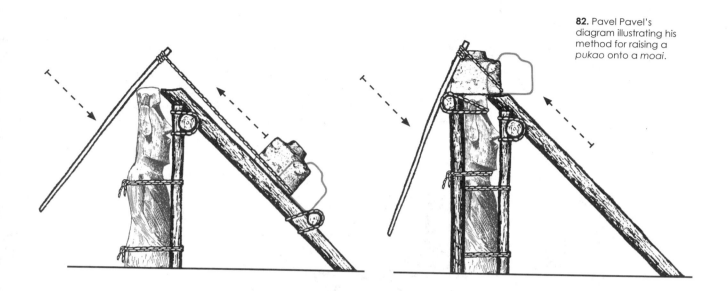

82. Pavel Pavel's diagram illustrating his method for raising a *pukao* onto a *moai*.

Their cylindrical shape implies that the head-dresses were often rolled from quarry to platform, using levers, and reworked there before being raised. Some were carved to a more elliptical cross-section, and a shallow mortise pecked into the base -this may have been to set it more firmly on the statue's flat head-, with a slight projection over the eyes (some of the *Anakena* figures even have tenons on their heads to fit these mortises). Some *pukao* take the form of a truncated cone, while others were given a narrower boss or knob at the top (ill. 79). All such modifications, of course, had the advantage of reducing the cylinder's weight.

The likely answer to the enigma came through experiments by Czech engineer Pavel Pavel who applied the same technique as he used to raise the 6-ton lintel of a replica Stonehenge trilithon: the method was surprisingly simple (ill. 82), and involved gradually pulling the *pukao* up sloping beams of wood. A concrete *pukao*, 1 m in diameter and weighing 900 kg, was raised onto the top of a 3 m concrete *moai* by only 4 men in 6 hours! [18]

González in 1770 reported that the cylinders contained a slight hollow on the upper surface in which the bones of the dead were placed. Roggeveen's party in 1722 observed a 'corona' of white balls or stones on them, some scholars believe these may in fact have been whitened bones, but many white, coral-encrusted beach cobbles have been found during work at *Anakena*, where it is likely they were used to decorate the platforms. Another possibility is that the white eyes, which were sometimes inserted into the statues' eye sockets, may have been stored on the *pukao* above. The phenomenon of the giant statues and platforms is clearly far more complex than it at first appears, and some major questions remain: for example, why were some statues quarried inside the crater of *Rano Raraku* when this would entail much extra effort to get them out of there even before starting the journey to the platforms? Did this add to their prestige? Possibly; but on the whole the statues inside the crater are smaller and less carefully made than those outside. Is it feasible, therefore, that those inside the crater were never intended to be removed, but were set up there permanently, facing the lake? This would help explain why there were far more statues left finished or unfinished at the quarry than could ever have been allotted to existing platforms. In fact one statue inside RR was dropped into a hole hollowed out of bedrock, which was labour-intensive and unnecessary if the placement were to be temporary [19].

The Belgian archaeologist Lavachery suggested that the unfinished statues were bas-reliefs -a theory also applied to El Gigante, as mentioned earlier- but he envisaged this as the first, primitive stage in an evolution of statue carving. It is, however, possible to propose an alternative view based on

hierarchy and one-upmanship: namely, that the whole spectrum of statues and platforms reflected the prestige of the commissioning groups and their wealth.

From this viewpoint, it could be argued that outlined or unfinished statues were the 'cheapest' option, involving nothing more than a little carving; those left unfinished inside the crater would be the least prestigious of all, being the least visible and not potentially movable. Presumably, work could resume later to finish the figure if funds were forthcoming. Completed and extracted statues would be more expensive, involving more carving and some effort in moving them: Routledge

noticed that there were fewer completed statues inside than outside. The place where figures were set up expressed the degree of prestige they reflected: those set up inside the crater were perhaps intended to stay there for ever, while those moved down to the plain and set upright may have been intended to remain there, but also were potentially transportable to platforms if the commissioning group were eventually to acquire the necessary resources. This would explain the sheer numbers of statues in and around the quarry, movement of which was obviously neither imminent nor anticipated. In fact, Love has suggested that many of these statues were commissioned by people who had already realised that there would

83. *Ahu Tongariki*, one of the most impressive megalithic monuments in Polynesia. Like others, its *moai* were knocked down during the wars, and the monument was finally destroyed by the tsunami of 1960. Their restoration, supported by Japan, was completed in 1995.

not be sufficient resources of timber, etc, to move them at all, but nevertheless wished to honour the ancestors by the carving of an image [20].

The most prestigious statues, of course, were those that were actually transported and erected on platforms. Here, as we have already seen, the factors of distance travelled, size and weight of statue, and size and splendour of platform all played a role in the prestige game. Some groups seem to have poured all their resources into acquiring a single enormous figure, like *moai Paro*. The really powerful centres took this to extremes, as in *Vinapu*'s superb masonry and *Tongariki*'s fifteen figures on a single platform, while the royal centre of *Anakena* featured statues with unique, elaborate designs carved on them.

Tongariki (ill. 83) was by far the biggest ceremonial structure ever built on the island; its central platform was almost 100 m long, and with the addition of two wings its total length was about 220 m. The average height of the seaward wall is 4 m, and it comprises more than 800 'irregular, unworked, crudely fitted basalt blocks' [21]. Its 15 statues are from 5.6 to 8.7 m tall, with an average weight of more than 40 metric tons (the largest, near the centre, is 88 metric tons), so that in total, with *pukao* in place, this monument was up to 14 m high! The final touch, apparently a late development, and perhaps triggered, once again, by one-upmanship, was the placing of head-dresses on top of the statues, a truly awesome and prestigious feat of engineering, commanding respect and reflecting the power of

83.1. At present the *ahu* have lost their colour, but it is possible that, like Maya temples, in the past they looked splendid like in this illustration (Lukas), full of colour and life.

the group responsible. As we have seen, only the biggest and richest platforms had such *pukao*.

Other touches of splendour included the occasional use of red scoria blocks to decorate parts of the platform, and perhaps (despite lack of solid evidence) the painting (ill. 83.1) of the statues: Dundas in 1871 reported of some of the fallen *moai* of *Vinapu* that '...some of them seem to have been decorated with paintings of canoes and other rude figures, done in red, black and white earths' [22], but this sounds like painting done after the statues came down. No early European visitor mentioned paint on the ordinary *moai*, but Métraux believed that some of the statues were painted [23]. Certainly when *Hoa Hakananai'a* (see below, p. 231) was first seen by Europeans in 1868, its back was painted red and white -most of the paint was inadvertently washed off when the statue was floated out to HMS *Topaze* [24].

Recent work on the island by Mieth and Bork has revealed evidence for pigment production on a massive scale on the slopes of Terevaka, on Poike, and elsewhere. They have found hundreds of pits up to 2.4 m in diameter and 0.4 m deep, full of reddish silt-like material. At Terevaka there seems to have been a huge outdoor workshop for the manufacture of special pigments, dyes or paints. The process involved some burning, which has been dated to the first half of the 13th century, with other phases in the 15th century. The pigment was a very pure biogenic iron oxide, obtained by burning plants high in iron content -probably rhizomes of the totora reed from the *Rano Aroi* swamp above. They calculate that 1 kg of pure iron oxide would have required 1.7 tons of fresh rhizome- so a great deal of work was involved, and the burning required an abundance of fuel, which seems to have been primarily grass [25].

Imagine, then, a finished platform of grey, white and sometimes red stone, on which stand a number of yellowish statues with bright white eyes and crowned by red cylinders and white stones. The statues and even the platforms may also have been painted, and smaller red figures stood in some forecourts. In other words, Easter Island was encircled by numerous impressive, vivid, highly colourful monuments testifying to the ingenuity, faith and communal spirit of its inhabitants.

What happened to tear this picture apart from within?

[1] Martinsson-Wallin 1994, 1996a, 2001; Martinsson-Wallin & Wallin 1998b; see also Heyerdahl & Ferdon 1961; Mulloy 1997; Love 1983; Seelenfreund 1988; Ayres 1988; Huyge & Cauwe 2002.

[2] Mulloy & Figueroa 1978; Huyge & Cauwe 2002; Love 2010.

[3] Love 1993, p. 104; 2010. Edwards & Edwards (2013, p. 317) estimate that it may have taken hundreds of workers 2-3 years to build the average *ahu moai*, and ethnographic evidence indicates that platforms were modified or rebuilt every three generations, or roughly every 100 years (ibid., p. 310).

[4] Cristino & Vargas 1998, 1999.

[5] Love 1993, p. 110.

[6] Mulloy & Figueroa 1978; see also Skjølsvold 1996.

[7] Van Tilburg 1986a.

[8] Mulloy & Figueroa 1978.

[9] Martinsson-Wallin & Wallin 1998a, 1998b, 2000.

[10] Liller 1990, 1991, 1993a, 1993b; Mulloy 1975.

[11] Métraux 1957, p. 166.

[12] Love 1990a, p. 17.

[13] Love 1993, p. 105; 2010.

[14] Skjølsvold 1961, p. 372; Heyerdahl et al. 1989.

[15] Love 2000, p. 118.

[16] Skinner 1967; Barrow 1967, p. 193.

[17] Mulloy 1970; Adam 1988.

[18] Pavel 1995, 2009. See also Lee 2012, 2013.

[19] Van Tilburg 2006, p. 17.

[20] Love 2010.

[21] Cristino & Vargas 1998, 1999.

[22] Dundas 2000, p. 39.

[23] Métraux 1957, p. 153.

[24] Van Tilburg 2006, p. 37; Horley & Lee 2008, pp. 113-4.

[25] Mieth & Bork 2015. Van Tilburg & Arévalo (2012, p. 78) encountered 800 gm of red pigment in their recent excavations of two *moai* in the inner quarry.

Group of islanders. Rapanui Press.

Part III

The aftermath

*Perhaps the thing
that most distinguishes
islands, at least
oceanic islands…
is their extreme
vulnerability
or susceptibility to
disturbance.*

Raymond Fosberg

Chapter 9

Crash go the ancestors

*I don't know how I am to make a fire
on that island,
there is no wood!*

Bailey, Katherine Routledge's ship's cook

If Captain Cook had stayed longer than the four days he spent there in 1774, there would probably never have been any mysteries of Easter Island. Cook was an astute observer and recorded what he saw with meticulous accuracy. He would probably have discovered the religious significance of the giant statues, the history of their downfall, and the meaning of the *rongo rongo*. He would certainly have described the island and its environmental state more fully than he did. But, as far as we know, neither Cook nor any other early visitor made these records. Easter Island was, as we have seen, visited by over a hundred ships -mostly whalers- between 1800 and 1900, but it is only a remote possibility that some unknown manuscript may survive. The history of Easter Island is therefore lost forever. Or is it? Even if written records are non-existent, and oral traditions of very limited use, there are records of another kind: those provided by archaeology and, as we have seen, by pollen analysis.

Violence erupts – toppled statues

We have a rough idea of when the islanders began to topple the statues; neither Roggeveen in 1722 nor González in 1770 mentions having seen fallen statues; the Dutch saw only a small part of the island during their one-day visit, but the Spanish saw considerably more during their six days, so it is a fair bet that all *moai*, or very nearly all, were still upright in 1770 (but since the Spanish sailed past the point from which the hugely impressive *Tongariki* platform with its 15 statues would have been visible, and since they made no mention of it, it is possible that the *Tongariki moai* were already down by 1770 [1]). Only four years later, however, when Captain Cook arrived, the situation was very different: he was the first to report that many statues had been overturned next to their platforms, and that the monuments were no longer maintained. Skeletal material was now strewn about the figures. One platform (probably at *Vinapu*) had three fallen and four upright figures, one of the latter having lost its head-dress [2].

Four statues were still standing in *Hanga Roa* (Cook's) Bay, and seven at *Vinapu*, when the Russian Lisjanskij visited in 1804 (he saw at least twenty-one upright statues altogether, on at least eight different monuments) [3], but his compatriot Kotzebue found them toppled in 1816 except for two survivors at *Vinapu*; all monuments on the Bay had been totally destroyed by 1825. The last eye-witness account we have of standing statues on the island is that of the French admiral Abel Dupetit-Thouars in 1838 who, on the west coast, saw '...a platform on which were set four red statues, equidistant from one another, their summits covered with white stones'; by 1868 the visiting English surgeon Linton Palmer reported that not a single *moai* remained upright, and the missionaries of the 1860s scarcely mention the statues at all. So between 1722, when the Dutch thought the statue cult was still underway, and 1774, when Cook thought it a thing of the past, something drastic had happened.

Cook's companion Forster suggested that the fallen statues at *Vinapu* could have toppled because of an earthquake; recently, geologist Oscar González-Ferrán has pointed out that Easter Island is in a very active earthquake zone, and since 80% of the *moai* have fallen to the west, he speculates they were toppled by an earth tremor [4]. However, there is absolutely no mention of such a recent and devastating catastrophe (or indeed of any tsunamis) in the island's rich oral traditions; on the contrary, tales relate how, for example, the *Tongariki* statues were thrown down by an evil priest; there are many stories of strife on the island, and Métraux was clearly told that the statues were deliberately toppled by people, and the islanders referred to 'the wars of the throwing down of the statues' [5]. Finally, it is worth mentioning that a quake with a magnitude of 6.3 occurred on the island in 1987, but had not the slightest effect on any re-erected statues! The same applies to 13 quakes in the region in June 2005, of 5.7 or less, and another 300 miles to the west in May 2006, of 5.6 [6].

The toppling was often no mean achievement, and must have involved ropes and a number of men, and perhaps the removal of rocks from the rubble foundations -this may be why *Paro*, the tallest and heaviest statue ever erected on a platform, was also the last to be overthrown, its huge head-dress coming to rest a few metres in front of it. But simple toppling or undermining was sometimes not enough. In one or two cases, rocks were placed so as to deliberately break the statues' faces. Most were toppled landward, perhaps to cover the eyes;

in one case, a statue resting face-upward had its eye area completely pulverized, again a task of considerable effort. These attacks on head and eyes probably reflect the location of the figures' *mana*, they were not just toppled but had their power totally extinguished: Cook wrote of the fallen statues that '...every one except one were broken by the fall and otherways defaced', while Geiseler reported in 1882 that '...they view the tipped over statues as being still alive; only the broken idols are thought of as dead and without any powers whatsoever' [7].

It is certain that statues had been destroyed at times throughout the centuries, to make way for new ones, with fragments (especially heads) being incorporated into new building phases in the platforms. Some figures were toppled into prepared excavations in platform ramps, and were then buried fully or partially. But the real piecemeal destruction eventually came about through feuding and wars between groups who had previously vied with each other in the size and splendour of their monuments. It was only fitting that the vanquished should therefore have humiliating damage inflicted on their proud symbols by the victors: outrages inflicted on these ancestral figures were symbolically inflicted on the whole group. Tit-for-tat acts of this kind would quickly have decimated the number of standing statues.

In recent years, some strange views have been presented concerning the throwing down of the statues: for example, Hunt and Lipo have claimed that 'in some cases toppling of statues may have been purposeful, but many more likely came down as a result of inattention and lack of maintenance' [sic], while Cauwe insists that they were all lowered gently and carefully, to be re-used in different ways (such as coverings for tombs), but that subsequent material stress and fatigue caused some breakage. It is doubtful that anyone seeing the broken statues at Vinapu and other platforms could agree that

84. Engraving by Pierre Loti dedicated to Sarah Bernhardt, 1872.

85. *Mata'a*: A weapon used only in Polynesia, as a spearhead or mace.

Right: *Ua*: The most characteristic weapons in Polynesia were the clubs. In *Rapa Nui* the longest is called *paoa* and the shortest *ua*.

gentle handling followed by stress and fatigue can possibly account for their condition, as Mulloy already showed very convincingly in his excavations at Vinapu. Besides, one might point out that, throughout the island's history, fragments of statues were constantly used in wall construction and platform-fill, so in fact it would have been a great help to the islanders to have them shatter into pieces when they fell – surely they were not all destined to be tomb roofs! Cauwe has also emphasised the fact that the *pukao* or head-dresses are often intact, but these are huge solid pieces of rock, which may have fallen onto soft soil. A fall of only a few metres would be most unlikely to have shattered most of them. And if, as Cauwe believes, it was important to preserve the statues' faces, why were they not lowered onto their backs, instead of thrown down into a prone position? [8]

Mata'a

A further, dramatic symptom of violence and strife is the sudden appearance in the late prehistoric period of weapons made of obsidian, a material used previously only for tools. *Mata'a* were large, stemmed flakes used hafted as daggers and as spearheads (ill. 85); the earliest known are two from a layer at *Ahu Nau Nau*, dating to AD 1220-1420 [9], but they really proliferated in the 18th and 19th centuries when they became the commonest artifact on the island. Owing to their size, only one or two could be obtained from each slab mined, but the sheer abundance of obsidian available led to no apparent decrease in quality over time, and thousands of *mata'a* were produced: Routledge reported finding hoards of fifty or sixty under stones in caves [10], while Mulloy's excavations uncovered 402 at *Vinapu* alone. The Dutch in 1722 had reported that the islanders were all unarmed, but in 1774 Cook's party saw a few clubs and spears. Forster said that '...some... had lances or spears made of thin ill-shaped sticks, and pointed with a sharp triangular piece of black glassy lava' [11]. Most weapons must have been kept hidden, however, since in 1786 La Pérouse claimed that the islanders were all unarmed. The Spanish visitors of 1770 saw conspicuous evidence of *mata'a* wounds on several natives (see below) [12].

Recently, claims have been made by a few researchers that the *mata'a* were not weapons at all, but were simply for cutting or processing plants. The idea that they could have been agricultural tools, however, is ludicrous – has any culture anywhere in the world ever used brittle glass implements for such work? The islanders had basalt and other hard materials for adzes and other heavy-duty tools. But, in the absence of metal, the only sharp material they had was obsidian, and it is obvious that they always used its flakes for cutting plants, etc – as mentioned above (p. 113), Bouman already noticed this in 1722. It is certainly true that, as analyses by Flas

86. *Ahu Tongariki* in 1985, before being restored. Photo: Eduardo Ruiz-Tagle.

and by Lipo et al. have shown, the *mata'a* have a highly varied range of types, shapes and sizes, and most would not have made good projectile points [13]. There may be numerous reasons for this – for example, many of them probably had multiple uses, constituting the islanders' 'Swiss army knife' – think of how many things a pocket knife or dagger would have been used for in prehistoric or medieval times. And the apparently very late invention of this tool type presumably meant that very few people were skilled enough to produce good ones, and many poorly-made specimens were thus manufactured by unskilled hands. As the vast majority of *mata'a* have been surface finds, it is unsurprising that their edges are usually somewhat damaged and have lost sharpness – while cleaning has obviously removed any chance of residues reflecting their possible uses.

Where use-wear analyses are concerned, it should be recalled that obsidian is a particularly difficult material from which to obtain accurate data. But even accepting the validity of the few published analyses, it is noteworthy that in each case only a very few *mata'a* were analysed, sometimes just fragments, and the vast majority were done on flakes. So to dismiss *mata'a* as weapons on the basis of such scant evidence, when hundreds, if not thousands, of them were made, seems somewhat illogical. [14] And if they were all simple kitchen utensils, why do they appear in such large numbers relatively suddenly and so late in the island's occupation? And why do they occur in large caches? As Englert, one of the foremost specialists of the island's ancient culture, put it, 'The weapons used by the islanders in their own conflicts were primitive but deadly. Both traditions and archaeological evidence suggest that some of them at least may have been newly developed at the time of the internal conflicts to meet the problems that arose. One such weapon was the *mata'a*, a large crudely percussion-flaked spearhead with a projecting tang... they used to be

scattered over the surface of the island in endless numbers. Tremendous quantities of them must have been made. Though obsidian tools of many kinds are found buried in the earlier archaeological deposits, the *mata'a* do not appear there. They seem to have come into use shortly before the arrival of the first Europeans... These large blades are described as producing ghastly wounds with their ragged, razor-sharp edges' [15].

It is simply astonishing that some researchers such as Mulrooney et al. have stated that the *mata'a* 'do not appear to have been used as weapons', a claim which blatantly ignores all the available evidence. Indeed, amid thousands of classic *mata'a*, only one miniature hafted scraper is known. This view is contradicted not only by the testimony of early visitors such as Forster, but also by many others; Eyraud, in his account of his arrival on the island in 1864, reported that 'The men were armed with a kind of spear made of a long stick and a sharp stone fixed at one extremity', and also mentioned 'men armed with spears' elsewhere. Thomson devoted no less than three pages to weapons and war: 'The native weapons in offensive and defensive operations were limited to obsidian-pointed spears, short clubs, and the throwing-stones....Two kinds of spears were used, one about 6 feet long for throwing and the other a shorter one... the various forms of obsidian points were secured by a lashing made from the indigenous hemp'; he also described the tradition concerning the invention of the obsidian spearpoint, and presented a large collection of obsidian spearpoints 'showing the nine classes into which they are divided by the natives... These spear-heads were fastened to poles about 8 feet long, by lashings of hemp, and formed the chief weapon used by the natives in their frequent strifes' [16].

Geiseler too stated clearly that 'The chief weapon was all along the spear... they bound onto an approximately 1 inch wide stick of [mulberry] an arrow-shaped, polished point of obsidian... The spear was a formidable weapon because of its sharp point.' According to Routledge, 'the chief weapon was made from obsidian... hoards [of *mata'a*] were occasionally found..', while Métraux presented a full account of obsidian spearpoints, including two in the British Museum with their original hafting, and also described the 'legend of the origin of the spears'. One should also not forget that in 1872 Pierre Loti acquired a specimen attached at the end of a long shaft, and mentioned that 'lances de silex' hung from house walls. And Ayres et al. stated that the *mata'a* is 'referred to traditionally by Easter Islanders as a weapon... that is, a point for a spear *(kaukau)* or thrusting lance *(vero)*, and hafted examples are known in ethnological collections' [17].

Finally, one should mention an account of the pursuit of a Peruvian slaver by an islander called Tori. Years later the Peruvian returned to Easter Island and offered gifts to his pursuer who had shouted to him to stand and fight. In the account it states 'Tori could easily have thrown his *mata'a* (spear) and have killed that young man, but he did not want to throw at the young man's back.' And Tori himself makes the following explanation: 'I could easily have thrown my *mata'a* at your back and have killed you but I didn't want to' and an intermediary repeats 'He didn't want to cut you with his *mata'a* from behind. You would now be dead with his *mata'a*. He didn't wish to cut you from behind' [18].

In view of all the above testimony, it baffles us how anyone can seriously claim that the *mata'a* 'do not appear to have been used as weapons,' or that this is entirely a late-European misinterpretation of these objects! This is special pleading at its very worst, as well as highly insulting to the many early researchers whose testimony is thus cast aside. And in fact there is even more evidence, as we shall now see.

Skeletal evidence for violence

It is equally baffling that Cauwe, like others, has claimed that 'aucun témoin ne rencontra d'hommes blessés ou portant d'autres séquelles inhérentes à de la violence'. As mentioned above, the Spanish visitors of 1770 saw conspicuous evidence of *mata'a* wounds on several natives: '...in some we observed sundry wounds on the body, which we thought to have been inflicted by cutting instruments of iron or steel, we found that they proceeded from stones, which are their only [weapons of] defence and offence, and as most of these are sharp edged they produce the injury referred to'. Geiseler stated that the islanders' spears 'caused deep, mostly fatal, and, in other cases, hard to heal wounds. One skull showed that it was pierced through by a single thrust of the spear'. The missionary Zumbohm wrote that wounds produced by *mata'a* were always fatal if they were deep, and Loti noted that violence on the island had included 'des coups de lance' [19].

Nor was violence restricted to men, since Sir Arthur Keith's study of skeletal material from the island revealed traces of violent blows on female skulls. Although several researchers have claimed recently that there is little evidence for violence on skeletal material from the island, in 1994 Owsley was cited as reporting that he had found multiple injuries and wounds, and 'depression fractures from blunt force trauma are frequent'. In a 2003 BBC TV documentary, he stated that, after examining more than 600 Easter Island skeletons, he realised from the extreme frequency of injuries he saw that he was looking at the evidence of people at war with themselves: 'When I compare the frequency of injuries that I have observed in the Easter Island population with other collections that I have worked with, it certainly shows the high end, it's the extreme. It was a period of social disintegration. You have got endemic warfare, it is chronic – they are slugging it out, there is no doubt about it.' More recent accounts have tried to play down such evidence – but, without quibbling about numbers, it should be mentioned that obsidian is ideal for cutting and slashing, and so it is extremely likely that many wounds (like those seen by the Spaniards) or deaths caused by such weapons would have left absolutely no trace on bones. We will never know, so trying to deny the presence of such weapons by that route is not particularly helpful or relevant [20].

Oral traditions claim that a major battle took place between the stocky *Hanau E'epe* and the slender *Hanau Momoko* at the '*Poike* Ditch', a 3.5 km (c. 2 miles) feature which almost isolates the *Poike* peninsula; it comprises a series of elongated trenches, 20 or 30 of which are still visible, each c. 100 m (c. 325 ft) long, 10 to 15 m (33 to 50 ft) wide, 2 or 3 m (6 to 10 ft) deep, and 5 m (16 ft) apart, with spoil-banks alongside. This intriguing feature of the Easter Island landscape has caused a lot of ink to flow. Islanders claim that it is called the 'Cooking Place of the *Hanau E'epe*' and was dug by that group and filled with brush either for defence or to roast the *Hanau Momoko*; however, the latter turned the tables, and it was the *Hanau E'epe* (who had retreated to *Poike* after an outbreak of killing) who eventually perished in flames there after a fierce battle.

Excavations during the Norwegian expedition of the 1950s found a zone of intensive burning in the ditch that was radiocarbon-dated to AD 1676±100, a figure that seemed to coincide with Englert's genealogical calculation that the battle had taken place in 1680 [21]. However, more recent excavations in the ditch uncovered only root and vegetable moulds and a tree hole with charcoal, at a depth of over 1 m (3 ft), which gave a radiocarbon date in the 11th century AD, which seems to cast the gravest doubt on this 'ditch' having been involved in a battle of the type and date mentioned in the traditions, particularly since no human bones or *mata'a* have ever been found in it [22].

Early researchers believed the ditch to be entirely natural, but since the digging of test pits most geologists and archaeologists agree that it is either a natural feature that has been artificially modified, or that it is entirely man-made. A series of ancient excavations are discernible, with the soil piled up along one side, but the ditch itself has been almost filled by centuries of erosion by water and wind. But what was it for? It is a most unlikely fortification, since it is discontinuous and could be bypassed at either end. One suggestion is that it was a series of ovens for preparing the food for workers in the nearby quarry of *Rano Raraku*; this would account for the ditch's names (it is also called 'the long earth oven of *Tavake*' [23]) as well as for the burnt material. An alternative explanation is that it was a ditch, well protected from the elements, in which crops such as bananas, sugar cane and *taro* were grown for the quarry workers, and irrigated by water running down the slopes of *Poike*. In this case, the burning would result from the disposal of stalks and leaves after the harvests.

A more convincing clue to warfare is the late adoption of the custom of taking refuge in caves and on the offshore islets [24]; none of the latter has a permanent water source, and they are difficult to reach across the pounding waves, so they were clearly not for permanent occupation. However, the refugees (as well as those who came here for fish or bird eggs; see p. 226) adapted the caves here, often building stone-walled entryways -some cave walls were fortified with kerbstones from the high-status elliptical houses, the *hare paenga*, an obvious and convenient prestige item to steal from one's enemies. It is thought that these low, narrow crawlways were designed to retain the heat and protect from wind and driving rain, rather than as defensive measures. However, excavations in an *Ana Kionga* (refuge cave) in the southwest part of Easter Island, found that it had been enlarged, purposely fortified and camouflaged: a small interior

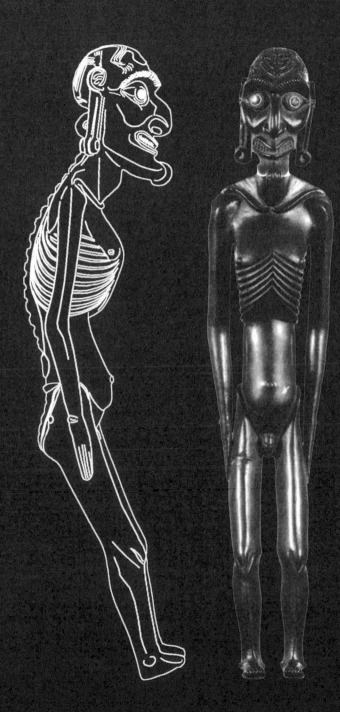

chamber had been walled off with stones, and an entrance tunnel built but concealed beneath debris from the enlargement. The cave, which yielded thousands of fish, rat and chicken bones from layers only 5 cm (2 in) deep, seems to have been used as a refuge for a brief period sometime after 1722 (as proved by the presence of a European glass bead).

Cauwe has stressed that no early European visitor witnessed a battle on the island – but these visits were so few, sporadic and brief that it would be amazing if a battle *had* been seen! – and has also pointed out the lack of fortifications as a further argument against the existence of conflict [25]. Why did the islanders not build defensive habitations, or even hilltop fortresses, like the Maori of New Zealand? They had some hills and plenty of stone at their disposal, even if timber was by now in short supply. The answer is simply that *Rapa Nui* has an abundance of large, usable underground hiding places which are often impossible to detect from the surface. Since it was not possible to flee in canoes from the warfare, as their ancestors might have done, refugees went underground or to the islets.

What clues do we have that point to possible causes for such strife? The most obvious evidence to look for is scarcity of food, and there are abundant indications in the archaeological and ethnographic record of significant changes in the islanders' diet through time, and perhaps even of famine: the well-known wooden statuettes from the island, known as *moai kava kava* (ill. 87) [26], depict men with goatee beards and hooked noses, but also hollow cheeks,

87. A *moai kava kava* with its characteristic hollow cheeks and prominent ribs; legends hold that such figures are in the likeness of two ghosts found sleeping in the top-knot quarry.

a spinal ridge and prominent emaciated ribs which are often seen as indicators of famine. However, the bottom half of these figures seems normal, healthy and well built, with rounded buttocks; they embody a complex symbolism, representing secondary gods, spirits of dead people or supernatural beings, and were used in dances to ward off evil spirits (Melville reported that Typee priests in the Marquesas kept little wooden figures as oracles).

Like all of the island's portable art objects, they have no date or stratigraphic provenance (except for one specimen which has been radiocarbon dated to c. AD 1390-1480, but of course that process dates the death of the tree, not necessarily the carving of the figure) [27]. Be that as it may, they certainly imply that the islanders were well acquainted with some of the physical results of mineral deficiency or starvation. We have already seen (p. 112) the dramatic change in the islanders' appearance and health between 1722 and 1774, perhaps even merely in the four years between the Spanish visit and that of Cook, who was the first to find the natives in a very poor and distressful condition: '...small, lean, timid and miserable', although in 1770 Aguera had already described the people as 'muy misera y humilde' [28]. Gill's X-ray analysis of the human skeletal remains from Ahu Nau Nau has found that the population, and especially the children, suffered repeated periods of stress and growth arrest, which could well be due to malnutrition (and/or perhaps also infectious disease introduced by Europeans); evidence has also been found on the island for abundant dental caries and bone porosity, which point to a carbohydrate-rich diet lacking in iron and calcium. Recent analysis by Polet of largely undated (17th-19th centuries?) skeletal material from 20 sites revealed some indicators of stress, such as dental hypoplasia and Cribra orbitalia, though within the range of other Pacific samples. More women displayed signs of stress than men [29].

The first European visitors reported that sea birds, fowls and fish were scarce by 1722 and particularly by the 1770s. Claude Nicolas Rollin in 1786 said that there were few chickens and few fish, while Captain Charles Bishop in 1795 reported that he obtained lots of sweet potatoes but very few fowls [30]. The Spanish said that chickens were bred in little runs scraped out in the ground and thatched over. Excavations at some sites have revealed a dramatic decrease in the numbers of chicken bones (compared with other foods) after AD 1650 (see above, p. 117), and also an increase in human bone fragments and teeth in late prehistoric times.

This has inevitably given rise to the spectre of cannibalism on the island as a solution to hunger. One can certainly discount some fanciful tales, such as that involving sailors who supposedly escaped the ferocious islanders in 1845 with teethmarks on their bodies [31]! Archaeologists have also been somewhat quick to reach conclusions of cannibalism based on the flimsiest of evidence -for example, the finding of 'innumerables huesos calcinados' (despite the early prominence of cremation!) or of bits of burnt bone by the crematorium at Anakena! Van Tilburg has stated that '...archaeological evidence for cannibalism is present on a few sites' and that '...apparent remains of cannibalistic activities are known on Rapa Nui from both ceremonial and non-ceremonial contexts', but she does not reveal what this evidence consists of! This is hardly surprising since, in fact, the evidence for the practice on the island is entirely narrative, and not archaeological [32].

Cannibalism is certainly very prominent in Rapa Nui's oral traditions, and the name of the painted cave of Ana Kai Tangata is often translated as 'eat man cave', though it could equally mean 'place where men eat'. Recent surveys of ethnography all over the world have failed to come up with much solid evidence for the existence of cannibalism (other than for survival) anywhere, in any period, so at first glance these emphatic oral traditions on Easter Island may have as little factual basis as those elsewhere. However, given the unique cultural developments in this isolated place turned in on itself, as well as the strife and undoubtedly serious shortages of food it experienced in late prehistory, the existence of cannibalism here cannot be totally discounted.

It is also worth noting that the legends explaining the end of the statue quarrying all point to quarrels over food as the cause: e.g. an old woman or witch was denied her rightful share of a giant lobster, and angrily caused all statue production to cease [33]. The tales are reckoned to indicate that it was a breakdown of the system of distribution, the exchange networks and the feeding of the craftsmen by the farmers and fishermen that finally halted the group co-operation that was so vital to the enterprise. The abandonment of work at *Rano Raraku* was not necessarily the sudden dramatic downing of tools so beloved of the mystery writers, but is likely to have been a more gradual (albeit relatively rapid) winding down and disintegration of the system [34]: in short, work quickly ground to a halt because of an ever-increasing imbalance between the production of essentials (food) and that of non-essentials (statues), and the abandonment of the work was probably caused by a shortage of both food and trees.

Where farming is concerned, Stevenson's work, based on excavation and obsidian dates, suggests that, after a concentration of agriculture on the coastal zone for the first few centuries after colonization, upland areas were first settled c. AD 1100, and more intensively occupied from c. 1425 -the appearance of larger field systems in the 1400s coincides with a sharp rise in the construction of religious structures. But the uplands were then abandoned from the late 1500s to 1710; the data from *Maunga Tari* on Mt *Terevaka* show an intensification

of agriculture between 1200 and 1600, as revealed in the use of locations and technologies that increased subsistence productivity while reducing the risk of crop failures or underproduction. It thus seems that the less productive areas of the island, with poorer soils, became occupied as the population relentlessly increased. The decline in agricultural productivity and subsequent population displacement are likely to have placed significant stress on the economic and political systems. The series of declines and increases in land-use in different areas seems linked to rainfall variations and soil quality, with the poorer environmental locations declining earlier. Stevenson's most recent work has confirmed that the intensity of land use decreased substantially in some areas of the island before European contact: 'Reductions in the intensity of land use before European contact in the dry northwest section of Rapa Nui and the region of nutrient-leached soils in upland areas would have contributed to increasing land pressure in other parts of the island and may have led to periods of conflict as land use was renegotiated. This argues against the notion of an island-wide precontact collapse, but does support the reality of a precontact decline in land use that probably was associated with declines in good production' [35].

One measure, possibly Introduced in the 1300s (i.e. long before the decline) to increase the productivity of the moisture-limited and excessively drained soils, was the creation of lithic mulched household gardens and fields -the rock cover served to protect the underlying soils and enhance its moisture retention capacity: as La Pérouse put it, '...ces pierres, que nous trouvions si incommodes en marchant, sont un bienfait de la nature; elles conservent à la terre sa fraîcheur et son humidité et suppléent en partie à l'ombre salutaire des arbres' [36]. Deforestation having removed protection of the soils and plants against wind and water erosion, the stone mulching was introduced to reduce evaporation and soil loss; it has been estimated that more than a billion stones were carried from basalt outcrops to the gardens, and, based on a study of more than 500 sites, that an area of 76 square km received the mulching, with an average intensity of about 150,000 stones per hectare, and the average distance from quarry or source to garden being 65 m; the physical effort involved in this may even have exceeded that involved in the *ahu/moai* phase, since it has been estimated that it would have required 100-150 people working daily for 400 years [37]!

There appears to be a change towards the end of the island's prehistory to a greater dependence on marine resources that could be gathered rather than fished, and even these were being overexploited: the increasing collection of the shellfish *Nerita* is thought to reflect overexploitation of the more highly prized *Cypraea*. By the historic period, fishing had become relatively unimportant, though its former prominence survived in the number of legends with fishermen as heroes. Excavations in some of the island's middens have revealed a slight decrease of fish remains relative to other resources from about AD 1400 to the present. Evidence of the use of rock shelters for activities connected with fishing (e.g. hook manufacture) also shows a marked decrease after AD 1500.

The major reason for the decline in fishing -enforced, as we have seen, by seasonal *tapu*, restrictions on marine resources by the high-status *Miru* clan- must be the limitations on offshore fishing caused by the decreasing number and size of canoes. The Orliacs have unearthed 2300 carbonized wood fragments from various sites, dating from the early 14th to the mid-17th century AD, and these include some useful species: for example, *Alphitonia zizyphoides*, which in Tahiti and in Fatu Hiva produces excellent, hard and resistant wood (*toi*) used for the construction of canoes; and *Elaeocarpus rarotongensis*, whose semi-hard wood was used in the Austral Islands for paddles and lances [38].

However, these finds give absolutely no indication of how abundant such species were, and while it is clear from the earliest levels at *Anakena* that the first islanders had sea-going canoes, since dolphin/porpoise bones are so plentiful, the rapid decline in this resource (their bones are rare or absent from sites on the island less than 500 years old [39]) points to a decreasing ability to get out to sea -it may be no coincidence that an early statue identified as the deity of tuna fishermen was eventually overthrown and buried in an *ahu*'s fill [40].

The decline in ability to fish at sea suggests that the island was never really rich in good canoe timber [41]. The Dutch in 1722 reported that the islander who came out to their ship had a boat made of small, narrow pieces of sewn planks of wood glued together with some organic material (ill. 16), and so light that one man could carry it easily. The other canoes were poor and frail, and so leaky that the islanders spent half their time baling. Bouman added that most natives came swimming out to them on bunches of reeds (*pora*), but there is absolutely no mention of any totora boats of Lake Titicaca style as promulgated by Heyerdahl (see above, p. 62). The first Western visitors saw very few canoes, and the largest was only 3 m (c. 10 ft) long. In 1770 González saw only two canoes. Four years later, Cook said the island had the worst canoes in the Pacific -small, patched and unseaworthy. He saw only three or four small canoes, 3 or 4 m (10 to 13 ft) in length and built of sewn planks of wood only up to 1 m (3 ft) long, and stated that most natives simply swam out. Forster wrote of the canoe which he sketched (ill. 88), '...the boat seemed to be a very wretched thing, patched together of several pieces... each of the men had a paddle made of more than one piece, which sufficiently proves the want of wood on this Isle' [42]. Beechey in 1825 saw three canoes on the beach which did not put to sea, while the Russian Kotzebue in 1816 had likewise seen three, each carrying two men. This is all a far cry from *Hotu Matu'a*'s vessel which legend claimed was 30 m (c. 100 ft) long and 2 m (6 ft) high, and carried hundreds of people. Canoes, including possible double-canoes and Polynesian sails, are clearly depicted in the islanders' rock art, proving that they were acquainted at some time with more impressive vessels, a fact also supported by the numerous canoe ramps found near platforms.

What, then, was the ultimate cause of all these changes? The answer must lie in deforestation, and particularly the disappearance of the palm. The first European visitors all commented on the island's bare, barren, treeless appearance: Roggeveen in 1722 described the island as '...destitute of large trees', and González in 1770 wrote, 'Not a single tree is to be found capable of furnishing a plank so much as six inches in width'; Forster in 1774 reported that '...there was not a tree upon the whole island which exceeded the height of 10 feet' [43]. So clearly, timber was in very short supply. Dupetit-Thouars in 1838 said that five canoes came out to his ship from the island, each carrying two men; what they

most wanted was wood. Even driftwood was looked on as a treasure of inestimable value, and a dying father frequently promised to send his children a tree from the kingdom of shades. It is highly significant that the Polynesian word rakau (tree, wood, timber) meant 'riches' or 'wealth' in old rapanui, a meaning recorded nowhere else [44].

Why, then, did the palm become extinct? Possibly the *coup de grâce* was administered by the sheep and goats introduced in the 19th and 20th centuries, but the species had clearly become rare before that, if Cook and La Pérouse are correct. One answer lies in tooth marks: every *Paschalococos* nut so far recovered from caves (Chapter 4) (but not those from *Anakena* or from burned soil layers [45]), had been gnawed by rodents. Both in Kew and in Orotava, Tenerife (where the wine palm is grown in the Botanic Gardens), it is difficult to recover many intact fruits: almost all have the same hole, surrounded by toothmarks, as one sees on the nuts from Easter Island caves. In each case, a hole large enough to eat out the kernel has been

88. Two rapanui men paddling a plank canoe. Forster's drawing, Cook second voyage, 1774.

88.1. Next page: Reconstruction of a canoe and its various elements. *Ika Rapa Nui*, Alfredo Cea, Rapanui Press.

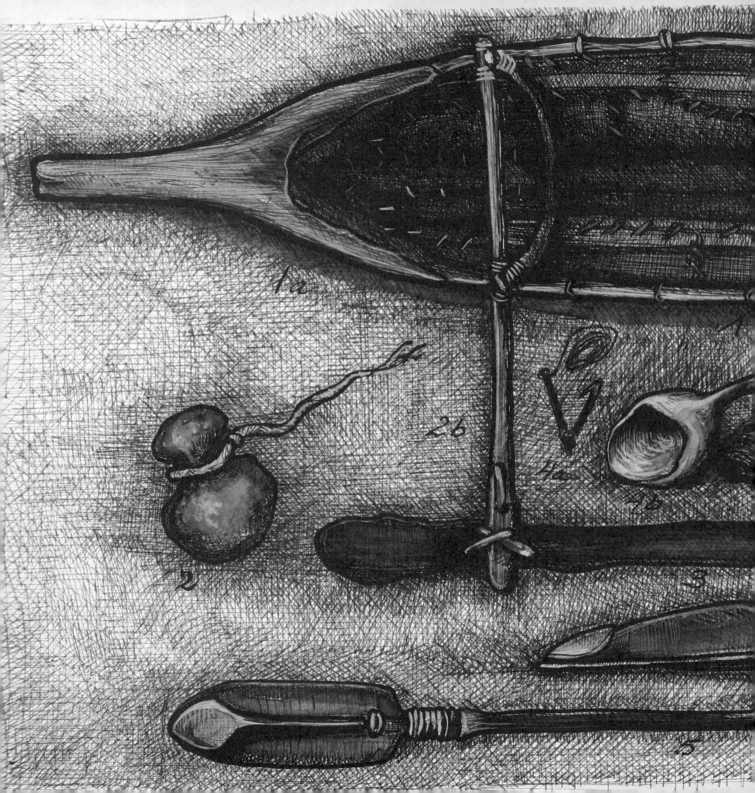

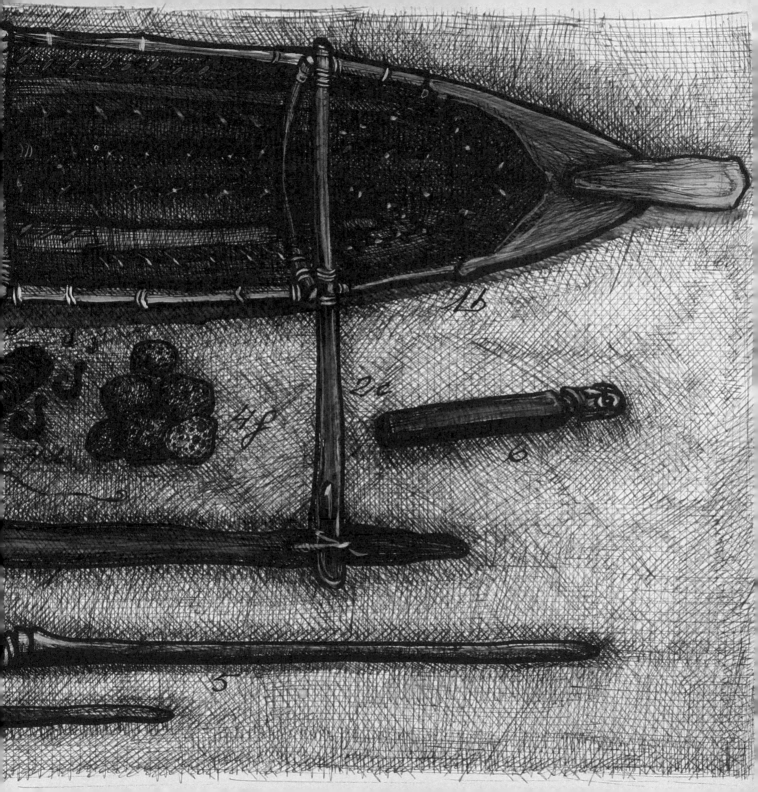

made, and the edge of the hole bears distinctive tooth marks. Some of the gnawed nuts found on Easter Island were submitted by Flenley to Dr A. J. Stuart of Cambridge University, a specialist on Britain's Quaternary mammals, in the hope that he would pronounce them the product of rats' teeth. He did not. He said the tooth marks were more the size that would be produced by the teeth of mice. This was disturbing, for mice are not abundant on Easter Island. It then transpired, however, that the archaeological dig at *Anakena* had turned up numerous remains of the Polynesian rat, *Rattus exulans*. The island's present rat, *Rattus rattus*, had been introduced only after European contact, when it had rapidly ousted the Polynesian rat.

The latter, as already mentioned, was regularly introduced, quite deliberately, by all Polynesian voyagers, wherever they settled. It was, in fact, a source of protein food for them. Furthermore, *Rattus exulans* is a very small species -mouse-sized, in fact. Dr Stuart's findings were now explicable. Clearly, the nuts in the caves had been gnawed by *Rattus exulans*, probably the only rodent on the island at the time. Reconstructing the likely course of events was facilitated by examining modern sagas of the introduction of rats to islands. Almost everywhere they had become a nuisance, and often they had been disastrous. The effects on ground-nesting birds were the best reported: the rats stole so many eggs that species became extinct. A case more apposite to that of the Easter Island palms was that of Lord Howe Island, home of the *Kentia* palm, that denizen of coffee-bars. Rats ate so many of the palm fruits that the export trade in seed was ruined and the regeneration of the species was totally prevented [46].

It therefore seems likely that it was the introduction of the Polynesian rat that may have prevented regeneration of the Easter Island palm and contributed ultimately to its extinction. But it was human activities that actually removed the trees themselves. Significant among these must have been building watercraft (e.g. at *Terevaka*): palms are not ideal for this role, because their timber is somewhat porous, but they can be made waterproof with materials like beeswax, and it is known that coconut trunks are used for dugout canoes in the Marquesas and elsewhere [47], and in any case palm trunks can make seaworthy rafts. It seems likely that the Easter Island palm was simply the best tree available for this purpose -it has been said that a boat or canoe made of it could have stood much physical abuse [48]- although some hardwood species were also available (see above, p. 196); and we know that the islanders occasionally made large canoes: not only do such vessels appear in their rock art, but regular visits are claimed to have been made to Salas y Gómez, 415 km (258 miles) ENE of Easter Island, probably to collect sea birds; and, as we have already seen, the large fish-hooks imply offshore fishing for sharks and other large species, which would be very dangerous from a small canoe.

Other possible causes of decline in palms could include general felling of forest for firewood and to produce agricultural land, and also the specific felling of palms for use as rollers or rails in the moving of the giant statues, as described in Chapters 6 and 7.

A recent suggestion by T. Hunt and C. Lipo is that the deforestation of the island was almost entirely the result of the activities of the introduced Polynesian rats [49]. This idea grew from the very large number of rat bones discovered in the early part of their archaeological sequence from *Anakena*, dating to c. AD 1200. They argued that the lack of predators on the island allowed the rats to proliferate to plague numbers, an attribute of introduced rodents in other locations (e.g. Australia). This explanation seems unlikely for several reasons [50]. Firstly, we know of no evidence that the rats ate anything on the island but the palm fruits. This could stop the reproduction of the tree, but not eliminate it rapidly. We do not know the age to which the *Rapa Nui* palm

89. Most of the canoe designs at Ra'ai have "end extensions". This specific design element may possibly represent supports used to fish with net or fishline. *The Rock Art of Easter Island*, Georgia Lee and Paul Horley, Rapanui Press.

could live, but its closest relative, the Chilean wine palm, is the world's longest lived palm tree, with a longevity of about 2000 years. Secondly, Polynesian rats have not yet succeeded in deforesting Fiji, or Rarotonga, or Tahiti, or New Zealand. Thirdly, the evidence of cut and carbonised palm tree bases on the *Poike* Peninsula (see p. 107) clearly shows that the destruction of the trees was by fire, which was immediately followed by agricultural activity. The pollen evidence shows that tree decline was always accompanied by charcoal. Fourthly, the *Anakena* excavation, as explained on p. 95, is almost certainly not revealing the earliest presence of people, or rats, on the island. Very probably, rats and palms had co-existed on the island for some centuries before that; and other plant species disappeared from the island which co-exist with rats elsewhere and are not known to be eaten by them.

One important result of the presence of rats, however, was their probable impact on the island's indigenous birds – here their effect could indeed have been devastating: for example, on Henderson Island it has been calculated that rats have killed 25,000 petrel chicks per year, and it should be remembered that Rapa Nui originally had numerous species of endemic birds as well as abundant breeding seabirds that migrated to the island (see Chapter 4, p. 108) [51].

The evidence

The evidence for decline of forest on the island comes from two main sources: pollen analysis and charcoal analysis. We now have pollen diagrams from all three of the crater swamps on the island, *Rano Raraku*, *Rano Aroi* and *Rano Kau*.

We might expect the results in these diagrams to be complementary to each other in helping us to reconstruct the palaeo-ecology of the island. In the first place, they are from different altitudes (*Rano Raraku* c. 75 m, *Rano Kau* c. 110 m, *Rano Aroi* c. 425 m), so that two should sample pollen from the lowland vegetation and one the upland vegetation. Secondly, they are of different diameters (*Rano Raraku* c. 500 m, *Rano Kau* c. 1000 m, *Rano Aroi* c. 200 m). This is important because it is well known that small sites tend to collect pollen mainly from local areas, whereas large sites tend to collect pollen from larger regions [52]. Also, it is known that cores from the edge of a large site collect pollen mainly from nearby dryland margins, whereas cores from the centre of a large site collect their pollen mainly from the region [53]. In addition, we know that small sites are more liable to disturbance than large sites, unless the latter include inflow streams (which none of the Easter Island craters does). Disturbance could include mixing of deposits by people wading in marginal sediments, inwash of older material exposed to erosion by forest clearance on the banks, burning of swamp vegetation, change of water surface level by interference with the outflow point (if any: only *Rano Aroi* has one at present). Apart from damaging the stratigraphic sequence, such disturbances can introduce older carbon and thus invalidate the radiocarbon dates [54]. Bearing all these points in mind, we can now proceed to review the pollen evidence from the three sites.

The *Rano Raraku* lake/swamp yielded a 12-metre core (RRA 3) dating back to c. 35,000 BP (before present), with pollen showing a long history of forest dominance [55]. Chemical analysis revealed, however, that during the last 2000 years there had been a huge increase in the amount of metallic ions entering the lake. Clearly something fairly dramatic had happened, even before the soil erosion of which there is visual evidence in the cores. The sort of changes suggested could be those which exposed the soil to more leaching within the crater without actually causing erosion: perhaps selective felling of trees. Alternatively, and perhaps additionally, the deforestation by burning of areas outside the crater could have provided smoke containing wood ash rich in minerals. A third possibility which could not yet be eliminated from the investigation was climatic change: an alteration in total rainfall, or in the intensity of rainfall, could have produced these effects. Most likely would have been an increase of seasonality, leading to a less dense vegetation cover and hence to more leaching in the wet season.

A look at the radiocarbon dates suggested that, although there were no actual inversions, some dates seemed to be too old when an age-depth graph was plotted: either that, or there had been a hiatus in deposition. Further interpretation of the upper part of this core was therefore suspended.

Daniel Mann and colleagues have now produced a good pollen diagram from almost the same point in *Rano Raraku* [56], with much better dating based on individual fruits of totora reed, rather than the bulk sediment used earlier. They clearly show deforestation, accompanied by charcoal, starting at about AD 1200. As explained later, however (see p. 252), there appears to be sediment missing from immediately below this date, as the next date, only 2 cm lower, is about 2000 BC. This suggests that a drought dried up the lake and prevented sedimentation. So again AD 1200 is only a minimum date for the start of deforestation.

The core analysed from *Rano Aroi* (ARO1) showed much lower values of tree pollen than *Rano Raraku* [57]. It also dated back to over 30,000 BP, and trees appeared to have been almost absent at some periods, including the peak of the last Ice Age around 18,000 BP. This was not really surprising at an altitude of c. 425 m in the sub-tropics. After that, trees became more common again until a depth of c. 1.5 m (after 2000 BP) when trees went into decline and charcoal appeared, having been totally

90. Taking a core sample in the *Rano Kau* crater.

90.1. A time-transect through the island showing vegetation, as reconstructed from pollen evidence.

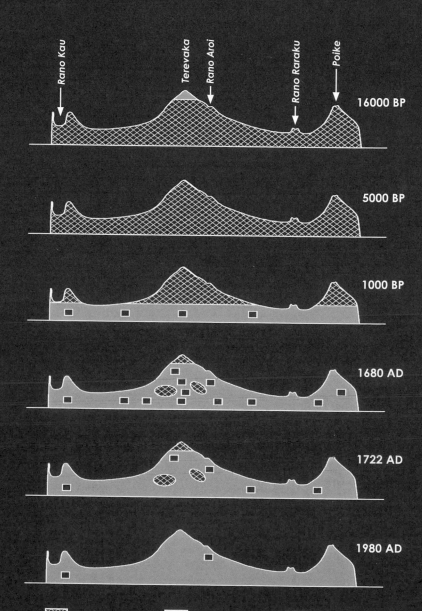

Rano Kau

Terevaka

Rano Aroi

Rano Raraku

Poike

16000 BP

5000 BP

1000 BP

1680 AD

1722 AD

1980 AD

absent before. Again, however, the dates suggest disturbance, this time on a massive scale, so that the topmost date at 0.45-0.75 m is beyond 18,000 BP. A talk with Gerardo Velasco revealed that there had been large-scale interference with this site in the 1920s. Teams of bullocks were used to drag peat from the centre to the banks, to facilitate water storage. Clearly, this crater also was unsuitable for a detailed study of the forest decline.

In desperation we turned to *Rano Kau*. Three cores were taken from this site, despite the difficulty of working at the bottom of a steep-walled crater, and on floating mats of vegetation which make coring very difficult. Core KAO1 was obtained near the edge, and although it gave a clear pollen record [58] it has been criticized because the radiocarbon dates were based on bulk sediment. The same was initially true of core KAO2, collected near the centre, but fortunately this was re-dated recently using totora fruits and other macrofossils. A third core, KAO3, obtained by Candace Gossen [59] at an intermediate position, has yielded an excellent sequence of 15 dates which show clearly that the floating mat is a part of the overall sequence: i.e. the mat has probably separated (floated) off from the sediment beneath, and little or no later sediment has penetrated between. This is explicable by the lack of inflow streams, so that there are no water currents moving sediment around in the lake. Final pollen results from core KAO3 are awaited with great interest. Meanwhile, the results from KAO2 are presented using a time scale derived from all its available calibrated carbon dates [60].

The pollen results (ill. 91) show that the sediment dates back to 10,000 BC, at which time there was a cool dry period on the island, presumably the end of the last ice age. Pollen of trees (especially palm) was slightly reduced and shrubs such as *toromiro* (*Sophora*) and *hau hau* (*Triumfetta*) were more abundant. There was a peak of charcoal which could imply a natural fire on the island, or perhaps more probably long-distance wind-blown charcoal from South America or Australia, where we know there were extensive natural fires at the time.

There then follows a long postglacial period when forest species, especially palms, dominated the vegetation. Sedimentation was slow at this time in the lake, perhaps because soil nutrients were largely locked up in the dense vegetation, thus discouraging algal growth in the lake. *Polygonum acuminatum* (*tavari*) made its appearance during this time. It is a swamp plant which still abounds round the edge of the lake today, and is found in South America and on several Pacific islands. Probably it was brought by birds.

A dramatic change occurs around 14 m depth, c. AD 100. Tree pollen (especially palm) starts to decline, more charcoal appears, *Sophora* has some higher values, and there are more ferns and grasses. The sedimentation rate becomes very rapid. The palm pollen graph enters a saw-tooth stage, suggesting alternating phases of forest destruction and forest recovery. Five of these phases occur in the lake sediment, and a further five in the floating mat, the topmost one showing the final extinction of the palm, and the total domination of the record by grasses and ferns, in the upper 30 cm of the mat. These data must surely represent successive phases of forest destruction and partial recovery. The later phases were doubtless caused by people, but the earlier ones could have been caused by volcanic fires. We know that there was outpouring of lava from *Maunga Hiva-Hiva* (3 km north-east of *Hanga Roa*) within the last 2000 years [61]. But early forest clearance by people may well have begun inside the crater, where the availability of fresh water and the favourable wind-free environment for tropical crops would have encouraged early settlement.

The rise in sedimentation rate around AD 100 suggests the arrival of more nutrients into the lake, thus stimulating plant growth in the swamp. Local forest burning would have provided these nutrients. The rise in sedimentation rate is in direct conflict with the apparent cessation of deposition in *Rano Raraku* at about the same time [62]. If there was a drought at *Rano Kau* interrupting deposition as at *Rano Raraku*, then it must have been before AD 100.

Could the fires evidenced at *Rano Kau* have been caused by lightning? Possibly, but the frequency of lightning on Pacific islands is generally low at present [63]. Could the charcoal have blown from outside *Rapa Nui*? Possibly, but it would hardly have been accompanied by enough wood ash to stimulate the sediment growth of which we have good evidence.

The current pollen evidence is therefore unable to determine the date of human arrival. Fortunately, investigations recently undertaken by Dr Troy Baisden and Dr Mark Horrocks (see below) will probably help to resolve this problem by analyzing further cores for phytoliths, starch grains, and ancient DNA.

The cores described above were collected from all three sites by John Flenley and Jim Teller [64]. Later, a core from *Rano Kau* was collected by Candace Gossen, and multiple cores from *Rano Raraku* [65]. The problem was that all these cores gave radiocarbon dates which were inconclusive. The result was that the evidence from these cores was often ignored by archaeologists. To solve the problem, new research by a group from New Zealand, headed by Troy Baisden (radiocarbon specialist) and Mark Horrocks (micropalaeontologist), and including David Feek (coring specialist) and John Flenley, was initiated by collecting new cores from all the main sites. These were subjected to high-resolution radiocarbon dating by Troy Baisden and to microfossil analysis (pollen, diatoms, phytoliths, starch grains and arthropods) by Mark Horrocks (see Ills. 92.1, 92.2, 92.3).

From *Rano Kau*, they investigated a core (KAO5) near the northwest shore of the swamp, below the ancient cliff-top village of *Orongo* [66]. This was carbon dated at 31 different levels, yielding reliable calibrated dates back to c. 13,000 BP and an excellent age-depth calibration curve (Ill. 92.2).

There were several clayey layers that appear to represent gardened terraces that have slumped into the lake. The data indicated large-scale deforestation, and replacement of Arecaceae (palms) with Poaceae (grass) and a mixed-crop production system including *Broussonetia papyrifera* (paper mulberry), *Colocasia esculenta* (taro), *Dioscorea alata* (greater yam), *Ipomoea batatas* (sweet potato), *Lagenaria siceraria* (bottle gourd) and *Musa* sp. (banana) (see ill. 92.3, 92.4).

The core also contained interesting insect remains. There were two species of ant (*Phaidole* sp. and *Tetramorium bicarinatum* (Nylander). One ant head was enough to provide a C14 date, and the *Tetramorium* head gave a result of c. 2500 BP (see ill. 92.1). This species has been found in modern Rapa Nui and was assumed to have been introduced by people, but it could have reached the island on floating logs. In addition, the ants could have fed on ancient carbon material in the sediment, so this date cannot be relied upon.

The new research from *Rano Raraku* [67] consisted partly of an investigation inside the crater to find evidence of lake level changes. Casts of wetland taxa (*Scirpus californicus* and fern rhizomes) were found up to 10 m above the current lake level, providing evidence of a higher lake level during the last Glacial period. Microfossils of taro, sweet potato, banana and possibly bottle gourd were found in a sediment core collected near the

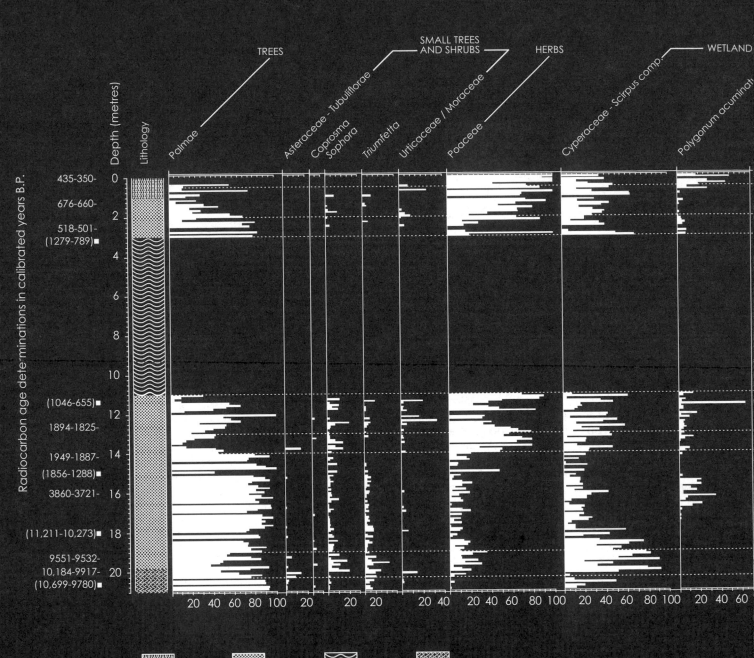

Organic detritus with roots   Coarse organic detritus   Fresh water   Consolidated organic detritus

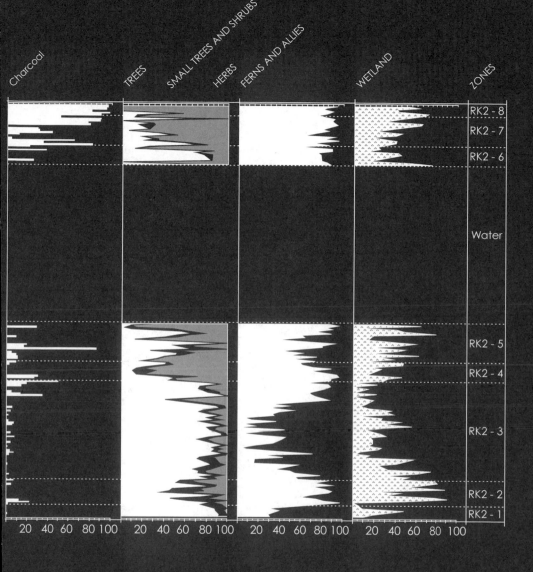

Charcoal · TREES · SMALL TREES AND SHRUBS · HERBS · FERNS AND ALLIES · WETLAND · ZONES

RK2 - 8
RK2 - 7
RK2 - 6

Water

RK2 - 5
RK2 - 4
RK2 - 3
RK2 - 2
RK2 - 1

20 40 60 80 100   20 40 60 80 100   20 40 60 80 100   20 40 60 80 100

KAO2, *Rano Kau*, Easter Island
Borehole two
Relative pollen diagram
Analysts: Kevin Butler and John Flenley
(After Butler and Flenley 2011)

91. The *Rano Kau* crater is a caldera, formed by the collapse of a volcanic cone into its own magma chamber. The swamp itself is largely a floating mat, often only a metre or so thick; if you were to fall through, it would probably be fatal, and one geologist has already disappeared there without trace.

This pollen diagram is from core KAO2, taken near the middle of *Rano Kau*. The lowest section is the lake sediment, then comes the water gap, and at the top the floating mat. The less reliable bulk sediment dates are shown in brackets, and the AMS dates without brackets. The palm (*Palmae*) pollen clearly dominates below 14 m (c. AD 100) and there is little grass (*Poaceae*) pollen or charcoal. Above 14 m palm and grass alternate in dominance and there are peaks of charcoal suggesting periodic destruction and partial recovery of the forest. Finally, within the top 1 m (the last few hundred years), the palm becomes extinct. For further interpretation see text.

western edge of the lake. The earliest evidence of gardening occurred at c. 627-513 cal. BP, immediately after large-scale forest clearance. The latter was evidenced in the pollen diagram which showed the disappearance of Arecaceae (palm) pollen and its replacement by Poaceae (grass) pollen (see ill. 92.3, 92.4).

The highest altitude wetland on Rapa Nui is *Rano Aroi*, at c. 425 m altitude, near the summit. This site was generally regarded as above the level for early agriculture, but still worth studying. Earlier studies [68] had shown that this site was probably above the altitude for the native Arecaceae (palm) forest, and was probably surrounded by Asteraceae scrub. The new research confirmed this, and also gave evidence of a prolonged dry phase which appears to have predated human settlement in the region. Polynesian activity is demonstrated by abundant microscopic charcoal fragments, beginning at 709 cal. BP and continuing until 330 cal BP. The cessation of gardening around this date (c. AD 1611) is interesting in relation to the end of *moai* production at *Rano Raraku* around this time (see Chapter 9).

So all the main sites for analysis of deposits (*Rano Kau, Rano Raraku* and *Rano Aroi*) have given relatively late dates for the start of horticulture. The tendency may be to assume that these are the dates for the arrival of people. They had brought crop plants with them, so surely they would immediately start to cultivate them? No doubt this is partially true. But consider carefully where the people had arrived. Rapa Nui, when they arrived, was probably the richest sea-bird island in the world. Sea-birds nested there in their thousands. For at least four months a year, this would provide a food supply. Young birds were just waiting to be cooked and eaten. Certainly, people would have to cut down timber to provide the fuel for the earth-ovens whose remains are abundant on the island. And for the remaining

92.1. *Musa* phytoliths; mounted in Caedex; transmitted light 600x; scale bar, for all: 20μm, **a, b**: Fossil *Musa* sp. leaf phytoliths from *Rano Kau* core, at 18.0 and 15.9 m depths, respectively. **c, d**: *Musa paradisiaca* leaf phytoliths from modern reference sample, showing typical rectangular/squarish base with side protuberances and cone.

Fossil ant heads from *Rano Kau* core; diameters measured from outer edge of eyes. **a**: *Pheidole* sp., 0.55 mm, from 11 m depth **b**: *Tetramorium bicarinarium*, 1.02 mm, from 11.00-11.05 m depth

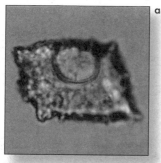
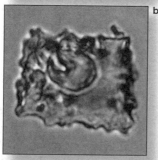
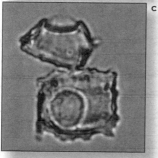
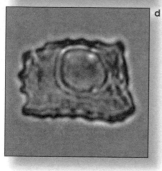

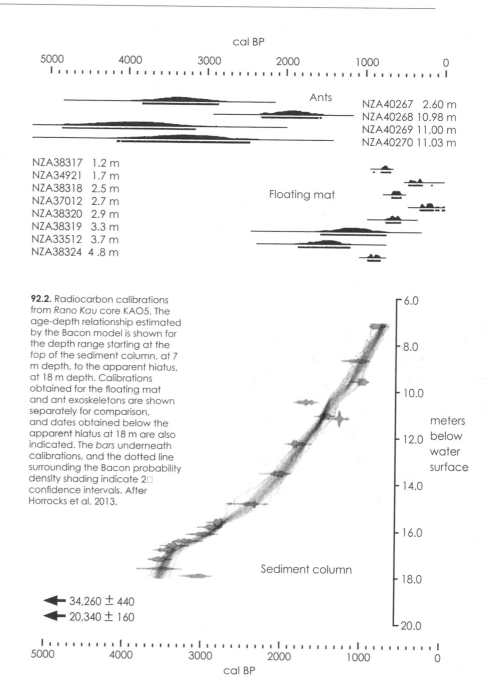

cal BP

5000   4000   3000   2000   1000   0

Ants

NZA40267   2.60 m
NZA40268 10.98 m
NZA40269 11.00 m
NZA40270 11.03 m

NZA38317   1.2 m
NZA34921   1.7 m
NZA38318   2.5 m
NZA37012   2.7 m
NZA38320   2.9 m
NZA38319   3.3 m
NZA33512   3.7 m
NZA38324   4 .8 m

Floating mat

92.2. Radiocarbon calibrations from *Rano Kau* core KAO5. The age-depth relationship estimated by the Bacon model is shown for the depth range starting at the *top* of the sediment column, at 7 m depth, to the apparent hiatus, at 18 m depth. Calibrations obtained for the floating mat and ant exoskeletons are shown separately for comparison, and dates obtained below the apparent hiatus at 18 m are also indicated. The *bars* underneath calibrations, and the dotted line surrounding the Bacon probability density shading indicate 2□ confidence intervals. After Horrocks et al. 2013.

6.0
8.0
10.0
12.0   meters below water surface
14.0
16.0
18.0
20.0

Sediment column

← 34,260 ± 440
← 20,340 ± 160

5000   4000   3000   2000   1000   0

cal BP

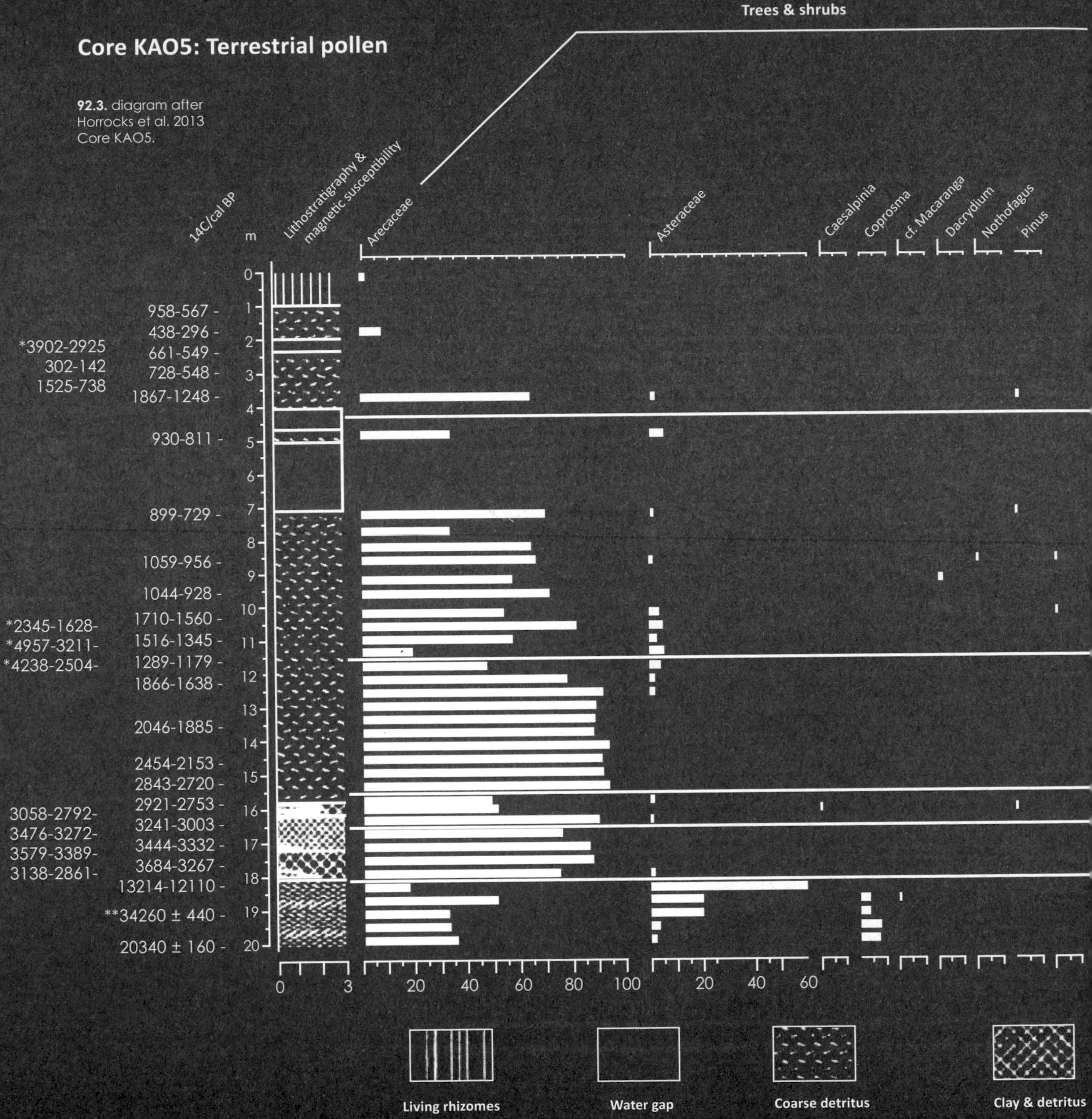

Core KAO5: Terrestrial pollen

92.3. diagram after
Horrocks et al. 2013
Core KAO5.

Trees & shrubs

14C/cal BP

m

Lithostratigraphy & magnetic susceptibility

Arecaceae

Asteraceae

Caesalpinia

Coprosma

cf. Macaranga

Dacrydium

Nothofagus

Pinus

958-567 -
438-296 -
*3902-2925   661-549 -
302-142   728-548 -
1525-738   1867-1248 -

930-811 -

899-729 -

1059-956 -

1044-928 -

1710-1560 -
*2345-1628-   1516-1345 -
*4957-3211-   1289-1179 -
*4238-2504-   1866-1638 -

2046-1885 -

2454-2153 -
2843-2720 -
2921-2753 -
3058-2792-   3241-3003 -
3476-3272-   3444-3332 -
3579-3389-   3684-3267 -
3138-2861-   13214-12110 -

**34260 ± 440 -

20340 ± 160 -

0   3   20   40   60   80 100   20   40   60

Living rhizomes   Water gap   Coarse detritus   Clay & detritus

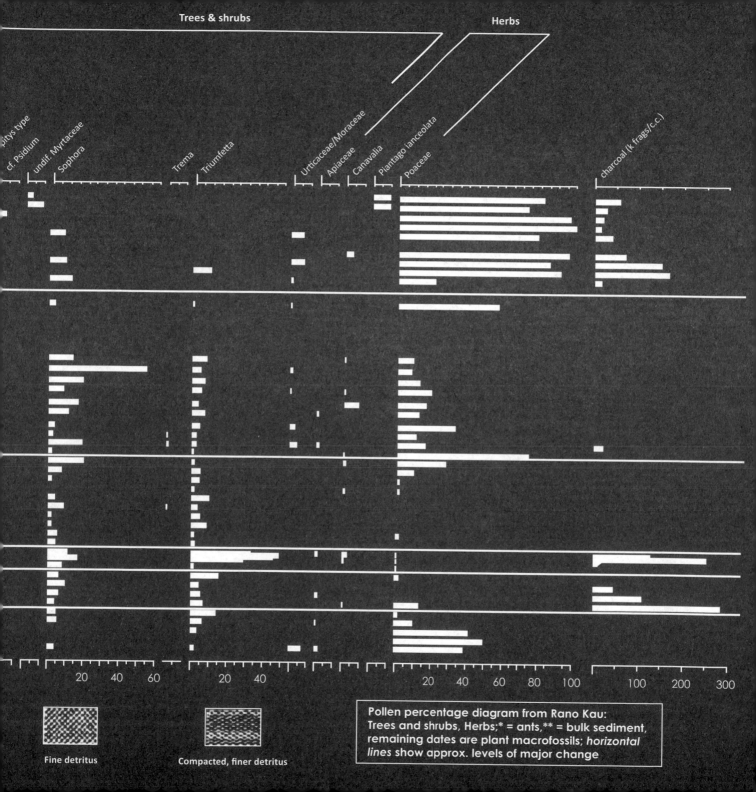

Pollen percentage diagram from Rano Kau:
Trees and shrubs, Herbs;* = ants,** = bulk sediment,
remaining dates are plant macrofossils; *horizontal
lines* show approx. levels of major change

Fine detritus

Compacted, finer detritus

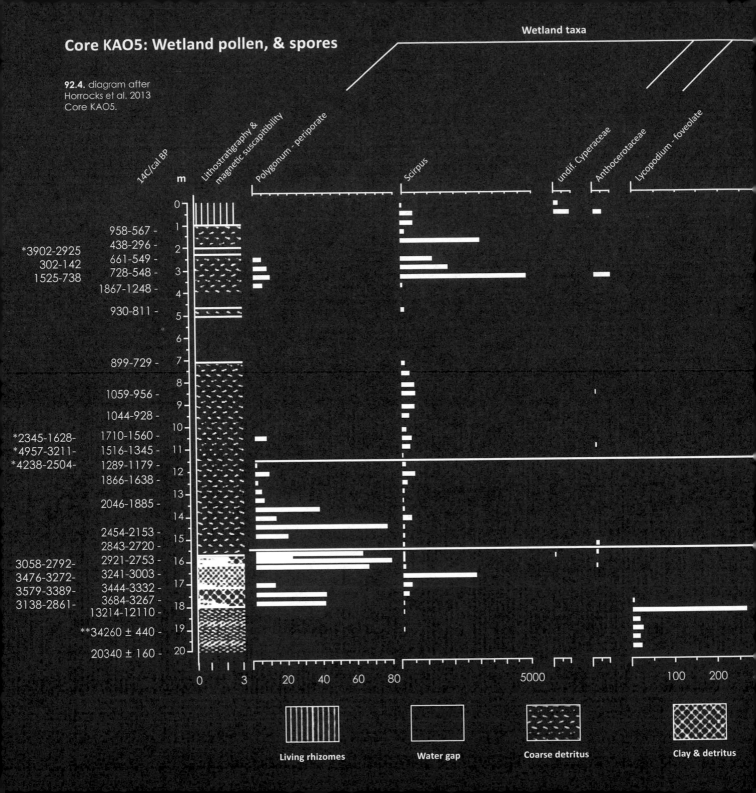

Core KAO5: Wetland pollen, & spores

92.4. diagram after
Horrocks et al. 2013
Core KAO5.

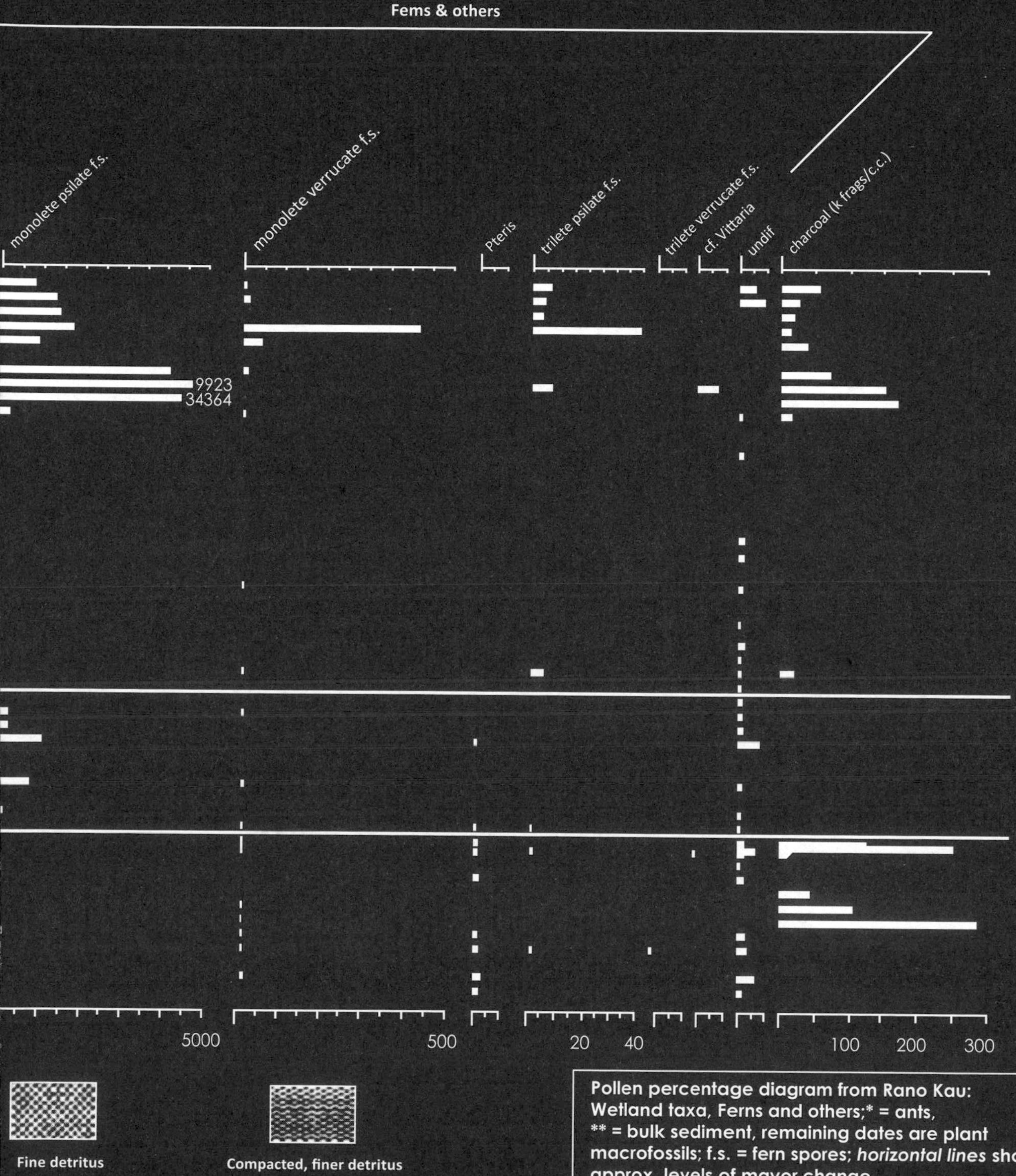

Fems & others

monolete psilate f.s.

monolete verrucate f.s.

Pteris

trilete psilate f.s.

trilete verrucate f.s.

cf. Vittaria

undif

charcoal (k frags/c.c.)

9923
34364

5000   500   20 40   100 200 300

Fine detritus   Compacted, finer detritus

Pollen percentage diagram from Rano Kau:
Wetland taxa, Ferns and others;* = ants,
** = bulk sediment, remaining dates are plant
macrofossils; f.s. = fern spores; *horizontal lines* show
approx. levels of mayor change

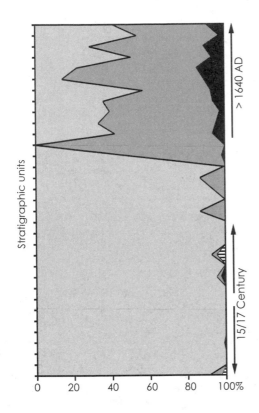

Stratigraphic units

> 1640 AD

15/17 Century

0   20   40   60   80   100%

Rhizome

Stem

Wood charcoal

Unknown

93. Types of charcoal found in archaeological sites on Easter Island. Early horizons (basal half of diagram) have almost all wood charcoal. Later horizons, after c. AD 1640 (upper part of diagram) have mostly charcoal stems (mainly grasses). After C. & M. Orliac.

Site	Altitude	Start of Forest Decline	Start of Horticulture
Rano Raraku	c. 75 m	625 – 513 cal. B.P.	625 – 513 cal B.P.
Rano Kau	c. 110 m	3680 – 2860 cal B.P.	750 ± 200 B.P.
Rano Aroi	c. 425 m	797 – 645 cal B.P.	281 cal B.P.

94. Summary of the radiocarbon dates for various events from the three main wetlands of Easter Island. Source: Horrocks et al. 2012, 2012a, 2013, 2015.

eight months, people could turn to fishing. Large fish (tuna, sharks, etc) were abundant offshore, so one would have to fell coastal trees and make canoes, but the supply of fish was immense. We know that all this happened, because excavations have yielded the bones of large fish and sea-birds [69]. Only when this natural bonanza started to come to an end did people really turn to agriculture. Obviously they had planted their crop-plants on arrival, but they did not need to clear large areas of forest and plant large numbers of crops until much later. That is the story throughout Polynesia. Even then, the islanders were so keen to eat sea-birds that they perhaps risked the hazardous sailing to Salas y Gómez, the reef over 400 km away, to obtain their favourite food. So the date of the start of horticulture is well after the date of the first arrival on Rapa Nui.

95. John Flenley at *Poike*, pointing out changes in the soil brought about by soil erosion. The original soil, below his left hand, has a blocky structure. The horizontal layers above his hand are soil brought down by slopewash erosion from higher up the slope and deposited here. Right: *Poike* eroded soil surface.

The other main evidence about the date of forest clearance has come from the excellent work on charcoal by Catherine Orliac [70]. By separately identifying over 30,000 charcoal fragments from archaeological sites on the island, she has been able to provide not only far more data on the nature of the original forest, but also a date for its decline. As shown in ill. 93, her information indicates that people were burning almost exclusively wood until c. AD 1640, but then changed over suddenly to stem and rhizome of herbaceous plants, presumably because wood was no longer available.

To sum up, it appears that forest clearance may have begun at least 1200 years ago (i.e. around AD 800 or earlier) inside the *Rano Kau* caldera, and progressively later at other sites. The forest may have been completely destroyed at some sites by c. AD 1400, but the last forest may have been cut for firewood around AD 1640. The forest was replaced mainly by crop plants, grasses and introduced weeds. In other words, although it has often been suggested -from La Pérouse in 1786 up to some present-day scholars- that the island's trees disappeared because of drought, the situation appears more gradual and complex than this. Droughts may indeed have played a role -after all, they still occur here frequently- but the activities of the human settlers were clearly a persistent and major factor, together with the depredations of their rats.

The loss of trees had consequences not only for fishing and statue-building. The loss of fertile forest soils must have caused a shortage of food. There is now good evidence of massive soil erosion on the deep soils of the *Poike* peninsula, following burning of the vegetation. Although most of the eroded soil was doubtless lost into the sea, sufficient was trapped in small sedimentary basins to reveal the sequence of events. At the bottom, in such basins, the original soil containing palm root casts is still present; above this is a layer containing charcoal and carbonized palm fruits, giving a radiocarbon date of AD 1256-1299; this charcoal layer was found over an area of several hectares. Above the charcoal layer is a sediment of many thin, horizontal layers of inwashed soil from upland areas around the basin [71].

Even water was affected: at *Ava O Kiri*, inland from *Ovahe*, there is a deep ravine that was clearly cut by running water in ancient times; these days it contains water only after heavy rain, but the ravine's depth shows that before deforestation the island must have had intermittent streams like this one. Geomorphology shows that there was a formerly perennial stream coming down from the slopes of *Terevaka*, and entering the sea at *Anakena* Bay, and it is certainly possible that deforestation led to its drying up [72]. The decline in water sources must have made those that remained extremely precious, which may explain the presence of carved face-petroglyphs at *Val Tapa Eru*, a spring inland from *Tepeu*.

Easter Island's small size and isolation made its human population especially sensitive to the effects of any environmental alterations, such as the loss of the non-renewable forest resources. When ecological disaster struck, they had nowhere to go, but had to sit it out, with the catastrophic results outlined at the start of this chapter.

The human population

Could population pressure lie behind the deforestation? As in any other part of the world, it is a daunting challenge to calculate the prehistoric population of Easter Island. Estimates are inevitably vague, and the situation is little better during the first period of European contact: Roggeveen in 1722 guessed at 'thousands', but his party went ashore only on one day. González in 1770 thought it was 900 or 1000 -one Spaniard was told that the land could not support more and that, when this number was reached, if somebody was born they killed someone over 60; certainly the Spanish saw no old people on the island [73]. Cook, only four years later, estimated the population at 600 or 700, and his naturalist Forster thought 900. However, since these first visitors saw very few women and children – the Spanish saw fewer than 70 women, while William Wales, part of Cook's party, reported seeing at least 500 men but no more than 6 or 8 women [74] – it is clear that much of the population was hidden from them, probably in their subterranean refuges: González actually reported that most islanders lived in underground caves with narrow entrances into which they sometimes had to crawl feet-first, while Forster stood on a hill near *Hanga Roa* and '...did not see above 10 or 12 huts, though the view commanded a great part of the island'.

La Pérouse, who came in 1786, saw a much more representative range of people -the islanders '...crawled out of their subterranean dwellings'- and estimated the population to be 2000. Lisjanskij, who saw 23 houses near the shoreline in 1804, guessed at a population of about 1800, while Beechey, in 1825, reckoned it was about 1500. Salmon, who spent many years on the island, told Thomson that its population between 1850 and 1860 was about 2000. It is known that the figure in 1862 was about 3000, just prior to the devastating arrival in 1862/3 of slave traders who took numerous islanders off to Peru; by 1872, there were only 110 people left on Easter Island [75]. By 1886, this had risen slightly to 155: 68 men, 43 women, 17 boys and 27 girls under 15; by 1915, there were 250 people. Since then, the population has grown, albeit with considerable contributions from Chile, to which the island has been attached since 1888; at the time of writing, the island has about 5000 residents, mostly concentrated in the main village of *Hanga Roa* [76].

In short, despite the low estimates of the first European visitors, it is likely that La Pérouse's estimate of 2000 was quite near the mark. So we have a boatload of settlers in the first centuries AD, and 2000 people some 1400 years later. What happened to population numbers during that time? The normal model applied to Polynesian islands is that the founder population grew exponentially and rapidly until stabilizing at a level just under the carrying capacity of the environment, with possible oscillations above that level. Some see the 18th-century population figures as evidence for an early settlement of East Polynesia, since any arrival after AD 600 would have allowed insufficient time for the population to rise to this level [77]. On Easter Island, however, one estimate is that numbers may have doubled every 150 years; some scholars even reckon that island populations with simple horticultural techniques, '...in food-rich environments and free of epidemic diseases and lethal predators (including other humans) could double or even triple their numbers' every generation, until they run out of land [78]. Clearly, on Easter Island something cracked and the system declined. Indeed, the mathematical model developed by Anthony Cole [79] suggests that there could have been numerous declines. Another possible influence on human population is periodic fish poisoning resulting from algal blooms [80].

Roggeveen reckoned that the island could have supported a larger population than was living there in 1722; and, as we have already seen, La Pérouse found that only one tenth of the island was being used to support the 2000 people. Cook's party noticed that much of the inner part of the island showed evidence of having been cultivated in the past, though, as mentioned earlier (p. 112), there would have been few traces visible of abandoned unordered fields even in the 1770s, and far fewer survive today.

To what figure could the prehistoric population have risen? Mrs Routledge was told by the natives that their ancestors had been 'thick as grass'; she was also informed that half the island -about 15,000 acres- could grow bananas and sweet potatoes, and if one allowed 2 acres per family of 5 to 7 individuals, this would give a potential population of 37,500 to 52,500, a highly theoretical figure which was probably never even approached in reality. Using population densities from Tahiti, Métraux reckoned on 13.7 people per square kilometre and hence a population of about 3000 or 4000. Most archaeologists who have worked on the island in recent years estimate that the prehistoric population may have reached 6000 to 8000, while some speculate about figures of 10,000 or even 20,000. For example, one model using a founding population of 50 in c. AD 800, and a growth of 0.7%, estimates a total of 15,000 people after 800 years, with a density of c. 150 people per square kilometre [81]. Population estimates are made particularly difficult by the uneven distribution of settlements, which were dense along the coast but sparser in the interior due to lack of irrigation.

Surveys of about 80% of *Rapa Nui* have estimated that this small island has more than 20,000 archaeological features and sites [82], and those are only the data visible on the surface. The southeast coast alone has 17 platforms within less than 3 km (less than 2 miles), and over 100 houses. This high population density probably reflects the high agricultural production of the south and east parts of the island, and the proliferation of major platforms in the 15th century on the south coast is thought to indicate an influx of people from other parts of the island together with a period of sustained population growth. One survey of the south coast's residential sites in each period has concluded that the population level remained fairly low until c. AD 1100, after which it doubled every century, only slowing down after 1400, with a decline setting in after a maximum c. 1600 [83].

There are a number of other archaeological indications of population increase: for example, coastal caves and rockshelters were not much used until c. AD 1400 [84], when their extensive utilization implies a greater exploitation of marine resources, which may reflect a rising number of mouths to feed and/or a decrease in productivity of the land resources, caused by excessive deforestation and leaching. There is a noticeable decline in food remains, especially marine foods, in the shelters after AD 1650, which may denote a significant fall in population and/or a lack of canoes for fishing.

A similar clue to the rise and fall of population lies in the dating of obsidian from habitation sites, which shows that the exploitation of obsidian sources rose from c. AD 1300 to 1650, and then decreased for the next fifty years before rising again. The first increase has been attributed to a rising population, while the drop may reflect a decline in numbers. The subsequent rise is thought to indicate a social change, either an increased clustering of population, with larger residential units, or perhaps a collapse of the previous system of territorial control over the quarries, leaving them open to all. Such a theory would fit the oral traditions which point to big socio-political changes on the island somewhere around AD 1680 [85], with a shift in religion, burial practices, architecture and leadership.

It is now time, therefore, to look more closely at some of the consequences of these major changes which reflect the will of a strong society to survive adversity through adaptation and innovation.

[1] Cristino & Vargas 1998, 1999; Edwards et al. 1996, p. 12.

[2] von Saher 1992, p. 36-38; Beaglehole 1961, p. 344.

[3] Lisjanskij 2004.

[4] Edwards et al. 1996; Edwards & Edwards 2013, p. 354; see also Martinsson-Wallin 2001, p. 74. Love 2010 has speculated that two palaeo-tsunamis may have hit *Ahu Te Pito Kura*; Edwards &

96. Engraving by Pierre Loti, 1872.

Edwards (2013, p. 40) claim that Anakena is very vulnerable to tsunamis and has been severely affected by them in the past 100 years; and Ramírez (pers. comm.) has witnessed the consequences of a series of tidal waves hitting the south coast in June 2006; and of one which caused the fall of a section of back-wall at *Ahu Vai Uri* in September 2009.

[5] Bahn 1995; Métraux 1957, p. 172. See also Vargas et al. 2006, pp. 157, 402.

[6] *Rapa Nui Journal* 19 (2), 2005, p. 154; and 20 (2), 2006, p. 149.

[7] Beaglehole 1961, p. 344; Geiseler 1995, p. 35.

[8] For a full study of the toppling issue, see Bahn 2015. See also Hunt & Lipo 2011, p. 153; Cauwe 2011; Mulloy 1961, pp. 109-11.

[9] Steadman et al. 1994, p. 87; Vargas et al. 2006, pp. 326, 392.

[10] Routledge 1919, p. 223.

[11] von Saher 1992, p. 35; 1994, p. 99. Spears were also mentioned by other members of Cook's party such as Wales and Pickersgill (see Foerster 2012).

[12] Ruiz-Tagle 2006, p. 63; Foerster 2012, p. 131.

[13] Hunt & Lipo 2007; Lipo et al. 2010, 2016; Flas 2015; Mulrooney et al. 2010. For a contrary view, see Flenley, Butler & Bahn 2007, pp. 101-2; Bahn 2015, pp. 145-47. Bloch (2012, p. 48) quotes Sergio Rapu as laughing: 'Don't tell me those obsidian tools were just for agriculture'.

[14] For use-wear analyses, see Church & Rigney 1994; Church & Ellis 1996; Church 1998.

[15] Englert 1970, p. 139.

[16] Mulrooney et al. 2010. For the miniature scraper, Ramírez, pers. comm. Eyraud 2008, p. 8; Thomson 1891, pp. 474-6, 532-33, 536.

[17] Geiseler 1995, pp. 72-73; Routledge 1919, p. 223; Métraux 1940, pp. 166-68, 376; for Loti, see Rapa Nui 2009, pp. 95-100; Ayres et al. 2000, p. 175.

[18] McCall 1976.

[19] Cauwe 2008, p. 52; 2011, p. 65; for the Spaniards, Anon 2004, p. 63, and Foerster 2012, p. 131; Geiseler 1995, pp. 72-73; for Zumbohm, see Métraux 1940, p. 165; for Loti, Rapa Nui 2009, p. 100.

[20] See e.g. Hunt & Lipo 2011, p. 94, 'the remains of prehistoric Rapanui show few signs of lethal trauma'. For Owsley, see Van Tilburg 1994, p. 107; and Owsley et al. 2015.

[21] Smith 1961, 1990; Heyerdahl & Ferdon 1961, p. 385; Baker 1967, p. 119.

[22] *Rapa Nui Journal* 4 (4), 1990/1, p. 56; 6 (1), 1992, p. 14. Vargas et al. 2006, pp. 368-91.

[23] Barthel 1978, p. 6.

[24] McCoy 1978.

[25] Cauwe 2011, pp. 62, 88.

[26] Forment 1991; Orliac & Orliac 1995a; Orliac & Orliac 2008. Where famine is concerned, Brown (1924, pp. 182-3) says: '…that they had periods of famine we know, not merely from the word for it in their language (*haka-maruahi*), but from their traditions; they were often reduced to eating the skins of bananas, the peelings of their tubers, the bark of the banana stem, and the root of the *tanoa*, or seaside convolvulus, although that inflamed the eyes and swelled the tissues and sometimes caused death….The gorging at their feasts of the whole produce of their land meant often subsequent famine' (though the source of these claims is unclear).

[27] Forment et al. 2001.

[28] The first quote is from Heyerdahl (1974, p. 200) but accurately conveys the epithets utilised by Cook and the Forsters when describing the islanders in 1774 (Bahn & Flenley 2008). For Aguera, see Foerster 2012, p. 122. There is, however, absolutely no evidence to support the claim by Hunt & Lipo (2011, pp. 158-9, 162-3) that there was a catastrophic population collapse after the Dutch visit, thanks to VD and epidemic diseases – as Boersema (2015, pp. 68, 124) shows, these supposed Dutch diseases are a figment of the imagination, and there is no sign of syphilis on the island till the late 18th century.

[29] Gill 2000, pp. 111, 116; Gill & Owsley 1993; Stefan & Gill 2015; Polet 2015.

[30] For Rollin, see Foerster 2012, p. 254. For Bishop, Roe 2005, p. 62.

[31] Fischer 1992a.

[32] Cervellino Giannoni 1993; Skjølsvold 1994, p. 112; Van Tilburg 1994, pp. 109-10. For a critique of all such claims, see Bahn 1997a; for oral traditions, see Routledge 1919, pp. 225-26.

[33] Routledge 1919, p. 182; Barthel 1978, pp. 277-78.

[34] Love 2010.

[35] Stevenson 1997, pp. 141-42; Wozniak 1998; Stevenson & Haoa 2008, pp. 174-76. See also Vargas et al. 2006, p. 230; Stevenson et al. 2015.

[36] Stevenson et al. 1999; see also La Pérouse 1997, p. 65.

[37] Bork et al. 2004; Mieth & Bork 2005, p. 62; 2015, p. 101.

[38] Orliac 2000, p. 216.

[39] Steadman et al. 1994.

[40] Huyge & Cauwe 2002.

[41] Steadman et al. 1994, p. 91; Wallin 1996.

[42] von Saher 1999, p. 43.

[43] von Saher 1992, p. 34.

[44] Fischer 2005, p. 44; Brown 1924, p. 153.

[45] Mieth & Bork 2010.

[46] N. M. Wace, personal communication.

[47] R. Green, personal communication.

[48] Gurley & Liller 1997, p. 84.

[49] Hunt & Lipo 2006, 2011.

[50] Flenley & Bahn 2007; Mieth & Bork 2010, 2015, p. 97; according to Bork (in Pelletier 2012, p. 110) of the 220 palm nuts found at *Ava Ranga Uka A Toroke Hau*, almost none had been gnawed by rats, so he is certain that rats were not responsible for the disappearance of the palm. See also Vogt in *Rapa Nui Journal* 28 (2), 2014, p. 92.

[51] Edwards & Edwards 2013, p. 60.

[52] Jacobson & Bradshaw 1981.

[53] Turner 1965.

[54] Pennington et al. 1976.

[55] Flenley et al. 1991.

[56] Mann et al. 2008.

[57] Flenley et al. 1991.

[58] Ibid.

[59] Gossen 2007.

[60] Flenley et al. 2007.

[61] González-Ferrán et al. 2004.

[62] Mann et al. 2008.

[63] Doswell 2002.

[64] Flenley et al. 1991.

[65] Gossen 2007; Cañellas-Boltà et al. 2012.

[66] Horrocks et al. 2012, 2013.

[67] Horrocks et al. 2012a.

[68] Flenley et al. 1991.

[69] Steadman et al. 1994; Hunt & Lipo 2011.

[70] Orliac 2000.

[71] Mieth et al. 2002.

[72] Steadman et al. 1994, p. 93; Martinsson-Wallin & Wallin 2000, p. 27.

[73] Mellén Blanco 1986, p. 103; Ruiz-Tagle 2006, p. 93. For a useful table of early population estimates, see Boersema 2015, p. 110.

[74] Foerster 2012, p. 198.

[75] *Rapa Nui Journal* 16 (1), 2002, p. 4 -the usually quoted figure of 111 included the census taker, who was not a resident! According to Edwards & Edwards (2013, p. 89), the figure of 110 was probably wrong, since the population in 1872 was 175, in 1880 it was 150 and in 1883 it was 167.

[76] *Rapa Nui Journal* 6 (3), 1992, p. 57; 14 (1), 2000, p. 23; 15 (1), 2001, p. 55.

[77] Kirch 2000, p. 232. Boersema's (2015, p. 112) detailed speculations about population growth on the island are rendered irrelevant by his assumption that settlement began as late as AD 1100!

[78] Bellwood 2001, p. 13.

[79] Cole & Flenley 2005, 2007, 2008.

[80] Rongo et al. 2009.

[81] Vargas et al. 2006, p. 401.

[82] Vargas 1998.

[83] Stevenson 1986; Stevenson & Cristino 1986.

[84] Shaw 1996.

[85] The date of AD 1680 was first settled on by Englert (basing himself on oral traditions) as the year of the *Poike* battle, and it seemed to coincide with a C14 date of AD 1676 from the ditch -see Vargas et al. 2006, pp. 299, 339. It then became entrenched in the literature in the chronological schemes devised for the island's prehistory (e.g. by Heyerdahl, see below, Chapter 11, p. 245; and in Stevenson & Haoa 2008, pp. 174-6). We place no particular faith in the precise year but certainly see the late 17th century as being correct.

nevitably, our information on social and political developments comes primarily from oral traditions and the reports of the first visitors. During at least the island's final prehistory, it was divided up into different clan territories (ill. 98) -with fairly blurred and overlapping edges owing to the lack of physical boundaries- though there was a centralized control of religious and economic activities through the *Miru*, a royal lineage descended from *Hotu Matu'a*, centred at *Anakena*, and headed by the hereditary chief, the *Ariki Henua*. Although the most important person on the island, he was, however, not really a king or political leader, but rather a religious symbol, the main repository of *mana*, or spiritual power; he was, as it were, to the *mana* born.

There was a rigid class structure, and all surplus produce was assigned to those of high status: the chiefs, priests, possessors of ritual knowledge and arts, and the warriors (*matato'a*). The emphasis was on continually increased production, and the authority to focus manpower on particular activities was supernaturally ordained. Effective networks of exchange must have arisen since, as shown earlier, different parts of the island specialized in particular activities (fishing, cultivation) or had access to crucial resources: tuff, scoria, basalt, obsidian, timber and paper mulberry, reeds, red ochre, coral for files, and even moss for caulking boats were all highly localized.

Within this framework, the islanders had laboured long and hard at clearing agricultural land of the ubiquitous stones and cultivating it, at tree-felling and carpentry, at fishing and, of course, at producing the spectacular platforms and statues. Throughout

eastern Polynesia, communal or specialist labour was employed on major subsistence projects, but Easter Island's peculiar environmental conditions seem to have largely precluded this outlet, and hence similar efforts were poured into esoteric pursuits: the monumental structures and statues. It appears that the craft specialists and ordinary workers were in no way driven under the lash to do all this, but instead were paid with cooked food, and they expected to derive supernatural rewards for their efforts -rather like the medieval cathedral builders of Europe. The work was accompanied by joyful feasts, and the spiritual power of the giant statues was thought to bring benefit to the communities that owned them.

Once the system crashed, for reasons outlined in the previous chapter, there were marked changes not only in subsistence and settlement patterns, with exchange networks disintegrating, but also in religion and politics: La Pérouse noted in 1786 that the island no longer had a chief. It seems that the warrior leaders rose to power out of the ever-increasing warfare, so that hereditary privilege was replaced by achieved status: some have even seen it as a revolt of the lower classes against the upper. Inter-group rivalry and competition had always been endemic, as seen in the construction of ever more splendid monuments, but these also required group co-operation, and until the crash it seems -from archaeological evidence as well as from oral traditions- that actual warfare was absent or extremely rare. Since persistent warfare (from simple raiding to major territorial conflict) is common and ubiquitous in Polynesia, one of the most remarkable features of Easter Island's culture is that peace may

97. Engraving of a rapanui chief, Pierre Loti, 1872.

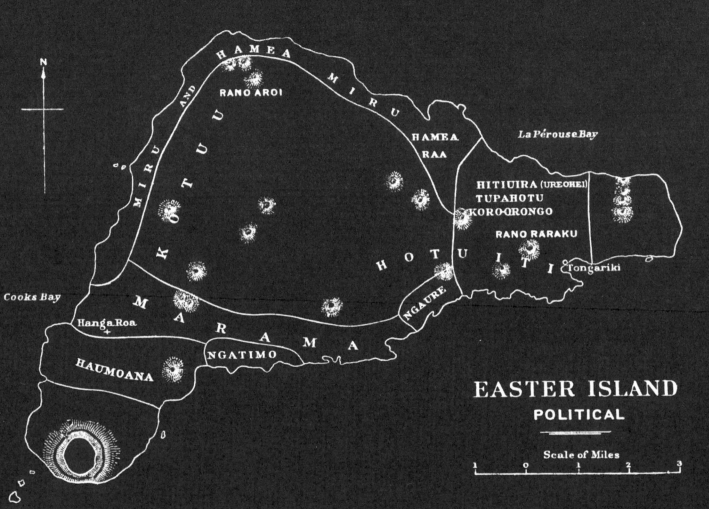

N

RANO AROI

MIRU AND HAMEA

MIRU

HAMEA RAA

La Pérouse Bay

KOTUU

HITIUIRA (UREOHE)
TUPAHOTU
KORO-ORONGO

RANO RARAKU

MIRU

HOTU I T I

Cooks Bay

Tongariki

NGAURE

Hanga Roa

M A R A M A

NGATIMO

HAUMOANA

EASTER ISLAND

POLITICAL

Scale of Miles

1   0   1   2   3

Note.—The dividing lines shown are not defined boundaries.

98. Mrs Routledge's map
showing the locations
of the island's territorial
groups; the boundaries
were approximate owing
to the often uniform terrain.

have reigned for over a millennium before crisis led to violence. Once the warriors had taken control, there was virtually persistent territorial conflict between two loose confederations of groups, the northwestern (*Tu'u*) and southeastern (*Hotu Iti*).

With the change came new methods of disposing of the dead. The cremation pits behind the platforms seem completely to have lost their significance, and burial became dominant: bodies were often left exposed for a while, and then the bones would be placed in family caves (cave burial appears to have begun c. 1700 [1]), in the new kinds of non-image platforms such as a wedge-shaped form or the semipyramidal kind, in crevices inside the ruined platforms, in their wings and ramps, in nooks beneath the toppled statues, in the hollows of their fallen head-dresses, or simply scattered in the plazas. Most of the bones seen by early visitors are probably from the post-contact period, since Routledge reported that, at the time of the great smallpox epidemic in the 1860s (introduced by the few surviving slaves brought back from Peru), corpses had been deposited any and everywhere; the French traveller Pierre Loti, in 1872, said the whole island was like an immense ossuary, and that merely to lift a bit of earth would reveal skulls and jaws. As recently as 1880, islanders were still stealing bodies at night from the Catholic cemetery, preferring to place the remains inside the platforms.

From a religion based on virtually deified ancestors in local kin groups (a typically Polynesian segmentary pattern), the islanders turned to a single deity, the creator god *Make Make* (a name that is widespread in the Marquesas), and to beliefs and rituals that were strongly focused on fruits and on fertility, including human fertility. They developed a system suited to precarious times whereby leadership alternated between groups from year to year based on a ritual egg-race. The winner of this 'election by ordeal' was consecrated as the sacred birdman (*tangata manu*) for a year, during which time his group received special privileges [2]. This was the system in place when the first Europeans arrived; the principal location of the new island-wide religion was the ceremonial village of *Orongo*.

Orongo: The scramble for eggs

The ceremonial village of *Orongo* [3] is a scenic wonder, perched on the rim between the spectacular, huge crater of *Rano Kau* and the precipitous drop to the ocean. It originally comprised one (or possibly two) *ahu*-like terraces and a plaza. These appear to have been abandoned shortly after AD 1400, when a series of stone houses began to be used. In its final phase, after the mid-16th century, *Orongo* contained about fifty contiguous, oval stone houses with corbelled roofs covered in earth, and arranged in a half-ellipse facing the islets (ill. 99 and 101). They have crawlway entrances, are from 6 to 12 m (20 to 39 ft) wide inside (with walls about 2 m [6 ft] thick), and between 1 and 2 m (3 and 6 ft) high inside. Their overall shape is like an inverted canoe (like the *hare paenga*). They often contained painted slabs (ill. 98), mostly with bird motifs. It has been suggested that they were built of thin, flat basalt slabs owing to the lack of timber by this time, but it is more probable that only stone could withstand the elements and strong winds on this exposed spot from one annual ceremony to the next.

It is thought that the ceremony began as a competition for divine blessing, but by the time it finally ended in 1878 it had altered and had degenerated into a test of skills, under the influence of the missionaries in the 1860s. It is not known precisely when the ritual began: Routledge obtained a list of eighty-six sacred birdmen ending in 1866 [4], so allowing for missing names one can estimate a start around 1760, although some scholars claim an origin several centuries earlier.

The object of the ceremony was to find a new birdman for the year, who became *Make Make's* representative on earth. Each candidate -ambitious warlords from dominant or victorious tribes rather than hereditary aristocrats- had a young man to represent him. Each September (i.e. in springtime), these unfortunate 'stunt-men' had to make their way down the sheer 300 m (1000 ft) cliff to the shore, and then swim 2 km (1.25 miles) on a bunch of reeds through shark-infested swells and strong currents to the largest and outermost islet, *Motu Nui* (3.6 ha [c. 9 acres]), where they awaited -sometimes for weeks- the arrival of a migratory seabird, the sooty tern. The aim was to find its first, elusive brown-speckled egg. The winner would allegedly shout the news to his employer on the clifftop at *Orongo* ('Shave your head, you have got the egg'), and then swim back with the egg securely held in a headband. The master now became the new sacred birdman, shaved his head, eyebrows and eyelashes, and had his head painted, while the losers cut themselves with *mata'a*.

The birdman went off to live in lazy seclusion for a year in an elliptical house at the foot of *Rano Raraku*, where he neither washed nor bathed, and refrained from cutting his nails -this must have helped ensure his seclusion! The egg was blown and then hung up for the year, after which it might be buried in a crevice at *Rano Raraku*, or thrown into the sea, or eventually buried with its owner (also at *Rano Raraku*), who meanwhile returned to ordinary life -the egg was thought to have magical powers, and to make food supplies more abundant [5]. In the final years of the ceremony the winner's group, who took up residence in *Mataveri* at the foot of *Rano Kau*, could raid and plunder other groups with impunity.

The birdman cult was really a most ingenious solution to a political problem. Intertribal warfare was rife. Any system of voting would just have put the largest tribe in permanent control. But with each tribe putting forward one 'champion', there was always the chance that even a small tribe could rule occasionally. Furthermore, the energies of the young men of the tribe, previously no doubt directed towards skirmishing with other tribes, were now diverted into training and competition within the tribe for the honour of being selected as the next year's 'champion'. It is almost as if the United Nations agreed that the country winning the most Olympic gold medals (or the football World Cup) could rule the world for the next four years. It might be a good alternative to world war.

Unlike normal dwellings, the *Orongo* houses were not closely associated with earth ovens, but instead a special cluster of ovens existed where food was prepared for participants in the ceremonies; they would have to take food out to the islets with them, or have it brought out by servants or relatives, because the *motu* had no water, and nothing to eat but fish, seaweed and berries. Each egg-seeker's food supply had to be jealously guarded to prevent it being poached by the others.

The new religious importance of the offshore islets, previously valued primarily for their obsidian and their sea birds, led to many of *Motu Nui's* twenty-one caves being modified for temporary occupation by the egg-seekers, and also being used for large numbers of burials. Eight of the caves had elaborate rock art on their walls, including birdmen and a

99. Houses in the ceremonial village of *Orongo*, and sailors from the USS *Mohican*, William Thomson's expedition, 1886, taking painted slabs from inside one of them. The upper one was returned by the Smithsonian and is now in the museum on the island, MAPSE.

Photos: Eduardo Ruiz-Tagle.

100. The giant crater of *Rano Ka*

103. Body paint, or *Takona*, during the *Tapati* celebrations

104. The unique basalt statue removed from a house at *Orongo* by the British in 1868, and now housed in London's British Museum. Its name, *'Hoa Hakananai'a'* means 'Friend which has been stolen'. The statue weighs 4 tons, stands 2.5 m (c. 8 ft) high, and bears remarkably rich decoration on its back including a raised ring and girdle, birdmen, paddles and vulvas.
Photos: Eduardo Ruiz-Tagle.

bright red mask of *Make Make*. A stockpile of red earthen pigments was found hidden in one cave, for rock art or perhaps for painting the bodies of initiates. One cave contained a 60 cm (2 ft) stone statue which, according to Routledge, marked a boundary between the territory of the northwestern and southeastern groups.

A much larger statue, known as '*Hoa Hakananai'a*' ('stolen friend' [6]), stood with its back to the sea inside one of the central *Orongo* houses, which must have been built around it: excavations revealed a great deal of charcoal in front of the entrance. The figure was buried to the chest, perhaps to lessen the necessary height of the building. Resembling a classic *moai*, it was carved in basalt -which required far more effort than carving tuff- and was richly decorated on its back with birdmen, dance-paddles, vulvas and other motifs, including traces of white and red paint. Its pointed base indicates that it was never meant to stand on a platform. This 4 ton statue, 2.5 m (8 ft) high, was removed -with ropes, levers, 300 sailors, 200 natives and considerable difficulty- in 1868 and now stands close to the Great Court of the British Museum (ill. 104) [7]. It has been argued that it was the prototype of all classical *moai*, but in view of its veneration at *Orongo* it seems far more likely that this was a very late carving, forming a crucial link between the old ancestor-worship and the new birdman cult. Its front is that of a classical *moai*, while its back bears all the motifs of this new phase, such as the birdman, the double-bladed

104.1 Tracings by Georgia Lee showing some of the many birdman carvings at *Orongo*. *The Rock Art of Easter Island*, Georgia Lee and Paul Horley, Rapanui Press.

105. Two *moai Tangata Manu*. Left British Museum and right Museum of St. Petersburg.

paddle (a symbol of power) and the vulva (for fertility) [8]. Other possible signs of transition were the birdman's residence at the old statue quarry, and the placing of head-dresses on some statues, which some scholars see as a sign that these figures represented warriors.

The rocks around *Orongo* are festooned with 1274 petroglyphs, particularly at a spot called *Mata Ngarau*, which has the heaviest concentration of rock art on the whole island, with much superimposition [9]. It is worth noting that the basalt here is very dense, so the figures took a great deal of time and effort to produce. The most striking motif is the birdman (ills. 104.1-109), sometimes holding an egg. No less than 473 birdmen are known so far, the vast majority (86 per cent) being at or near *Orongo* -they rarely occur elsewhere, and then only in the earlier, more sinuous form (e.g. at *Anakena*); the later, fuller form, which often obliterates the earlier design, is entirely restricted to the environs of *Orongo*, and it has been convincingly suggested that each is a portrait of a winning contestant. Some are partly covered by houses, so they predate at least some of the buildings.

Many of these later, crouching figures, with hands and feet clearly depicted, also have the hooked bill and gular pouch of a frigate bird, although the ritual involved the sooty tern. Frigate birds were important in Pacific cults as far away as the Solomon Islands, being magnificent flyers and also notorious for being territorially and sexually rapacious -the male's red pouch under the beak is blown up like a balloon during courtship and mating. One can readily understand their significance for the islanders, for quite apart from the importance of the colour red, the birds' behaviour must have mirrored that of the islanders themselves, raiding and pillaging as a way of life, demolishing their neighbours' nests, and even stealing twigs (perhaps reflecting the islanders' desperation for timber).

106. View of the three islets, *Motu Kao Kao, Motu Iti* and *Motu Nui*, from *Orongo*, and rocks carved with petroglyphs of the *Tangata Manu*. Right, Katherine Routledge, 1914.

107. Originally the bird associated with the cult was the *makohe* or frigate bird (*Fragata minor*); later this was changed to the *manutara* or sooty tern (*Sterna fuscata* and *Sterna lunata*), shown in the photo.

It is likely that frigate birds were frequent visitors to Easter Island in the past, but today their visits are an extremely rare event, probably because they nest in trees: in 1983, forty frigate birds were seen in the skies, but none came to nest. Moreover, a frigate lays an egg only once every two years, and, if disturbed, will not return to nest. This helps to explain why the more reliable annual arrival of the sooty tern on *Motu Nui* was adopted as the basis of the cult: it may have been an acceptable second-best, since both birds are web-footed species with forked tails, though the tern has a straight beak and no pouch. A tern will lay up to three eggs per year if the first two are collected, and may form big colonies. Even the tern, however, is no longer reliable, perhaps owing to overexploitation in the past: in 1983, only one pair nested on the islet.

The symbolism of birds is largely self-evident; we have already mentioned their ability to fly wherever they liked and hence leave the island, unlike the natives. A combination of human and bird elements is consistent in Oceanic art from the islands of southeast Asia through Melanesia to Polynesia, and is usually associated with gods or ancestral spirits -it will be recalled that the *moai* have winglike hands (p. 138). The emphasis on bird symbols is understandable in these islands which generally lack large land mammals. Birds always occupy a prominent place in Oceanic mythology; they were often thought to have a mystical relationship with the gods, acting as messengers or as transporters of souls: sea birds were particularly symbolic since they united land, sea and sky. It is worth remembering that bird-headed humans are also known even further afield in space and time: one need only mention the ancient Egyptian gods Horus and Thoth, or the bird-headed man painted in the French cave of Lascaux, perhaps c. 15,000 BC. As shown above, the birdman concept was by no means a late arrival on the island but predated the *Orongo* houses and underwent some development. The concept of the birdman and *Make Make* may therefore have begun as a subordinate ideology: oral tradition claims that *Hotu Matu'a* brought the worship of *Make Make* with him; the birdman cult's eventual adoption and dominance probably reflect the need of the warrior class to justify and legitimize its rule.

The new egg cult was probably stimulated in part by the dwindling of the bird population and hence the need to protect one of the island's decreasing sources of protein. There are myths describing *Make*

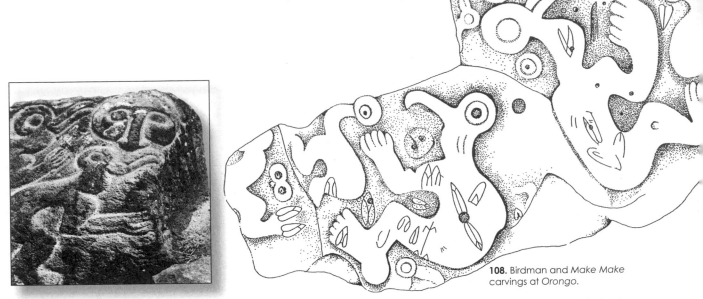

108. Birdman and *Make Make* carvings at *Orongo*.

109. Note the *komari* (vulvas) engraved on top of the birdmen. *The Rock Art of Easter Island.*

Make and other gods driving birds from Easter Island to *Motu Nui* so they would be safe from men. In this regard, it is significant that the few islanders who accompanied Métraux to *Motu Nui* devoured over a hundred eggs there in half an hour.

Goggle-eyed mask-faces are another common motif in the *Orongo* area's rock art, and are usually thought to represent *Make Make*, though they could be other gods, ancestors or particular individuals. Some have deliberately mismatched eyes. As in the rest of Polynesia, it is believed that round eyes (as on the birdmen and some masks) denote supernatural beings, whereas oval eyes (as on the statues) occurred on natural beings. Some mask-faces have long noses which make them resemble male genitalia, but it is female genitalia which really dominate here.

The vulva (*komari*) is the commonest figurative motif in the island's rock art [10], and of the 564 found so far (not including those carved on stone pillows, figurines, skulls, etc.) no less than 334 are at *Orongo*, constituting 30 per cent of all petroglyphs at the site. Not one occurs at *Anakena* which, being the traditional seat of the old royal power, may have resisted the trappings of the new order like the birdman and the fertility cult. At *Orongo*, the vulvas are even found engraved inside the ceremonial houses. They vary from 4 to 130 cm (1.5 to 51 in) in size. It is known that girls had their clitoris deliberately lengthened from an early age, with the longest and finest destined to attract the best warriors as husbands [11]. At special ceremonies girls would stand on two rocks at *Orongo* to be examined by priests, and those judged best would have their genitalia immortalized in stone. This emphasis on fertility appears to be one of the last phases of *Rapa Nui* culture, since vulvas are superimposed at least forty-eight times on late-style birdman engravings, while one fragment of fallen statue was deeply and finely recarved into a huge bas-relief vulva, 46 cm (18 in) long and 25 cm (c. 10 in) wide, and set up in a prominent place.

The island has a remarkable wealth of rock art: about a thousand sites, more than 4000 petroglyphs, and hundreds of images, clustering around coastal religious centres such as *Orongo* and *Anakena*, with very little in the interior where there are few suitable rock-surfaces. It is impressive not only for its abundance and diversity in a small island, but also for the superb quality shown in some of its designs and executions, from simple engravings to elaborate bas-reliefs, all of which may originally have had colour in their grooves. Paintings, as mentioned earlier, survive inside *Orongo* houses as well as in some caves: the famous cave of *Ana Kai Tangata* (see p. 194) contains some beautiful late paintings of terns so high up that scaffolding must have been required [12].

Much of the rock art is probably quite late; carvings, especially of canoes, and cupmarks are a frequent sight on fallen statues and their cylindrical *pukao* where they may be a sign of defeat; fifteen European ships were also depicted, including a three-master on the chest of a statue standing at the foot of *Rano Raraku*. The clustering of particular motifs in certain places or areas could also be seen as territorial marking by conquering groups during the warfaring period: the urge to mark one's clan superiority and supremacy over others clearly became a driving force on the island. Like the island's amazing richness and variety of small portable carvings, the rock art shows that the craftsmanship which produced the giant figures for centuries did not die out completely; stone and wood could still be carved with consummate skill in other ways by the 'guilds' of mastercarvers. Some of the motifs in *Rapa Nui's* art also provide a link with the one genuine mystery that remains from the island's past.

Rongo Rongo

The enduring enigma of Easter Island is the rongo rongo phenomenon: Is it really a form of writing? And more crucially, did the islanders invent it for themselves?

It comprises parallel lines of incised characters, many of them bird symbols, hooks, etc. Every alternate line is upside down, and the overall impression is of a tightly packed mass of uniform, skilfully inscribed hieroglyphics [13].

According to legends, *Hotu Matu'a* himself could read and write the characters and brought sixty-seven inscribed tablets to the island with him [14], but since the same legends also attribute many of *Rapa Nui's* indigenous plants to him, we should discount them as a reliable source on this matter. The more pertinent point to bear in mind is that not one of the early European visitors ever mentioned the tablets or the characters -yet some of them spent days exploring ashore, and entered native houses. The earliest written mention of the phenomenon [15] is that of Eugène Eyraud, the missionary, who wrote to his superior in 1864: 'In all their houses one can find tablets of wood or sticks with many kinds of hieroglyphic signs... Each figure has its own name; but the little they make of these tablets makes me incline to think that these signs, the rest of the primitive script, are for them at present a custom which they preserve without searching the meaning. The natives do neither know how to read nor write...' Eyraud's claim that the tablets were to be found in every house is strangely at odds with the silence on this matter from previous visitors and with Mrs Routledge's belief that they used to be kept apart in special houses and were very strictly *tapu*.

The obvious conclusion is that the 'script' was a very late phenomenon, directly inspired by the visit of the Spanish under González in 1770, when a written proclamation of annexation was offered to the chiefs and priests for them to 'rubriquen en forma de sus caracteres' (sign by a mark in the form of their characters) -was this their first experience of speech embodied in parallel lines? The document survives, and the marks placed on it (ill. 112) are pretty nondescript except for a vulva, and a classic

④

⑤

⑥

110. Some of the 25 tablets conserved in museums around the world. Each is designated here with a letter and a name.

① **Text E**, *Keiti*. Destroyed, reproductions in the Smithsonian, Washington and the Museum of Quai Branly, Paris.

② **Text R**, *Atua Matariri*, Smithsonian, Washington.

③ **Text G**, *Mu'a Au Mingo Ata'i Hoa Au*, or 'The Small Santiago Tablet', MNHN, Santiago.

④ **Text B**, *Aruku Kurenga*, SS.CC Collection, Rome.

⑤ **Text D**, Échancrée. SS.CC, Collection, Rome.

⑥ **Text C**, *Mamari*. SS.CC, Collection, Rome.

bird motif at the bottom which is identical to rock art images and similar to characters on the tablets.

The dilemma, as yet unresolved, is therefore as follows: were the islanders already producing their 'script' before the European arrivals, or did they devise a method of using written symbols as mnemonics after they had seen the annexation document? Throughout the world, in the 18th, 19th and early 20th centuries, first encounters with writing frequently led almost immediately to the local elaboration of invented scripts [16]. One piece of evidence is that many of the motifs found on the tablets are well represented in the island's wealth of rock art. Some scholars therefore see this as possible proof of *rongo rongo* being an ancient phenomenon on the island, although there is no archaeological evidence for this and no inscriptions on stone are known; but others argue equally convincingly that, once the islanders, inspired by the Spanish document, had decided to adopt a method of 'script', they would most probably use the motifs with which they were already familiar, rather than invent a new set [17]. In other words, the similarities of *rongo rongo* symbols with rock art motifs provide no solution to the puzzle. Besides, if the 'script' already existed, why did the chiefs and priests not use more of its motifs on the Spanish document?

Whatever its origin, the *rongo rongo* phenomenon now survives only as markings on 25 pieces of wood scattered around the world's museums. Some signs also survive on paper in makeshift 'books' from the end of the 19th and early 20th centuries, but these were considered by the islanders to be an 'inferior form of script'. The 25 wooden objects contain over 14,000 'glyphs', including one incised staff (which probably represents the original *rongo rongo* artifacts; the driftwood boards are likely to have been elaborated later on the model of the staffs). They were probably originally called *kouhau ta*, or 'written staffs'; another name, *Kohau motu*

mo rongo rongo, is a recent invention, translated by Sebastian Englert as 'the lines of inscriptions for recitation'. This is often shortened to *kouhau rongo rongo* ('wooden board for recitation') [18], which Métraux believed to mean 'chanter's staff' and hence to indicate a link with Mangareva and the Marquesas where staves were used to beat the rhythm of chants.

Examination of eleven pre-1886 *rongo rongo* carvings [19] has shown that six were made from the sacred tree *makoi* (*Thespesia populnea*) which is generally thought to be introduced to the island. A further four were carved from *Podocarpus*, which probably arrived as driftwood. Most other wood carvings were of *toromiro*.

The term *rongo rongo* (chants, recitations) did not exist in *Rapa Nui* before the 1870s, and was certainly brought from Mangareva by people who returned after abandoning the Catholic mission there: in Mangareva the rongorongo was a class of high-ranking experts charged with the memory and recitation of sacred *marae* chants; it is therefore highly likely that the concept came to *Rapa Nui* with its first settlers, and the same may well be true of the 'script'.

All the surviving pieces are over 125 years old: many look quite unused, and besides, some are fragments of wood foreign to the island, and even include a European oar. It is therefore probable that they all postdate European contact. Although a myth has arisen that the Peruvian slave raids of 1862 removed the last islanders who could truly understand the

111. Petroglyphs and *rongo rongo*:
1. Anthropomorphic signs.
2. Different types of birds.
3. Birdmen and objects of material culture.
The Rock Art of Easter Island,
Georgia Lee and Paul Horley. Rapanui Press.

Human figure

Hanga Oteo and 'Anakena

Db3   Pr9

Head with headgear and ear adornments

1

'Ōmohi and Vai Tara Kai 'Ua

Hr3   Pr3   I10

Figure with inward-pointing hands

'Ana o Keke

I10   Br1

Leg

'Ōrongo (Locus 6)

Pr4   Br8   Br7

Frigate bird

2

Papa Tataku Poki, Tongariki

Db4   Br2

Long-neck bird(?)

'Ōrongo (Loci 17 and 31)

Cb2   Ab8   Cb9

Frigate bird in diving stance

Rano Raraku

Aa4   Ab1

Bird with a "backward" neck

'Ōrongo (Locus 17)

Aa3   Ab3

Birdman

3

'Ōrongo (Locus 12)

Br7   I14   Br3

Ceremonial paddle 'ao

'Ōrongo (inside a house)

Ev5   I3   I4   Aa6

Birdman with an egg

'Ōrongo (Locus 11)

I9   Db5   Hr2

Pectoral rei miro

Hua

Ra3   Gr5   I6   I12

111.1. Part of the Santiago staff, showing the vertical lines incised among the glyphs.

112. The marks placed on the Spanish proclamation by the islanders in 1770. Right, *Mamari* staff glyphs.

tablets -knowledge of them was confined to the royal family, chiefs and priests, and every person in authority was carried off to Peru- this is actually not true; many of the older people seem to have avoided the raid, but most if not all of them later succumbed to the smallpox and virulent pneumonia brought back by one of the few survivors [20].

Thomson's informant on the subject in 1886 had never owned or made a tablet, but had been a servant of the chief who possessed *rongo rongo*, and had surreptitiously memorized some texts. Mrs Routledge could find only a handful of 'man-in-the-street' informants who had merely heard readings as children but had no personal knowledge of the 'script'; there were no experts left. It has been said that the islanders were like illiterate parishioners being asked about hymnals; they honoured and revered the objects and their texts, but in the absence of their religious leaders they could provide little information.

In the 1930s, Métraux offered 1000 pesos merely for information about new tablets, but without success. Many had been destroyed: the islanders told Thomson that the missionaries made them burn these heathen objects, though other islanders strenuously denied this [21]. One missionary was told that the natives were using them to light their kitchen fires, and even in pre-missionary days they were often destroyed in wars or deliberately burned: one chief's funeral pyre was said to have been composed of *rongo rongo* tablets, while others were buried with the honoured dead. Englert believed that many tablets, once their existence had been noticed by Eyraud, had been hidden in sacred caves to protect these *tapu* symbols of paganism from the new faith.

Bishop Jaussen of Tahiti took a great interest in the boards, and had his missionaries send some to him: indeed, far from having the tablets burned, it is largely thanks to the missionaries' efforts that we have any tablets to study at all. Jaussen attempted to have one read, or rather chanted, by an islander called Metoro [22], but the results, while providing some valuable clues, are by no means a Rosetta Stone -it has been said that the untutored Metoro was like a schoolboy trying to explain a university textbook, and his readings were clearly full of inaccuracies. Nevertheless, they show that the boards were rotated as they were read -hence the glyphs' arrangement in a 'reversed boustrophedon' (see p. 68), meaning that the characters formed a continuous sequence and the board was rotated through 180 degrees at the end of every line. A subsequent attempt was made in 1874 to have an islander read a text, but on three successive Sundays he provided three different versions of the same text!

According to Alfred Métraux, and later Thomas Barthel, who was to become the foremost specialist in *rongo rongo*, there are about 120 basic elements in the glyphs, mostly stylized outlines of objects or creatures, but these are combined to form between 1500 and 2000 compound signs [23]. They were incised with an obsidian flake and a shark's tooth [24]. The most abundant motif is the sooty tern figure, including sitting birdmen with a sooty tern head. Barthel and other scholars reached the conclusion that the motifs represent a rudimentary phonetic writing system, in which picture symbols were used to express ideas as well as objects. In other words, the individual glyphs do not represent an alphabet or even syllables, as in other scripts, but are 'cue cards' for whole words or ideas, plus a means of keeping count, like rosary beads. Each sign was a peg on which to hang a large amount of text committed to memory. There are no articles, no conjunctions, no sentences. The missing words had to be filled in by the reader as the tablet's content was sung -this would explain why the untutored provided different versions of a single text. They might be vaguely aware of the subject matter, but the details had to be improvised.

That being the case, there is little chance of our ever being able to produce full and accurate translations, unless the meagre collection of tablets is ever boosted by unexpected new finds from the island. Nonetheless, Barthel and others made great progress in identifying certain symbols and assessing the subject matter of different texts: one fragment, for example, seems to be a lunar calendar. They believed that they also include king-lists, religious and cult texts, hymns in honour of the gods, instructions to priests, lists of murdered men, creation legends, etc.

In 1995 Steven Fischer announced that he had cracked the structure of many of the *rongo rongo* inscriptions [25] -his claim received 'unlimited endorsement' from Thomas Barthel just before his death, but inevitably it has failed to convince some other researchers who have fixed ideas of their own about the script. Fischer's 'Rosetta Stone' was the Santiago Staff, a 2 kg wooden sceptre, 126 cm by 6.5 cm, which once belonged to an Easter Island *ariki* or leader and which bears the biggest collection of glyphs (2300) (ill. 111.1). Interspersed with its normal glyphs are about 103 irregularly spaced vertical lines, and Fischer noticed that these divided groups of 3 or multiples of 3 glyphs; he then also noticed

that the first in almost every group of 3 glyphs bore a 'phallic suffix', a motif which was first identified as a phallus by a rapanui informant in the 1870s. On the basis of a recitation by an old islander in 1886 and what is known of chants and beliefs from other parts of Polynesia, he sees the staff's inscription as a creation chant, a cosmogony -a whole succession of copulations, which account for the creation of everything in the world. The first glyph in each triad is thus the copulator, the second is the copulatee, and the third is the offspring resulting from the copulation.

Subsequently, he came to the conclusion that no less than 15 of the 25 known *rongo rongo* artifacts (60%) also consist wholly or in part of cosmogonies or procreation triads; but in 12 of the 15 cases the phallic suffix has been dropped. He thus feels that the script is a mixed writing system which is both logographic (i.e. the 3 glyphs in each triad represent physical objects) and also semasiographic (i.e. the phallic suffix represents an act without recourse to language).

If Fischer is correct, then we now know what most of the inscriptions say, even though we cannot read them yet. But almost all the surviving inscriptions appear to have a marked preoccupation with fertility, copulation and procreation, which fits with the phenomenon's late date [26]. Be that as it may, and whether or not the islanders developed their 'script' alone or under outside influence, it remains a crowning glory of this unique culture, one of the most highly evolved Neolithic societies in human history.

[1] Shaw 1996.

[2] Esen-Baur 1983, 1993.

[3] Routledge 1920; Mulloy 1997 (Bulletin 4, 1975, *Investigation and restoration of the ceremonial center of Orongo, Easter Island*); Davis Drake 1992.

[4] Routledge 1917a.

[5] Davis Drake 1992, p. 31.

[6] Fischer 1991.

[7] Van Tilburg 2006.

[8] Ramírez & Huber 2000, p. 40; Horley et al. 2013, pp. 22-23.

[9] Lee 1986, 1992, 1997; Horley et al. 2013.

[10] Lee 1987, 1992, 1997.

[11] Edwards & Edwards 2013, pp. 261, 265.

[12] Lee & Horley 2013.

[13] Davis Drake 1988-90; Fischer 1997.

[14] Englert 1970, p. 74.

[15] Heyerdahl erroneously reported that the first indication we have of the tablets' existence is that a *rei miro* (a large, crescent-shaped, carved wooden pendant) inscribed with *rongo rongo* characters reached New Zealand by 1851; however, he had confused this object with a Maori wooden box. See Fischer 1997, p. 8; Van Tilburg 1992, p. 93.

[16] See Fischer 2005, p. 63, for a list.

[17] Fischer 1997, pp. 552-53.

[18] Fischer 1990.

[19] Orliac 2010; Orliac & Orliac 2008.

[20] Fischer 1997, pp. 9-10, 562.

[21] For the island's first missionaries, see Dederen 1990.

[22] Routledge 1919, pp. 247-48.

[23] Métraux 1940; Barthel 1978.

[24] Fischer 1997, pp. 386-87.

[25] Fischer 1995, 1995a, 1997, 1998, 2010. Bafflingly, Cauwe (2008, p. 100) attributes the discovery of the *rongo rongo* triads to Thomson in 1891!

[26] Fischer 2005, p. 64.

113. Rongo rongo symbols of Mamari tablet.

Chapter 11

The island that self-destructed

Easter Island... fell victim to the ravages of human beings, who caused the island's deforestation, which led to the extinction of all the native trees and birds. The land suffered the most damage, and if the human inhabitants had had sufficient technological means, they would have caused profound changes to the sea around the island.

Jan Boersema 2015, p. 44.

It is common and convenient in archaeology to divide cultures or periods into three, such as Lower/Middle/Upper. Easter Island is no exception to the rule, and it was no surprise when the first attempt (by the Norwegian expedition of the 1950s) to trace the whole course of the island's history resulted in a three-phase scheme: Early (AD 400-1100), Middle (1100-1680) and Late (1680-1722). Subsequent work has questioned this scheme, only to replace it with others of a similar nature, such as Settlement (up to AD 1000), Expansion (1000-1500) and Decadence (1500-1722). An alternative chronological labelling system might be: Altars, Statues, Burials; or Architecture, Sculpture and Rock Art.

A more detailed 4-phase sequence has now been developed on the basis of agricultural production:

1) AD 800-1100, occupation of coastal areas.
2) 1100-1425, occupation of the whole coast, initial settlements become ceremonial centres, and inland field systems become established.
3) 1425-1680, maximum population, most intensive agricultural production.
4) 1680-1750, abandonment of remote field systems [1].

The 'golden age' of platform and statue building appears to start in the mid-12th century, and the island's 'cultural peak' occurred in the 15th century. It is reckoned that no more statues (or at least very few) were erected on platforms after c. AD 1500. Geiseler was told in 1882 by the oldest inhabitants that the last statues were carved about 250 years earlier [2] -and that, economically and demographically, it was all downhill after that.

Behind the spectacular constructions and sculptures lay a religious motivation, a tribal pride in display [3], and an intensely competitive instinct that was characteristic of Polynesia. In most cultures, complexity seems to be closely connected to the intensity of interaction, and opportunities to exchange ideas, with one's neighbours. When such interaction and opportunities are lacking, one normally expects to find the very simplest of cultural adaptations. Easter Island is of enduring fascination because it flagrantly violates that rule.

114. Engraving based on a drawing by Pierre Loti, 19th century.

Yet as the tremendous effort of carving, constructing and transporting the island's numerous monuments increased, it inevitably meant that the food producers had to support ever-growing numbers of non-food producers. As the population grew, and these monumental religious activities intensified, the problem can only have grown worse. Deforestation and depletion of vegetation through burning and cutting must have led to leaching and soil erosion, more wind damage, increased soil evaporation and a reduction in crop yields. The decreased water retention by the ever-diminishing plant cover had a negative effect on water supply, with the drying up of springs and previously reliable streams. The loss of large timber eventually led to an abandonment of deep-sea fishing, and hence a further loss of badly needed protein. The islanders' counter-measures -such as the garden enclosures and lithic mulch to retain precious soil moisture- reveal the kind of predicament in which they found themselves. It is theoretically possible that a drought made things worse, but clearly the islanders brought disaster upon themselves by gradually destroying a crucial resource, the palm, and unwittingly preventing its regeneration through having imported rats. A delicate balance was put under strain and finally upset. The environmental degradation was irreversible.

The amazing peace of a thousand years -unique in Polynesia- was shattered, as old rivalries were no longer expressed in competitive construction but rather in raids, violence and destruction, aimed presumably at the acquisition of arable land or simply of food and other resources. The island-wide exchange mechanisms and the co-operation of large numbers of people required to produce the religious monuments all collapsed.

The story of Easter Island is one of amazing achievement followed by, as Patrick Kirch puts it, a 'downward spiral of cultural regression'. A remarkable and unique culture, displaying tremendous continuity combined with invention and development, crumpled under the pressures of environmental destruction and, perhaps, of overpopulation; as Kirch has said, it '...temporarily but brilliantly surpassed its limits and crashed devastatingly' [4]. Unlike the inhabitants of other islands, the Easter Islanders could not escape in big canoes -in destroying their forests they had cut themselves off from the outside world even more than they had already been cut off by geography. Many of the Polynesian islands took particular skills to unparalleled heights: in Hawai'i it was featherwork, in the Marquesas tattooing, while woodcarving was outstanding in New Zealand, Hawai'i and elsewhere. Easter Island achieved eminence not only in woodwork, tattoos, feathers, and *tapa*-work (paper-mulberry cloth), but also in rock art and the extraordinary *rongo rongo* phenomenon. All of these were an integral part of its culture. But the island's supreme communal efforts were poured into the giant statues and platforms -the most spectacular religious building compulsion known anywhere in Polynesia. In fact, as William Mulloy once remarked, it was a compulsion that became a little insane: 'It came to take up so much of the force of the culture that such important activities as farming and fishing were neglected, and the people didn't have enough to eat. You can carry statue-making only so far.' Or, as Métraux put it, this was a 'mania for the colossal' [5].

The present-day Easter Islanders live amid the ruins of their ancestors' remarkable accomplishments. Mulloy saw his restoration of the monuments as a means of reaffirming the identity and dignity of the islanders. It would be a truly spectacular sight if all the statues could be re-erected on their platforms. Nevertheless, nature, despite the abuse she has suffered on the island, will eventually reclaim everything: quite apart from the possibility of volcanic eruption, it is inevitable

that not only will all the statues be worn away, dissolved back into the soil by the sun, rain and wind, but, in some millions of years, the waves and winds will batter the island itself to nothing.

[1] Stevenson & Haoa 2008, pp. 174-6.
[2] Geiseler 1995; Skjølsvold 1996, p. 104.
[3] Sahlins 1955.
[4] Kirch 1984, p. 264.
[5] Métraux 1957, p. 152.

115. Scene from the film *Rapa Nui* by Kevin Reynolds. Statue similar to the giant *moai Te Tokanga*, as if it had finally been completed and transported to an *ahu*. Photo: Eduardo Jara.

Chapter 12

The last enigma

Repeatedly and with remarkable resilience, the Rapanui devised new cultural solutions to the environmental setbacks that they themselves were causing.

Andreas Mieth & Hans-Rudolf Bork 2015, p. 108.

Perhaps the greatest of all the Easter Island enigmas remains to be considered fully: why did the civilization decline? At least five explanations (apart from those of the lunatic fringe, such as those involving extra-terrestrial visitors) have been advanced.

Van Tilburg has suggested that the prolonged isolation led to cultural downfall [1]. This has a certain plausibility, in that we know the effects of isolation on individuals can be very destructive. Certainly the rapanui isolation was exceptionally prolonged -possibly about 1000 years. The problem is that the theory is difficult to test, so that we have no real evidence for it at present.

A related idea comes from the theory of landscape known as prospect-refuge theory [2]. According to the theory, landscape views contain elements which are symbolic to the human viewer in three ways: as prospect, refuge and hazard. A prospect, such as a wide open land space or seascape, may suggest the possibility of exploration and perhaps settlement and food supply. To live safely there (in early stages of human development) it was desirable to have refuge symbols such as caves, or (later) buildings. The third element -hazard symbols, such as cliffs, rapids, rocky beaches- provides that

excitement without which life becomes boring. J. H. Appleton has argued that, for happiness and mental health, it is important to have a balance of such things in one's environment. Imbalance can lead to activity to correct for this. For instance, urban landscapes are very restricted on prospect and hazard, but over-provided with refuge symbols (buildings). The result is urban crime, where bored young people take to drugs or theft because life is too restricted and too safe. Outward-bound courses help to cure this [3]. Perhaps on Easter Island life was originally balanced. With big canoes, the ocean offered prospects for fishing and exploration. The forest, and lava caves, offered refuge, and there were hazards in cliffs and rocky beaches. When the forest was all gone, and there were no more big canoes, the ocean became a massive, restrictive hazard, and life became unbalanced, resulting in the outbreak of warfare.

Another idea is climatic change, as suggested by Grant McCall and others [4]. The argument is that a major drought or series of droughts caused crop failure and precipitated the famine and warfare, etc. McCall points out that the island experienced periodic droughts in the 20th century, and that these could have been more severe during the period AD 1400-1900, known as the Little Ice Age.

116. Engraving of a destroyed *ahu*, Cook expedition, 1774.

Many areas of the temperate world experienced droughts at this time [5], but there is little evidence from the sub-tropics of either hemisphere.

Candace Gossen has carried out a most interesting analysis of the cellulose in two plants (*Scirpus californicus* and *Polygonum acuminatum*) that grow in the floating mat of *Rano Kau*. The original idea was presented by Wolfe & Beuning [6], and uses the fact that the surface water in the lake will contain varying proportions of ^{16}O and ^{18}O. In dry weather the water molecules with ^{16}O will tend to evaporate at a faster rate than those with ^{18}O, since the ^{18}O water molecules are heavier.

The same will also apply to the hydrogen atoms in the water molecules. Those water molecules with deuterium (^2H) in them will evaporate more slowly than those with ^1H in them, because they are heavier. Since the water molecules are absorbed by those plants living in the water surface and made by them into cellulose, these plants will contain a record of climate conditions over time.

Dr Gossen uses this (combined with radiocarbon dating) to reconstruct the climate over the last few thousand years. She argues that enrichment of ^{18}O means there is more evaporation than input of rainfall [7], and thus identifies several significant dry events in the last 20,000 years. Interestingly, none of these appears to cause deforestation.

A last significant event indicated by these data is a cool and dry period starting around 545 BP, and lasting perhaps 200 years. This coincides with the Little Ice Age of Europe. It also coincides with the depletion of palm trees on Rapa Nui, but the effect is deemed to be unlikely to have caused deforestation [8], though it could have affected horticulture, and might have triggered stone mulching.

The Little Ice Age hypothesis has received strong support from some quarters [9], but unfortunately much of the evidence for climatic change in the South Pacific is based on indications of a drop in sea level. There is no doubt that there was a small drop in world sea level during the Little Ice Age. It resulted from the abstraction of water from the oceans to provide ice for the slight expansion of glaciers and ice sheets at that time, in temperate, sub-polar and polar regions [10], but that does not mean there was necessarily a change in the climate in sub-tropical regions. Moreover, the dates don't quite fit. The Little Ice Age began around AD 1400; but this was the time when Easter Island's civilization was about to enter its most flourishing phase.

It is true, however, that a number of Pacific islands seem to have been abandoned in this period (c. AD 1400), perhaps because of an unreliable water supply [11]. These include Pitcairn and Henderson, a mere 2250 km from *Rapa Nui*. Hunter-Anderson goes even further and attributes both the cultural decline and the decline of trees to the droughts [12]. We regard the latter as highly unlikely, for the pollen evidence shows that even the Last Ice Age (c. 18,000 BP), which was a much more severe event than the Little Ice Age, did no more than reduce the density of the palm forest in the lowlands of *Rapa Nui*, though it pushed the altitudinal forest limit below *Rano Aroi* [13]. But the idea that climatic change is involved in the cultural decline is quite plausible. Unfortunately, there is no good independent evidence for major droughts at the time required. The swamp at *Rano Kau* continued to grow -rather rapidly, in fact, perhaps because of its in-washed nutrients from the denuded slopes around it- throughout the period. There is a slight possibility of a hiatus in deposition at *Rano Raraku*, but the dates are vitiated by in-washed carbon, as explained above (chapter 9), so one cannot be sure. On balance, we are inclined to think that

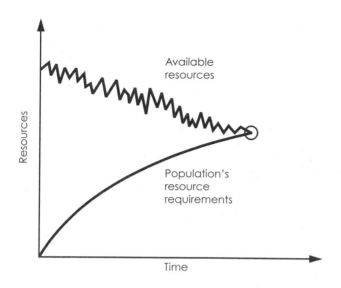

117. A model in which the island's resources are progressively depleted (e.g. by deforestation) but also vary in relation to periodic droughts. The island's population increases steadily and so do its resource requirements. Crisis is reached much sooner than if the resources were not being depleted.

probably there were major droughts in the relevant time period. But we envisage these as being more in the nature of proximate causes (triggers), with the underlying, fundamental cause being deforestation produced by increasing population. Had the deforestation not occurred, the population could probably have survived the droughts intact by utilizing moist, organic-rich forest soils for cultivation, and palm fruits as starvation food.

The charcoal remains unearthed by the Orliacs [14] have been regarded as evidence for a pronounced drought around AD 1680. But what these data actually show is a change from the burning of wood to the burning of grass, which may be explained simply by the supply of wood being exhausted from deforestation. It is not independent evidence of drought. Certainly, the development of the *umu pae* has been seen as an adaptive solution to the progressive shortage of wood [15], since the earliest are open, extended, slightly concave ovens, very different from the characteristic later form, and while the early examples contain big pieces of charcoal, the later ones contain small charcoal fragments from thin branches as well as grass, showing a gradual deterioration in the quality of combustion materials.

The fact that there is some slight renewal of the use of wood later could be explained in any number of ways, e.g. exploitation of a new source area (the offshore islets?), regeneration of some tree species (but not palms) from cut stumps, growth of new trees from seeds in the ground, etc.

Some attempts at invoking drought as the explanation have involved the El Niño phenomenon (see p. 51 and 87) [16]. This climatic event occurs every 4-7 years in western South America, and comprises a greater rainfall than usual in this region, combined with a higher-than-usual sea temperature, which is disastrous for the anchovy fishery off Peru. In between El Niño years, there may be extremes in the opposite direction, known as La Niña. We now know that this is all part of a larger variability in the circulation of ocean water and the atmosphere, so the entire phenomenon is now called ENSO (El Niño–Southern Oscillation). ENSO events not only bring rainfall to South America, they also bring droughts to the Western Pacific (Tahiti, Cook Islands, Samoa, Tonga, Fiji, New Zealand, Australia). Hence it has been argued that a stronger than usual ENSO event could have brought a disastrous drought to Easter Island. The problem with this idea is that ENSO involves a kind of see-saw of warm surface water from one side of the Pacific to the other, near the Equator. As Ferran McIntyre has pointed out, Easter Island is just about on the fulcrum of the see-saw, but to the south of it, and should therefore experience little change compared with the western and eastern Pacific regions -indeed, the largest El Niño of the 20th century, and probably of the millennium, in 1997 went completely unnoticed on *Rapa Nui* [17].

We at last have fairly clear, dated evidence of a former drought on the island. This comes from *Rano Raraku*, where Daniel Mann recovered a core c. 100 m from the southern edge of the lake. The dates from this core [18] were taken from fruits of the totora reed, or from palm pollen, and appear to avoid the problems of earlier dating using bulk sediment. The new dates show normal deposition up to about 4000 years ago. There is then a gap in deposition up to about AD 1200. The gap in sedimentation almost certainly signals a drought, although it is not clear how long this lasted, as there appears to have been some erosion of sediment during that period. It seems the drought cannot have been too major, since there is no evidence for one at that time in the *Rano Kau* core (see Chapter 9). In fact, sedimentation was extra rapid over that period in *Rano Kau*.

There is some possibility of a slight connection between Easter Island weather and ENSO. This came from a study of cores collected from an offshore coral *Porites lobata* [19]. The calcium carbonate of which the coral skeleton is made contains oxygen of two stable isotopes, O16 and O18. The ratio of these gives an indication of the temperature of the water at the time of formation. The results suggested some degree of correlation with the known ENSO record for the last 50 years. If this is so, then it is possible that ENSO droughts could have affected Easter Island a little. We now have a long record of ENSO events provided by a core from Laguna Palcacocha in the Ecuadorean Andes [20]. The core data give the frequency of ENSO events per century, and show that such events increased in frequency from a low value of c.3 per century in AD 900-1000 to a peak value of 25 per century around AD 1100-1300. Since ENSO events frequently lead to local droughts, the possibility of droughts around AD 1100-1300 on Easter Island must be entertained. This does not, however, fit with the finding of Mann et al. [21] that drought ended before AD 1200.

A third possible explanation is that the cultural decline resulted from disruption caused by European contact before AD 1722. Although the latter date is the one usually accepted for the island's 'discovery' by the western world, there were many ships (mainly Spanish) around in the Pacific for at least a century before this, and possibly almost two centuries [22]. The English pirate Edward Davis claimed in 1687 to see land west of South America at 27 degrees S (see above, p. 17). But the land described was a low sandy island, so it does not sound like *Rapa Nui* at all. It is not impossible, however, that the Spanish archives may contain evidence of earlier contact, and certainly such contact could well have been disastrous for the population, as it was on many islands in the Pacific [23]. But this version of events would not square well with the island legends of famine and internal warfare.

Recently a fourth explanation has been put forward, which claims that all the island's ills can be laid at the door of the European visitors from 1722 onwards [24]. While nobody can deny or minimise the many and varied negative effects which contact with Europeans eventually brought to the island, this theory completely ignores the massive body of varied evidence presented in this book, which proves that the island's culture had declined before 1722 [25].

The fifth explanation is that the civilization's decline was brought about by an ecological disaster resulting from the over-use of biological resources such as timber, shellfish and birds. By over-use, we mean use in a non-sustainable manner. The fact that the Easter Island civilization declined not long after the demise of the forests does not necessarily establish a connection between the two. Associations in time -even if established statistically- are not necessarily causal connections. In the case of Easter Island, however, there are some grounds for believing that the connection could be causal. In the first place, the events are in the right order. A cause must precede its effect. If decline of the forests is to *cause* decline of the civilization, then decline of the forests must happen *first*, as indeed the dating of the *Rano Kau* pollen diagrams suggests that it did.

Secondly, there is a possible causal connection. That is to say, we can think of a mechanism or model for connecting the cause and effect. Such a model is illustrated in ill. 118. Starting at the centre of the diagram, with forest and human immigration, we can see how these could interact to produce the elements which contributed to population decline. Forest clearance for the growing of crops would have led to population increase, but also to soil erosion and decline of soil fertility. Progressively more land would have to be cleared. Trees and shrubs would also be cut down for canoe building, firewood, house building, and the timbers and ropes needed in the movement and erection of statues. Palm fruits would be eaten, thus reducing

regeneration of the palm. Rats, introduced for food, fed on the palm fruits (see pp. 200-201), probably multiplied rapidly, and completely prevented palm regeneration. The over-exploitation of prolific seabird resources would have eliminated these from all but the offshore islets. Rats could have helped in this process by eating eggs. The abundant food provided by fishing, seabirds and rats would have encouraged rapid initial human population growth. Unrestrained human population growth would later put pressure on availability of land, leading to disputes and eventually warfare. Non-availability of timber and rope would make it pointless to build further statues. A disillusionment with the efficacy of the statue religion in providing the wants of the people could lead to the abandonment of this belief. Inadequate canoes would restrict fishing to inshore waters, leading to further decline in protein supplies. The result could have been a general famine, warfare, and decline of the whole economy, leading to a marked population decline.

Most of this is, of course, hypothesis. Nevertheless, there is evidence that many features of this model did in fact occur. There certainly were deforestation, famine, warfare, decline of civilization, and population decline (ill. 118). There could be other explanations. There could have been a major drought. But it seems odd that the forest should survive for 35,000 years -including the major climatic fluctuations of the last Ice Age (the forest was greatly reduced before 10,000 BP, at least in the uplands; see pollen diagram, pp. 206-207) and the postglacial climatic peak- only to succumb to drought once people arrived on the island. That would be just too great a coincidence to believe. There could have been an invasion by a new group of people. A disease could have been introduced. But neither of these would explain all the history of the island, nor is there any convincing independent evidence for either.

The ecological disaster hypothesis would gain further support if it were possible to put this model on a mathematical basis. This has in fact been done by economic theorists James Brander and M. Scott Taylor [26]. They found that when plausible estimates of initial population, timber supply, rates of use, etc, were fed into a Malthusian computer model, a population crash was inevitable (ill. 120). This was so, however, because the timber was being used as if it were a non-renewable resource like coal or oil. They conclude that the Easter Island palm was slow-growing. Ian Mahon produced a very similar result from a different mathematical model, albeit likewise using the Lotka-Volterra predator-prey equation [27].

Now, we are not great believers in mathematical models. Indeed one of us (JRF) is on record as saying 'There are lies, damned lies, statistics, and finally there are mathematical models.' Nor are we strong proponents of economics. We in fact incline more to the view that economics must be the most ancient profession, since God created the world from chaos, so there must have been economists first to produce the chaos. Nevertheless, when separate authors are convinced that the Lotka-Volterra is an appropriate model, and both their analyses produce results which resemble the real-world data, it suggests that they could be on the right track.

A more recent model [28] suggests there could have been repeated declines of the Easter Island economy, perhaps as many as eight of them. Whether these could be related to occasional droughts, population pressure, over-use of resources, internal warfare or some other cause is uncertain.

All of this propels us towards the idea of Easter Island as a microcosm, a miniature model of the planet Earth. Certainly the Earth is isolated in space in a way analogous to Easter Island's isolation in the Pacific. Attempts have been made to model the economics of the entire Earth. Early attempts by the Club of Rome [29] led to predictions of disaster on a grand scale in the 21st century. In the first edition of this book [30] we followed Mulloy (see pp. 11-12) in pointing out the analogy with Easter Island, and gained some notoriety from this.

However, the Club of Rome models were widely criticized on the grounds that they did not adequately allow for sufficient further discoveries of mineral deposits and improved techniques of recovery (e.g. for oil). Also, they did not adequately take into account substitution, i.e. the replacement of one commodity by another as stocks are exhausted. This concept may be extended to cover also the development of improved techniques, using human ingenuity to develop more efficient and less wasteful ways of exploiting the environment. This, of course, is the purpose behind the search for sustainability, as promulgated at the Rio Summit meeting [31].

The Club of Rome authors have produced a revised set of models taking these criticisms into account [32]. It now appears (ill. 121) that there is a range of predictions, depending largely on how soon the world implements sustainable practices in agriculture, industry and other parts of the economy. Sustainability is, apparently, possible.

In this connection, it is interesting to make comparisons briefly between Easter Island and some other islands. As it happens, these islands are also in the Pacific, though less isolated than Easter. Perhaps some islands have had a history even more extreme than *Rapa Nui*. Pitcairn and Henderson have already been mentioned as islands which were totally abandoned (or the population all died), perhaps because of lack of a reliable water resource. A more modern example is Nauru, where the island was physically destroyed by phosphate mining and the population had to be resettled elsewhere.

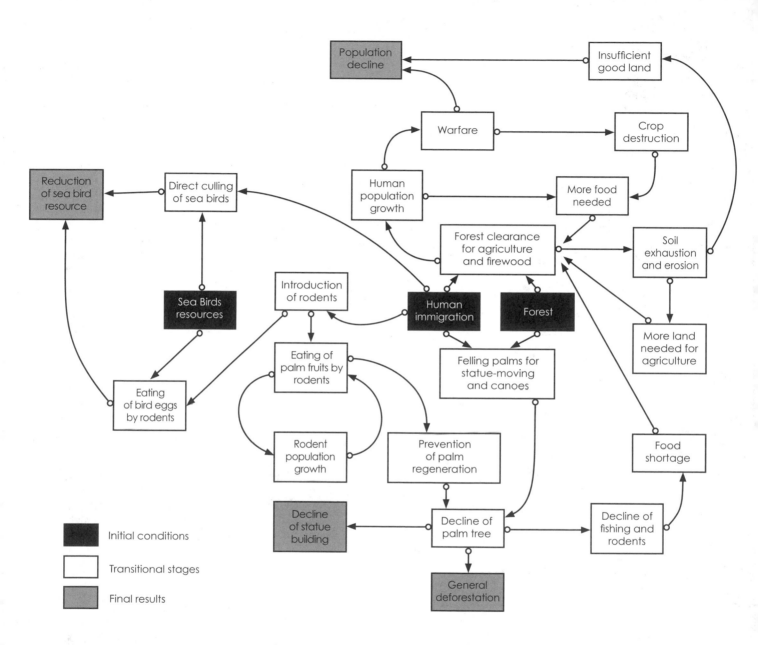

118. A model showing how human immigration could have interacted with the indigenous Easter Island resources to produce the elements that led to the decline of the civilization and to population decrease.

There are, however, some islands which seem to have been able to move towards sustainability. Their story has been beautifully told by Patrick Kirch [33]. Mangaia is an island in the Southern Cooks group, about 200 km southeast of its nearest neighbour, Rarotonga. Like Easter, it is a volcano, but a much older one. The result is that the topography is gentle, and the basalt (lateritic) soils are deep. The chief peculiarity of the place is the makatea, a ring of coral limestone (actually a raised coral reef) which surrounds the basalt heart. This limestone has been deeply eroded by the tropical climate to form an almost impenetrable coastal ring up to 2 km wide of sharp limestone pillars, some 50 m high. Between the basalt and the limestone is an annular valley, which is the most fertile part of the island, and much used for irrigated *taro* growing. Archaeology and palynology suggest initial colonization of a forested island about 2400 years ago, and the introduction at that time of pigs, dogs, chickens and rats. But when Cook's expedition visited the island in AD 1777, the islanders had neither pigs nor dogs, and possibly not chickens either. Excavation and oral records suggest the people were reduced to living on rats. There were also many human bones, not in burial situations, and it seems ritual sacrifice, and bodily mutilation of defeated enemies (if not actual cannibalism) were occurring. A summary of events is shown in ill. 121, for comparison with Easter Island. One can conclude that Mangaia also had an ecological crisis, and that it was survived only by adopting extreme measures of population control such as human sacrifice.

A slightly happier story emerges from Tikopia. This tiny island is a 'Polynesian outlier': the culture is Polynesian, but the island is situated in the Solomon Islands, the rest of which are staunchly Melanesian.

It seems the island has been inhabited for c. 2900 years, but it has survived sustainably by a system of 'orchard gardening' which has allowed root crop production under a canopy of coconuts, breadfruit

119. Natives of Tikopia, sketched by Danvin and engraved by Massard, 1836.

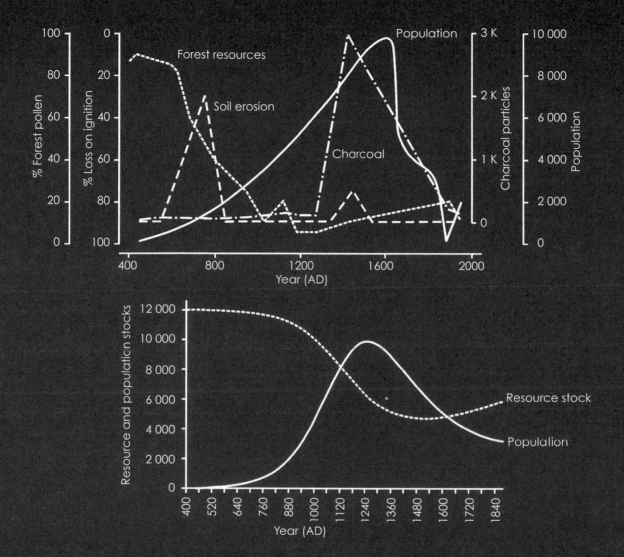

120. Top: The *Rano Kau* pollen record, as shown in core KAO 1 (Flenley et al. 1991) (forest resources) combined with an estimated population graph, and with stratigraphic evidence of disturbance (soil erosion and charcoal).

Bottom: A Malthusian computer model for Easter Island population and resources, showing that a population decline was inevitable. After Brander and Taylor 1998.

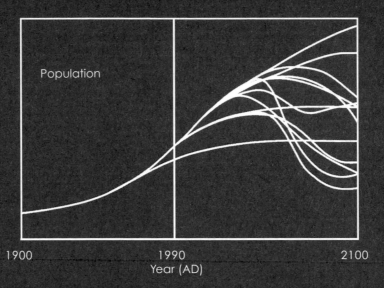

Population

1900   1990   2100

Year (AD)

121. Above: The Club of Rome's revised computer models for the population of the Earth. Whether or not sustainability is achieved depends on decisions taken now. After Meadows et al. 1992.

Opposite, top: The course of events on *Mangaia* (Southern Cook Islands), reconstructed from archaeological and palynological data. Note the population crash and recovery.

Opposite, bottom: The course of events on Tikopia, a Polynesian outlier in the Solomon Islands. Note the relative stability of population in the last millennium. Both after Kirch 1997.

and other economic trees. Archaeology shows that the island's prehistory started with over-use of bird resources and forest destruction in much the same way as Easter and Mangaia. But about AD 1600, it is recorded in oral traditions that a decision was reached to eliminate pigs, because of their destruction of crops, and the heavy timber requirements to protect gardens against this. The summary in ill. 121 suggests that Tikopia is a model of self-sufficiency. Actually, this is not entirely true, as it is still taking its protein requirements from the ocean in the form of fish and shellfish. Also,

there was a human cost. The mechanisms of population control included celibacy, prevention of conception, abortion, infanticide, sea voyaging (usually suicidal), and occasionally the expulsion of some proportion of the population. Zero population growth became a cultural ideology.

So is there still a message from the Pacific about sustainability on Earth? We think there is. Clearly Tikopia encourages us to believe that sustainability is possible for the Globe. But we must realize that even on a rather well-provided island like Tikopia

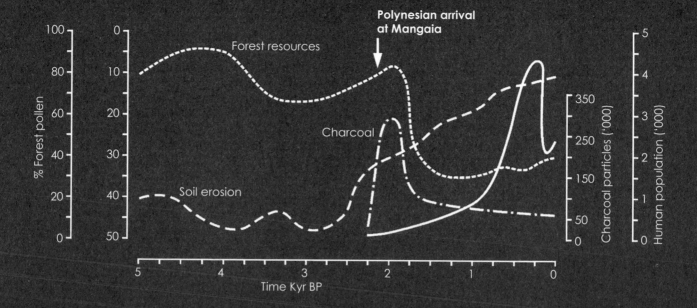

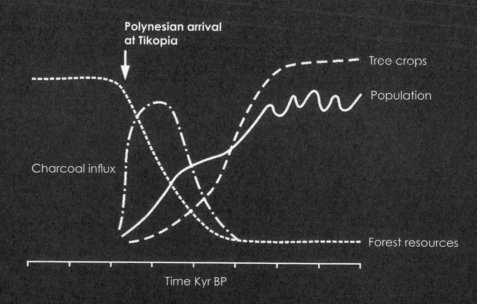

(fertile soil, tropical climate, diverse flora) extreme measures were necessary. Meat eating had to be abandoned, and strict population control was essential. The quality of life was definitely reduced, but the people and their culture survived. The alternatives illustrated by Mangaia and Easter are too horrible to contemplate. Patrick Kirch makes another telling point: perhaps Tikopia survived because it is the smallest of the three. Everybody knew each other, so it was difficult for rival factions to develop as they did on Easter and Mangaia. The message to Earth is clear: communicate, control, conserve -or face a grim future.

Could we not search for sustainability -and thus achieve stability- of population, resource use, and economic activity? It seems that human personality is against us. The person who felled the last tree on Easter Island knew it would lead ultimately to disaster for subsequent generations but went ahead and swung the axe. We have already mentioned Métraux's account of how the islanders gorged themselves on eggs when visiting the *Motu Nui* islet; he also reported that he saw the single *toromiro* tree surviving inside *Rano Kau* (ill. 123), and that '...during our stay the natives were jealously watching the growth of this tree, waiting for the right moment to cut it down and turn it into statuettes and other "curios"' [34]; even in 1984, the few terns that arrived on the island were eagerly captured and eaten. It seems the islanders' attitude to resources remains unchanged. However, we should not like our favouring of the ecological disaster model for Easter Island to be taken to imply any criticism of the *Rapa Nui* people, or any suggestion that their management of resources was worse than other people's, that they were less environmentally conscious or ecologically competent than other humans -even though, rather than exceeding the carrying capacity of the island, they 'brought the carrying capacity crashing down upon themselves' [35].

It is even possible that both the megalithic cult and the birdman cult were in fact extremely ingenious ideas to redirect the aggressive energies of the young men away from inter-village warfare and into inter-village peaceful rivalry. The physical effort and technological ingenuity involved in constructing, moving and erecting the *moai*, and in training for the hazardous swim to and from *Motu Nui* and the subsequent cliff climb, would certainly have used up a great deal of energy and time. There is good evidence of inter-village rivalry in the size and style of the *ahu*, and in the birdman cult. Unfortunately, both cults contributed to the decline of natural resources. Perhaps such things are analogous with the present-day rivalry between sporting teams in soccer, rugby, and internationally in the Olympic Games. President Kennedy's moon race was spectacular in its defusing of the Cold War. Once again, *Rapa Nui* could be a lesson to us all.

The fact is that all people everywhere have degraded their environments. Some environments are more sensitive than others. As MacIntyre reminds us, there are plenty of other examples of massive deforestation in human history -for various reasons, such as the building of warships or the construction of buildings- and, referring to what he calls 'ecostupidity', he notes that '...the damage wreaked by Polynesians on the larger and more resilient islands of Hawai'i and New Zealand does not encourage one to believe that the rapanui treated their biota any better' [36].

In the twenty-four years since our book first appeared, a great deal of wishful thinking and special pleading has been published by those who still desperately seek a South American connection, or who reject the notion that the islanders were isolated, or who deny that the statues were deliberately toppled, or who cannot bring themselves to believe that the islanders destroyed the forests, regardless of the clear evidence of what they did to the birds and other resources both on

122. Engraving of a native of Mangaia, Cook voyage, by William Sharp, London, 1885.

123. "Woman sitting under the last toro-miro (?) tree on the island; Orongo, Rapa Nui (Easter Island)". Photo by Dr. Alfred Metraux. 1934-35, Bishop Museum.

Rapa Nui and elsewhere. But Remote Oceania *had* to undergo significant environmental modification if people were to inhabit it successfully, and in exploiting their environments the settlers did not always manage their resources wisely -prehistoric human interactions with island environments have often had drastic effects on island ecosystems and the people living in them [37]. It is pointless to look back and apportion blame. We must look forward and seek sustainability.

[1] Van Tilburg 1994.
[2] Appleton 1975.
[3] Flenley 2007.
[4] McCall 1993, 1994; see also Hunter-Anderson 1998.
[5] Grove 1988.
[6] Wolfe & Beuning 2001.
[7] Gossen 2011: 126.
[8] Gossen 2011: 141.
[9] Nunn 1994, 1999, 2000, 2001; Nunn & Britton 2001.
[10] Grove 1988.
[11] Irwin 1992.
[12] Hunter-Anderson 1998.
[13] Flenley et al. 1991.
[14] Orliac 2000.
[15] Vargas 1998, pp. 128-29.
[16] e.g. Orliac 2000.
[17] MacIntyre 2001, 2001a.
[18] Mann et al. 2008.
[19] Mucciarone & Dunbar 2003.
[20] Moy et al. 2002.
[21] Mann et al. 2008.
[22] Langdon 1975.
[23] Moorehead 1966.
[24] Rainbird 2002; Peiser 2005; Hunt 2006, 2007. In *The Australian* of 18 Feb. 2016, Lipo claimed that 'The collapse was entirely triggered by Europeans'!

[25] Flenley & Bahn 2007; Flenley, Butler & Bahn 2007; see also Vargas et al. 2006, pp. 233, 401-2, concerning the major population crash before the arrival of Europeans, caused by internal factors.
[26] Brander & Taylor 1998.
[27] Mahon 1998.
[28] Cole & Flenley 2008.
[29] Meadows et al. 1972.
[30] Bahn & Flenley 1992.
[31] World Commission 1987.
[32] Meadows et al. 1992.
[33] Kirch 1997; Erickson & Gowdy 2000.
[34] Métraux 1957, p. 62.
[35] MacIntyre 1999a, p. 36. Brown (1924) was a particularly harsh critic of the islanders, mentioning (p. 148) that a missionary had recently planted two or three acres with vines, but they had cut them down for firewood; how (p. 178) they wiped out the pigs, goats and sheep left by La Pérouse, as well as rabbits that were introduced later -in fact, he even wrote 'have [the Australians] ever tried the introduction of a colony of Easter Islanders into their continental island as a cure for the rabbit pest?' His general conclusion (pp. 182-3) was quite damning: 'No Polynesian people was ever so improvident, although the cessation of the taboo, the basis of the chiefly organization and power, has, by removing the compulsion to work, brought out the tendency of the village communism of Polynesia to idleness and lack of forethought in providing for the future. As long as the Polynesians were long-voyagers they knew the evils of improvidence. And the awful example of this vice is that since the catastrophe the natives could not and did not make long voyages... The natives had not even the forethought to ask the gods for success in their raising of food; only when the crops were in danger of dying did they go to the king and get him to send an ariki paka to pray for rain'.
[36] MacIntyre 1999a, p. 37.
[37] Kirch 2000; Anderson 2002, p. 376.

124. Eucalyptus forest, *Maunga Terevaka* sector.
Photo: Eduardo Ruiz-Tagle.

Acknowledgements for the 1st edition

The initial interest of Paul Bahn in the story of Easter Island was kindled at an early age by television documentaries about Thor Heyerdahl's pioneering expedition and his experiments in carving and erecting statues. Later, this interest was developed in archaeological studies at Cambridge and, during the same years, by further television programmes such as a BBC *Chronicle* which took Colin Renfrew to the island, and *The Ascent of Man* which did the same for Jacob Bronowski. The fact that Bronowski had, alas, nothing very flattering or informative to say about the prehistoric islanders did not detract from the visual impact of their achievements or from the ever-growing desire to go and see for oneself.

That chance finally arrived in 1985 when, thanks to a J. Paul Getty postdoctoral fellowship in the history of art and the humanities, it was possible to start planning a first visit to the island. At that point, in the course of researching the subject, it was realized that by an amazing and lucky coincidence John Flenley -the very person who had recently made a most important breakthrough in Easter Island studies through pollen analysis- taught at the University of Hull, Bahn's home town.

In 1977, on finishing a research fellowship at the Australian National University, Flenley took a circuitous route back to England. As he was writing a book about tropical rain forests at the time, he resolved to go via South America, which he had never previously visited. The obvious way to do this was to fly to Tahiti and then transfer to the LanChile flight to Easter Island and Santiago in Chile. At last his own childhood ambition to visit Easter Island was to be achieved, and he decided to stop over there for two weeks, having obtained permission from the Governor to do research on the island. The important results obtained during that short stay are set out in Chapters 4 and 9.

On Bahn's return from the island in 1986, he took the advice of Graham Massey at the BBC and submitted to the then editor of *Horizon*, Robin Brightwell, a synopsis for a new television documentary on recent Easter Island research. This eventually became a successful double programme for *Horizon* in 1988 (and for *Nova* in the USA in 1989), with Bahn as archaeological consultant, and with Flenley's work featured.

We would like to express our deep appreciation for the help and documentation provided by many friends in Europe, in particular Michel and Catherine Orliac; the late André Valenta and his Paris group; Georg Zizka in Frankfurt; Annette Parkes; Pat Winker. Our thanks for documentation are also owed to Horst Cain and Annette Bierbach, Shirley Chesney, Steven Fischer, Roger Green, Johan Kamminga and Pam Russell.

Currently, the great majority of Easter Island scholars are to be found in the United States, and here above all we would like to thank Georgia Lee, founder-editor of the invaluable and indispensable *Rapa Nui Journal*; and also William Ayres, Alan Davis Drake, George Gill, Bill Hyder, Patrick Kirch, Sharon Long, Charlie Love, Chris Stevenson and JoAnne Van Tilburg. For photographs, we are grateful to Georgia Lee, Scott Baker, George Gill, Bill Hyder, Sharon Long, Charlie Love, Emily Mulloy, Mark Oliver, Isabella Tree and Jacques Vignes.

125. Polynesian man.
Mauricio Rugendas (1802-1858).

Technical help was given to Flenley by Sarah M. King (pollen counting), Maureen Martin (pollen preparation), Joan Jackson and Christopher Chew (chemical preparation), Keith Scurr and Karen Puklowski (diagrams), and Glynis Walsh (typing).

On the island itself, Flenley would like to thank Gerardo Velasco (Director of CORFO, the Chilean Government's Agricultural Development Organization in *Rapa Nui*) and his wife Margherita (an islander of high birth) for accommodation and much other help; Yolanda Ika and her mother for accommodation; Sergio Rapu for help and discussions; Claudio Cristino for useful discussions, and also Earthwatch volunteers Ernest Igou, Sally Goodhue, Kathy Marine and Mike Symond.

Flenley would also like to acknowledge research grants from the British Natural Environment Research Council; the NERC Radiocarbon Laboratory (Dr D. D. Harkness); and Professor Jim Teller for his research collaboration.

Acknowledgements for the 2nd edition

For help and documentation over the past ten years, we not only continue to be grateful to the above friends and colleagues, but would also like to thank the following: Peter Baker, Elena Charola, Francina Forment, Erika Hagelberg, Dirk Huyge, Bill Liller, Grant McCall, Francisco Mellén Blanco, Mike Pitts, Maria Eugenia Santa Coloma, Pavel Pavel, and José Miguel Ramírez. We are also grateful to Peter Bellwood, whose excellent review of our first edition pointed out several minor factual errors which had escaped us and which have been corrected here. We are very grateful to Mike Williams for permission to reproduce his cartoon. For photographs, we are indebted to Don and Elaine Dvorak for their remarkable pictures taken from a kite. Flenley would like to thank Kevin Butler for

help with pollen counting, Olive Harris for typing, and is also grateful to Professor Yoshinori Yasuda of the Centre for Japanese Studies, Kyoto, Japan, for a visit to the island in 1995, and to Japanese NHK television for a further visit in 2000. And finally, we would like to thank our agent Sheila Watson, as well as George Miller and the staff at Oxford University Press, for helping to bring this new edition to fruition.

Acknowledgements for the 3rd edition

Warmest thanks to Sonia Haoa; to Nico Haoa, Yan Araki and all the staff at the Hotel Otai; to Eduardo Ruiz-Tagle, *Rapanui Press*, for accepting the task of publishing this third edition in Chile, in both English and Spanish, and to our friend José Miguel Ramírez for his excellent translation. We thank Gerardo Velasco for help with collection of material for radiocarbon dating; Dr Christine Prior for dating these and other samples, and Massey University for financing this; Kevin Butler for help with palynology and cartography; and David Feek for help with digitization. We are also grateful to Professor Y. Yasuda for financing the visit to the island by JRF and others in 2005, and the preceding workshop in New Zealand. Finally, our gratitude as always to our agent Mandy Little, and also to Andante Travels for providing one of us (PB) with the opportunity to visit the island even more frequently!

Acknowledgements for the 4th edition

Once again we are profoundly grateful to Eduardo Ruiz-Tagle at Rapanui Press Editorial, and to the staff at Rowman & Littlefield for producing this volume. John Flenley is also very grateful to Denise Stewart for typing and much other help, and to Claire Minton for computer assistance. John Flenley also wishes to thank Troy Baisden and Mark Horrocks for including him in their research visit to the island in 2009, and in their resulting publications.

References

Adam, J-P. 1988. *Le Passé Recomposé*. Seuil: Paris, pp. 143-54.

Alden, B. 1982. Le *Toromiro*, l'arbre des Pascuans, fleurit toujours in Suède, pp. 119-23 in (A. Valenta, ed.) *Nouveau Regard sur l'île de Pâques*. Moana: Paris.

Alden, B. 1990. Wild and introduced plants on Easter Island. A report on some species noted in February 1988, pp. 209-16 in (H. Esen-Baur, ed.) *State and Perspectives of Scientific Research in Easter Island Culture*. Courier Forschungsinstitut Senckenburg: Frankfurt, No. 125.

Allen, M. S. 2006. New ideas about Late Holocene climate variability in the Central Pacific. *Current Anthropology* 47 (3): 521-535.

Anderson, A. 1989. *Prodigious Birds. Moas and Moa-Hunting in Prehistoric New Zealand*. Cambridge University Press: Cambridge.

Anderson, A. 2001. Towards the sharp end: the form and performance of prehistoric Polynesian voyaging canoes, pp. 29-35 in (C. Stevenson et al., eds), *Pacific 2000. Proceedings of the Fifth International Conference on Easter Island and the Pacific*. Easter Island Foundation: Los Osos.

Anderson, A. 2002. Faunal collapse, landscape change and settlement history in Remote Oceania. *World Archaeology* 33 (3): 375-90.

Anon 2004. *Easter Island: The first three expeditions*. Rapa Nui Press: Santiago.

Appleton, J. H. 1975. *The Experience of Landscape*. Wiley: Chichester.

Arnold, M., Orliac, M. & Valladas, H. 1990. Données nouvelles sur la disparition du palmier (cf. Jubaea) de l'île de Pâques, pp. 217-19 in (H. M. Esen-Baur, ed.) *State and Perspectives of Scientific Research in Easter Island Culture*. Courier Forschungsinstitut Senckenburg: Frankfurt, No. 125.

Ayres, W. S. 1971. Radiocarbon dates from Easter Island. *Journal of the Polynesian Society* 80: 497-504.

Ayres, W. S. 1979. Easter Island fishing. *Asian Perspectives* 22: 61-92.

Ayres, W. S. 1985. Easter Island subsistence. *Journal de la Société des Océanistes* 80: 103-24.

Ayres, W. S. 1988. The Tahai settlement complex, pp. 95-119 in (C. Cristino *et al.*, eds) *First International Congress. Easter Island and East Polynesia. Vol. 1. Archaeology*. Universidad de Chile, Instituto de Estudios Isla de Pascua.

Ayres, W. S., Spear, R. L. & Beardsley, F. R. 2000. Easter Island obsidian artifacts: typology and use-wear, pp. 173-90 in (C. M. Stevenson & W. S. Ayres, eds) *Easter Island Archaeology. Research on Early Rapanui Culture*. Easter Island Foundation: Los Osos.

Baer, A., Ladefoged, T. N., Stevenson, C. M. & Haoa, S. 2008. The surface rock gardens of prehistoric *Rapa Nui*. *Rapa Nui Journal* 22 (2): 102-9.

Bahn, P. G. 1990. Juggling dates and swivelling statues. *Rapa Nui Journal* 4 (2): 24.

Bahn, P. G. 1993. The archaeology of the monolithic sculptures of Rapanui: a general review, pp. 82-85 in (S. R. Fischer, ed.) *Easter Island Studies*. Oxbow Monograph 32: Oxford.

Bahn, P. G. 1993a. *Rapa Nui* Rendez-Vous, a personal view. *Rapa Nui Journal* 7 (3): 45-48.

Bahn, P. G. 1994. Celibate Settlers and Forgetful Fishermen: a reply to George Gill. *Rapa Nui Journal* 8 (2): 40.

Bahn, P. G. 1995. Where Giants Walked. *Rapa Nui Journal* 9 (2): 62.

Bahn, P. G. 1997. Talking turkey in Albuquerque. *Rapa Nui Journal* 11 (4): 163-64.

Bahn, P. G. 1997a. Easter Island or (Man-) Eaters Island? *Rapa Nui Journal* 11 (3): 123-25.

Bahn, P. G. 2015. The end of the Moai – did they fall or were they pushed?, pp. 135-52 in N. Cauwe & M. De Dapper, eds) *Easter Island: Collapse or Transformation? A State of the Art.* (Conference, Brussels, November 2012). Royal Academy for Overseas Sciences: Brussels.

Bahn, P. & Flenley, J. 1992. *Easter Island, Earth Island*. Thames & Hudson: London & New York.

Bahn, P. G. & Flenley, J. R. 1994. Reply to Robert Langdon. *Rapa Nui Journal* 8 (1): 11-12.

Bahn, P. G. & Flenley, J. 2008. Letter to the editor. *Rapa Nui Journal* 22: 147.

Baker, P. E. 1967. Preliminary account of recent geological investigations on Easter Island. *Geological Magazine* 104 (2): 116-22.

Baker, P. E. 1993. Archaeological stone of Easter Island. *Geoarchaeology* 8 (2): 127-39.

Baker, S. J. & Gill, G. W. 1997. A modification of results of the osteological analysis of the Norwegian Expedition to Easter Island. *Rapa Nui Journal* 11 (2): 53-57.

Balfour, H. 1917. Some ethnological suggestions in regard to Easter Island, or Rapanui. *Folklore* 28: 356-81.

Ballard, C., Brown, P., Bourke, R. M. & Harwood, T. (eds) 2005. *The Sweet Potato in Oceania: a Reappraisal*. Ethnology Monographs 19 / Oceania Monograph 56. Univ. of Pittsburgh & Univ. of Sydney.

Barnes, S., Matisoo-Smith, E. & Hunt, T. 2006. Ancient DNA of the Pacific rat (*Rattus exulans*) from *Rapa Nui* (Easter Island). *Journal of Archaeological Science* 33: 1536-40.

Barrow, L. J. 1998. The birdman in art and mythology in Marginal Polynesia -Easter Island, Hawai'i and New Zealand, pp. 346-51 in (C. Stevenson *et al.*, eds), *Easter Island in Pacific Context. South Seas Symposium*. Easter Island Foundation: Los Osos.

Barrow, T. 1967. Material evidence of the bird-man concept in Polynesia, pp. 191-213 in (G. A. Highland *et al*, eds) *Polynesian Culture History*. Bishop Museum Special Publication 56, Honolulu.

Barthel, T. S. 1958. Female stone figures on Easter Island. *Journal of the Polynesian Society* 67: 252-55.

Barthel, T. S. 1978. *The Eighth Land. The Polynesian Discovery and Settlement of Easter Island*. University Press of Hawai'i: Honolulu.

Beaglehole, J. C. (ed.) 1961. *The Journals of Captain James Cook on his Voyages of Discovery. Vol. II. The Voyages of the* Resolution *and* Adventure *1772-1775*. Cambridge University Press: Cambridge. Hakluyt Society, extra series XXXV.

Beck, J. W., Hewitt, L., Burr, G. S., Loret, J. & Torres, F. 2003. Mata Ki Te Rangi: Eyes toward the heavens -climate and radiocarbon dates, pp. 93-111 in (J. Loret & J. T. Tanacredi, eds) *Easter Island: Scientific Exploration into the World's Environmental Problems in Microcosm*. Kluwer Academic / Plenum: New York.

Bellwood, P. 1978. *Man's Conquest of the Pacific*. Collins; Auckland. Bellwood, P. 1987. *The Polynesians*. (Revised ed.) Thames & Hudson: London.

Bellwood, P. 2001. Polynesian prehistory and the rest of mankind, pp. 11-25 in (C. Stevenson et al., eds) *Pacific 2000. Proceedings of the Fifth International Conference on Easter Island and the Pacific*. Easter Island Foundation: Los Osos.

Bittmann, B. 1984. Fishermen, mummies and balsa rafts on the coast of Northern Chile, pp. 53-96 in (M. Druss & B. Bittmann, eds), *Archaeological Investigations in Chile: Selected Papers*. Occasional Publications in Anthropology and Archaeology Series 19, Museum of Anthropology, University of Northern Colorado.

Bloch, H. 2012. If they could only talk. *National Geographic* 222 (1), July: 30-49.

Boersema, J. J. 2015. *The Survival of Easter Island, Dwindling Resources and Cultural Resilience*. Cambridge University Press: Cambridge.

Bork, H-R. & Mieth, A. 2003. The key role of *Jubaea* palm trees in the history of *Rapa Nui*: a provocative interpretation. *Rapa Nui Journal* 17 (2): 119-22.

Bork, H-R., Mieth, A. & Tschochner, B. 2004. Nothing but stones? A review of the extent and technical efforts of prehistoric stone mulching on *Rapa Nui*. *Rapa Nui Journal* 18 (1): 10-14.

Brander, J. A. & Taylor, M. S. 1998. The simple economics of Easter Island: a Ricardo-Malthus model of renewable resource use. *American Economic Review* 88 (1): 119-38.

Brown, J. M. 1924. *The Riddle of the Pacific*. London: Unwin.

Butinov, N. A. & Knorozov, &. V. 1957. Preliminary report on the study of the written language of Easter Island. *Journal of the Polynesian Society* 66: 5-17.

Butler, K. & Flenley, J. 2001. Further pollen evidence from Easter Island, pp. 79-86 in (C. M. Stevenson *et al.*, eds) *Pacific 2000. Proceedings of the Fifth International Conference on Easter Island and the Pacific*. Easter Island Foundation: Los Osos.

Butler, KR & Flenley, JR 2011. The Rano Kau 2 Pollen Diagram: palaeoecology revealed. *Rapa Nui Journal* 24(1), 5-10.

Cain, H. & Bierbach, A. 1997. The term *Mo'ai* as a key to the idea behind the phenomenon. *Rapa Nui Journal* 11 (3): 103-8.

Cañellas-Boltà, N. *et al.* 2012. Macrofossils in Raraku Lake (Easter Island) integrated with sedimentary and geochemical elements: towards a palaeoecological synthesis for the past 34,000 years. *Quaternary Science Reviews* 34: 113-26.

Carlquist, S. 1967. The biota of long-distance dispersal: plant dispersal to Pacific islands. *Bull. Torrey Bot. Club* 44: 129-62.

Cauwe, N. (ed.) 2008. *Ile de Pâques. Faux mystères et vraies énigmes.* Editions du CEDARC: Treignes.

Cauwe, N. 2011. *Easter Island: The Great Taboo. Rebuilding its History after Ten Years of Excavations.* Versant Sud: Louvain-la-Neuve.

Cauwe, N. & De Dapper, M. 2015. The road of the Moai, an interrupted travelator? pp. 9-57, in N. Cauwe & M. De Dapper, eds) *Easter Island: Collapse or Transformation? A State of the Art.* (Conference, Brussels, November 2012). Royal Academy for Overseas Sciences: Brussels.

Caviedes, C. N. & Waylen, P. R. 1993. Anomalous westerly winds during El Niño events: the discovery and colonisation of Easter Island. *Applied Geography* 13: 123-34.

Cea, Alfredo. 2016. *Ika Rapa Nui.* Rapanui Press, Rapa Nui: 6.

Cervellino, M. 1993. Investigación arqueológica in la Caverna Ana Kai Tangata, Isla de Pascua. *Rapa Nui Journal* 7 (2): 52-54.

Chapman, P. 1998. *An Examination of East Polynesian Population History.* Unpublished Ph.D. thesis, University of Otago.

Chapman, P. & Gill, G. W. 1997. Easter Islander origins: non-metric cranial trait comparison between Easter Island and Peru. *Rapa Nui Journal* 11 (2): 58-63.

Chapman, P. M. & Gill, G. W. 1998. An analysis of Easter Island population history, pp. 143-50 in (C. Stevenson *et al.*, eds), *Easter Island in Pacific Context. South Seas Symposium.* Easter Island Foundation: Los Osos.

Church, F. 1998. Upland, lowland, citizen, chief: Patterns of use-wear from five Easter Island sites, pp. 312-15 in (C. Stevenson, G. Lee & F. J. Morin, eds) *Easter Island in Pacific Context (South Seas Symposium: Proceedings 4th International Conference on Easter Island and East Polynesia).* Los Osos, Easter Island Foundation.

Church, F. & Ellis, J. G. 1996. A use-wear analysis of obsidian tools from Ana Kionga. *Rapa Nui Journal* 10 (4): 81-88.

Church, F. & Rigney, J. 1994. A microwear analysis of tools from Site 10-241 Easter Island, an inland processing site. *Rapa Nui Journal* 8 (4): 101-5.

Clark, R. 1983. Review of R. Langdon & D. Tryon, 'The Language of Easter Island'. *Journal of the Polynesian Society* 92: 419-25.

Clow, C. M., Stefan, V. H., Gill, G. W. & Owsley, D. W. 2001. Cranial and facial form descriptions and comparisons of several Polynesian and Peruvian samples, pp. 437-46 in (C. M. Stevenson *et al.*, eds) *Pacific 2000. Proceedings of the Fifth International Conference on Easter Island and the Pacific*. Easter Island Foundation: Los Osos.

Cole, A. & Flenley, J. 2005. Human settlement of Easter Island, a Far-from-Equilibrium model, pp. 35-54 in (C. M. Stevenson, *et al.*, eds) *The Reñaca Papers: VI International Conference on Rapa Nui and the Pacific*. Easter Island Foundation: Los Osos.

Cole, A. & Flenley, J. 2007. Human settlement of Easter Island - a competing hypothesis. *Earth and Environmental Science Transactions of the Royal Society of Edinburgh* 98: 101-116.

Cole, A. & Flenley, J. 2008. Modelling human population change on Easter Island far-from-equilibrium. *Quaternary International* 184: 150-265.

Commendador, A. S. *et al.* 2013. A stable isotope (∂13C and ∂15N) perspective on human diet on Rapa Nui (Easter Island) ca AD 1400-1900. *American Journal of Physical Anthropology* 152: 173-85.

Conte Oliveros, J. 1994. *Isla de Pascua. Horizontes, Sombríos y Luminosos. (Historia Documentada)*. Centro de Investigación de la Imagen: Santiago.

Cotterell, B. & Kamminga, J. 1990. *Mechanics of Pre-Industrial Technology*. Cambridge University Press: Cambridge.

Cristino, C. & Izaurieta, R. 2006. Easter Island: total land area of Te Pito o Te Henua. *Rapa Nui Journal* 20 (1): p. 81.

Cristino, C. & Vargas, P. 1998. Archaeological excavations and reconstruction of Ahu Tongariki, pp. 153-58 in (P. Vargas Casanova, ed.) *Easter Island and East Polynesian Prehistory*. Universidad de Chile: Santiago.

Cristino, C. & Vargas, P. 1999. Ahu Tongariki, Easter Island: Chronological and sociopolitical significance. *Rapa Nui Journal* 13 (3): 67-69.

Cristino, C., Vargas, P., Izaurieta, R. & Budd, R. (eds) 1988. *First International Congress. Easter Island and East Polynesia. Vol. 1. Archaeology*. Universidad de Chile, Instituto de Estudios Isla de Pascua.

Cummings, L. S. 1998. A review of recent pollen and phytolith studies from various contexts on Easter Island, pp 100-106 in (C. M. Stevenson, G. Lee & F. J. Morin, eds) *Easter Island in Pacific Context*. Easter Island Foundation: Los Osos.

von Däniken, E. 1969. *Chariots of the Gods?* Souvenir Press: London.

Davis Drake, A. 1988-90. A layman's guide to Rongorongo. *Rapa Nui Journal* 2 (3) to 4 (1).

Davis Drake, A. 1992. *Easter Island. The Ceremonial Center of Orongo*. Cloud Mt Press: Old Bridge, NJ.

Dederen, F. 1990. L'évangélisation de l'île de Pâques, pp. 103-23 in (B. Illius & M. Laubscher, eds), *Circumpacifica. Band II, Ozeanien, Miszellen. Festschrift für Thomas S. Barthel*. Peter Lang: Frankfurt.

Delhon, C. & Orliac, C. 2010. The vanished palm trees of Easter Island: new radiocarbon and phytolith data, pp. 97-110 in (P. Wallin & H. Martinsson-Wallin, eds) *The Gotland Papers. Selected papers from the VII International Conference on Easter Island and the Pacific: Migration, Identity and Cultural Heritage*. Gotland, Sweden, 20-25 August 2007. Gotland University Press 11.

Diamond, J. 2004. Twilight at Easter. *New York Review of Books* 51 (5): 4-7.

Diamond, J. 2005. *Collapse. How Societies Choose to Fail or Succeed*. Viking Press: New York.

Diamond, J. 2007. Easter Island revisited. *Science* 317: 1692-94.

DiSalvo, L. H. & Randall, J. E. 1993. The marine fauna of Rapanui, past and present, pp. 16-23 in (S. R. Fischer, ed.), *Easter Island Studies. Contributions to the History of Rapanui*. Oxbow Monograph 32: Oxford.

Dodd, E. 1972. *Polynesian Seafaring*. Dodd, Meade & Co.: New York.

Doswell, C. A. 2002. In the line of fire: first global lightning map reveals high-strike zones. *National Geographic Magazine* 202 (2): viii.

Dransfield, J., Flenley, J. R., King, S. M., Harkness, D. D. & Rapu, S. 1984. A recently extinct palm from Easter Island. *Nature* 312: 750-52.

Du Feu, V. M. & Fischer, S. R. 1993. The *rapanui* language, pp. 165-68 in (S. R. Fischer, ed.) *Easter Island Studies*. Oxbow Monograph 32: Oxford.

Dundas, C. M. 2000. The Easter Island reports of Lt. Colin M. Dundas, 1870-71. *Rapa Nui Journal* 14 (2): 37-41.

Dyer, G. 2005. Is World War III overdue? *The Manawatu Standard* newspaper, 6 May, p. 12.

Edwards, E. & Edwards, A. 2013. *When the Universe was an Island. Exploring the Cultural and Spiritual Cosmos of Ancient Rapa Nui*. Hangaroa Press: Hanga Roa.

Edwards, E., Marchetti, R., Dominichetti, L. & González-Ferrán, O. 1996. When the Earth trembled, the statues fell. *Rapa Nui Journal* 10 (1): 1-15.

Emory, K. P. 1972. Easter Island's position in the prehistory of Polynesia. *Journal of the Polynesian Society* 81: 57-69.

Englert, S. 1948. *La Tierra de Hotu Matu'a. Historia y Etnología de la Isla de Pascua*. Imprenta San Francisco: Santiago.

Englert, S. 1970. *Island at the Center of the World*. Scribners: New York.

Erickson, J. D. & Gowdy, J. M. 2000. Resource use, institutions and sustainability: a tale of two Pacific island cultures. *Land Economics* 76 (3): 345-54.

Esen-Baur, H-M. 1983. *Untersuchungen über den Vogelmann-kult auf der Osterinsel*. Franz Steiner Verlag: Wiesbaden.

Esen-Baur, H. (ed.) 1989. *1500 Jahre Kultur der Osterinsel.* Verlag Philipp Von Zabern: Mainz.

Esen-Baur, H. M. (ed.) 1990. *State and Perspectives of Scientific Research in Easter Island Culture.* Courier Forschungsinstitut Senckenburg: Frankfurt, No. 125.

Esen-Baur, H-M. 1993. The *Tangata Manu* of Rapanui, pp. 147-52 in (S. R. Fischer, ed.) *Easter Island Studies. Contributions to the History of rapanui in Memory of William T. Mulloy.* Oxbow Monograph 32: Oxford.

Etienne, M., Michea, G. & Díaz, E. 1982. *Flora, Vegetación y Potencial pastoral de Isla de Pascua.* Univ. de Chile, Fac. de Ciencias Agrarias, Veterinarias & Forestales, Boletín Técnico No. 47.

Eyraud, E. 2008. *Easter Island 1864.* Imprenta Andina: Santiago.

Ferdon, E. 1966. *One Man's Log.* Allen & Unwin: London.

Ferdon, E. N. Jr. 2000. Stone chicken coops on Easter Island. *Rapa Nui Journal* 14 (3): 77-79.

Finney, B. 1985. Anomalous westerlies. El Niño and the colonization of Polynesia. *American Anthropologist* 87: 9-26.

Finney, B. 1991. Myth, experiment, and the reinvention of Polynesian voyaging. *American Anthropologist* 93: 383-404.

Finney, B. 1993. Voyaging and isolation in *Rapa Nui* prehistory. *Rapa Nui Journal* 7 (1): 1-6.

Finney, B. 1994. Polynesia-South America round trip canoe voyages. *Rapa Nui Journal* 8 (2): 33-35.

Finney, B. 1994a. The impact of Late Holocene climate change on Polynesia. *Rapa Nui Journal* 8 (1): 13-15.

Finney, B. 2001. Voyage to Polynesia's land's end. *Antiquity* 75: 172-81.

Finney, B. & Kilonsky, B. 2001. Closing and opening the Polynesian Triangle: *Hokule'a's* voyage to *Rapa Nui,* pp. 353-63 in (C. Stevenson et al., eds), *Pacific 2000. Proceedings of the Fifth International Conference on Easter Island and the Pacific.* Easter Island Foundation: Los Osos.

Finney, B. *et al.* 1989. Wait for the west wind. *Journal of the Polynesian Society* 98: 261-302.

Fischer, S. R. 1990. 'Rongorongo mechanics' reviewed. *Rapa Nui Journal* 4 (3): 44-45.

Fischer, S. R. 1991. Has the British Museum a 'stolen friend' from *Rapa Nui? Rapa Nui Journal* 5 (4): 49-51.

Fischer, S. R. 1992. Homogeneity in old Rapanui. *Oceanic Linguistics* 31: 181-90.

Fischer, S. R. 1992a. At the teeth of savages. *Rapa Nui Journal* 6 (4): 72-73.

Fischer, S. R. (ed.) 1993. *Easter Island Studies. Contributions to the History of rapanui in Memory of William T. Mulloy.* Oxbow Monograph 32: Oxford.

Fischer, S. R. 1993a. The calling of H.M.S. *Seringapatam* at rapanui (Easter Island) on 6 March 1830. *Pacific Studies* 16 (1): 67-84.

Fischer, S. R. 1995. Preliminary evidence for cosmogonic texts in Rapanui's *Rongorongo* inscriptions. *Journal of the Polynesian Society* 104: 303-21.

Fischer, S. R. 1995a. Further evidence for cosmogonic texts in the *Rongorongo* inscriptions of Easter Island. *Rapa Nui Journal* 9 (4): 99-107.

Fischer, S. R. 1997. *Rongorongo. The Easter Island Script. History, Traditions, Texts.* Clarendon Press: Oxford.

Fischer, S. R. 1998. Reading Rapanui's *Rongorongo*, pp. 2-7 in (C. Stevenson *et al.*, eds) *Easter Island in Pacific Context. South Seas Symposium.* Easter Island Foundation: Los Osos.

Fischer, S. R. 2005. *Island at the End of the World: The Turbulent History of Easter Island.* Reaktion Books: London.

Fischer, S. R. 2010. Preliminary internal evidence for series of procreation triads in Easter Island's Rongorongo corpus, pp. 225-230 in (P. Wallin & H. Martinsson-Wallin, eds) *The Gotland Papers. Selected papers from the VII International Conference on Easter Island and the Pacific: Migration, Identity and Cultural Heritage.* Gotland, Sweden, 20-25 August 2007. Gotland University Press 11.

Fischer, S. R. & Love, C. M. 1993. Rapanui: The geological parameters, pp. 1-6 in (S. R. Fischer, ed.), *Easter Island Studies. Contributions to the History of Rapanui.* Oxbow Monograph 32: Oxford.

Fisher, M. J. & Fisher, D. E. 2000. *Mysteries of Lost Empires.* Macmillan (Channel 4 Books): London.

Fitzpatrick, S. M. & Callaghan, R. 2009. Examining dispersal mechanisms for the translocation of chicken (*Gallus gallus*) from Polynesia to South America. *Journal of Arch. Science* 36: 214-23.

Flas, D. 2015. The Mata'a and the "collapse hypothesis", pp. 59-75 in (N. Cauwe & M. De Dapper, eds) *Easter Island: Collapse or Transformation? A State of the Art.* (Conference, Brussels, November 2012). Royal Academy for Overseas Sciences: Brussels.

Flenley, J. R. 1993. The present flora of Easter Island and its origins, pp. 7-15 in (S. R. Fischer, ed.), *Easter Island Studies. Contributions to the History of Rapanui.* Oxbow Monograph 32: Oxford.

Flenley, J. R. 2007. For the beauty of the Earth. *Stimulus* 15: 21-25.

Flenley, J. R. 2010. A palynologist looks at the colonization of the Pacific, pp. 15-34 in (P. Wallin & H. Martinsson-Wallin, eds) *The Gotland Papers. Selected papers from the VII International Conference on Easter Island and the Pacific: Migration, Identity and Cultural Heritage.* Gotland, Sweden, 20-25 August 2007. Gotland University Press 11.

Flenley, J & Bahn, P. 2002. *The Enigmas of Easter Island.* Oxford University Press: Oxford.

Flenley, J. & Bahn, P. 2007. Conflicting views of Easter Island. *Rapa Nui Journal* 21 (1): 11-13.

Flenley, J., Butler, K. & Bahn, P. G. 2007. Respect versus contempt for evidence: reply to Hunt and Lipo. *Rapa Nui Journal* 21 (2): 98-104.

Flenley, J. R. & King, S. M. 1984. Late Quaternary pollen records from Easter Island. *Nature* 307: 47-50.

Flenley, J. R., King, S. M., Teller, J. T., Prentice, M. E., Jackson, J. & Chew, C. 1991. The Late Quaternary vegetational and climatic history of Easter Island. *Journal of Quaternary Science* 6: 85-115.

Foerster, R. 2012. *Rapa Nui, primeras expediciones europeas*. Rapa Nui Press: Santiago.

Forment, F. 1991. *Les Figures* Moai Kavakava *de l'île de Pâques*. Working Papers in Ethnic Art 5, Dept. of Ethnic Art, University of Ghent: Ghent.

Forment, F., Huyge, D. & Valladas, H. 2001. AMS 14C age determinations of *rapanui* (Easter Island) wood sculpture: *moai kavakava* ET 48.63 from Brussels. *Antiquity* 75: 529-32.

Forster, G. 2000. *A Voyage around the world* (N. Thomas & Berghof, eds). Vol. I. University Press of Hawaii: Honolulu.

Geiseler, W. 1995. *Geiseler's Easter Island Report. An 1880s Anthropological Account*. (Trad. W. S. & G. S. Ayres). Asian and Pacific Archaeology Series No. 12. Social Science Research Institute, University of Hawaii at Manoa.

Gill, G. W. 1988. William Mulloy and the beginnings of Wyoming osteological research on Easter Island. *Rapa Nui Notes* 7: 9/13.

Gill, G. 1990. Easter Island rocker jaws. *Rapa Nui Journal* 4 (2): 21.

Gill, G. W.1994. On the settlement of Easter Island: in response to Paul Bahn. *Rapa Nui Journal* 8 (1): 16-18.

Gill, G. W. 1998. Easter Island settlement: current evidence and future research directions, pp. 137-42 in (C. Stevenson *et al.*, eds), *Easter Island in Pacific Context. South Seas Symposium*. Easter Island Foundation: Los Osos.

Gill, G. W. 2000. Skeletal remains from Ahu Nau Nau: Land of the Royal Miru, pp. 109-24 In (C. M. Stevenson & W. S. Ayres, eds) *Easter Island Archaeology. Research on Early rapanui Culture*. Easter Island Foundation: Los Osos.

Gill, G. W. 2001. Basic skeletal morphology of Easter Island and East Polynesia, with Paleoindian parallels and contrasts, pp. 447-56 in (C. M. Stevenson *et al.*, eds) *Pacific 2000. Proceedings of the Fifth International Conference on Easter Island and the Pacific*. Easter Island Foundation: Los Osos.

Gill, G. W. 2015. East-Polynesian and Paleoindian parallels and contrasts in skeletal morphology, pp. 269-85 in Stefan, V. H. & Gill, G. W. (eds) 2015. *Skeletal Biology of the Ancient Rapanui (Easter Islanders)*. Cambridge University Press: Cambridge.

Gill, G. W., Haoa, S. & Owsley, D. W. 1997. Easter Island origins: implications of osteological findings. *Rapa Nui Journal* 11 (2): 64-71.

Gill, G. W. & Owsley, D. W. 1993. Human osteology of Rapanui, pp. 56-62 in (S. R. Fischer, ed.), *Easter Island Studies*. Oxbow Monograph 32: Oxford.

Golson, J. (ed.) 1962. *Polynesian Navigation*. Memoir 34, The Polynesian Society: Wellington. Supplement to the *Journal of the Polynesian Society*.

Golson, J. 1965/6. Thor Heyerdahl and the prehistory of Easter Island. *Oceania* 36: 38-83.

Góngora, J., Rawlence, N. J., Mobegi, V. A., Jianlin, H., Alcalde, J. A., Matus, J. T., Hanotte, O., Moran, C., Austin, J. J., Ulm, S., Anderson, A. J., Larson, G. & Cooper, A. 2008. Indo-European and Asian origins for Chilean and Pacific chickens revealed by mtDNA. *Proc. Nat. Acad. Sci. USA* 105 (30), July 29, pp. 10308-13.

Gossen, C. 2007. The mystery lies in the *Scirpus*. *Rapa Nui Journal* 21 (2): 105-110.

Gossen, C. L. 2011. *Deforestation, drought and humans. New discoveries of the Late Quaternary Palaeoenvironment of Rapa Nui (Easter Island)*. Ph.D. Thesis, Portland State University, U.S.A.

Gossen, C. & Stevenson, C. 2005. Prehistoric solar innovation and water management on *Rapa Nui*, in (D. Y. Goswami, S. Vijayaraghavan & R. Campbell-Howe, eds) *Proceedings of the 2005 Solar World Congress, the 34th ASES Annual Conference and 30th National Passive Solar Conference*, August 2005, Orlando, Florida (only available on CD).

Grau, J. 1996. Jubaea, the palm of Chile and Easter Island? *Rapa Nui Journal* 10 (2): 37-40.

Grau, J. 2000. *Palmeras*. Oikos: Santiago.

Green, R. C. 1988. Subgrouping of the *rapanui* language of Easter Island in Polynesian and its implications for East Polynesian prehistory, pp. 37-57 in (C. Cristino *et al.*, eds), *Easter Island and East Polynesia*. Vol. 1, *Archaeology*, First Int. Congress, Hanga Roa 1984. Univ. de Chile, Inst. de Estudios Isla de Pascua.

Green, R. C. 1998. *Rapanui* origins prior to European contact. The view from Eastern Polynesia, pp. 87-110 in (P. Vargas, ed.) *Easter Island and East Polynesian Prehistory*. Univ. de Chile: Santiago.

Green, R. C. 2000. Origins for the *rapanui* of Easter Island before European contact: solutions from Holistic Anthropology to an issue no longer much of a mystery. *Rapa Nui Journal* 14 (3): 71-76.

Green, R. C. 2001. Commentary on the sailing raft, the sweet potato and the South American connection. *Rapa Nui Journal* 15 (2): 69-77.

Grove, J. M. 1988. *The Little Ice Age*. Methuen: London.

Guerra, A, 2006a. Las estructuras domesticas de *Rapa Nui* (I): Las olvidadas de la arqueología. *Revista de Arqueología* 300: 34-39.

Guerra, A, 2006b. Las estructuras domesticas de *Rapa Nui* (II): Levantamiento, registro & manutención. *Revista de Arqueología* 301: 36-43.

Guerra, A. & Stevenson, C. 2005. Arqueología de la agricultura prehistórica. *Rapa Nui*. Resultados de la Campaña Vaitea 2001-2002. *Revista de Arqueología* 293: 26-35.

Gurley, R. E. & Liller, W. 1997. Palm trees, Mana and the moving of the moai. *Rapa Nui Journal* 11 (2): 82-84.

Hagelberg, E. 1993/4. Ancient DNA studies. *Evolutionary Anthropology* 2 (6): 199-207.

Hagelberg, E. 1995. Genetic affinities of prehistoric Easter Islanders: reply to Langdon. *Rapa Nui Journal* 9 (1): 16-19.

Hagelberg, E. 2014. Molecular genetics and the human settlement of the Pacific, pp. 132-42 in (I. Hoëm, ed.) *Thor Heyerdahl's Kon-Tiki in New Light*. The Kon-Tiki Museum Occasional Papers 14, Oslo.

Hagelberg, E. 2015. Genetic affinities of the Rapanui, pp. 182-201 in (V. H. Stefan & G. W. Gill, eds) *Skeletal Biology of the Ancient Rapanui (Easter Islanders)*. Cambridge University Press: Cambridge.

Hagelberg, E., Quevedo, S., Turbon, D. & Clegg, J. B. 1994. DNA from ancient Easter Islanders. *Nature* 369: 25-26.

Hasse, K. M., Stoffers, P. & Garbe-Schonberg, C. D. 1997. The petrogenetic evolution of lavas from Easter Island and neighbouring seamounts, Near-Ridge Hotspot Volcanoes in the Southeast Pacific. *Journal of Petrology* 38: 785-813.

Heiser, C. B. 1974. Totoras, taxonomy and Thor. *Plant Science Bulletin*, 22-26.

Heyerdahl, T. 1950. *The Kon-Tiki Expedition*. Allen & Unwin: London.

Heyerdahl, T. 1952. *American Indians in the Pacific*. Allen & Unwin: London.

Heyerdahl, T. 1958. *Aku-Aku. The Secret of Easter Island*. Allen & Unwin: London.

Heyerdahl, T. 1974. *Sea Routes to Polynesia*. Futura Books: London.

Heyerdahl, T. 1989. *Easter Island: The Mystery Solved*. Souvenir Press: London.

Heyerdahl, T. & Ferdon, E. Jr. (eds) 1961. *Reports of the Norwegian Archaeological Expedition to Easter Island and the East Pacific. Vol. 1: The Archaeology of Easter Island*. Allen & Unwin: London.

Heyerdahl, T. & Ferdon, E. Jr (eds) 1965. *Ibid: Vol. 2: Miscellaneous Papers*. Allen & Unwin: London.

Heyerdahl, T., Sandweiss, D. H. & Narvaez, A. 1995. *Pyramids of Túcume. The Quest for Peru's Forgotten City*. Thames & Hudson: London.

Heyerdahl, T., Skjølsvold, A. & Pavel, P. 1989. The 'walking' moai of Easter Island, pp. 36-64 in *Occasional Papers of the Kon-Tiki Museum 1*.

Hill, A. V. S. & Serjeantson, S. W. (eds) 1989. *The Colonization of the Pacific: A Genetic Trail*. Clarendon Press: Oxford.

Hoare, M. E. (ed.) 1982. *The Resolution Journal of Johann Reinhold Forster 1772-1775. Vol. III.* Hakluyt Society, 2nd series No. 154. Hakluyt Society: London.

Horley, P. & Lee, G. 2008. Rock art of the sacred precinct at Mata Ngarau, 'Orongo. *Rapa Nui Journal* 22 (2): 110-16.

Horley, P., Lee, G. & Bahn, P. 2013. Return of the Birdman. Bringing back colour to Easter Island's sacred cult. *Current World Archaeology* 62, Dec/Jan: 16-22.

Horrocks, M. & Wozniak, J. A. 2008. Plant microfossil analysis reveals disturbed forest and a mixed-crop dryland production system at Te Nui, Easter Island. *Journal of Archaeological Science* 35: 126-42.

Horrocks, M. *et al.* 2012. Microfossils of Polynesian cultigens in lake sediment cores from Rano Kau, Easter Island. *Journal of Palaeolimnology* 47: 185-204.

Horrocks, M. *et al.* 2012a. Fossil plant remains at Rano Raraku, Easter Island's statue quarry: evidence for past elevated lake level and ancient Polynesian agriculture. *Journal of Palaeolimnology* 47: 767-83.

Horrocks, M. *et al.* 2013. Pollen, phytoliths, athropods and high-resolution 14C sampling from Rano Kau, Easter Island: evidence for late Quaternary environments, ant (Formicidae) distributions and human activity. *Journal of Palaeolimnology* 50: 417-32.

Horrocks, M. *et al.* 2015. A plant microfossil record of Late Quaternary environments and human activity from Rano Aroi and surroundings, Easter Island. *Journal of Palaeolimnology* 54: 279-303.

Howells, W. 1973. *The Pacific Islanders*. Weidenfeld & Nicolson: London.

Hubbard, D. K. & Garcia, M. 2003. The coral reefs of Easter Island a preliminary assessment, pp. 53-77 in (J. Loret & J. T. Tancredi, eds) *Easter Island: Scientific Exploration into the World's Environmental Problems in Microcosm*. Kluwer: New York.

Hunt, T. L. 2006. Rethinking the fall of Easter Island. *American Scientist* 94 (5): 412-19.

Hunt, T. L. 2007. Rethinking Easter Island's ecological catastrophe. *Journal of Arch. Science* 34 (3): 485-502.

Hunt, T. L. & Lipo, C. R. 2006. Late colonization of Easter Island. *Science* 311: 1603-06.

Hunt, T. L. & Lipo, C. 2007. Chronology, deforestation, and 'collapse'. Evidence vs. faith in *Rapa Nui* prehistory. *Rapa Nui Journal* 21 (2): 85-97.

Hunt, T. & Lipo, C. 2011. *The Statues that Walked. Unraveling the Mystery of Easter Island*. Free Press: New York.

Hunter-Anderson, R. L. 1998. Human vs climatic impacts on *Rapa Nui*: did the people really cut down all those trees?, pp. 85-99 in (C. M. Stevenson *et al.*, eds) *Easter Island in Pacific Context: South Seas Symposium*. Easter Island Foundation: Los Osos.

Huyge, D. & Cauwe, N. 2002. The Ahu O Rongo project: archaeological research on *Rapa Nui*. *Rapa Nui Journal* 16 (1): 11-16.

Irwin, G. 1989. Against, across and down the wind. *Journal of the Polynesian Society* 98: 167-206.

Irwin, G. 1990. Human colonisation and change in the remote Pacific. *Current Anthropology* 31: 90-94.

Irwin, G. 1992. *The Prehistoric Exploration and Colonisation of the Pacific*. Cambridge University Press: Cambridge.

Irwin, G., Bickler, S. & Quirke, P. 1990. Voyaging by canoe and computer: experiments in the settlement of the Pacific Ocean. *Antiquity* 64: 34-50.

Jacobson, G. L. & Bradshaw, R. H. W. 1981. The selection of sites for paleovegetational studies. *Quaternary Research* 16: 80-96.

Jennings, J. D. (ed.) 1979. *The Prehistory of Polynesia*. Harvard University Press: Cambridge, Mass.

Jones, T. & Klar, K. A. 2005. Diffusionism reconsidered: Linguistic and archaeological evidence for prehistoric Polynesian contact with southern California. *American Antiquity* 70 (3): 457-84.

Jones, T. L., Storey, A. A., Matisoo-Smith, E. & Ramírez-Aliaga, J. M. (eds) 2011. *Polynesians in America: pre-Columbian contacts with the New World*. Altamira Press: Lanham.

Kirch, P. V. 1984. *The Evolution of the Polynesian Chiefdoms*. Cambridge University Press: Cambridge.

Kirch, P. V. 1997. Microcosmic histories: island perspectives on 'global' change. *American Anthropologist* 99: 30-42.

Kirch, P. V. 2000. *On the Road of the Winds. An Archaeological History of the Pacific Islands Before European Contact*. University of California Press: Berkeley.

Kirch, P. V., Christensen, C. C. & Steadman, D. n.d. Extinct achatinellid snails from Easter Island: biogeographic, ecological and archaeological implications.

Kirch, P. V. & Ellison, J. 1994. Palaeoenvironmental evidence for human colonization of remote Oceanic islands. *Antiquity* 68: 310-21.

Kjellgren, E. (ed.) 2001. *Splendid Isolation. Art of Easter Island*. Metropolitan Museum of Art: New York.

Klemmer, K. & Zizka, G. 1993. The terrestrial fauna of Easter Island, pp. 24-26 in (S. R. Fischer, ed.), *Easter Island Studies. Contributions to the History of Rapanui*. Oxbow Monograph 32: Oxford.

Kvam, R. Jr. 2013. *Thor Heyerdahl. Mannen og mytene*. Gyldendal: Oslo.

Ladefoged, T., Stevenson, C., Vitousek, P. & Chadwick, O. 2005. Soil nutrient depletion and the collapse of *Rapa Nui* society. *Rapa Nui Journal* 19 (2): 100-105.

Ladefoged, T. *et al*. 2010. Soil nutrient analysis of Rapa Nui gardening. *Arch. Oceania* 45: 80-85.

Langdon, R. 1975. *The Lost Caravel*. Pacific Publications: Sydney. (2nd edition, *The Lost Caravel Re-explored*, Brolga Press: Canberra).

Langdon, R. 1988. Manioc, a long-concealed key to the enigma of Easter Island. *The Geographical Journal* 154: 324-36.

Langdon, R. & Tryon, D. 1983. *The Language of Easter Island: its Development and Eastern Polynesian Relationships*. Institute for Polynesian Studies: Laie, Hawai'i.

Lanning, E. P. 1970. South America as a source for aspects of Polynesian culture, pp. 175-82 in (R. C. Green & M. Kelly, eds), *Studies in Oceanic Culture History*, vol. 2. Pacific Anthropological Records 11.

La Pérouse, J-F. de 1997. *Voyage autour du Monde sur l'Astrolabe et la Boussole (1785-1788)*. La Découverte: Paris.

Lavachery, H. 1935. *Ile de Pâques*. Grasset: Paris.

Lavachery, H. 1939. *Les Pétroglyphes de l'île de Pâques*. 2 vols. De Sikkel: Antwerp.

Lee, G. 1986. The birdman motif of Easter Island. *Journal of New World Archaeology* 7: 39-49.

Lee, G. 1987. The cosmic Komari. *Rock Art Research* 4: 51-55.

Lee, G. 1992. *The Rock Art of Easter Island. Symbols of Power, Prayers to the Gods*. Monumenta Archaeologica 17, Inst. of Archaeology, UCLA.

Lee, G. 1997. Petroglyph motif distribution in East Polynesia. *Rapa Nui Journal* 11 (1): 5-9.

Lee, G. 2004. *Rapa Nui*'s sea creatures. *Rapa Nui Journal* 18 (1): 31-38.

Lee, G. & Catany, T. 1995. *Rapa Nui. Histoire de l'île de Pâques*. Editions Olizane: Geneva.

Lee. G. & Horley, P. 2013. The paintings of Ana Kai Tangata cave, Easter Island. *Rapa Nui Journal* 27 (2): 11-32.

Lee, G. & Liller, W. 1987. Easter Island's 'sun stones': a critique. *Journal of the Polynesian Society* 96: 81-93 (& in *Archaeoastronomy* 11, 11pp).

Lee, G. & Stasack, E. 1999. *Spirit of Place. Petroglyphs of Hawai'i*. Easter Island Foundation: Los Osos.

Lee, V. R. 1998. *Rapa Nui* rocks: impressions from a brief visit. *Rapa Nui Journal* 12 (3): 69-72.

Lee, V. R. 1999. *Rapa Nui* rocks update. *Rapa Nui Journal* 13 (1): 16-17.

Lee, V. R. 2012. Awakening the giant. *Rapa Nui Journal* 26 (2): 5-16.

Lee, V. R. 2013. *Ancient Moonshots. Megalithic Mysteries from before Technology*. Sixpac Manco Publications: Cortez.

Levison, M., Ward, R. G. & Webb, J. W. 1973. *The Settlement of Polynesia, A Computer Simulation*. ANU Press: Canberra.

Lewis, D. 1972. *We, the Navigators. The Ancient art of Landfinding in the Pacific*. ANU Press: Canberra.

Lewis, D. 1974. Wind, wave, star and bird. *National Geographic* 146 (6): 746-54.

Liller, W. 1990. The lost observatories of *Rapa Nui*, pp. 145-59 in (H. M. Esen-Baur, ed.) *State and Perspectives of Scientific Research in Easter Island Culture*. Courier Forschungsinstitut Senckenburg: Frankfurt, No. 125.

Liller, W. 1991. New archaeoastronomical results from *Rapa Nui*. *Rapa Nui Journal* 5 (1): 1, 4-6. Liller, W. 1993. A survey and documentation of the *Moai* of Rapanui, pp. 86-88 in (S. R. Fischer, ed.) *Easter Island Studies*. Oxbow Monograph 32: Oxford.

Liller, W. 1993a. The monuments in the archaeoastronomy of Rapanui, pp. 122-27 in (S. R. Fischer, ed.) *Easter

Island Studies. Contributions to the History of rapanui in Memory of William T. Mulloy. Oxbow Monograph 32: Oxford.

Liller, W. 1993b. *The Ancient Solar Observatories of Rapanui. The Archaeoastronomy of Easter Island.* Easter Island Foundation/Cloud Mt Press: Old Bridge, NJ.

Liller, W. 1995. The oldest *Toromiro* in the world. *Rapa Nui Journal* 9 (3): 65-68.

Lipo, C. P. & Hunt, T. 2005. Mapping prehistoric statue roads on Easter Island. *Antiquity* 79: 158-68.

Lipo, C. P., Hunt, T. L. & Hundtoft, B. 2010. Stylistic variability of stemmed obisidian tools (*mata'a*), frequency seriation, and the scale of social interaction on Rapa Nui (Easter Island). *Journal of Arch. Science* 37 (10): 2551-61.

Lipo, C. P., Hunt, T. L. & Rapu, S. 2013. The 'walking' megalithic statues (*moai*) of Easter Island. *Journal of Archaeological Science* 40 (6): 2859-66.

Lipo. C. P. *et al.* 2016. Weapons of war? Rapa Nui *mata'a* morphometric analyses. *Antiquity* 90: 172-87.

Lisjanskij, U. 2004. Travel round the world onboard the ship *Neva* performed in 1803, 1804, 1805 and 1806. *Rapa Nui Journal* 18 (2): 118-25.

Long, S. A. & Gill, G. W. 1997. Facial features of the ancient *Rapa Nui*. *Rapa Nui Journal* 11 (2): 72-74.

Love, C. M. 1983. Easter Island research. *Chilean University Life* 16, Spring, 3-8.

Love, C. M. 1984. *The Katherine Routledge Lantern Slide Collection of Easter Island and the South Pacific.* Western Wyoming College.

Love, C. M. 1990. How to make and move an Easter Island statue, pp. 139-40 in (H. M. Esen-Baur, ed.) *State and Perspectives of Scientific Research in Easter Island Culture.* Courier Forschungsinstitut Senckenburg: Frankfurt, No. 125.

Love, C. M. 1990a. The interpretation of site 5-72, an Easter Island Ahu. *Rapa Nui Journal* 4 (2): 17-19.

Love, C. M. 1993. Easter Island *ahu* revisited, pp. 103-11 in (S. R. Fischer, ed.) *Easter Island Studies. Contributions to the History of rapanui in Memory of William T. Mulloy.* Oxbow Monograph 32: Oxford.

Love, C. M. 2000. More on moving Easter Island statues, with comments on the NOVA program. *Rapa Nui Journal* 14 (4): 115-18.

Love, C. M. 2004. Getting to know you. *Rapa Nui Journal* 18 (2): 132-34.

Love, C. M. 2010. The Easter Island cultural collapse, pp. 67-86 in (P. Wallin & H. Martinsson-Wallin, eds) *The Gotland Papers. Selected papers from the VII International Conference on Easter Island and the Pacific: Migration, Identity and Cultural Heritage.* Gotland, Sweden, 20-25 August 2007. Gotland University Press 11.

MacIntyre, F. 1999. Walking Moai? *Rapa Nui Journal* 13 (3): 70-78.

MacIntyre, F. 1999a. Is humanity suicidal? Are there clues from *Rapa Nui*? *Rapa Nui Journal* 13 (2): 35-41.

MacIntyre, F. 2001. ENSO, climate variability and the Rapanui. Part I. The basics. *Rapa Nui Journal* 15 (1): 17-26.

MacIntyre, F. 2001a. ENSO, climate variability and the Rapanui. Part II. Oceanography and *Rapa Nui*. *Rapa Nui Journal* 15 (2): 83-94.

Mahon, I. 1998. Easter Island: the economics of population dynamics and sustainable development in Pacific context, pp. 113-19 in (C. M. Stevenson *et al.*, eds) *Easter Island in Pacific Context: South Seas Symposium.* Easter Island Foundation: Los Osos.

Mann, D., Chase, J., Edwards, J., Beck, W., Reanier, R. & Mass, M. 2003. Prehistoric destruction of the primeval soils and vegetation of *Rapa Nui* (Isla de Pascua, Easter Island), pp. 133- 53 in (J. Loret & J. T. Tanacredi, eds) *Easter Island: Scientific Exploration into the World's Environmental Problems in Microcosm.* Kluwer Academic / Plenum: New York.

Mann, D., Edwards, J., Chase, J., Beck, W., Reanier, R., Mass, M., Finney, B. & Loret, J. 2008. Drought, vegetation change and human history on *Rapa Nui* (Isla de Pascua, Easter Island). *Quaternary Research* 69: 16-28.

Martin, P. S. & Steadman, D. W. 1999. Prehistoric extinctions on islands and continents, pp. 17-55 in (R. D. E. MacPhee, ed.) *Extinctions in Near Time.* Kluwer Acad/Plenum: New York.

Martinsson-Wallin, H. 1994. *Ahu -The Ceremonial Stone Structures of Easter Island: Analyses of Variation and Interpretation of Meanings.* Aun 19, Societas Archaeologica Upsaliensis: Uppsala.

Martinsson-Wallin, H. 1996. The eyes of the Moai, lost and re-discovered. *Rapa Nui Journal* 10 (2): 41-43.

Martinsson-Wallin, H. 1996a. Variation and meaning of Easter Island ahu. *Rapa Nui Journal* 10 (4): 93-98.

Martinsson-Wallin, H. 2001. Construction-destruction-reconstruction of monumental architecture on *Rapa Nui*, pp. 73-77 in (C. M. Stevenson *et al.* eds) *Pacific 2000. Proceedings of the Fifth International Conference on Easter Island and the Pacific.* Easter Island Foundation: Los Osos.

Martinsson-Wallin, H. & Crockford, S. 2002. Early settlement of *Rapa Nui*. *Asian Perspectives* 40 (2): 244-78.

Martinsson-Wallin, H. & Wallin, P. 1994. The settlement/activity area Nau Nau East at Anakena, Easter Island, pp. 122-216 in *Kon-Tiki Museum Occasional Papers vol. 3*, Oslo.

Martinsson-Wallin, H. & Wallin, P. 1998. Excavations at Ahu Hek'i'i, La Pérouse, Easter Island, pp. 171-77 in (C. M. Stevenson, *et al.*, eds) *Easter Island in Pacific Context. South Seas Symposium.* Easter Island Foundation: Los Osos.

Martinsson-Wallin, H. & Wallin, P. 1998a. Excavations at Anakena. The Easter Island settlement sequence and change of subsistence?, pp. 179-86 in (P. Vargas, ed.) *Easter Island and Polynesian Prehistory.* Universidad de Chile: Santiago.

Martinsson-Wallin, H. & Wallin, P. 1998b. Dating of Ahu structures within the La Pérouse area. *Rapa Nui Journal* 12 (3): 85.

Martinsson-Wallin, H. & Wallin, P. 2000. Ahu and settlement: archaeological excavations at Anakena and La Pérouse, pp. 27-43 in (C. M. Stevenson & W. S. Ayres, eds) *Easter Island Archaeology. Research on Early rapanui Culture*. Easter Island Foundation: Los Osos.

Matisoo-Smith, E., Roberts, R. M., Irwin, G. J., Allen, J. S., Penny, D. & Lambert, D. M. 1998. Patterns of prehistoric mobility in Polynesia indicated by mtDNA from the Pacific rat. *Proc. Nat . Acad . Sci. USA* 95: 15145-50.

Maunder, M. 1997. Conservation of the extinct *Toromiro* tree, *Sophora toromiro*. *Curtis's Botanical Magazine* 14 (4): 226-31.

Maunder, M., Culham, A., Bordeu, A., Allainguillaumes, J. & Wilkinson, M. 1999. Genetic diversity and pedigree for *Sophora toromiro* (*Leguminosae*): a tree extinct in the wild. *Molecular Ecology* 8: 725-38.

Mazière, F. 1969. *Mysteries of Easter Island*. Collins: London.

McCall, G. 1976. European impact on Easter Island: response recruitment and the Polynesian experience in Peru. *Journal of Pacific History* 11 (2): 90-105.

McCall, G. 1990. *rapanui* and outsiders: the early days, pp. 165-225 in (B. Illius & M. Laubscher, eds), *Circumpacifica. Band II, Ozeanien, Miszellen. Festschrift für Thomas S. Barthel*. Peter Lang: Frankfurt.

McCall, G. 1993. Little Ice Age: some speculations for Rapanui. *Rapa Nui Journal* 7 (4): 65-70.

McCall, G. 1994. *Rapanui. Tradition and Survival on Easter Island*. 2nd ed. Allen & Unwin: St Leonards.

McCoy, P. C. 1973. Excavation of a rectangular house on the east rim of Rano Kau volcano, Easter Island. *Archaeology & Physical Anthropology in Oceania* 8: 51-67.

McCoy, P. C. 1976. *Easter Island Settlement Patterns in the Late Prehistoric and Protohistoric Periods*. Bulletin 5, Easter Island Committee, International Fund for Monuments Inc.: New York.

McCoy, P. C. 1976a. A note on Easter Island obsidian cores and blades. *Journal of the Polynesian Society* 85: 327-38.

McCoy, P. C. 1978. The place of near-shore islets in Easter Island prehistory. *Journal of the Polynesian Society* 87: 193-214.

Meadows, D. & Randers, J.1992. *Beyond the Limits*. Universe Books: New York.

Meadows, D. H., Meadows, D. L., Randers, J. & Behrens, W. W. 1972. *The Limits to Growth*. Earth Island Limited: London.

Mellén Blanco, F. 1986. *Manuscritos y Documentos Españoles para la Historia de la Isla de Pascua*. Biblioteca CEHOPU: Madrid.

Meroz, Y. 1995. Comment on the two *hanau*. *Rapa Nui Journal* 9 (1): 7-8.

Métraux, A. 1940. *Ethnology of Easter Island*. Bulletin 160, Bishop Museum Press: Honolulu (reprinted 1971).

Métraux, A. 1957. *Easter Island*. André Deutsch: London.

Mieth, A. & Bork, H-R. 2003. Diminution and degradation of environmental resources by prehistoric land use on Poike Peninsula, Easter Island (*Rapa Nui*). *Rapa Nui Journal* 17 (1): 34-41.

Mieth, A. & Bork, H-R. 2004. *Easter Island - Rapa Nui. Scientific Pathways to Secrets of the Past*. Christien-Alberts-Universität: Kiel.

Mieth, A. & Bork, H-R. 2005. Traces in the soils: interaction between environmental change, land use and culture in the (pre)history of *Rapa Nui* (Easter Island), pp. 55-65 in (C. M. Stevenson *et al.*, eds) *The Reñaca Papers: VI International Conference on Rapa Nui and the Pacific*. Easter Island Foundation: Los Osos.

Mieth, A. & Bork, H-R. 2010. Humans, climate or introduced rats -which is to blame for the woodland destruction on prehistoric *Rapa Nui* (Easter Island)? *Journal of Arch. Science* 37: 417-26.

Mieth, A. & Bork, H-R. 2012. *Die Osterinsel Auf Tour*. Springer Spektrum: Berlin.

Mieth, A. & Bork, H-R. 2015. Degradation of resources and successful land-use management on prehistoric Rapa Nui: two sides of the same coin, pp. 91-113 in (N. Cauwe & M. De Dapper, eds) *Easter Island: Collapse or Transformation? A State of the Art*. (Conference, Brussels, November 2012). Royal Academy for Overseas Sciences: Brussels.

Mieth, A., Bork, H-R. & Feeser, I. 2002. Prehistoric and recent land use effects on Poike Peninsula, Easter Island (*Rapa Nui*). *Rapa Nui Journal* 16 (2): 89-95.

Moorehead, A. 1966. *The Fatal Impact: an account of the invasion of the South Pacific 1767-1840*. Penguin: Harmondsworth.

Moreno-Mayar, J. V. *et al.* 2014. Genome-wide ancestry patterns in Rapanui suggest pre-European admixture with Native Americans. *Current Biology* 24 (21): 2518-25.

Moy, C. M., Seltzer, G. O., Rodbell, D. T. & Anderson, D. M. 2002. Variability of El Niño-Southern Oscillation activity at millennial timescales during the Holocene epoch. *Nature* 420: 162-165.

Mucciarone, D. A. & Dunbar, R. B. 2003. Stable isotopes record of El Niño-Southern Oscillation events from Easter Island, pp. 113-132, Chapter 7, in (J. Loret & J. T. Tancredi, eds) *Easter Island: Scientific Exploration into the World's Environmental Problems in Microcosm*. Kluwer: New York.

Mulloy, E. R. 1993. The long and short of it: some thoughts on the meaning of the names hanau eepe and hanau momoko in *rapanui* tradition. *Rapa Nui Journal* 7 (4): 71-72.

Mulloy, W. 1961. The ceremonial center of Vinapu, pp. 93-180 in (T. Heyerdahl & E. Ferdon Jr., eds) *Reports of the Norwegian Archaeological Expedition to Easter Island and the East Pacific. Vol. 1: The Archaeology of Easter Island*. Allen & Unwin: London.

Mulloy, W. 1970. A speculative reconstruction of techniques of carving, transporting and erecting Easter Island statues. *Archaeology & Physical Anthropology in Oceania* 5 (1): 1-23.

Mulloy, W. 1974. Contemplate the Navel of the World. *Americas* 26 (4): 25-33, republished in *The Easter Island Bulletins of William Mulloy*, World Monuments Fund: New York & Easter Island Foundation: Houston, 1997, pp. 89-95.

Mulloy, W. 1975. A solstice oriented *ahu* on Easter Island. *Archaeology & Physical Anthropology in Oceania* 10: 1-39.

Mulloy, W. 1997. *The Easter Island Bulletins of William Mulloy*, World Monuments Fund: New York & Easter Island Foundation: Houston.

Mulloy, W. 1997a. Preliminary culture-historical research model for Easter Island, pp. 97-111 in *The Easter Island Bulletins of William Mulloy*, World Monuments Fund: New York & Easter Island Foundation: Houston.

Mulloy, W. & Figueroa, G. 1978. *The A Kivi-Vai Teka Complex and its Relationship to Easter Island Architectural History*. Asian and Pacific Archaeology Series No. 8, Social Science Research Institute, University of Hawaii at Manoa.

Mulrooney, M. A. 2012. *Continuity or Collapse? Diachronic Settlement and Land Use in Hanga Ho'onu, Rapa Nui (Easter Island)*. Ph.D. Thesis, University of Auckland.

Mulrooney, M. A. 2013. An island-wide assessment of the chronology of settlement and land use on Rapa Nui (Easter Island) based on radiocarbon data. *Journal of Arch. Science* 40: 4377-99.

Mulrooney, M. A., Ladefoged, T. N., Stevenson, C. M. & Haoa, S. 2010. Empirical assessment of a pre-European societal collapse on *Rapa Nui* (Easter Island), pp. 141-154 in (P. Wallin & H. Martinsson-Wallin, eds) *The Gotland Papers. Selected papers from the VII International Conference on Easter Island and the Pacific: Migration, Identity and Cultural Heritage*. Gotland, Sweden, 20-25 August 2007. Gotland University Press 11.

Nunn, P. D. 1994. *Oceanic Islands*. Blackwells: Oxford.

Nunn, P. D. 1999. *Environmental Change in the Pacific Basin: chronologies, causes, consequences*. Wiley: New York.

Nunn, P. D. 2000. Environmental catastrophe in the Pacific Islands around AD 1300. *Geoarchaeology* 15 (7): 715-40.

Nunn, P. D. 2001. Ecological crises or marginal disruptions: the effects of the first humans on Pacific islands. *New Zealand Geographer* 57 (2): 11-20.

Nunn, P. D. & Britton, J. M. R. 2001. Human-environment relationships in the Pacific islands around AD 1300. *Environment and History* 7: 3-22.

Orefici, G. (ed.) 1995. *La Terra dei Moai. Dalla Polinesia all'Isola di Pasqua*. Erizzo: Venice.

Orliac, C. 1993. Le *Toromiro*, l'arbre des Dieux, pp. 388-401 in *Les Mystères Résolus de l'île de Pâques*. Cercle d'Etudes sur l'île de Pâques et la Polynésie, Editions STEP: Evry.

Orliac, C. 2000. The woody vegetation of Easter Island between the early 14th and the mid- 17th centuries AD, pp. 211-20 in (C. M. Stevenson & W. S. Ayres, eds) *Easter Island Archaeology. Research on Early rapanui Culture*. Easter Island Foundation: Los Osos.

Orliac, C. 2010. Botanical identification of 200 Easter Island wood carvings, pp. 125-140 in in (P. Wallin & H. Martinsson-Wallin, eds) *The Gotland Papers. Selected papers from the VII International Conference on Easter Island and the Pacific: Migration, Identity and Cultural Heritage.* Gotland, Sweden, 20-25 August 2007. Gotland University Press 11.

Orliac, C. & Orliac, M. 1995. *Silent Gods. The Mysteries of Easter Island.* Thames & Hudson: London / Abrams: New York.

Orliac, C. & Orliac, M. 1995a. *Bois Sculptés de l'île de Pâques.* Editions Parenthèses: Marseille.

Orliac, C. & Orliac, M. 1998. Evolution du couvert végétal à l'île de Pâques du 15e au 19e siècle, pp. 195-200 in (P. Vargas, ed.) *Easter Island and Polynesian Prehistory.* Universidad de Chile: Santiago.

Orliac, C. & Orliac, M. 2008. *Treasures of Easter Island.* Editions D/ Editions Louise Leiris: Paris.

Orliac, M. 1989. Le palmier des Pascuans. *Saga Information* (Société Amicale des Géologues Amateurs), Paris, 94: 60-64.

Orliac, M. 1993. Le palmier des Pascuans, pp. 402-413 in *Les Mystères Résolus de l'île de Pâques.* Cercle d'Etudes sur l'île de Pâques et la Polynésie, Editions STEP: Evry.

Østreng, W. 2014. The science vision and practice of Thor Heyerdahl in critical light, pp. 71-93 in (I. Hoëm, ed.) *Thor Heyerdahl's Kon-Tiki in New Light.* The Kon-Tiki Museum Occasional Papers 14, Oslo.

Owsley, D. W., Mires, A-M. & Gill, G. W. 1983. Caries frequency in deciduous dentitions of protohistoric Easter Islanders. *Bulletin of the Indo-Pacific Prehistory Association* 4: 143-47.

Owsley, D. W., Mires, A-M. & Gill, G. W. 1985. Carious lesions in permanent dentitions of protohistoric Easter Islanders. *Journal of the Polynesian Society* 94: 415-22.

Owsley, D. W. *et al.* 2015. Evidence for injuries and violent death, pp. 222-52 in (V. H. Stefan & G. W. Gill, eds) 2015. *Skeletal Biology of the Ancient Rapanui (Easter Islanders).* Cambridge University Press: Cambridge.

Palmer, J. L. 1868. Observations on the inhabitants and the antiquities of Easter Island. *Ethnological Society, London, Journal* 1: 371-77.

Palmer, J. L. 1870. A visit to Easter Island, or *Rapa Nui. Proceedings of the Royal Geographical Society* 14: 108-19.

Palmer, J. L. 1870a. A visit to Easter Island, or *Rapa Nui*, in 1868. *Journal of the Royal Geographical Society* 40: 167-81.

Pavel, P. 1990. Reconstruction of the transport of moai, pp. 141-44 in (H. M. Esen-Baur, ed.) *State and Perspectives of Scientific Research in Easter Island Culture.* Courler Forschungsinstitut Senckenburg: Frankfurt, No. 125.

Pavel, P. 1995. Reconstruction of the transport of the *moai* statues and *pukao* hats. *Rapa Nui Journal* 9 (3): 69-72.

Pavel, P. 2009. *Rapa Nui. The man who made the statues walk*. VN Publishing: Strakonice.

Peiser, B. 2005. From genocide to ecocide: the rape of *Rapa Nui*. *Energy and Environment* 16: 513-39.

Pelletier, M. 2012. *Ile de Pâques. Terra Incognita*. Editions de la Martinière: Paris.

Pennington, W., Cambray, R. S., Eakins, J. D. & Harkness, D. D. 1976. Radionuclide dating of the recent sediments of Blelham Tarn. *Freshwater Biology* 6: 317-31.

Polet, C. 2015. Starvation and cannibalism on Easter Island? The contribution of the analysis of Rapanui human remains, pp. 115-33 in (N. Cauwe & M. De Dapper, eds) *Easter Island: Collapse or Transformation? A State of the Art*. (Conference, Brussels, November 2012). Royal Academy for Overseas Sciences: Brussels.

Porteous, J. D. 1981. *The Modernization of Easter Island*. Dept. of Geography, University of Victoria, B. C.

Powell, W. A. 1869. Easter Island. The London *Times*, 21 January (published in *Rapa Nui Journal* 21 (1), May 2007, pp. 58-60.

Rainbird, P. 2002. A message for our future? The *Rapa Nui* (Easter Island) eco-disaster and Pacific island environments. *World Archaeology* 33 (3): 436-51.

Ralling, C. 1990. *The Kon-Tiki Man*. BBC Books: London.

Ramírez, J. M. & Huber, C. 2000. *Easter Island. Rapa Nui, a land of Rocky Dreams*. Alvimpress Editores: Santiago.

Ramírez, J. M. & Matisoo-Smith, E. 2008. Polinesios in el sur de Chile in tiempos prehispánicos: evidencia dura, nuevas preguntas & una nueva hipótesis. *Clava* 7: 85-100.

Rapa Nui. L'Ile de Pâques de Pierre Loti. 2009. Les Cahiers de la Girafe, Les Editions du Muséum de Toulouse: Toulouse.

Raphael, M. 1988. Die Monumentalität in der Bildhauerkunst am Beispiel eines Kopfes von der Osterinsel, pp. 462-526 in *Tempel, Kirchen und Figuren. Studien zur Kunstgeschichte, Ästhetik und Archäologie* (by M. Raphael). Suhrkamp: Frankfurt.

Roe, M. (ed.) 2005. The Journal and Letters of Captain Charles Bishop on the North-West Coast of America, in the Pacific and in New South Wales. 1794-1799. *Rapa Nui Journal* 19 (1): 61-63.

Rolett, B. & Diamond, J. 2004. Environmental predictors of pre-European deforestation on Pacific islands. *Nature* 431: 443-46.

Rongo, T., Bush, M. & Woesik, R. van 2009. Did ciguatera prompt the late Holocene Polynesian voyages of discovery? *Journal of Biogeography* 36: 1423-32.

Roullier, C. *et al.* 2013. Historical collections reveal patterns of diffusion of sweet potato in Oceania obscured by modern plant movements and recombination. *Proc. Nat. Acad. Sciences* 110 (6): 2205-10.

Routledge, K. 1917. Easter Island. *The Geographical Journal* 49: 321-49.

Routledge, K. 1917a. The bird cult of Easter Island. *Folklore* 28: 337-55.

Routledge, K. (Mrs S.) 1919. *The Mystery of Easter Island. The Story of an Expedition.* Sifton, Praed & Co.: London.

Routledge, K. 1920. Survey of the village and carved rocks of Orongo, Easter Island, by the Mana Expedition. *Journal of the Royal Anthropological Institute of Great Britain* 50: 425-51.

Ruiz-Tagle, E. (ed.) 2006. *Easter Island: The first three expeditions.* (2nd ed.) Rapanui Press: *Rapa Nui.*

von Saher, H. 1990. Some details of the journal of Jacob Roggeveen. *Rapa Nui Journal* 4 (3): 33-35, 45.

von Saher, H. 1990/1. Some details from the journal of Captain Bouman on the discovery of Easter Island. *Rapa Nui Journal* 4 (4): 49-52.

von Saher, H. 1992. More journals on Easter Island. *Rapa Nui Journal* 6 (2): 34-39.

von Saher, H. 1993. Roggeveen and Bouman: an inventory of all the narratives. *Rapa Nui Journal* 7 (4): 77-82.

von Saher, H. 1993a. Preparations for Belgian diving expedition to Easter Island. *Rapa Nui Journal* 7 (2): 30-31.

von Saher, H. 1994. The complete journal of Captain Cornelis Bouman, Master of the ship *Thienhoven* forming part of the fleet of Jacob Roggeveen, from 31 March to 13 April 1722 during their stay around Easter Island. *Rapa Nui Journal* 8 (4): 95-100.

von Saher, H. 1994a. Austronesian megalith transport today: no hypotheses, just facts-figures- photographs. *Rapa Nui Journal* 8 (3): 67-70.

von Saher, H. 1999. The search for the original 1774 Easter Island manuscript of Johann Reinhold Forster. *Rapa Nui Journal* 13 (2): 42-43.

Sahlins, M. 1955. Esoteric efflorescence in Easter Island. *American Anthropologist* 57: 1045-52.

Scaglion, R. 2005. *Kumara* in the Ecuadorian Gulf of Guayaquil? pp. 35-41 in (C. Ballard *et al.,* eds) 2005. *The Sweet Potato in Oceania: a Reappraisal.* Ethnology Monographs 19/Oceania Monograph 56. Univ. of Pittsburgh & Univ. of Sydney.

Seelenfreund, A. 1988. *Ahu Tautira:* architectural changes and cultural sequence of the ancient ceremonial platform on Easter Island. *Clava* 4: 69-81.

Sharp, A. 1957. *Ancient Voyagers in the Pacific.* Penguin: Harmondsworth.

Sharp, A. 1961. Polynesian navigation to distant islands. *Journal of the Polynesian Society* 70: 221-26.

Sharp, A. (ed.) 1970. *The Journal of Jacob Roggeveen.* Clarendon Press: Oxford.

Shaw, L. C. 1996. The use of caves as burial chambers on Easter Island. *Rapa Nui Journal* 10 (4): 101-3.

Shepardson, B. L. 2013. *Moai. A new look at old faces.* Rapa Nui Press: Santiago.

Shepardson, B., Shepardson, D., Shepardson, E., Chiu, S. & Graves, M. 2008. Re-examining the evidence for late colonization on Easter Island. *Rapa Nui Journal* 22 (2): 97-101.

Skinner, H. D. 1955. Easter Island masonry. *Journal of the Polynesian Society* 64: 292-94.

Skinner, H. D. 1967. Cylindrical headdress in the Pacific region, pp. 167-89 in (G. A. Highland *et al.*, eds) *Polynesian Culture History*. Bishop Museum Special Publication 56, Honolulu.

Skjølsvold, A. 1961. The stone statues and quarries of Rano Raraku, pp. 339-79 in T. Heyerdahl & E. Ferdon Jr. (eds) *Reports of the Norwegian Archaeological Expedition to Easter Island and the East Pacific. Vol. 1: The Archaeology of Easter Island*. Allen & Unwin: London.

Skjølsvold, A. 1993. The dating of *rapanui* monolithic sculpture, pp. 89-95 in (S. R. Fischer, ed.) *Easter Island Studies*. Oxbow Monograph 32: Oxford.

Skjølsvold, A. 1994. Archaeological investigations at Anakena, Easter Island, pp. 5-121 in *The Kon-Tiki Museum Occasional Papers*, vol. 3.

Skjølsvold, A. 1996. Age of Easter Island settlement, *Ahu* and monolithic sculpture. *Rapa Nui Journal* 10 (4): 104-9.

Skjølsvold, A. & Figueroa, G. 1989. An attempt to date a unique, kneeling statue in Rano Raraku, Easter Island. *Occasional Papers of the Kon-Tiki Museum, Oslo* 1: 7-35.

Skottsberg, C. 1956. *The Natural History of Juan Fernández and Easter Island, vol. 1*. Almquist & Wiksells: Uppsala.

Smith, C. S. 1961. The Poike ditch, pp. 385-91 in T. Heyerdahl & E. Ferdon Jr. (eds) *Reports of the Norwegian Archaeological Expedition to Easter Island and the East Pacific. Vol. 1: The Archaeology of Easter Island*. Allen & Unwin: London.

Smith, C. S. 1961a. Two habitation caves, pp. 257-71 in T. Heyerdahl & E. Ferdon Jr. (eds) *Reports of the Norwegian Archaeological Expedition to Easter Island and the East Pacific. Vol. 1: The Archaeology of Easter Island*. Allen & Unwin: London.

Smith, C. 1988. A small pottery scam. *Rapa Nui Journal* 2 (3): 3-4.

Smith, C. S. 1990. The Poike ditch in retrospect. *Rapa Nui Journal* 4 (3): 33-37.

Smith, C. S. 1993. The Norwegian Expedition to Easter Island in retrospect, pp. 79-81 in (S. R. Fischer, ed.), *Easter Island Studies*. Oxbow Monograph 32: Oxford.

Spriggs, M. & Anderson, A. 1993. Late colonization of East Polynesia. *Antiquity* 67: 200-17.

Steadman, D. W. 1989. Extinction of birds in Eastern Polynesia: a review of the record, and comparisons with other island groups. *Journal of Archaeological Science* 16: 177-205.

Steadman, D. 1995. Prehistoric extinctions of Pacific island birds: biodiversity meets zooarchaeology. *Science* 267: 1123-31.

Steadman, D. 1997. Extinctions of Polynesian birds, pp. 105-23 in (P. Kirch & T. Hunt, eds), *Historical Ecology in the Pacific Islands.* Yale University Press: New Haven.

Steadman, D. 1999. The prehistoric extinction of South Pacific birds, pp. 375-86 in (J-C. Galipaud & I. Lilley, eds) *The Pacific from 5000 to 2000 BP.* Institut de Recherche pour le Développment: Paris.

Steadman, D. W. 2006. *Extinction and Biogeography of Tropical Pacific Birds.* University of Chicago Press: Chicago.

Steadman, D., Vargas, P. & Cristino, C. 1994. Stratigraphy, chronology and cultural context of an early faunal assemblage from Easter Island. *Asian Perspectives* 33 (1): 79-96.

Stefan, V. 2001. Origin and evolution of the *rapanui* of Easter Island, pp. 495-522 in (C. M. Stevenson *et al.,* eds) *Pacific 2000. Proceedings of the Fifth International Conference on Easter Island and the Pacific.* Easter Island Foundation: Los Osos.

Stefan, V. H. & Gill, G. W. (eds) 2015. *Skeletal Biology of the Ancient Rapanui (Easter Islanders).* Cambridge University Press: Cambridge.

Stephen-Chauvet, Dr 1935. *L'Ile de Pâques et ses Mystères.* Editions Tel: Paris.

Stevenson, C. M. 1986. The socio-political structure of the southern coastal area of Easter Island: AD 1300-1864, pp. 69-77 in (P. V. Kirch, ed.) *Island Societies.* Cambridge University Press: Cambridge.

Stevenson, C. M. 1988. The hydration dating of Easter Island obsidians. *Clava* 4: 83-93.

Stevenson, C. M. 1997. *Archaeological Investigations on Easter Island. Maunga Tari: an upland agricultural complex.* Easter Island Foundation: Los Osos.

Stevenson, C. M. & Cristino, C. 1986. Residential settlement history of the *Rapa Nui* coastal plain. *Journal of New World Archaeology* 7: 29-38.

Stevenson, C. M. & Haoa, S. 1998. Prehistoric gardening systems and agricultural intensification in the La Perouse area of Easter Island, pp.205-213 in (C. M. Stevenson, G. Lee & F. J. Morin, eds) *Easter Island in Pacific Context.* Easter Island Foundation; Los Osos.

Stevenson, C. M. & Haoa, S. 2008. *Prehistoric Rapa Nui. Landscape and Settlement Archaeology at Hanga Ho'onu.* Easter Island Foundation: Los Osos.

Stevenson, C. M., Jackson, T. L., Mieth, A., Bork, H-R. & Ladefoged, T. N. 2006. Prehistoric and early historic agriculture at Maunga Orito, Easter Island (*Rapa Nui*), Chile. *Antiquity* 80: 919-36.

Stevenson, C. M., Ladefoged, T. & Haoa, S. 2002. Productive strategies in an uncertain environment: prehistoric agriculture on Easter Island. *Rapa Nui Journal* 16 (1): 17-22.

Stevenson, C., Ladefoged, T. N., Haoa, S. & Guerra, A. 2005. Managed agricultural production in the Vaitea Region of *Rapa Nui*, Chile, pp. 125-136 in (C. M. Stevenson, Ramirez, J. M., Morin, F. J. & Barbacci N., eds) *The Reñaca Papers: Proc. VI International Conference on Easter Island.* Easter Island Foundation: Los Osos.

Stevenson, C., Lee, G. & Morin, F. J. (eds) 1998. *Easter Island in Pacific Context. South Seas Symposium. Proceedings of the 4th Int. Conference on Easter Island and East Polynesia, Albuquerque 1997.* Easter Island Foundation: Los Osos.

Stevenson, C., Lee, G. & Morin, F. J. (eds) 2001. *Pacific 2000. Proceedings of the Fifth International Conference on Easter Island and the Pacific.* Easter Island Foundation: Los Osos.

Stevenson, C. M., Ramirez, J. M., Morin, F. J. & Barbacci N (eds) 2005. *The Reñaca Papers: VI International Conference on Rapa Nui and the Pacific.* Easter Island Foundation: Los Osos.

Stevenson, C. M., Shaw, L. C. & Cristino, C. 1983/4. Obsidian procurement and consumption on Easter Island. *Archaeology in Oceania* 18/19: 120-24.

Stevenson, C. M., Shaw, L. C. & Cristino, C. 1988. Obsidian procurement and consumption on Easter Island, pp. 83-94 in (C. Cristino *et al.* ed.) *First International Congress. Easter Island and East Polynesia. Vol. 1. Archaeology.* Universidad de Chile, Instituto de Estudios Isla de Pascua.

Stevenson, C. M., Wozniak, J. & Haoa, S. 1999. Prehistoric agricultural production on Easter Island (*Rapa Nui*), Chile. *Antiquity* 73: 801-12.

Stevenson, C. M. *et al.* 2015. Variation in Rapa Nui (Easter Island) land use indicates production and population peaks prior to European contact. *Proc. Nat. Acad. Sciences* 112 (4): 1025-30.

Storey, A. A., Ramírez, J. M., Quiroz, D., Burley, D. V., Addison, D. J., Walter, R, Anderson, A. J., Hunt, T. L., Athens, J. S., Hynen, L. & Matisoo-Smith, E. A. 2007. Radiocarbon and DNA evidence for a Pre-Columbian introduction of Polynesian chickens to Chile. *Proc. Nat. Acad. Sci. USA* 104: 10335-339.

Storey, A., Quiroz, D., Beavan, N. & Matisoo-Smith, E. 2011. Pre-Columbian chickens of the Americas: a critical review of the hypotheses and evidence for their origins. *Rapa Nui Journal* 25 (2): 5-19.

Suggs, R. C. 1951. *The Island Civilizations of Polynesia.* New American Library: New York.

Sutton, D. G., Flenley, J. R., Li, X., Todd, A., Butler, K., Summers, R. & Chester, P. I. 2008. The timing of the human discovery and colonization of New Zealand. *Quaternary International* 184; 109-121.

Theroux, P. 1992. *The Happy Isles of Oceania.* Putnam: New York.

Thomson, W. S. 1891. 'Te Pito te henua, or Easter Island.' *Report of the U.S. Nat. Museum for the year ending June 30, 1889,* 447-552. Smithsonian Inst.: Washington.

Thorsby, E. 2010. Evidence of an early Amerindian contribution to the Polynesian gene pool on Easter Island, pp. 285-296 in (P. Wallin & H. Martinsson-Wallin, eds) *The Gotland Papers. Selected papers from the VII International Conference on Easter Island and the Pacific: Migration, Identity and Cultural Heritage.* Gotland, Sweden, 20-25 August 2007. Gotland University Press 11.

Thorsby, E. 2012. The Polynesian gene pool: an early contribution of Amerindians to Easter Island. *Phil. Trans. R. Soc. B.* 367: 812-19.

Thorsby, E. 2014. Genetic traces of an early contribution of Amerindians to Easter Island, pp. 120-31 in (I. Hoëm, ed.) *Thor Heyerdahl's Kon-Tiki in New Light*. The Kon-Tiki Museum Occasional Papers 14, Oslo.

Treister, K, Vargas Casanova, P. & Cristino, C. 2013. *Easter Island's Silent Sentinels. The Sculpture and Architecture of Rapa Nui*. University of New Mexico Press: Albuquerque.

Turner, J. 1965. A contribution to the history of forest clearance. *Proceedings of the Royal Society B*, vol. 161: 343-54.

Valenta, A. (ed.) 1982. *Nouveau Regard sur l'île de Pâques*. Editions Moana: Corbeil, France.

Van Balgooy, M. M. J. 1971. *Plant Geography of the Pacific*. Blumea Supplement (Vol. 6).

Van Tilburg, J. A. 1986. *Power and Symbol: the stylistic analysis of Easter Island monolithic sculpture*. Ph.D. Dissertation, UCLA.

Van Tilburg, J. A. 1986a. Red scoria on Easter Island. *Journal of New World Archaeology* 7: 1-27.

Van Tilburg, J. A. 1994. *Easter Island. Archaeology, Ecology and Culture*. British Museum Press: London.

Van Tilburg, J. A. 1996. Mechanics, logistics and economics of transporting Easter Island (*Rapa Nui*) statues. *Rapa Nui Journal* 10 (4): 110-15.

Van Tilburg, J. A. 2006. *Remote Possibilities. Hoa Hakananai'a and HMS Topaze on Rapa Nui*. British Museum Press: London.

Van Tilburg, J. A. & Arévalo Pakarati, C. 2012. Rano Raraku: a brief overview of six seasons of excavations, three seasons of conservation interventions, and a heritage management program, 2010-2012. *Rapa Nui Journal* 26 (2): 75-81.

Vargas, P. (ed.) 1998. *Easter Island and East Polynesian Prehistory*. Universidad de Chile: Santiago.

Vargas, P. 1998a. *Rapa Nui* settlement patterns: types, function and spatial distribution of households structural components, pp. 111-30 in (P. Vargas, ed.) *Easter Island and Polynesian Prehistory*. Universidad de Chile: Santiago.

Vargas, P., Cristino, C. & Izaurieta, R. 2006. *1000 Años en Rapa Nui. Arqueología del asentamiento*. Editorial Universitaria, Universidad de Chile: Santiago.

Vezzoli, L. & Acocella, V. 2009. Easter Island, SE Pacific: an end-member type of hotspot volcanism. *Geology Society of America Bulletin* 121 (5/6): 869-86.

Vignes, J. 1982. Les yeux des statues, pp. 183-87 in (A. Valenta, ed.) *Nouveau Regard sur l'île de Pâques*. Editions Moana: Corbeil, France.

Vogt, B. & Moser, J. 2010. Ancient Rapanui water management: German archaeological investigations in Ava Ranga Uka A Toroke Hau, 2008-2010. *Rapa Nui Journal* 24 (2): 18-26.

Vogt, B. *et al.* 2015. The Quebrada Vaipú sacred landscape and the practice of taboo on pre-contact Easter Island. Abstract for *Cultural and Environmental Dynamics. 9th International Conference on Easter Island and the Pacific.* June 2015. Ethnological Museum Dahlem, Berlin.

Wallin, P. 1996. A unique find on Easter Island. *Rapa Nui Journal* 10 (4): 99-100.

Weisler, M. I. & Green, R. C. 2008. The many sides of Polynesian archaeology in reference to the colonization process in Southeast Polynesia. *Rapa Nui Journal* 22 (2): 85-87.

Wenger, D. & Duflon, C-E. 2011. *L'Ile de Pâques est Ailleurs.* Editions F. Dawance Sarl: Geneva.

Wolfe, B. & Beuning, K. 2001. Carbon and Oxygen Isotope Analysis of Lake Sediment Cellulose: Methods and Applications, pp. 373-400 in (W. M. Last & J. P. Smol. eds) *Tracking Environmental Change Using Lake Sediments. Volume 2. Physical and Geochemical Methods.* Klewer Academic Publishers: Dordrecht, The Netherlands.

Wolff, W. 1948. *Island of Death.* (reprinted 1973). Hacker Art Books: New York (pp. 149-61).

World Commission on Environment and Development 1987. *Our Common Future (The Bruntland Report).* Oxford University Press: London.

Wozniak, J. A. 1998. Settlement patterns and subsistence on the northwest coast of Easter Island. A progress report, pp. 171-78 in (P. Vargas, ed.) *Easter Island and Polynesian Prehistory.* Universidad de Chile: Santiago.

Wozniak, J. A. 1999. Prehistoric horticultural practices on Easter Island: lithic mulched gardens and field systems. *Rapa Nui Journal* 13: 95-99.

Wozniak, J. A., Horrocks, M. & Cummings, L. 2010. Plant microfossil analysis of deposits from Te Nui, *Rapa Nui*, pp. 111-124 in (P. Wallin & H. Martinsson-Wallin, eds) *The Gotland Papers. Selected papers from the VII International Conference on Easter Island and the Pacific: Migration, Identity and Cultural Heritage.* Gotland, Sweden, 20-25 August 2007. Gotland University Press 11.

Yen, D. 1974. *The Sweet Potato and Oceania.* Bishop Museum Bulletin 236, Honolulu.

Zizka, G. 1989 Naturgeschichte der Osterinsel, pp. 21-38 in (H. Esen-Baur, ed.) *1500 Jahre Kultur der Osterinsel.* Verlag Philipp Von Zabern: Mainz.

Zizka, G. 1989a. *Jubaea chilensis* (MOLINA) BAILLON, die chilenische Honig- oder Coquitopalme. *Der Palmengarten* (Frankfurt) 1: 35-40.

Zizka, G. 1990. Changes in the Easter Island flora. Comments on selected families, pp. 189-207 in (Esen-Baur, H., ed.) *State and Perspectives of Scientific Research in Easter Island Culture.* Courier Forschungsinstitut Senckenburg: Frankfurt, No. 125.

Zizka, G. 1991. Flowering plants of Easter Island. *Palmarum Hortus Francofurtensis* 3: 1-108.

75.2. *Moai*, on the interior slopes of the
Rano Raraku statue quarry. Photo: Paul Bahn.

Analytical index

tuff 30, 65, 127, 128, 145, 148, 153, 159, 165, 169, 170, 223, 231
Tukuturi 46, 64, 65, 75, 131
turtles 35, 108, 121, 122, 173

U

umu pae 103, 116, 251

V

Vai Atare 120
Vai Mata, ahu 173
Vai Tapa Eru 216
Vaitea 106
Vai Uri 134, 220
Van Tilburg, Jo Anne 14, 23, 138, 145, 151, 155, 157, 159, 165, 181, 194, 220, 243, 249, 265
Velasco, Gerardo 101, 103, 106, 204
Vignes, Jacques 101, 103, 138
Vinapu, ahu 46, 48, 53, 60, 62, 65, 103, 113, 121, 132, 143, 168, 170, 173, 174, 180, 181, 185, 186, 188
Von Däniken, Erich 141, 145, 151, 175, 173
vulvas, see *komari* 231, 234, 230, 234

W

Ward, R. Gerard 83
warfare, see *mata'a* 10, 13, 78, 191, 192, 193, 223, 226, 249, 252, 253, 254, 255, 261
water sources 107, 192, 216
Webb, John W. 83
winds 5, 18, 32, 38, 43, 44, 51, 52, 81, 82, 83, 86, 87, 88, 114, 116, 225, 247
Wolff, Werner 153, 165

Y

Yen, Douglas 59, 75

Z

Zumbohm, Gaspard 191, 220
Zuñiga, Joaquín de 43, 51

303